FOCUS ON BUSINESS

The new edition

Cornelsen

Focus on Business The new edition wurde im Auftrag des Verlages entwickelt von David Clarke, Witten und Michael Macfarlane, Oxford.

Berater/in:
Barbara Quante, Lippstadt
Hans Oestreich, Lemgo
Horst-Ralf Steinbach, Werther

Projekleitung:	Jim Austin
Außenredaktion:	Chris Caridia, Publishing Services, Berlin; Christine House, Berlin; Sigrid Janssen, Hannover
Redaktionelle Mitarbeit:	Laura Spratling
Wörterverzeichnisse:	Oliver Busch
Bildredaktion:	Gertha Maly
Layout und technische Umsetzung:	Oxford Designers & Illustrators, Oxford
Illustrationen:	Oxford Designers & Illustrators, Oxford
Umschlaggestaltung:	werkstatt für gebrauchsgrafik, Berlin
Umschlagfoto:	Gettyimages / W. Krecichwost (Normandy Bridge, Le Havre, Frankreich)

Erhältlich sind auch
Audio-CD
ISBN 978-3-464-05003-3

Workbook
ISBN 978-3-464-05002-6

Workbook key
ISBN 978-3-464-05006-4

Handreichungen für den Unterricht
ISBN 978-3-464-05005-7

www.cornelsen.de

1. Auflage, 4. Druck 2009/06

Druck: CS-Druck CornelsenStürtz, Berlin

ISBN 978-3-464-05000-2

Inhalt gedruckt auf säurefreiem Papier aus nachhaltiger Forstwirtschaft.

Vorwort

Mit dieser Neuausgabe von **FOCUS ON BUSINESS** bekommt das lang bewährte Lehrwerk neue und aktualisierte Inhalte und ein neues Gesicht. Voraussetzung für die Arbeit mit **FOCUS ON BUSINESS** ist der mittlere Bildungsabschluss. Das einbändige Lehrwerk bereitet auf die Abschlussprüfung der weiterführenden kaufmännischen Schulen vor. Ferner geht die Neuausgabe gezielt auf die Anforderungen des europäischen Referenzrahmens ein und führt die Lernenden schrittweise auf die Stufe B2.

FOCUS ON BUSINESS besteht aus einem **Refresher Course**, einem **Main Course** und einem **Business Communication Course**.

Refresher Course

Im **Refresher Course** werden Grammatikgrundkenntnisse im situativen Rahmen einer Jugendzeitschrift – ‚Coolio' – aufgefrischt. Die Units stellen die Mitarbeiter/innen dieser Zeitschrift vor und präsentieren ihre Themenseiten. Einem kurzen, visuell attraktiv gestalteten Eingangstext folgen Verständnisfragen *(Looking at the text)*, Vokabelarbeit *(Working with words)*, Grammatikübungen *(Looking at grammar)* und eine abschließende Übersetzung.

Main Course

Im Zentrum der acht Units des **Main Course** stehen zentrale Themen des Wirtschaftslebens und ihre Wechselwirkungen mit der Gesellschaft.

Den Units liegt folgender Aufbau zugrunde:

Focus führt durch motivierende Aufgaben und Fragen in das Thema der Unit ein.

Business and Society bietet jeweils einen Text oder Dialog, der den gesellschaftlichen Bezug des Wirtschaftslebens veranschaulicht. Im folgenden *Background Briefing* wird eine Zusammenfassung zum Thema bzw. statistisches Material angeboten. Dieser Abschnitt kann der Vertiefung dienen, ist aber fakultativ.

People and Business zeigt – oft mittels Fallstudien aus dem Arbeitsalltag – die individuelle Sicht auf die Vernetzung von Menschen und Wirtschaft. Die aus dem Berufsalltag stammenden Texte vermitteln praxisnah das relevante Vokabular und bieten zugleich vielfältige kommunikative Situationen.

Den Texten folgen jeweils Verständnisfragen *(Looking at the text)*, Übungen zum Wortschatz *(Working with words)*, zur Grammatik *(Using language at work)*, zur Schreibfertigkeit *(Writing)* und zur Hörfertigkeit *(Listening)*.

Tasks options bietet handlungsorientierte Übungen, die im situativen Kontext die mündlichen wie auch die schriftlichen kommunikativen Fähigkeiten schult.

Grammar checkpoint bietet kontextgebundene Grammatikübungen. Zur Vertiefung oder als Überblick dient die Begleitgrammatik am Ende des Buches.

Business Communication Course

In den zehn *Files* des **Business Communication Course** stehen *secretarial activities* und Handelskorrespondenz im Mittelpunkt.

Die fünf *Files* zur Handelskorrespondenz enthalten Muster authentischer englischer Geschäftsbriefe und schulen die Fähigkeit, Briefe auf Englisch selbstständig zu verfassen. Es stehen die eher klassischen Stichwortbriefe und Übersetzungen im Vordergrund, die jedoch eng mit den moderneren Formen der Bürokommunikation wie E-Mails und Telefaxen verknüpft sind.

Andere *Files* konzentrieren sich auf die mündliche Kommunikation im Büroalltag wie *Making contacts* oder *Arranging appointments*. Das Schreiben von E-Mails wird auch gesondert in einem *File* behandelt. In einem Glossar können die wichtigsten Wirtschaftsbegriffe nachgeschlagen werden.

Der Abschnitt **Exam Practice** besteht aus vier Prüfungen, die ganz gezielt auf die Abschlussprüfung vorbereiten. Enthalten sind Textaufgaben, Mediation-, Handelskorrespondenz- und Höraufgaben.

Anhang

Der ausführliche Anhang bietet Extras wie eine Begleitgrammatik, Lernhilfen mit Tipps und Kniffen, ein chronologisches sowie ein alphabetisches Wörterverzeichnis und sämtliche Hörverständnistexte.

Inhalt

Refresher Course

Main Course

Business Communication Course

Anhang

Refresher course

Auffrischung von Grundkenntnissen
mit der Jugendzeitschrift Coolio ...

Here's this week's edition

Coolio

About us

Quite a lot of you have told us that you'd like to know more about the people behind Coolio, the UK's most exciting magazine for 16 to 20-year-olds. In this week's edition we've asked five people to introduce themselves to you.

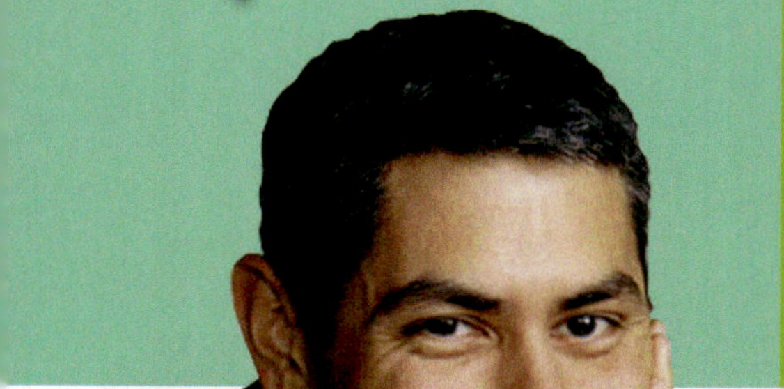

Making contact

1.2 Four readers are looking for partners for their leisure activities. Below are some early replies.

1 Hi. My name's Matt Ward and I live in St Ives in Cornwall. I'm looking for somebody who enjoys my favourite sport, kite-surfing. It's easier than windsurfing because you don't use a sail. Interested?

2 I'm Kate Conway from Glasgow. I spend a lot of time writing programs for computers, but it can be a bit lonely. Would you like to join me? At the moment I'm working on a program to help people to find their dream partner.

3 Hello. I'm Lee Yates from Brixton, London. I've been mad about motorbikes for years. I've just bought a second-hand Harley on eBay and now I'm planning to have a lot of fun with it. So what are you waiting for? Biking's a great way to make mates.

4 Hi. My name's Jasmin Khan and I'm from Bradford. I'd love to find somebody who's interested in jazz dance. When you're dancing, you don't have time to think of anything except what you're doing, so it's a wonderful way to switch off. And do you know what? I keep really fit that way.

Readers' emails

a Anyhow, I think it's a great idea, and I'd love to have a go.

b Hey, maybe we could sell it to a software giant and make ourselves a million!

c I haven't thought of doing anything like that before.

d I only passed my test last month. Is that a problem?

e Why not? I've wondered about having a go ever since we moved to the coast.

f I find those fitness places so boring. Maybe I should try what you do instead.

A

Looking at the texts

1 **Answer the questions.**

1 Find partners. Link the emails with the requests 1–4, and say how you know. (Be careful: two emails don't match the requests.)

Now you 2 Do you do any of the activities? If not, what do you do in your free time?

B

Working with words

2 **Complete the sentences with adjectives from the requests and emails.**

1 Why not try cross-country skiing? It's … for beginners than downhill.
2 Evening classes are good for … people who want to meet others.
3 Janna goes swimming every day. She's absolutely … about it.
4 The team is quite good, I suppose, but it is certainly not …, is it?
5 I should be more active. I'm not very … at the moment.
6 Chess is not … . It's the most fascinating game I know.

3 **Look at the texts and complete the expressions with the missing prepositions. (The text is given after the expression.)**

1 to look … a person to do an activity with (introduction)
2 to work … a project **2**
3 to wait … a person to answer **3**
4 to think … doing an activity **4**
5 to switch … and relax **4**
6 to wonder … doing an activity **e**
7 to move … a place **e**

C

Looking at grammar (1): the simple present

Begleitgrammatik p. 194

1 Matt **lives** on the coast and **enjoys** kite-surfing.
2 You **do not** / **don't use** a sail to go kite-surfing.
3 **Is** that a problem?
4 **Do** you **know** something? I keep really fit.

■ **Form**
Wie der Infinitiv, außer in der **3. Person Singular** (*he/she/it*), die auf *-s* endet [1];
Verneinung Verneintes Hilfsverb (*can't/mustn't/…*) oder eine verneinte Form von *be* bzw. *don't* oder *doesn't* [2];
Fragen Hilfsverb (*can/must/…*) oder eine Form von *be* bzw. *do/does* + Subjekt + Infinitiv [3] [4];

■ **Gebrauch**
Für gegenwärtige Situationen bzw. Handlungen, die **immer** bzw. **immer wieder** passieren [1] – [4];
Signalwörter *always* • *often* • *generally/normally/usually* • *regularly* • *sometimes* • *occasionally* • *seldom* • *never* • *at weekends* • *every day/week* • *on Mondays / Tuesdays* • *on weekdays* • *now and then* • *during the week*

4 **Use the ideas below and *Signalwörter* from the list on page 9 to say what you normally do – or don't do – in your everyday life. (You can add other things too.)**

argue with my parents • catch the bus • come home late • do homework • drink alcohol • get up • go clubbing / dancing / shopping • go to school / to the movies / to the pub / to bed • leave for school / the house • listen to music / the radio • meet (a) friend(s) • play • practise • read • surf • tidy up • take the train • walk • watch TV / a DVD • …

REMEMBER
Dick **often** goes kite-surfing **at the weekend**.
• Wo stehen kurze Adverbien der Häufigkeit wie *often, sometimes, always, …*?

EXAMPLES
I **usually go** to bed at about 11 o'clock **during the week**.
I **often go** clubbing **at the weekend**.
I **don't watch** TV **every week**.

5 **Ask your partner questions about his or her everyday life. Then change roles.**

EXAMPLES
When do you get up?
How do you get to school?
What do you do in your free time?
Where do you go shopping?

Looking at grammar (2): the present progressive

Begleitgrammatik p.194

1 I'**m writing** a computer program at the moment.
2 Jasmin **isn't dancing** right now.
3 **Are** the boys **cleaning** their bikes now?

■ **Form**
am/is/are + *-ing*-Form des Vollverbs [1];
Verneinung *am/is/are* + *not* + *-ing*-Form des Vollverbs [2];
Fragen *am/is/are* + Subjekt + *-ing*-Form des Vollverbs [3];

■ **Gebrauch**
Für Handlungen, die im Moment des Sprechens/Schreibens tatsächlich im Gange sind [1] – [3];
Signalwörter *at present* • *at the moment* • *currently* • *(right) now*

6 **Put the verbs into the correct form of the present progressive.**

1 Can I speak to Ms Bond, please? – Sorry. She … (interview) some job applicants at the moment.
2 Do you know where the visitors are now? – I think they … (talk) to Lucy.
3 What ... (you/do)? – I … (try) to find the address of Carr & Co.
4 Can you two help me with the invoices, please? – Can't it wait until later? We … (prepare) the summer catalogue.
5 Jane … (not work) in the office this week. She … (visit) clients.

7 **When the boss comes into the office, she isn't very pleased. Use the present progressive to describe the picture.**

chat at coffee machine • comb hair • do keep-fit exercises • eat pizza • file letters • flirt behind rubber plant • ~~look angry~~ • look at motorbike catalogue • paint fingernails • ~~play cards~~ • read newspaper • ~~stand at door~~ • surf holiday pages on the Internet • try on shoes • water plants

EXAMPLES The boss **is standing** at the door and she **is looking** very angry.
Josh and Chelsea **are playing** cards.

Looking at grammar (3): the present perfect

Begleitgrammatik p. 195

1 I **have** / **I've** just **bought** a second-hand motorbike.
2 Matt **has not** / **hasn't joined** a bikers' club yet.
3 Kate and Sue **have known** each other for ten years.
4 **Have** you **seen** Jasmin since last weekend?

- **Form**
  have oder *has* + 3. Form des Vollverbs (unregelmäßige Verben: S. 263) [1];
  Verneinung *haven't/hasn't* + 3. Form des Vollverbs [2];
  Fragen *have/has* + Subjekt + 3. Form des Vollverbs [4];
- **Gebrauch**
  Für Handlungen, die gerade passiert sind [1] oder in der Vergangenheit anfingen, aber noch andauern [2] – [4];
  Signalwörter *just* [1] • *still not* • *not yet* [2]; *for* (Zeitdauer) [3] • *since* (Zeitpunkt) [4]

8 **Put the verbs into the correct form of the present perfect.**

1 Janna … (just/phone) to say that they … (cancel) her flight.
2 … (you/book) our holiday yet?
3 We … (still/not decide) what to do this summer.
4 The Bentons … (just/buy) a new motor caravan for their holiday.
5 Thank heavens our tickets … (arrive) at last.
6 I … (not be) to the travel agent's yet.

9 **Use the present perfect to say what has just happened.**

EXAMPLE Tom **has just been** to the doctor's.

Tom/be

1 Ellie/find

2 Greg/write

3 Ben/help

4 Annie/switch off

5 Janna/buy

6 Kate/sell

10 **Complete with the present perfect and *for* or *since*.**

1 I … (use) eBay … I got connected to the Internet.
2 Matt … (not live) in St Ives … many years.
3 Jasmin and Kavita … (know) each other … they began jazz dance classes.
4 We … (not be) to the movies … ages.
5 Joshua … (wonder) about whether to learn how to kite-surf … months.
6 How many jobs … (you/have) … you left school?
7 She … (not keep) very fit … she stopped playing volleyball.
8 … (they/plan) every club tour … the last five years?

11 **Translate the sentences.**

1 Ich spiele jede Woche Tennis und ich spiele auch im Moment.
2 Die Kleins wohnen in Münster. Sie wohnen dort seit Jahren.
3 Jasmin telefoniert gerade mit ihrem Freund. Sie telefonieren jeden Tag, weil er zurzeit in Schottland arbeitet.
4 Ich arbeite seit drei Wochen in einem Computerladen. Ich arbeite immer freitags und samstags.
5 Ich schreibe mit einer Freundin ein Computerprogramm. Wir arbeiten seit Anfang des Monats zusammen.

NEWS AND VIEWS

Work experience

1.3 Clare Davis interviewed Lee Owen and Julie Mills, both 18, about their three-week work experience. Lee worked at an electronics retailer and Julie at a law firm. Read on to find out more.

Clare Well, let me start with you, Lee. You worked at an electronics store, right?

Lee Yes, that's right. I was at Elektra in Lime Street.

Clare I see. And did you find it useful?

Lee Well, yes and no. I spent the first ten days in the office and the second in the shop, which was great. I really enjoyed that. But I didn't learn much when I was working in the office. A few people told me what *they* were doing, but most of the time I just watched. It was really boring.

Clare Yes, but that's office work, isn't it? And what about the shop? I suppose you had more to do there.

Lee Oh, the shop was great. I spent some time shelf-filling, of course, but I also helped customers who had problems or didn't understand something. I liked that, you know, helping people, being part of a team. I was doing something useful when I was in the shop, you see.

Clare Well, thanks for that, Lee. Now what about you, Julie? You worked at a law firm, didn't you?

Julie That's right. My Aunt Sheryl got me a job at the firm where she works – at Abbott & Partners in Parker Street.

Clare And how did you get on?

Julie Oh, I had a brilliant time. It's only a small place so everybody has to do everything. You don't have time to get bored. I did everything from making coffee and filing to making appointments and even writing letters for the lawyers.

Clare What? You wrote letters to clients?

Julie Well, yes. When the secretaries were taking dictations, say, they asked me to write a few letters. Only easy ones, of course, and they're all in the computer. I just filled in names, addresses and dates, that's all.

Clare Very good. So what did you get out of your work experience, Julie?

Julie Well, I now know what I want to do when I leave school. I'm going back to Abbott & Partners as a trainee.

A Looking at the texts

1 Link a sentence part from list A to one from list B to make true statements. If you get it right, the letters in list B make a word.

A

1 In the shop, Lee felt part of a team and …
2 Julie didn't have time to get bored because …
3 Julie was obviously good because …
4 Julie was lucky because her aunt got her …
5 Lee didn't enjoy his first ten days at Elektra …
6 Lee wasn't given anything useful to do …
7 While Lee's work experience was a mix of …
8 Clare was surprised when Julie said …

B

s Abbott & Partners have given her a place as a trainee.
m and often just watched other people.
t a place at the law firm where she worked.
e good and bad, Julie's was just good.
u she did a little bit of everything.
r that she even wrote letters for the lawyers.
c was able to help customers.
o when he was in the office.

■ The word is … .

Now you 2 Tell the class about your own work experience. These words will help you.

(not) be allowed to do sth • ask for a different place because … • be (un)lucky because … • feel in the way • find sth boring/difficult/interesting/useful • get experience in • watch others doing sth • work as (job)

B Working with words

3 Replace the words in *italics* with a word of similar meaning. You can find the words in the text in the same order.

1 We want you to *begin* your work experience in the office, Lee.
2 Elektra is an electronics *shop* in Liverpool.
3 Lee really *liked* his ten days working in the shop.
4 A secretary at least *informed* Lee what she was doing.
5 Of course, watching somebody doing office work is *not very interesting.*
6 Lee helped customers who had *difficulties.*
7 Julie was responsible for *arranging* appointments for clients.
8 The firm is looking for three *apprentice* office workers.

C Looking at grammar (1): the simple past

Begleitgrammatik p.195

1 Lee **worked** at an electronics store last week.
2 He **spent** his first week in the office.
3 The office workers **didn't give** Lee anything to do.
4 **Did** you **find** your work experience useful?

- **Form**
  regelmäßige Verben: Infinitiv + *-ed* [1]; **unregelmäßige** Verben: Sonderform (unregelmäßige Verben: S. 263) [2];
  Verneinung *didn't* + Infinitiv [3];
  Fragen *did* + Subjekt + Infinitiv [4];
- **Gebrauch**
  Für Handlungen und Situationen, die in der Vergangenheit abgeschlossen wurden [1] – [4];
  Signalwörter *yesterday* • *the day before yesterday* • *in 1998/2004* • *last week/month/ Christmas* • *two/three days/weeks/months ago* • *at that time / in those days*

4 **Complete the text with verbs from the box. Use the simple past.**

ask (2x) • be • call • come • give • go • have • say • see (2x) • talk • want • work

Dear Mrs Bond

We are sorry to inform you that we *asked* 1 your pupil, Frank Gibson, to leave yesterday. We never like doing this, but unfortunately in this case we …2 no other choice. We …3 to him several times about his negative attitude to work and …4 him many chances to improve, but unfortunately he carried on just as before.

During the ten days he …5 for us, he was late four times. Two days ago, he …6 into the office nearly two hours late and then …7 to leave 90 minutes early to go to the dentist's. We allowed him to go, of course, but then I …8 him in a café in town.

When I …9 him about this, he …10 very rude and virtually …11 me a liar. 'I …12 to the dentist's,' he …13. 'You …14 my twin brother, Charlie.'

In the circumstances, we are sure you will agree that

5 **Julie helped one of the partners at the law firm, Alex Harper. This is a page from his diary. Use the simple past to say what he and others did last Friday.**

EXAMPLE Alex took his car to Apex Motors at 8 o'clock.

FRIDAY – 4 OCTOBER

08:00	take car to Apex Motors
09:00	plan next week's work (with Ben, Sue)
09:30	
10:00	call Grant Summers, New York (about visit to UK)
10:30	check contracts (Jack Webb)
11:00	
11:30	meet Jürgen Hoffmann (about new project for German company)
12:00	discuss work experience programme (with Sarah Davis)
12:30	lunch (Alison Fox; Red Lion pub)

6 **Work with a partner. Use information from Alex's diary to make negative statements. Add further information if necessary.**

EXAMPLE Ben and Sue **didn't discuss** court schedules. They planned next week's work.

7 **Use the simple past to ask your partner what he or she did *yesterday / last weekend / last summer / last Christmas / …* . Then change roles.**

go biking/camping/dancing/drinking/swimming • go to a/the disco / the leisure centre / the movies / a party / the pub • go on holiday • have a date • listen to CDs / the radio • meet sb • play computer games / basketball/cards/football • surf the net • watch a DVD / TV • …

EXAMPLES

Did you go to the pub on Saturday?

Yes, I did. / No, I didn't. I went to the movies.

What did you do at the weekend?

Nothing much. I stayed at home.

Looking at grammar (2): the past progressive

Begleitgrammatik p.195

1 Lee didn't learn much when he **was working** in the office last week.
2 While I **was working** in the shop, I helped customers with their questions.
3 Julie **wasn't working** when the boss came in.
4 What **were** you **doing** when the boss asked you to write a letter?

- **Form**
  was/were + *-ing*-Form des Vollverbs [1] [2];
  Verneinung *was/were* + *not* + *-ing*-Form des Vollverbs [3];
  Fragen *was/were* + Subjekt + *ing*-Form des Vollverbs [4];
- **Gebrauch**
  Für Handlungen, die zu einem bestimmten Zeitpunkt *(when)* oder während eines bestimmten Zeitraumes *(while)* in der Vergangenheit im Gange waren

8 **A** **What was happening when Jeff Gibbs was on his way to work? Make sentences with the past progressive.**

EXAMPLE *A girl was speaking on her mobile phone.*

1 girl / speak / mobile phone

2 two boys / help / old lady / road

3 police / stop / all heavy trucks

4 small crowd / demonstrate / factory gates

5 workers / build / new office block

6 woman / take / dog / walk

B **Use the past progressive to say what the office workers were doing at 12 o'clock. Add any missing words.**

1 Mandy / file / invoice – Liz / type / letter
2 Ben and Jane / talk / visitor – Martin / write / email
3 Ted / make / coffee – Chelsea and Tom / study / catalogue
4 Josh and Maggie / tidy / stationery cupboard – Barbara / book / hotel room
5 Andrea / read / report – Alan and Mike / have / their lunch break
6 Ann / send / fax – Lucy / photocopy / document

9 **Complete the text with the simple past or the past progressive.**

It was nearly closing time at Elektra. Lee and Sarah …1 (get) ready to go home. Suddenly the door …[2] (open) and a man …[3] (come) into the shop. He …[4] (wear) a mask and he …[5] (hold) something in his right hand. Was it a gun?

Sarah …[6] (stand) with her back to the room so she …[7] (not see) what was happening behind her. The man …[8] (catch) hold of her and held her tightly.

Lee …[9] (tell) the man that the till was empty. In fact, the manager …[10] (take) the money to the bank at that moment. But the thief …[11] (not believe) him. 'No tricks,' he said, 'or the girl gets hurt.' Then Lee …[12] (see) that the man …[13] (point) a gun at Sarah's head.

Lee …[14] (look) at the gun. Then he …[15] (smile). 'Come on, mate. That's a toy gun. I …[16] (buy) my kid brother one yesterday.'

10 **Translate the sentences.**

1 Julie hatte viel Spaß, als sie Alex Harper half.
2 Als die Chefin hereinkam, gingen wir gerade nach Hause.
3 Gestern haben die Auszubildenden Coolio besucht.
4 Es gibt keine Karten mehr. Wir haben gestern alle verkauft.
5 Letztes Jahr kaufte die Firma neue Büromöbel.
6 Zu jener Zeit arbeitete Lee in einem Elektrogeschäft in Lime Street.

Time out

Why not get in touch with Anjali Sharma's summer hotline with questions and ideas about holidays? Here's what two of our readers have to say about their plans.

1.4

To: summer@coolio.co.uk
Subject: plans
From: Cathy Edwards >cathy.edwards@uknet.co.uk<
Sent: Wed 23.05.— 10:58

Dear Anjali

I'm leaving school next July and then I'm taking time out, six months or so, to see the world. My problem is that I just can't decide where to go. I was thinking of some exotic destination that I won't have the chance to visit again – Africa or Latin America, perhaps?

The trouble is that my parents, who are going to help me financially, are totally against these places. I'm going to work some of the time and they say I won't find a suitable job in poorer parts of the world. They want me to go to Australia or North America. They say it will be easier to find a good job in a rich English-speaking country, and it will be safer there as well.

But that's not the point, is it? Those places are just like Europe! That's exactly why I'd like to go somewhere completely different. What do you think? Do you have any bright ideas?

Cathy Edwards

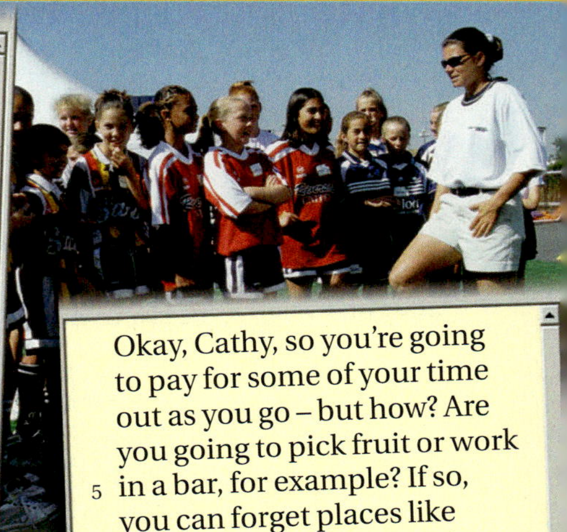

Okay, Cathy, so you're going to pay for some of your time out as you go – but how? Are you going to pick fruit or work in a bar, for example? If so, you can forget places like Africa – and safety really is a problem, especially for girls. Please believe this or I can see that you're going to have a lot of nasty surprises.

Anjali

Hi Anjali

I'm sure you're trying to help people with your summer hotline, but which planet are you living on? There's just no way that I or anybody I know will be able to go on holiday this summer. We're going to have to work to earn a bit of money before school or college starts again in September. Why don't you get real?

Henry Parks

Hi, Henry. I read your email and you're half right. Sure, a lot of people won't be able to have a holiday away from home this or any other year, and a lot of them will have to take a temporary job just to survive. But have you ever thought of combining work with pleasure? Do what I did last year. Search 'holiday jobs' on the net and you'll be surprised by what you find.

Anjali

A Looking at the text

1 Answer the questions.

1 Why is Cathy more interested in going to Brazil, for example, than Canada?
2 Why are Cathy's parents against her choice of a more exotic destination?
3 How will Cathy feel when she reads Anjali's advice?
4 What is Henry's opinion of Coolio's summer hotline?
5 What does Anjali mean when she says that Henry is only 'half right'?
Now you 6 What kind of holiday do you like best? Why?

active holiday • beach holiday • camping • package holiday • sightseeing holiday • study holiday • touring holiday • working holiday • …

B Working with words

2 Find the words or expressions on page 18.

1 to contact somebody
2 period away from school or work
3 verb: 'decision'
4 very colourful and unusual
5 opportunity
6 absolutely, completely
7 noun: 'safe'
8 not permanent
9 to integrate, to join together
10 adjective: 'to surprise'

3 Complete this email with words from Cathy's email.

File Edit View Insert Format Tools Message Help

Hello Cathy
Now, let me just get this right. When you …[1] school in July, you're not going to start work or go to college like most other school-leavers, but …[2] time out 'to see the world'. And – poor you – there lies your first big 'problem'. You just can't …[3] where to go! Your parents want you to go somewhere '…' [4], 'English-speaking' and '…' [5], Canada, for example. But you're wondering whether you should choose somewhere more '…' [6], an African country, say. And that's the 'trouble', as you call it. Daddy's helping '…' [7] and he's …[8] you going to a poor African country where you wouldn't be able to find a …[9] job. Really, Cathy! That's not a '…' [10]. That's called luck!
Mandy Butler

C Looking at grammar: future forms

Grammatik p.196

1 It **will be** safer in Australia or North America.
2 My parents **are going to help** me financially.
3 **I'm leaving** school next July.
4 School **starts** again in September
5 My parents say I **won't find** a suitable job.
6 **Are** you **going to pick** fruit?
7 I can see that you**'re going to have** a lot of nasty surprises.

- **Form**

will-future → *will* + Infinitiv für alle Personen [1]
going to-future → *am/is/are going to* + Infinitiv [2] [7]
present progressive → present progressive + Zukunftsadverb [3]
simple present → simple present + Zukunftsadverb [4]

Verneinung

will-future → *will not / won't* + Infinitiv [5]
going to-future → *am/is/are* + *not* + *going to* + Infinitiv

Fragen

will-future → *will* + Subjekt + Infinitiv
going to-future → *am/is/are* + Subjekt + *going to* + Infinitiv [6]

- **Gebrauch**

going to-future → Absichten, Pläne oder Vorhaben [2] [6]; unmittelbar bevorstehende Ereignisse, für die es schon Anzeichen gibt [7]
present progressive → zeitlich fest geplante Handlungen oder Abmachungen [3]
will-future → Vorhersagen oder Vermutungen über die Zukunft [1] [5]
simple present → durch Fährpläne, Programme festgelegte zukünftige Geschehen [4]
Beachten Sie: Oft können diese Formen ohne Bedeutungsunterschied verwendet werden.

4 What is going to happen? Use verbs from the box.

call somebody • clean • have lunch • ~~land~~ • leave • snow

EXAMPLE The plane **is going to** land.

1

2

3

4

5

5 **Make sentences with *going to* or the present progressive. Use the present progressive when there is an adverb of future time.**

EXAMPLES Mandy / move / her own flat
Mandy **is going to move** into her own flat.

Ben take / a day off / next Monday?
Is Ben **taking** a day off next Monday?

1 Cathy's father / talk / her / about / plans / when he gets home from work
2 we / not have / holiday / away / home / next summer
3 you / find / job / as soon as you leave school?
4 Cathy's parents are happy now. She / work / summer camp / Florida
5 Barbara / fly / Munich / Friday / or / she / go / car?
6 I heard on TV that thousands / British school-leavers / take / time out

6 **Choose the correct future tense.**

1 *Are you attending / Will you attend* the fair in Leipzig next March, Jim?
2 *Are you really going to leave / Will you really leave* school to get a job, Julie?
3 That's enough! *I'm going to tell / I'll tell* the boss that you smoke in my office.
4 *David is taking / David will take* a train tomorrow because he doesn't like flying.
5 *Lucy will have / Lucy's having* a meeting with her boss tomorrow.
6 Have you heard? *We are going to rent / We will rent* offices in Moscow next summer.
7 Mike says *he is lending / he will lend* me some cash until tomorrow.
8 Slow down! *That car in front is going to stop / That car in front will stop.*
9 The weather forecast says *it is raining / it will rain* at the weekend.

7 **Translate the sentences. The pictures will help you.**

1 Nächste Woche fahren wir nach Dresden, um unsere neue Fabrik zu besuchen.
2 Bist du sicher, dass du die Stelle bekommen wirst?
3 Ich habe nicht vor, in den Ferien zu arbeiten.
4 Ich weiß noch nicht, ob ich einen Ferienjob machen werde.
5 Haben Mary und Bob vor, die Firma zu verlassen?
6 Leider werden wir nicht zu Hause sein. Donnerstag fliegen wir nach Italien.

Cathy **is going to fly** to New York.

The plane **leaves** at 06:00.

She **will have to get** the next plane.

You are what you eat

1.5 Do you eat more fatty food and take less exercise than is good for you? Do you know what your 'body mass index' is? Read what Conny Hunt and Sally Webb write to Coolio's fitness expert, Josh Miller.

How's your weight? Work out your body mass index or 'bmi' to find out.

The **body mass index** (bmi) is a good guide to healthy weight. To find out your **bmi**, take your **weight** in kilos and divide it by the square of your **height** in metres.

Example Kim weighs 54 kg and is 1.63 m tall. Her bmi is $54 \div 1.63^2 = 54 \div 2.6569 = 20$, which is normal for a woman according to this table:

Classification	men	women
underweight	<20	<19
normal weight	20–25	19–24
overweight	25–30	24–30
obese	30–40	30–40
extremely obese	>40	>40

Note: age also plays a small role, but not among younger people.

Hi Josh

My boyfriend Tommy thinks all this propaganda about a 'healthy lifestyle' is too much. 'You must eat more fruit' and 'you mustn't drink alcopops' and 'you should do more exercise' – it really annoys him. But I'm not so sure. I think these people may be right. To be honest, a lot of what they say applies to me. I'm definitely not as fit as I should be.

I get out of breath when I have to cycle uphill or even climb a lot of stairs. I don't smoke and I'm not really 'fat'. In fact, I always thought I had a fairly healthy lifestyle. But I was kidding myself. I can see that now. I can't go on living as I have been or I could have health problems in later life. I must eat less and have a healthier diet, and I should do much more physical exercise as well. And do you know something? Since I realized that, I have felt much happier with myself.

Conny Hunt

Dear Josh

I'm a trainer at Fitness First, a gym here in Manchester. I find that a lot of people don't really understand what a 'healthier lifestyle' means. They think that they'll have to spend hours on a fitness machine or doing some sport like athletics to get fit. But in fact you needn't do anything like that at all. Just 20 minutes' exercise a day is enough. You can get that by walking or cycling to school or by using stairs instead of lifts. And a lot of young people think that they'll no longer be able to enjoy a burger and fries or a few beers. They think that they'll just have to eat salads and they'll only be allowed to drink mineral water. But we're talking about a balanced diet. Of course you can eat burgers, but you shouldn't only eat burgers.

Sally Webb

A Looking at the text

1 Who is talking? How do you know?

A health expert

Conny Hunt

Josh Miller

Sally Webb

Sally Webb's boss

Conny's boyfriend

1 I can't stand these health fanatics. They never stop.
2 I'm pleased. I didn't think readers would be interested in health issues.
3 Do you know what a healthy lifestyle is?
4 I advise people to eat better and exercise more.
5 When I accepted that I had a problem, I felt much better in myself.
6 We need healthy, fit young people to work here.

Nowy a1

7 What is your bmi? Are you happy with that?
8 Who do you agree with more – Conny or her boyfriend? Say why (not).

B Working with words

2 Complete the letter with words from the box.

careless • dangerous • higher • ill • medical • public • tolerant • unhealthy • unnecessary

Sir or Madam – Obesity is not a private but a ...[1] thing because we all have to pay obese people's ...[2] medical costs. The fact is that higher ...[3] costs are almost always caused by a person's ...[4] and irresponsible lifestyle. These costs are often completely ...[5]. Look at motorcycling, for example, or any ...[6] sport. And what about people who injure themselves because of ...[7] driving? Or become ...[8] through too much stress? I think we should be ...[9] towards people like this and let them lead their own lives. On the other hand, I don't want to have to pay for them!
Becky Wood, Exeter

C Looking at grammar: modal verbs

Begleitgrammatik p.197

- **can / could / be able to / be allowed to**
  Wir verwenden *can/could* im Englischen genau wie ‚können/könnten' im Deutschen. Für das zukünftige ‚werden können' verwenden wir jedoch *will be able to* (Fähigkeit) und *will be allowed to* (Erlaubnis) als Ersatzverben:
  – They think they **will** no longer **be able to enjoy** a burger.
  – Soon we **will** only **be allowed to drink** mineral water.
- **must / have to**
  In neutralen Situationen verwenden wir *have to*. Wollen wir betonen, dass es sich um eine Verpflichtung handelt, verwenden wir *must*:
  – I get out of breath when I **have to cycle** uphill. (neutral)
  – People **must eat** more fruit. (betont)
- **must / have to: Vergangenheit und Zukunft**
  Must wird nur in der Gegenwart gebraucht. Wir verwenden *have to* für die anderen Zeiten:
  – I **had to cancel** my appointment yesterday.
  – People think they **will have to spend** hours on a fitness machine.
- **mustn't / don't have to / needn't**
  Wir verwenden *mustn't* um ein Verbot auszudrücken. Hat man aber die freie Wahl, dann verwendet man *needn't* oder *don't have to*:
  – Children **musn't drink** alcopops.
  – You **needn't do / don't have to do** anything very energetic at all.
- Die übrigen englischen Modalverben verwendet man genau wie die deutschen Entsprechungen.

3 **Complete these sentences with *have to, must, mustn't* or *needn't*.**

1 You … buy expensive equipment to keep fit. You … just do more exercise, that's all.
2 Some people think that they simply … lose weight to be popular.
3 You … tell me that I … eat so many burgers. I know that already, thanks!
4 Sally … work on Sunday, so she … come in at all on Monday.
5 Some parents say their children … play outside because the streets aren't safe.
6 These children … stay indoors, which is not good for their health.

REMEMBER
musn't = *nicht dürfen*
needn't = *nicht müssen / nicht brauchen*

4 **Think of your lifestyle. Say what you *must/mustn't* do, what you *needn't* do and what you *should, could* or *may* do. The words in the box will help you.**

buy a fitness machine • cycle to the shops / youth club • do more exercise • (not) drink alcohol / mineral water / sweet drinks • (not) eat fast food / healthy food / sweets / TV snacks • go jogging / skiing / swimming • join a gym / sports club • lose weight • take dog for walk • take up a sport • (not) use buses / lifts / stairs • walk to school / town

5 **What would you say? Link sentences 1–6 and a–f.**

1 Ask somebody to do something.
2 Cancel an appointment and say why.
3 Give advice on a healthier lifestyle.
4 Give somebody a choice.
5 Offer somebody a drink.
6 Show somebody a possible danger.

a 'Be careful – you mustn't put your fingers in the machine.'
b 'Can I get you a coffee or would you prefer something stronger?'
c 'Could you show me how to adjust this exercise bike, please?'
d 'I can't come to yoga tomorrow. I have to work Mondays.'
e 'Of course you needn't go to a gym but it's more fun.'
f 'You should eat less and do more exercise.'

6 **Your keep-fit club is organizing a walking tour with one night at a campsite. Talk about the arrangements and make suggestions.**

I	could	buy an up-to-date map.
We	must	check the first aid kit.
Somebody	mustn't	decide on a route.
	should	find out about places of interest.
	shouldn't	fix a time and place to start the tour.
		organize transport of tents to the campsite.
		photocopy the route map and programme.
		reserve places at the campsite.
		tell everybody to bring food and drinks with them.

7 **Complete these sentences using the German in brackets.**

1 It's a pity but I … my appointment tomorrow. *(ändern müssen)*
2 Doctors say that people … much less salt and sugar. *(essen sollen)*
3 According to my bmi, I … at least ten kilos. *(verlieren müssen)*
4 Shops … beer to children, but what about alcopops? *(nicht verkaufen dürfen)*
5 A ban on smoking … smokers to give up smoking. *(helfen könnten)*
6 I'm afraid I … hours at a gym. *(nicht verbringen können)*
7 We … 30 minutes for our fitness trainer yesterday. *(warten müssen)*
8 I'm sorry. I … swimming next Friday after all. *(kommen können)*

8 **Translate the sentences.**

1 Die Gesundheitsexperten meinen, dass wir viel weniger Salz und Süßstoffe verwenden sollen.
2 Sally, darf ich dir meine Schwester vorstellen? Sie ist Sportstudentin und könnte dir helfen.
3 Du musst heute Abend Auto fahren. Du darfst nicht zu viel trinken!
4 Er kann nicht so gut schwimmen, weil er zu viel raucht.
5 Musst du wirklich jedes Wochenende zum Training gehen? Warum kannst du nicht zu Hause bleiben?
6 Du brauchst nicht so viel Zeit im Fitnessstudio zu verbringen. Du bist schon sehr schlank.

Getting about

1.6 Eddy Morris takes a look at our attitudes to cars – and what they say about us as people. Where do you stand?

1 A lot of young people put a car or at least a scooter right at the top of their 'must have' list, ahead of things such as fashionable clothing, holidays in the sun and the latest in electronic gadgets. How about you? What would you buy, if you had the money?

2 In Arizona, 16-year-old drivers have a one-in-four chance of having an accident, many of them fatal or causing permanent injury. But almost all these so-called 'accidents' aren't really accidents at all. They are easily avoidable. Tony Sanchez of Arizona's highway patrol says , 'If these teenage drivers had been more careful and had not driven so fast, most of these accidents wouldn't have happened.'

3 The German government is thinking about a two-year probationary period for new drivers. If the idea becomes law, cars driven by new drivers will carry a big red A (for *Anfänger*) to warn other drivers. And if new drivers break the traffic laws, they'll automatically lose their licences and have to retake their driving test. This idea was introduced in France a few years ago and there are now far fewer accidents among young drivers.

4 London resident: 'Some families in our street have three or four cars. Don't these people see that we can't possibly go on like this? If we don't limit car ownership, nobody will be able to go anywhere. There will be permanent gridlock. And what about the environmental costs? Climate change and so on? Things would get better very quickly if we limited car ownership to a maximum of two cars per household.'

5 Psychologists say that to some young people, particularly boys, cars are much more than just a way to get from A to B. They're also an expression of personality. 'Petrol costs so much nowadays that I don't use my car much,' said one 18-year-old. 'But that's not the point. My car's everything to me. And I spend a lot of my free time working on it. It says who I am. If I didn't have a car, I would be a nobody.'

A Looking at the texts

1 Answer the questions.

1 Match the captions below to the five photos. Then say which text each photo illustrates.
A big red A? • Arizona • Gridlock! • Top of the list • My car's everything
2 What do the texts say about these aspects of car ownership:
environmental costs • personal mobility • leisure aspect •
personal importance • road safety

Now you

3 Would you buy your own set of wheels if you had the money?
4 What do you think of the idea of a two-year probationary period for new drivers?
5 Look in a Monday edition of your local paper. Are there any reports of road accidents over the weekend? If so, tell the class the details.

B Working with words

2 Complete the sentences with words from list A (first gap) and from list B (second gap). Then match the cartoon to one of the sentences.

A	B
avoidable	big fall
break	careless driving
don't limit	do the test
personal mobility	electronic gadgets
probationary period	fatal accident
good chance	gridlock
single households	means of transport
young men	much difference

1 … means much more to many young people than such things as …, say.
2 In Arizona, 16-year-olds have a … of having a … while at the wheel of a car.
3 Tony Sanchez: 'Almost all traffic accidents are … . They are caused by … or driving too fast.'
4 In France, the … for new drivers has already led to a … in accidents among the young.
5 If new drivers … the traffic laws during their probationary period, they have to … again.
6 London resident: 'Can't you see that if we … car ownership, we will have permanent …?'
7 Traffic expert: 'As many households in big towns are …, a limit of one car per household wouldn't make … .'
8 Psychologist: 'A big problem is that for many young people, particularly …, cars are much more than simply a … .'

C Looking at grammar: *if*-sentences

Begleitgrammatik p.200

1 If new drivers **break** the traffic laws, they **will lose** their licences.
2 Things **would get** better very quickly if we **limited** car ownership.
3 If I **didn't have** a car, I **would be** a nobody.
4 If they **had been** more careful, the accidents **wouldn't have happened**.
5 **Would** you **buy** your own wheels if you **had** the money?

■ Form

Zeitenfolge der drei Typen von *if*-Sätzen:

	if-Teil	Hauptteil	
Typ I	*if* + present	*will* / *can* / *may*	+ Infinitiv
Typ II	*if* + past	*would* / *could* / *might*	+ Infinitiv
Typ III	*if* + past perfect	*would have* / *could have* / *might have*	+ 3. Form

Der *if*-Teil kann vor [1] oder nach [2] dem Hauptteil stehen.
Steht der *if*-Teil zuerst, setzt man danach ein Komma.

■ Gebrauch

Bedingung im *if*-Teil, Folge im Hauptteil;
Erfüllung der Bedingung:

– sicher bzw. sehr wahrscheinlich:	Typ I	[1]
– möglich, aber unwahrscheinlich:	Typ II	[2] [3] [5]
– unmöglich, weil schon geschehen:	Typ III	[4]

3 **Say what type (I, II or III) the following *if*-sentences are.**

1 If a bus picked me up at home and took me to my office, I'd use it.
2 If petrol prices go up much more, we'll have to sell our car.
3 If public transport doesn't improve, of course people won't use it.
4 If you had phoned, I'd have picked you up at the station.
5 Most accidents wouldn't happen if all drivers were more careful.
6 There will be no countryside left if they go on building more and more roads.
7 We wouldn't have missed our train if you hadn't overslept.
8 Would Jim have won the grand prix if his car hadn't broken down?
9 Would you buy an old scooter if you needed transport to work?

4 **Work with a partner. First link the *if*-sentences, A and B. Then put the verbs into the correct tense.**

A

1 If everybody … (have) a car,
2 The police would not have stopped you
3 If new drivers have an A on their cars,
4 If people … (not drive) so fast,
5 … (you/buy) a scooter
6 If new drivers … (break) the traffic laws,
7 Drivers … (not go) so fast
8 If the price of petrol had gone up,

B

a if there were more speed cameras.
b if you find a cheap one?
c if you … (stop) at the traffic lights.
d other drivers … (help) them.
e there would be nowhere to park them.
f the roads would be safer.
g they'll have to do the test again.
h we … (sell) our car.

5 **Complete with the right *if*-sentences.**

EXAMPLE If you … (ask) teenagers what they want most, many … (say) a car. *(wahrscheinlich)*
If you **ask** teenagers what they want most, many **will say** a car.

1 If the number of cars … (keep on) increasing, nobody … (be able to) go anywhere. *(wahrscheinlich)*
2 … Frank (repair) my car this weekend if he … (have) time? *(wahrscheinlich)*
3 If there … (be) more speed limits in Germany, there … (be) fewer accidents. *(unwahrscheinlich)*
4 Janna … (buy) a scooter if she … (have) more money. *(unwahrscheinlich)*
5 The driver … (live) if somebody … (call) an ambulance. *(unmöglich)*

6 **Read the dialogues and decide which type of *if*-sentence to use. Then put the verbs into the correct tense.**

1 A Luckily the traffic was light yesterday so the ambulance came quickly.
B You're right. If it … (not come) at once, Tom … (die).
2 A Frank's crazy driving really scares me. He went through a red light today.
B Really? If he … (not be) careful, I have no doubt he … (lose) his licence one day.
3 A Come on, Lucy. If we … (not leave) right now, we … (be) late again.
B Okay. Let's go.
4 A If I … (win) the lottery, the first thing I … (do) is buy a Harley Davidson.
B Dream on. That's not very likely, is it?
A Perhaps not, but one thing's for sure – if you … (not play), you definitely … (not win).

7 **Translate the sentences.**

1 Wenn wir früh genug landen, rufe ich dich an.
2 Sie wären rechtzeitig angekommen, wenn sie den Zug genommen hätten.
3 Hätte ich einen Stadtplan, könnte ich dir zeigen, wo das Auto geparkt ist.
4 Wenn ich ein Auto kaufen würde, würde ich ein gebrauchtes kaufen.
5 Wenn der rote Scooter noch zu haben ist, wirst du ihn kaufen?
6 Wenn er nicht so schnell gefahren wäre, hätte die Polizei ihn nicht angehalten.

EUROPE AT WORK

Focus

a

b

c

d

e

f

A **When Luke flew from London to Amsterdam to see his girlfriend, Andrea, these were some of the people who helped him:**

airline check-in clerk (1)
air ticket bookings clerk (2)
bank clerk (3)
flight attendant (4)
florist (5)
hairdresser (6)
nightclub manager (7)
sales assistant (8)
taxi driver (9)
waiter (10)

1 Match people in the photos to six of the jobs.
2 Say how you think all ten people helped.
3 Put them in the order that you think he saw them.

EXAMPLE *First, I expect the air ticket bookings clerk arranged Luke's ticket.*

B **Say which of jobs 1–10 (or any other job) you would/would not like to do and why. Choose from these words and expressions.**

It would/wouldn't be (very) …
(un)challenging • (un)creative • (in)secure • (un)stressful • interesting/boring • varied/repetitive • well-paid/badly-paid

I'd have to/I wouldn't have to … • I could/couldn't …
be friendly and helpful all the time • be independent • build a good career • deal with customers • do things my own way • do what my boss told me to do • get a good salary • get good company benefits • have a lot of fun • help people • make my own decisions • meet a lot of people • travel a lot • wear a uniform • work flexible/irregular/long/unsocial hours

A People and business

BCC File 6 (Job applications)

1.7 ▶ Look at the photos. Can you guess what sort of work do Ben and Marita do? Read to check.

Different routes to the right job

Ben Hale's story I left school without any plans, and I just started work at a local factory

that made car seats for Honda in Swindon. At first it was only a temporary job but then I moved to stock control because I'd done ICT at school. It was a boring, dead-end job but the pay was OK, so I stayed.

I was there for four years. Then they decided to move production to Poland and make us all redundant. Three months later, six huge trucks arrived from Warsaw. In a week, all the equipment went, and so did 140 jobs.

I was out of work, and that was the push I needed. I decided I really wanted a job with a future. I joined an 'access' programme at Oxford College of Further Education for people who want to return to education, and then I went straight on to an information technology course there.

My redundancy pay covered living expenses for a while, but then I needed a part-time job, and that was hard.

Things worked out well though. BMW were expanding just as I was finishing. I applied for an IT job there, and got it. I've been working there for several months now – in full-time, permanent work at last.

That's unless BMW decide to move to Poland, too! (222 words)

Marita Schneider's story After a secretarial course at home in Dortmund, I decided to go abroad for a while. I wanted to get a further business qualification and also get some international experience.

I applied to colleges in Britain which offered business courses. I was lucky and a few months later, I joined the International Study course at Oxford CFE for a year. The course I took combined English, Business Studies and ICT. It was just what I needed. Then I did a one-year Business Studies diploma course at the same college. And thanks to the EU, it was all free.

It was hard work, but I enjoyed my time at college. It was very international and I made a lot of friends from other countries.

Towards the end of the course, I began sending out CVs and letters of application and filling in application forms. Then, pretty soon, I got some interviews – and a job offer from

Mediscan, a local medical equipment manufacturer. I've been with them for six months now, and they're a good employer. The hours are a bit longer than at home, but the salary is good. They've been training me to work in Export Sales, and it's a really challenging job. (201 words)

BACKGROUND BRIEFING Preparing for work

CFE (college of further education): In every medium-sized town, they offer many types of education and training, e.g. school exam courses, full-time vocational courses, part-time evening classes, and often also international study programmes – free for full-time EU students.

ICT (information and communications technology): school subject

CV (curriculum vitae): part of a job application, giving work experience (American English: resumé)

1 Looking at the text

A Say whether the following are true, false or not stated in the text. Correct the false statements.

1 Ben worked at the car seat factory for a little over four years.
2 The company moved production to Poland because it was cheaper there.
3 He went to university to study information technology.
4 Marita went straight to Oxford after her *Abitur*.
5 The courses she studied did not cost her anything.
6 She will probably stay in Britain permanently.
7 Both Ben and Marita needed courses to prepare them before they studied for their main qualifications.
8 In the end, each managed to get a good job in or near Oxford.

B Say what you think.

1 What sort of job do you hope to have ten years from now? Start like this:
I'd like a job that will … For example, I think I'd like to be a …
2 What steps will you need to take to get there?

2 Working with words

A Complete the network with words from the texts. Lernhilfe p.210

Networks are a great way of building word fields.

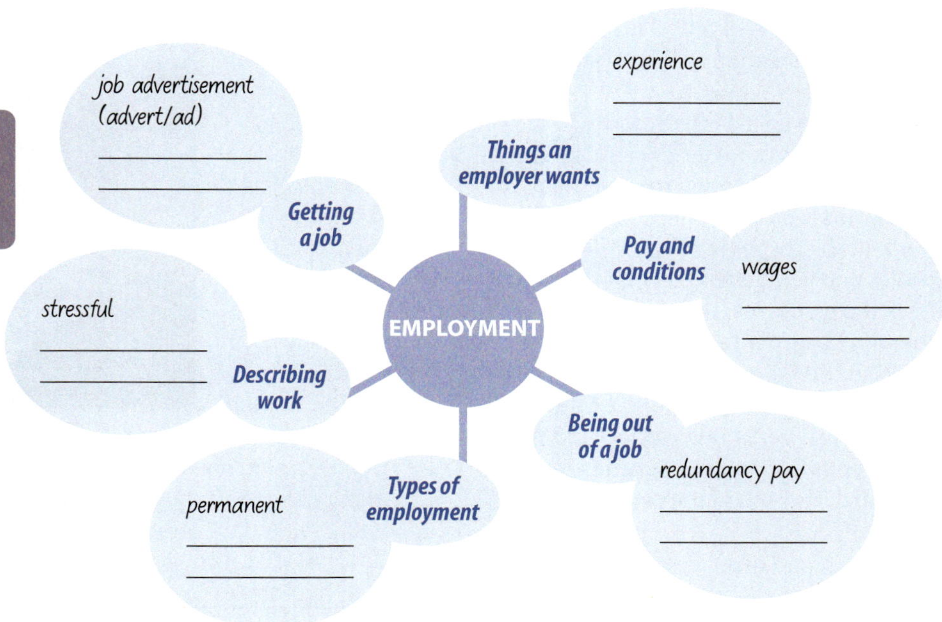

B **Now complete the dialogue. Use words and phrases from the network.**

Ian So what have you been doing since they made us …[1] at the factory?

Ben Well, I wanted to improve my chances of a job with a future, so I went to college to get a proper IT …[2]. Then I got my new job at BMW.

Ian Great! People say they're a good …[3].

Ben Yes, they're OK. The …[4] are fine – good money, good holidays, all that sort of thing. What about you though?

Ian Well, I spent my …[5] on a round-the-world holiday. That made me want to join the travel industry. But it wasn't easy. For ages, I was …[6] most of the time. I did several …[7] jobs, but they never lasted long. I also sent off hundreds of …[8], and filled in loads of …[9], but people never invited me to any …[10]. It was because my …[11] just showed that I was a factory worker. But then I got a …[12] job at weekends at a travel agency. They liked me, and they gave me a …,[13] …[14] job. I've been working there for eighteen months now, and I love it. I get the chance of cheap travel, too!

CULTURE CHECK Forms of address

Read the conversations. Decide the following.

1 When and where were these things said?
2 What rules do the the speakers follow? Who can and cannot suggest using first names?
3 In the same situations in Germany, what forms of address would people use?

Situation 1

A Please come in and take a seat, Miss Schneider. Marita Schneider, isn't it?
B Yes, Ms Brant.
A Well, I'm glad you managed to find us all right. So, let's begin.

Situation 2 (30 minutes later)

A Congratulations! You've got the job.
B Fantastic! Thank you, Ms Brant.
A Oh, please call me Sue. We're very informal here, Marita.

INFO

1 *Mr*, *Mrs*, *Miss* and *Ms* are the usual formal titles used when dealing with clients or customers. We can use *Ms* [məz]/[mɪz] for all women whether they are married or not, and this is common in US English. In Britain, *Ms* is usually written, but it can be used in formal spoken situations. Ms Brant knows from Marita's CV that she is not married and, being British, she chooses to use *Miss*.
2 In many companies, staff use first names with each other – even between junior and senior staff. This may seem very informal, but it is not really. It has nothing like the closeness of the German *du*.
3 As in Germany, changing from formal style to first names must come from the senior person, e.g. from Sue Brant to Marita Schneider.

1.8
1.9

3 Listening

A Listen to Part 1 and answer these questions.

1 Who and where are the speakers?

2 What is going to happen?

B Now listen to Part 2. Where are departments a–g?

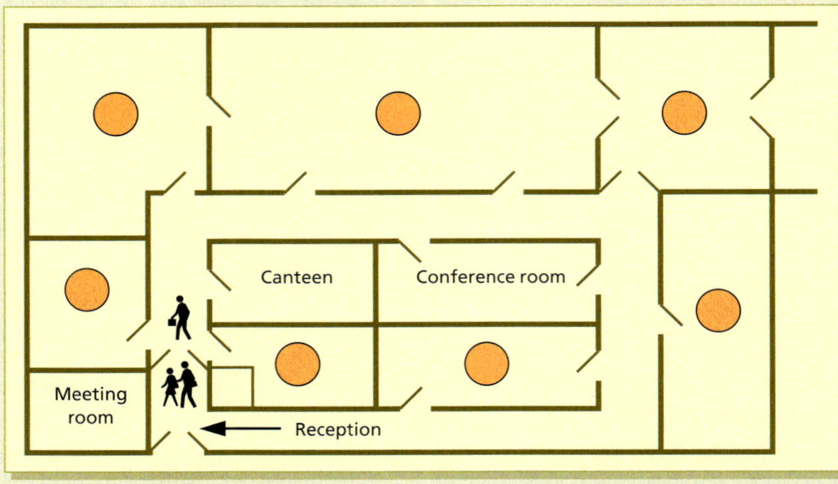

a **Distribution:** distribution staff get the products to the customers

b **Finance:** accountants control the costs

c **Marketing:** market research staff find out what the market wants; marketing planners decide on new products

d **Personnel:** personnel manager deals with staff pay and conditions; staff development officers do staff training

e **Production:** production workers make the products; quality controllers check that all products are perfect

f **Research and Development:** product designers develop new products

g **Sales:** sales staff sell the products; publicity staff arrange the advertising

1.9

4 Using language at work

A Showing visitors around. Listen to Part 2 again. Say which of these you hear.

1 a … let's go this way, round the meeting room …
  b … let's go this way, past the meeting room …

2 a This is the Personnel Department straight ahead.
  b This is the Personnel Department on our right.

3 a The Personnel Manager is the person who …
  b The Personnel Manager is the one that …

4 a The staff development officers are the people that …
  b The staff development officers are the ones who …

5 a I suppose that's the department that looks after the money ...
  b I suppose that's the department which looks after the money ...

B Work with a partner. Copy the plan on page 191 twice. One plan is your company. Label the departments a–g as you wish.

Partner A: show your visitor round, like Marita.

Then swop roles.

B Business and society

1.10

- List the English names of as many EU member states as you can. Which countries have joined most recently?
- Unemployment – particularly youth unemployment – is high in many parts of Europe. What about your own local situation? Is it easy to find jobs?

The new Europe

Europeans are on the move, but is Europe?

Deirdre O'Dwyer

The night before his departure, Slovakian computer parts buyer Michal Adamca, 28, had a goodbye party with friends and family at his home in Bratislava.

It was a happy-but-sad evening. The future looked good after so many tough years of change from communism. However, it was hard to leave everything he knew to build that better future far from home.

Three days later, Michal was at his new job with Planet PC, a large computer retail chain with branches across Britain and beyond. He was one of many who arrived after the EU expanded in 2004 and grew overnight from 15 countries to 25. Most new members were poorer than the older ones, and new EU citizens like Michal were soon travelling to better economic opportunities.

With his skills and ambition, Michal was welcome at Planet PC, Manchester. And for him it meant a salary six times bigger than his previous pay as a technical support manager and also a big career opportunity.

His new employer was not the only British organization that wanted staff from the new central European member states. The economy was growing steadily, unemployment was low, and there were large numbers of job vacancies for skilled workers like Michal. These jobs quickly attracted thousands of people.

The situation was similar in Ireland, but not in other countries. For years, French, German and Italian growth has remained slow and unemployment – especially youth unemployment – very high. This was why Michal chose to move to a country further away from home: there were simply more opportunities.

Why do these economies behave so differently from Britain's and Ireland's? Is it because the English-speaking countries are more like their transatlantic cousins? There, the free-market economy means lower taxes but less job protection and less social security than in most European countries. It is easier for companies to fire people but also easier to hire and to grow.

People like Michal have survived far worse times than most Europeans and Americans. They are ready to take risks and fight hard for success, and the free-market model suits them. Michal says, 'One day I aim to return home as the first director of Planet PC, Slovakia.'

Will the old Europe learn to be a little more like Michal and the new Europe?

(381 words)

BACKGROUND BRIEFING Employment trends

Britain Germany EU (15) USA

Fig 1

Total unemployment (% of workforce)

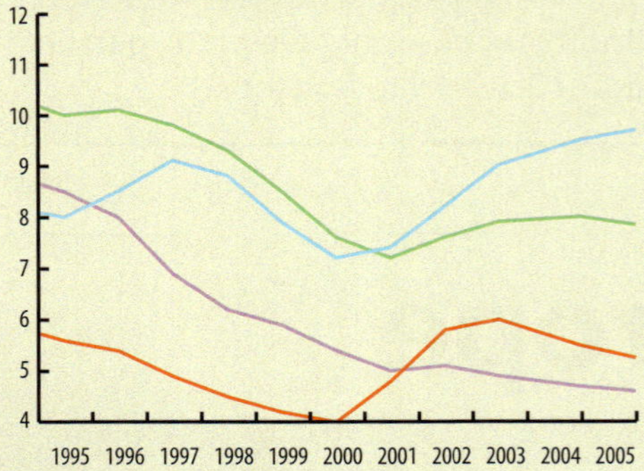

Fig 2

Youth unemployment (% of workforce)

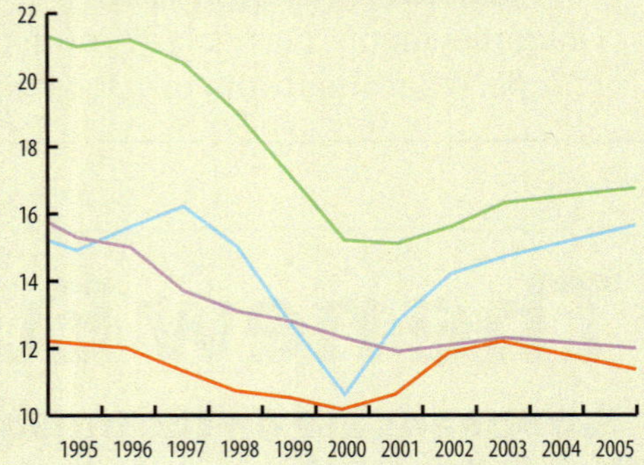

5 Looking at the text

A Decide which of these people might say the following? Explain why.

a Brussels politician • a young, unemployed European • Michal • Michal's boss at Planet PC • Michal's mother-in-law

1 'I can understand why he's doing it, but it's going to be very hard for my daughter and the little ones.'
2 'You work hard to do well at school, and then you work even harder at college, and then at the end of it all – unemployment!'
3 'His English isn't that great, but his technical knowledge is. I wish I could find two more like Michal just for this store here in Manchester.'
4 'EU citizens must have the freedom to work anywhere in Europe. Remember the big picture: we're building a new, re-united Europe!'
5 'The people here have helped me start a new life, but I'm counting the days till I can get back home for two weeks in August.'

B Think about it.

1 Explain the sub-title of the text *Europeans are on the move, but is Europe?*
2 Look at the two graphs in **Background Briefing**. What two points in the text do they tell you more about?

C Say what you think.

6 Writing: interpreting charts

A Use this language to describe the graphs below.

rise	slightly
increase	slowly
grow	steadily
	quickly

remain	steady
	unchanged

fall	slightly
decrease	slowly
shrink	steadily
	quickly

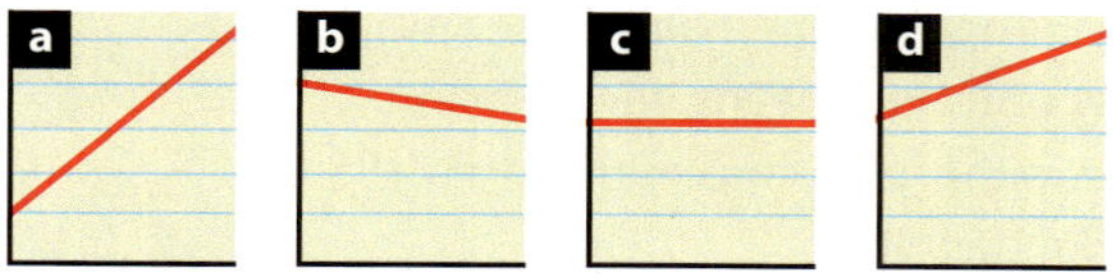

In Graph a, the figures rose …

B Complete the following text about Figure 1 in BACKGROUND BRIEFING. Use information from the graph and the language above.

The graph in Figure 1 shows *total unemployment*[1] between the years …[2] and …[3] in the EU, …[4], …[5] and the …[6].

Britain: Unemployment in Britain fell steadily from 9% to about …[7] between …[8] and 2001. It remained fairly steady from then until 2003. After that it decreased again slowly during the next …[9] years to around …[10]%.

C Write another paragraph about the EU average, Germany or the USA.

D Use information in Figure 2 to write about youth unemployment.

7 Working with words

A Complete the table with words from the text.

Verb	Noun
…	expansion
employ	…
…	choice
economize	…

Verb	Noun
protect	…
…	survival
succeed	…
direct	…

! When you collect words like this, you get two words for the price of one. (Or even three, if you collect verb, noun and adjective!)

B Complete this advert for the job that Michal really wants. Use words above.

Director[1] **Planet PC (Slovakia)**

Planet PC is now …[2] across the EU. In particular, our new operations in the fastest-growing …[3] of Poland and Hungary are experiencing …[4].
We are now looking for an energetic and experienced person to lead our …[5] into Slovakia. This person will …[6] an operation which will …[7] approximately 50 staff. To …[8], the new Director will need excellent Slovak and English as well as strong general management abilities.

C Should Michal get the job? What might his strengths and weaknesses be?

C Task options

8 Choosing a summer project

Work with a partner. You have decided to work as volunteers in Europe next summer. Euro-Serve has many different projects.

ABOUT EURO-SERVE

Euro-Serve offers young Europeans the chance to see other parts of Europe and meet other Europeans. We run many different sorts of projects in the following countries: Austria, Spain, Britain, Sweden, Hungary, Italy

About our projects

Austria
* Caring for elderly people
* Repairing mountain paths for walkers

Spain
* Organizing activities at a children's summer camp
* Working on an experimental desert farm

Britain
* Doing office work for an international charity
* Volunteering on organic farms

Sweden
* Analyzing the results of a tree survey
* Repainting and other DIY work for elderly people

Hungary
* Taking part in an archaeological dig
* Repairing a children's home

Italy
* Working with injured wild animals
* Cooking at a summer camp for teenagers

1 Read Euro-Serve's booklet, and agree which countries you would like to visit.
2 Read about the projects in your chosen countries and decide which ones interest you.

I'd	quite like	to visit	(country, place).
	really love	to see a bit of	
	prefer	to get to know	

I wouldn't mind trying ...	It	seems	quite challenging.
I don't like the idea of ...		might be	very boring.
I'd rather try ...		could be	hard work.

3 Choose the project that you like best. Explain your decision to the class.

We've	decided	to go to ...	because ...
	agreed		since ...
And we've	chosen	...	as ...
	decided on	...	because ...

Grammar checkpoint

1 Simple past and perfect tenses

Begleitgrammatik p.196

Put the verbs into the best tense – present perfect progressive, present perfect or simple past.

Sam I'm looking for today's post, Mum. Have you seen [1] (*you/see*) it?
Mum Yes, it …[2] (*just/arrive*). And look, there's one for you.
Sam Ah! I think this is the one I …[3] (*wait*) for.
Dad Is it the answer to one of your job applications?
Sam Yes, it's from TopTec.
Mum Poor boy! You …[4] (*try*) so hard to get another job. It's about time for some good news.
Dad From TopTec? …[5] (*you/not have*) an interview there a few weeks ago?
Sam Yes, and I think I …[6] (*do*) quite well at that interview, but you just never know. I …[7] (*worry*) about it for the last three weeks!
Mum Well, you'd better open it!
Dad And? What …[8] (*they/decide*) – yes or no?
Sam Wow! The answer is yes! They …[9] (*give*) me the job!

2 Adverbs and adjectives

Begleitgram. p.198

Add the adjectives to the sentences. Change them into the correct forms where necessary. (Some are irregular!)

1 Silke's an … worker, and she's done the job … … . (*excellent, real, good*)
2 You're talking too … . Could you … speak a little more …, please? (*fast, possible, slow*)
3 Stop! Don't switch on yet. The instructions … say that it's … to check everything … first. (*clear, important, careful*)
4 Stefan never looks very … in his job, but he … works very … . (*happy, actual, hard*)
5 …, profits have risen …, even though sales have fallen … … . (*surprising, steady, slight*)
6 You have to speak in a … way – even to customers who are … and speak to you … . (*friendly, difficult, unpleasant*)
7 Dieter always used to come to work …, but just …, he's started getting to the office very … . (*early, late, late*)
8 …, Barbara … realized that there was a fire, and she … called for help. (*fortunate, quick, immediate*)

3 Relative and contact clauses

Begleitgrammatik p.199

Complete the story with relative pronouns (*who, which, that*) where necessary.

The letter …[1] Sam received from TopTec went on to say: 'Please see my assistant, Pat Smith, in Room 256, West Block, at 8.30 on September 9. Pat is the person …[2] will look after you on Day 1. Please find enclosed a site map …[3] will help you find us. Please remember to wear the ID label …[4] we are also enclosing.'

* * *

It was 8.20, and Sam was at the main entrance. He felt in his pocket, and then he realized he had forgotten to put the map and ID label in the pocket of the new jacket …[5] he was wearing. Luckily, the security man …[6] he spoke to at the entrance produced a new label – but only after he had called Personnel. Now it was 8.25!

He rushed in. Where was West Block? He asked a girl …[7] was walking past, and she pointed. It was miles away! He started to run.

Outside West Block he asked a man …[8] was carrying a ladder, 'Where can I find Pat Smith, please?' It was 8.29!

'Down there.' The man pointed to some steps …[9] ran down under the building.

Sam rushed down and found himself in front of a large, unfriendly man …[10] was wearing overalls …[11] were covered in oil. 'I'm looking for Pat Smith,' Sam gasped.

'That's me,' the man said. 'So – they've finally given me the help …[12] I've been asking for.' He pointed. 'Put those overalls on.'

'But I thought you were a woman!'

The man stared. 'You're making a bad start, boy,' he said angrily.

2 REACHING THE MARKET

Focus

a

b

c

d
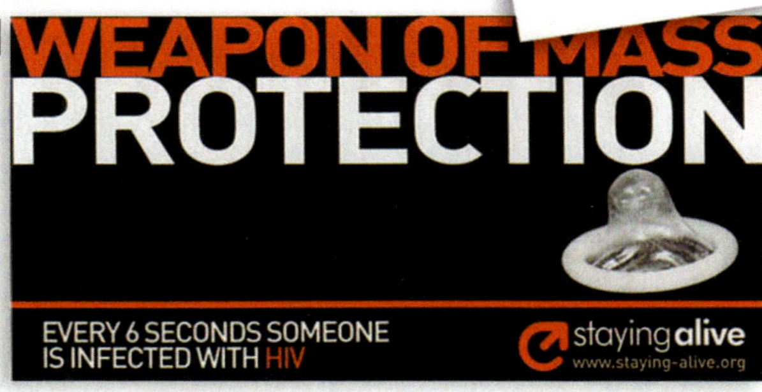

e

A Advertising never leaves us alone. Where have you seen or heard advertisements in the last 24 hours? What sort of adverts were they?

> pop-up Internet ads • neon signs • posters • brochures • leaflets • TV • radio commercials • full-page ads • small classified ads • newspapers • sponsorship (football shirts, etc.)

B What do you think of these adverts? Use adjectives like these.

> boring • clever • glamorous • funny • shocking • silly • strange • disgusting

C The aims of advertising vary. For example: to present products, promote brands or to make the public think. What do the adverts in the picture do?

D Adverts use images and/or words (often a 'play on words') for their message. Explain the messages in these adverts.

A People and business

1.11

- If you go to a party this weekend, what will you probably wear?
- Would you have worn the same things to the same party a year or two ago? What has changed – you, or fashion, or both?

Youth market movers

Whatever New Yorker Kate Lawrence wears, people notice. It might be something she herself has made, or it might be an odd combination of things she has put together. Her friends may not always like Kate's latest creation, but then they just accept Kate's unusual taste and say: 'That's kind of strange, but it looks OK on you.' Other times, though, they cannot wait to copy her.

All over America, clothing manufacturers are turning to inventive 'cutting-edge' kids like Kate. They know that they are wearing today what millions of others will want to wear tomorrow.

This youth market is big business. There are over 40 million in the 15–24 age group, and between them they spend over $350 billion a year. That is an average of $8,750 each!

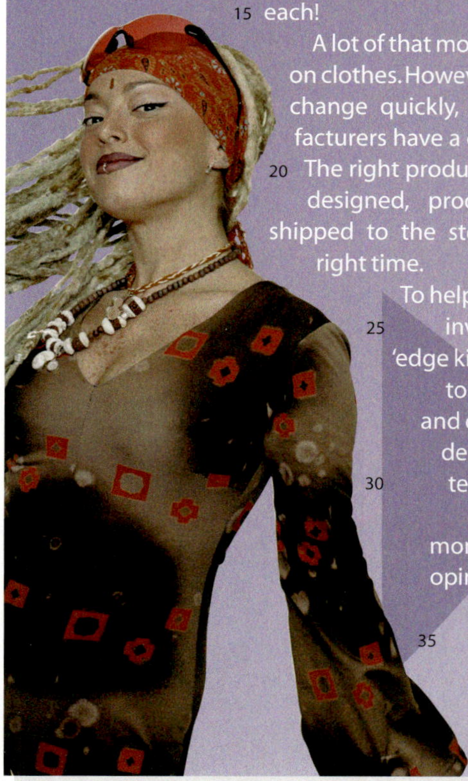

A lot of that money is spent on clothes. However, fashions change quickly, and manufacturers have a difficult job. The right product has to be designed, produced and shipped to the stores at the right time.

To help, they often invite creative 'edge kids' like Kate to join groups and discuss new designs. These teenagers are paid good money for their opinions. These are noted carefully by market researchers and are very helpful in deciding new directions. Kate has joined several such groups recently, and she really enjoys it.

'Influencers' are the second important group. They do not invent new trends, but they are quick to adopt ones they see and like. They have status among their friends, and their choice of clothing quickly becomes the choice of others. Equally, the things they *don't* choose never become mainstream – the 'gothic look', for example.

Sam Oleksi is an influencer. He constantly looks for things that are new, and he shops everywhere. People sometimes laugh at his latest outfit, but they may well buy the same thing a few months later. By that time, of course, Sam has moved on.

Like Kate, Sam earns money from his fashion sense. He often completes questionnaires for manufacturers, and he gets paid around $40 per hour for this.

Edge kids and influencers together make up fewer than one out of five of their generation. However, their importance is far greater than their numbers. It is they who largely decide what will soon be worn by the other 80%. (377 words)

BACKGROUND BRIEFING World trade in clothes and textiles

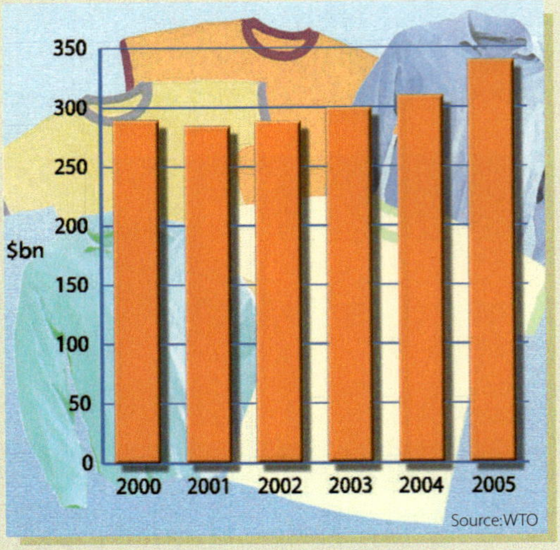

A lot of the clothes that Sam and Kate buy come from factories in China. Until the end of 2004, the World Trade Organization (WTO) allowed developed countries to protect themselves from cheap Chinese imports through quotas. In 2005, imports of clothing increased dramatically, flooding the EU and USA. New temporary controls were therefore set up. However, longer-term, China's share of world clothing exports is estimated to grow from the present 20% to 47% in 2010. Clothing and textile industries in developed economies are under extreme pressure.

1 Working with the text

A Explain these numbers from the text and BACKGROUND BRIEFING.

over 40 million • $8,750 • $40 • one in five • 31/12/04 • 47%

B Copy and complete the following notes. (You will need them later.)

1 Points of similarity between 'edge kids' & influencers
- Interest in clothes: Both love new fashion ideas.
- Effects on others: ...
- Market research: ...

2 Point of difference
- Creating new ideas / Choosing new ideas: ...

C Say it in other words. Match these words and phrases from the text with a–h below.

Youth market movers (text title) • an odd combination (line 2) • unusual taste (line 4) • 'cutting-edge' kids (line 7) • such groups (line 38) • influencers (line 40) • mainstream (line 47) • may well (line 53)

a a strange set
b meetings of this sort
c people who cause big changes
d people who have an effect on others
e young fashion leaders
f are likely to
g accepted as normal by most people
h a strange interest or liking

D Say what you think.

2 Working with words

A Complete the table with words from the text.

	Verb	Noun	Adjective
1	create	creation	creative
2	...	invention	...
3	...	...	productive
4	...	help	...
5	...	...	chosen

! Remember we said you could get three words for the price of one? Well, here we go!

B Now complete the sentences with words above.

1 *Creative* teenagers like Kate Lawrence think differently to other people. Her fashion ... often seem mad to her friends.
2 'Thanks, everyone, for a very ... meeting. You're going to see a lot of your ideas in our new ... in the coming months.'
3 'Which colour would you ...?' – 'Well, it's not my ..., but if it were, I'd go for blue.'
4 'Thanks for all your ... with this design. Lots of your ideas have been very ... .'
5 Shanghai Textile have ... a new type of man-made cloth. It's very strong, and I think this is an ... that will change the world textile industry.

C Study the table below. Then express the proportions below in the other two ways.

	1	2	3
10%	10 per cent	a tenth	*one out of ten
50%	50 per cent	a half	*one out of two
66%	66 per cent	two thirds	two out of three
75%	75 per cent	three quarters	three out of four
80%	80 per cent	four fifths	four out of five
*Also with 'one': *one in two, one in five*, etc.			

1 They make up fewer than <u>one out of five</u> of their generation.
2 It is they who decide what will be worn by the other <u>80%</u>.
3 As many as <u>three quarters</u> of the T-shirts we wear are produced in the Far East.
4 Up to <u>nine out of ten</u> of our company's new designs are never manufactured.
5 In our local shopping mall, around <u>33 per cent</u> of the stores sell clothing.
6 Nearly <u>two thirds</u> of those stores sell mainly to young people.

3 Writing

Read your notes for exercise 1B again. Then write a summary in two paragraphs. Start the paragraphs with these sentences.

One: *There are several points of similarity between 'edge kids' and 'influencers'.*
Two: *There is also an important difference between edge kids and influencers.*

Use some of these words.

Both groups ... • They both ... • ... also ... •
In addition, ... • ..., but ... • However, ... • While ...,

B Business and society

1.12

Do you think brands are important?

WHAT BRAND ARE YOU?

Look, they're drinking Pepsi, not Coke! Are you more Timberland than Nike? What would you think of me if I rode a Harley Davidson? We often choose a brand because of what it says about us.

But how do brands do this? First of all, they are made up of names, logos, slogans, designs and colours that we recognize immediately. They are fixed in our minds, at least partly by frequent advertising. But the ones we like are kept there by our positive feelings for them. We buy them because we trust them to be the best.

'The best' may just mean reliable quality at a reasonable price. But a strong brand often means something much more emotional. It may make us believe we are the person we really want to be – tough, cool, special, feminine, whatever. And other people will believe so too.

When we buy a particular brand instead of its competitors, we are promised things, and the brand must keep its promise. If the brand does not 'deliver', our brand loyalty can soon be lost and we will look for another product. No wonder companies like Coca-Cola advertise so much and fight so hard to keep their brands strong.

So how does an advert for a brand work? Look at this example.

- Above all, Nokia wants us to know that this is a high-quality product – an object of desire that shows the world the elegantly simple, modern, good taste of its owner. The beautiful image suggests a creation at the edge of technology. **(1)**
- The slogan at the top right leads us to the words on the left. This is no cheap, plastic phone. It is made with the traditional skill that goes into jewellery and watchmaking – a work of art as much as it is a phone. **(2)**
- All this suggests that the telephone technology inside is also the finest. If we want to know more, then the website provides full details. **(3)**
- But do we? Aren't we already sure of the high quality? After all, we know that the 8800 comes from the world's biggest mobile phone maker, and that Nokia is still, as always, 'connecting people'. **(4)**

(360 words)

BACKGROUND BRIEFING The advertising industry

After several bad years, world expenditure on advertising in 2005 was about $358bn and rising. The USA is about 45% of the total, and spending there is also rising faster than in Europe.

In America, the industry accounts for 1.4% of the whole economy, while for Europe the figure is just 0.8%.

Online advertising is the fastest-growing advertising medium today, and many US agencies now spend more on this than any other, including TV. Worldwide online advertising expenditure is expected to reach $16.1bn by 2009.

On average, advertising adds about 3% to the cost of goods and services.

Advertising expenditure by region 2004

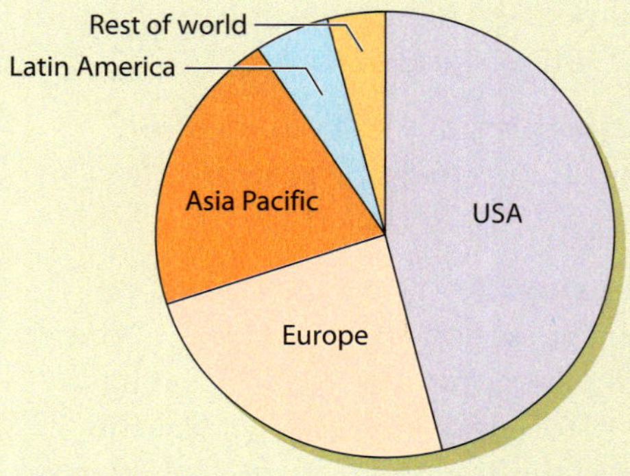

Advertising expenditure: % growth 2004

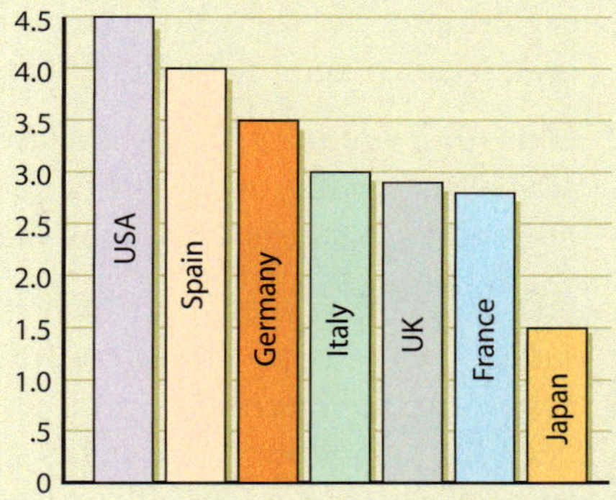

4 Looking at the text

A Answer the questions on the text and BACKGROUND BRIEFING.

1 What helps us recognize a product among its competitors?
2 Define a 'strong brand'.
3 What is the suggestion behind the last sentence in the text (line 32)?
4 What two points of comparison does BACKGROUND BRIEFING make between advertising in the USA and Europe?

B Match a–e in the advert in the text to (1)–(4) in the analysis.

C Think about it.

1 Read the dictionary definitions. Then say what the title of the text might mean.
2 Think of two well-known brands – of cars, for example. What images of themselves do the customers of each brand have?

brand *n* 1 a mark made with a hot, metal tool especially on cows to show who owns them. 2 a particular kind or type: *She has an unusual brand of humour.* 3 a product or group of products with a special name and all produced by the same company.

D Say what you think.

5 Working with words

A Find the opposites of the following in the text.

1 negative (paragraph 2)
2 worst (paragraph 2)
3 weak (paragraph 3)
4 ordinary (paragraph 3)
5 masculine (paragraph 3)
6 won (paragraph 4)
7 traditional (point 1)
8 ugly (point 1)

B Zara Cooper is co-director of the London advertising agency CooperWeston. Use the words above and their opposites to complete her talk with staff at the end of the year.

'Well, everybody, just a few words before the party begins. Generally speaking, it's been quite an *ordinary*[1] sort of year – fairly successful but without too much excitement. But there have been some …[2] moments to remember, too, such as our Gold Medal from the Media Council. Congratulations to all of you!

Like other agencies, we've had fairly …[3] growth of just 2.5% in TV and radio advertising while, on the other hand, there's been extremely …[4] growth – 18% – in our online business. Long may that continue!

Like every other year, there have been some ups and downs. Just last week, we sadly …[5] the Cappo Coffee contract. But on the other hand, we have just …[6] the very valuable Greenway Foods account. The most important event all year has been the end of our relationship with Galloway Tobacco. In one way, it was the …[7] event of the year since Galloway was our biggest multinational client. However, we believe it was also the …[8], as none of us wanted to promote smoking any more. This has also ended the …[9] attacks our agency has sometimes suffered, and it now allows us to present a much more …[10] image of ourselves.'

6 Using language at work

Begleitgrammatik p.200

Zara Cooper wants a publicity leaflet for new clients. Use her notes and rewrite the list of points in the passive so the language is more formal.

EXAMPLE 1 *As a first step, a general advertising concept is prepared …*

1 As a first step, we prepare a general advertising concept for the client.
2 We then present the concept (often in competition with other agencies).
3 If the client chooses our concept, we can then discuss further development of the ideas.
4 If we complete this stage successfully, we then have to agree a detailed schedule for completion.
5 After we sign a contract, we make one of our experienced team of account executives responsible for the project.
6 Clients may discuss commercial matters with our Business Manager, but they should deal with all project communications through the account executive.

1.13

7 Reading and listening

A Match advertising agency jobs and job descriptions a–d.

Account executive | Creative team (copywriter and designer) | Business manager | Media planner

a Deals with the financial side of clients' accounts, including payments and contracts.
b Organises schedules: when and where to advertise, including the mix of radio, TV, print and other media.
c Manages a project, linking the client and the creative team and media planners, advising and reporting in all directions.
d Works closely together to develop an advertising concept, producing the words and creating the 'look'.

B Listen to the conversations. Which of the jobs above do Terry, David and Petra do? Listen again and explain the situations.

1.13

8 Using language for life

Meeting people. Listen to the start of each conversation. Say which of these you hear.

1 a How are you?
  b How's everything with you?
2 a It's nice to meet you.
  b It's lovely to meet you.
3 a It's good to meet you, too, …
  b It's great to meet you, too, …
4 a Not bad, thanks. And you?
  b Not too bad, thanks. Yourself?

9 Writing

BCC File 1 (letter layout)

CooperWeston Ltd has offered you two weeks' work experience. You have the chance to 'shadow' a person in any of the jobs in exercise 7A. Write a short, formal thank-you letter to the director, Ms Zara Cooper.

- Write your own address and the addressee's name and address (52–54 Bedford Row, London, WC1 4LR). Start (and finish) appropriately.
- Refer by date to Ms Cooper's letter and thank her for offering you the chance.
- Explain which job you would like to shadow, and why this would be very useful. (Think about your interests, abilities or future career hopes. See Unit 1, page 30.)
- Finish by saying that you look forward to meeting Ms Cooper and the staff at CooperWeston and to starting your work experience with them on (date).

CULTURE CHECK Appropriate greetings

It is your first day at CooperWeston. Your new section head, Ann Reece, introduces you to Zara Cooper's partner, Tony Weston. Should you reply with a), b) or c)? What could Mr Weston and you say next? (Look back at exercise 8.)

Ann R Mr Weston, this is (your name).
Mr W How do you do?
You a) Fine, thank you. How do you do?
 b) I'm fine, thanks. How are things going?
 c) How do you do?

Later you see a young employee, Tania Day, who you know quite well. Which greeting do you use? How could she reply?

You a) Good morning, Tania!
 b) Hi, Tania! How are you?
 c) Hello, Tania! How do you do?

C Task options

10 Listening and speaking

1.14

A **Here, Zara Cooper, co-director of the London advertising agency CooperWeston, explains the AIDA advertising formula. Listen and note what AIDA stands for. Why is the ad below a good example of AIDA?**

B **Work with a partner. Find an advert and analyze it as Zara Cooper did with the mobile ring tone advert.**

11 Discussion and writing

With a partner work as the creative team – copywriter and designer – on an advert.

1 Produce a poster for one of the following:
   a a famous tourist sight in your town or region
   b a concert for a big German band visiting Britain for the first time and playing in London, Bristol, Manchester and Glasgow
2 Present your advert to the rest of the class. They are:
   a members of your local tourist information organization
   b the band members, manager and other back-up team members
3 At the end, take a class vote to decide which of the ads wins.

Grammar checkpoint

1 Passive 1

Begleitgrammatik p.200

David, an account executive at CooperWeston, wrote these notes on 20th January about the recent Starlight campaign. Write them as a formal report, using the passive. Use past, present and future forms as necessary.

We were asked to make a presentation in early November.

1 Early November: Starlight asked us to make a presentation.
2 1st December: Creative team presented basic concept.
3 8th December: Starlight chose us to do campaign.
4 Same day: Boss asked me to manage the account.
5 Since then: Have kept client up to date with progress through daily contact.
6 10th January: Finalized TV, magazine and poster campaign dates.
7 Last few days: Media Planning Dept have booked TV commercial slots for early April.
8 Today: Have just agreed final script for TV commercial and artwork for magazine campaign.
9 This week: Planning people are booking magazine space for early April to early May.
10 2nd–5th February: Make film commercial in Mexico, and show it on TV for first time – 1st April.

Name tags must be worn.

2 Passive 2

Begleitgrammatik p.200

Put these instructions into the passive. Where might you see them?

1 You may take up to five kilos on board as hand luggage.
2 People must wear name tags at all times when in this building.
3 You need to check oil and water levels and tyre pressures every week.
4 You should contact the company within 24 hours of an accident.
5 We will send you your new personal identification number (PIN) in the near future. You can then use the PIN as it is, or you can change it to a number of your choice. But you must not choose an easy number such as 1111.

3 Passive 3

Begleitgrammatik p.200

Put the following questions and answers into the passive. Leave out the agent (*by* ...) where you think it is not important.

Facts about advertising

1 Q When did people first use printed advertisements?
  A They produced the first ones in Strasbourg in 1466.
2 Q Where did somebody open the first advertising agency in the world?
  A Somebody started it in England in 1786.
3 Q Who set up the first American advertising agency?
  A An Englishman, Volney B Palmer, began the first one.
4 Q How much do US companies spend on advertising per year?
  A They spend over $150 billion on it every year.
5 Q Why do people invest so much in advertising?
  A Because good-quality advertising greatly increases sales.
6 Q Who runs ad campaigns for things like safe driving?
  A The government usually runs campaigns like that.

3 THE ROAD TO THE FUTURE

Focus

A **Look at the newspaper headline and photo and do these tasks.**

1 Describe the scene.
2 Imagine yourself as one of these commuters. Would you be calm and relaxed, anxious and worried about losing time, or frustrated and angry?
3 What might you say to yourself (or to anyone else in the car)?
Think about: present speed, distance to go, possible causes of the tailback, the number of cars on the roads.
Also think about: getting to work/appointments, children getting to school, a boyfriend/girlfriend to meet, a plane/train to catch.

B **Why do these people commute by car? Do you agree with them?**

Julie Miller, office manager: 'I don't have time to take the train as it takes at least 15 minutes longer. I know that sounds silly, but those are 15 minutes I need to do something else.'

Raul Ramirez, cellphone technician: 'I'd rather be in my car, listening to music, than be shoulder-to-shoulder with strangers on some kind of public transport.'

Andrea Goldstein, banker and mother of two: 'I'd love to take the bus home, but unless the driver is going to stop at the day care, dry cleaning and video store, I've got no use for it.'

C **Work with a partner and do these tasks.**

1 List good and bad things about:
a) having your own car;
b) using public transport.
2 Decide whether, as a commuter, you would:
a) use a car like Julie Miller and the others;
b) use public transport.

A People and business

1.15

- Is overcrowding on the roads a problem anywhere in your region?
- What, if anything, is the government doing about traffic congestion?

Gridlock!

DAVID DALE We're just getting news of total gridlock in and around London after several bad accidents. Nadia Shah brings us the latest. Nadia.

NADIA SHAH David, I'm here on the A4 into West London, and I'm with Peter Drake, a truck driver. Peter, what's it like?

PETER DRAKE Terrible! I've only moved 100 metres in the last hour. I don't know when I'll be able to make my first delivery.

NADIA SHAH What's the answer?

PETER DRAKE More roads. We pay the highest fuel taxes in Europe, so give us more roads!

NADIA SHAH Thanks, Peter! Now to Gill Bell, who's in a very full people carrier.

GILL BELL It's awful. I'm on the school run with my own and two neighbours' children. I'm worried about all the exhaust emissions. They're bad for our planet and for our children's health.

NADIA SHAH True, but your car sharing system is great.

GILL BELL Thanks, but look. How many other full cars can you see? None! If more drivers shared, there'd be far fewer vehicles on the roads, much less pollution, and we'd all move a lot faster.

NADIA SHAH So, David, it's a bad situation. Back to you.

DAVID DALE Thanks. Well, I have with me Tessa Parr, Secretary of State for Transport. Tessa Parr, should you spend drivers' taxes on more roads?

TESSA PARR We *are* spending a lot, but that isn't the real answer. This is a very serious situation. There were 20 million cars on the roads in 1990 and by 2025 there will be 40 million if we do nothing. Chaos! We could never build enough roads to keep up.

DAVID DALE So we need to control the amount of traffic. What are other countries doing?

TESSA PARR Various things, but nothing works perfectly. Austrians have to buy permits to use their motorways. But then they often make more journeys than necessary just to get their money's worth. The French pay road tolls, so they cross into Germany and avoid the charges. America encouraged car sharing in the past, but it was never very popular.

DAVID DALE And here, drivers in London pay a big congestion charge, but we've *still* got today's gridlock!

TESSA PARR We need new answers. People who have to drive must be able to drive efficiently. We must also cut environmental and health damage.

(377 words)

BACKGROUND BRIEFING Cars and congestion charging

- Globally, nearly 100,000 new cars are produced every day.
- In developed economies, about 25% of CO_2 emissions are from road traffic.
- In Britain, 55% of people drive themselves to work. Only 6% of workers travel as car passengers.
- London's congestion charging scheme:
  – cars are charged £8.00 per day to enter;
  – led to a 30% reduction in congestion;
  – bus travel up by 38%;
  – about 65% of money taken in charges is used to improve public transport;
  – much traffic has in fact been pushed onto roads around central London;
  – nearly 65% of small businesses in and close to the zone have suffered falling sales and many have considered moving out of the zone.

1 Looking at the text

A Say whether the following are true, false or not in the text and Background Briefing. Correct the false statements.

1 Today's gridlock caused the accidents.
2 Peter Drake's first delivery is in central London.
3 There will be a 100% increase in cars between 1990 and 2025.
4 Tessa Parr wants to spend less on road building, not more.
5 All Austrian drivers have to buy permits.
6 If London had not introduced the congestion charge, the gridlock today would be even worse.
7 Tessa Parr wants to find a way to control the amount of traffic on the roads.
8 In the UK, 55% of people go to work by car.
9 Congestion charging has brought benefits and problems.

B Explain the following. Look carefully at the context.

1 the A4 (line 5)
2 fuel taxes (line 12)
3 bad for our planet (line 20)
4 Secretary of State for Transport (line 34)
5 enough roads to keep up (line 43)
6 to get their money's worth (line 51)

C Say what you think.

2 Working with words

Read about Peter Drake's work, and complete the description with the best preposition in brackets.

Peter lives just west of London, but he drives his 40-tonne truck all ...[1] *(through, over)* the country. Last Monday, he drove ...[2] *(into, from)* central London early to avoid the congestion charge. There, he picked up his first load, turned ...[3] *(round, over)*, drove ...[4] *(out of, towards)* London and ...[5] *(up, through)* the M1 motorway ...[6] *(away from, to)* Leeds.

On Tuesday, he picked up another load in Leeds and took the M62 ...[7] *(across, from)* there ...[8] *(towards, down)* Manchester, south-westwards ...[9] *(along, over)* the Pennine Mountains.

On Wednesday, he left early for Birkenhead and Liverpool. After one drop in Birkenhead, he drove ...[10] *(through, under)* one of the tunnels that run ...[11] *(under, along)* the River Mersey, and he made another drop in Liverpool.

On Thursday, he travelled north, driving ...[12] *(into, across)* the Scottish border at lunchtime and reaching Glasgow that evening.

On Friday, he drove back home via Newcastle. He drove ...[13] *(under, past)* Edinburgh and then ...[14] *(along, up)* the east coast, reaching Newcastle at midday. Finally, he travelled home ... [15] *(down, over)* the M1.

3 Using language at work

Work with a partner. Develop a role-play, using expressions from exercise 2.

Partner A: You are Peter Drake, and you have just delivered a load to a factory in Germany. This is your first trip to Germany, and you need directions to your next destination.

Partner B: Help Peter. Tell him the different routes he could take. Advise the best / quickest / simplest route.

Before you start, agree Partner A's destination – somewhere about 100 kilometres away. If possible, use a map of the area where you live.

Start like this:

A Excuse me, but could you give me directions to (destination), please?
B Yes, of course. Go out of the factory gates and turn ...

4 Writing

A Match sentences 1–8 and a–h.

1 Traffic congestion in Britain is getting worse because
2 Building more roads is not the answer as
3 Other countries have tried various schemes to control traffic, but
4 Austrians use their motorways more than necessary in order to
5 Some French drivers cross into Germany so as to
6 Car sharing in America was not very successful as
7 New answers to the problem of congestion are needed since
8 The new way forward must allow people to drive efficiently and

a the old answers have not worked very well.
b avoid paying tolls on their own roads.
c it would be impossible to construct enough.
d also reduce unnecessary and damaging use of the roads.
e people refused to continue doing it for very long.
f the number of cars on the roads is rising fast.
g they have not been very successful.
h feel they are getting their money's worth for the permits they have to buy.

B Write out the sentences in 4A as a summary. Add these expressions.

Again, … • For example, … • However, … • In particular, … • It therefore seems that … • Then again, …

CULTURE CHECK Being indirect

INFO

English speakers are usually less direct than German speakers. They try to make requests, instructions, opinions, etc. 'softer'. This is partly through intonation but also through the words they use. They use polite expressions and also sound less definite.

Gill Bell has recently moved to London and heard about the neighbours' scheme to share the school runs. All the neighbours are expected to take part. Read the conversation and choose the less direct replies for Susan.

Gill: Susan, I've heard there's a school-run scheme.
Susan: a) That's right. Would you like to join it?
b) That's correct. And we expect you to join it.
Gill: I'm a bit frightened of driving in the London rush hour.
Susan: a) If you're a good driver, it isn't a problem.
b) It's hard, but I'm sure you'll be able to manage.
Gill: Well, when would you like me to take the children?
Susan: a) On Monday.
b) Perhaps you could do the school run on Monday.

B Business and society

1.16

If you were the German minister for transport, how would you try to reduce a) traffic congestion and b) emissions?

DRIVERS FACE ROAD PRICING BY SATELLITE

Transport Secretary Tessa Parr has presented a scheme for a new type of road tax.

'Road pricing' will instead be based on location, time of day and distance driven. A driver on a quiet country road will pay £0.02 per mile. However, a driver on a busy main road in the rush hour will pay as much as £1.34 per mile. Parr believes this is the only way to avoid national gridlock within 15 years.

The technology is not very different from the satellite navigation systems many cars now have. Satellites will track each vehicle's 'black box', and record location, time and distance travelled. Drivers will then be charged automatically.

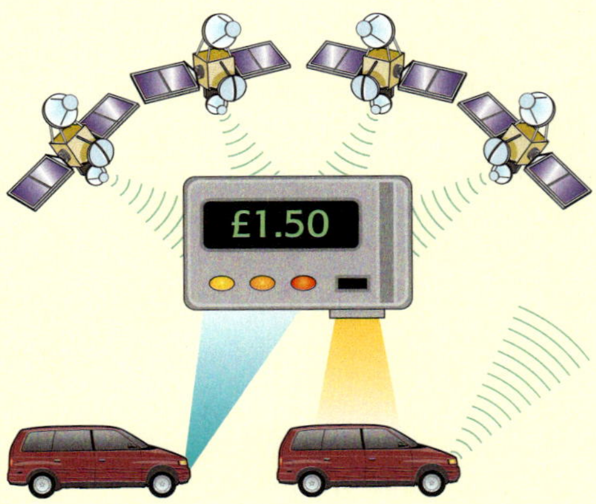

'Road pricing' has been criticized though. For some it means a 'Big Brother' society. "But," Parr argues, "if you've nothing to hide from the police, what's the problem?" Others fear it will destroy road hauliers, but Parr believes that costs will balance, provided that road hauliers avoid rush hour on the busiest roads. Still, others say it is unfair on urban commuters. However, Parr believes that everyone gains from a scheme that will reduce traffic congestion by 50%.

(190 words)

TOWARDS ZERO EMISSIONS

Fuel prices are high, and CO_2 emissions have to fall. Finally, the car owner and the green environmentalist want the same thing – a car that does not 'cost the earth' to run. Several technologies are racing to provide that car.

Electric vehicles are known for low performance and limited range, but the Reva NXG is improving on that. With a speed of 120 kph and a range of 200 km, the Reva plugs into the wall to recharge, costs £0.01 per kilometre to run and produces no emissions. The problem? The power station that supplies its electricity.

Hybrid petrol-electric vehicles like Toyota's Prius cleverly turn energy from the car's movement into electricity. It then supports the petrol engine, for instance on hills. These cars perform just as well as petrol-engine cars, and their fuel economy is up to 50% better.

But prototype vehicles powered by fuel cells are the greatest hope. The basic fuel is hydrogen, which combines with oxygen to produce power and – the only waste product – water. This is wonderful, except for one thing: like Reva's electricity, the hydrogen has to be manufactured, and this means emissions. When, however, renewable energy sources can do the job, we will finally have an environmentally friendly car with low running costs.

(211 words)

BACKGROUND BRIEFING Global energy supplies

The World Energy Council's analysis

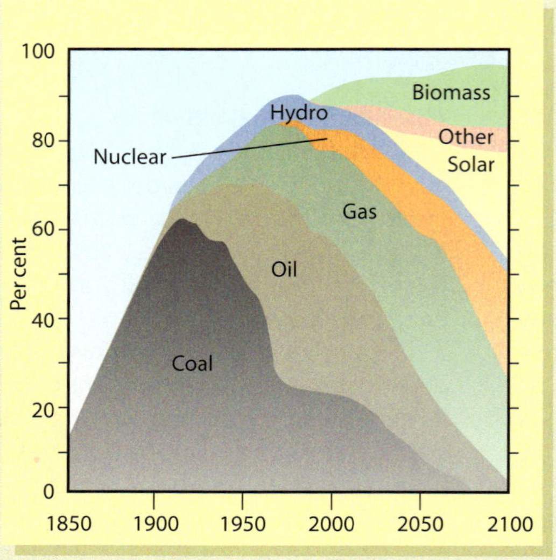

Some signs of the times

- WEC figures predict falling oil supplies.
- Oil prices recently doubled in two years.
- In America, much higher petrol prices have shocked the nation.
- Sales of large private cars fell dramatically between 09/04 and 09/05. In 2005, 24% of US drivers considered buying a hybrid.
- Worldwide sales of Toyota's hybrid Prius at the end of 2005 were approximately 300,000.
- Other car makers previously rejected hybrid technology but are now racing to match the Japanese. In 2005, DaimlerChrysler, General Motors and BMW agreed to share development work.

5 Looking at the text

A Answer the questions on the texts.

1 If road pricing is introduced, how much would a driver be charged for a ten-mile journey in London at 8.00 a.m. on a Monday?
2 Why will rural drivers pay much less to drive if road pricing is introduced?
3 What do the car navigation and road pricing technologies have in common?
4 How much would it cost to do a ten-kilometre journey in a Reva?
5 Why will fuel cell technology probably win against hybrid technology in the end?
6 What environmental problem do both electric cars and fuel cells have at the moment?
7 How could the problem be solved?

B Answer the questions on BACKGROUND BRIEFING.

1 From looking at the WEC chart, do you think oil prices will in the end fall, stay about the same, or rise much further? Why?
2 What did European and American car makers agree in 2005? Why?

C Say what you think.

6 Working with words

A **There are several 'word pairs' in the texts on page 55. Match these 'partner' words below, and then check your answers in the texts.**

congestion • fuel • main • road • pricing • zero

1 ... tax
2 road ...
3 ... road
4 traffic ...
5 ... emissions
6 ... prices

B **Match these other partners to words 1–6 above.**

accident ... • CO_2 • country • diesel • fuel • greenhouse gas • haulier • income • lights • oil • road • side • tolls

fuel / ... / ... → tax

road → *pricing* / ... / ...

Collect other word pairs like this. Use your dictionary to add partner words.

7 Listening

1.17

A **The TV discussion on traffic problems continues later. This time David Dale and his guests are talking about possible future solutions. Listen to the speakers and answer these questions.**

1 Who do the two main speakers represent?
2 What do they agree and disagree about?

B **Listen again and summarize the arguments on both sides.**

8 Using language for life

1.17

A **Arguing a point of view. Listen to the discussion again and say which of these sentences you hear.**

1 a I really believe this is the right answer.
  b I really think this is the right way forward.
2 a I don't disagree that there's a real problem.
  b I agree that there's a serious problem.
3 a But I'm sorry to say I don't quite agree.
  b But I'm afraid I can't really agree.
4 a I'm sorry, but I simply can't accept that argument.
  b I'm afraid I just don't accept that argument.
5 a I'm absolutely sure things will be fine.
  b I'm quite sure everything will be all right.
6 a But that's exactly my point.
  b But that's just what I'm saying.

B **Work with a partner and continue the discussion. Use these notes.**

Tessa Parr's views

- road pricing – make people use public transport
- money from road pricing – pay for better public transport
- work out in the end – cut traffic by 5% and congestion by 50%

Simon Way's views

- public transport not developed enough – couldn't cope
- take ages – people can't afford to commute – have to leave jobs
- too hard for ordinary people – must find a better way

C Task options

9 Reading and role-play

A **Study the map and factsheet and then prepare to do the role-play.**

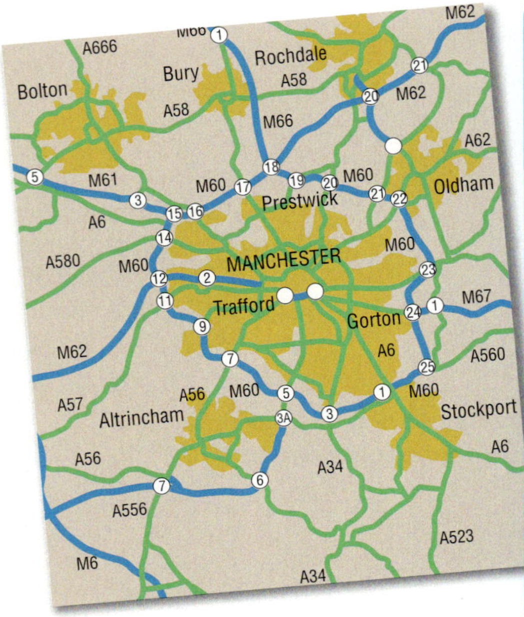

MANCHESTER FACTSHEET

Population: (central Manchester) 450,000; (Greater Manchester) 2.7 million. The traditional industrial heart of England, and also Britain's second largest commercial centre. The Greater Manchester conurbation contains many other old industrial towns.

Manchester transport situation

1 In the morning rush hour, 85% of commuters travel by car (national average: 61%).
2 Manchester has the UK's least developed city bus service. Fares are very expensive.
3 Traffic congestion makes bus services unreliable, so many people drive and congestion gets even worse.
4 Greater Manchester's tram system covers only part of the city. Its extension would greatly reduce congestion. But the city needs government financial help.
5 Congestion charging could reduce traffic by 13% and raise up to £32.5m per year to improve public transport.

B **Work in a group of four. You are at a meeting on congestion charging in Manchester. Choose one of these roles on page 192:**
the commuter • the businessperson • the Ministry of Transport official • the city councillor

C **By the end, you must all agree. Compare your decision with other groups. Take a class vote to decide the best one.**

10 Discussion

On page 51, you read about traffic congestion. Do you think traffic congestion charging would help? Discuss arguments for and against this.

11 Writing

BCC File 1 (letter layout)

Following the Manchester meeting, write a letter to the local newspaper to put forward your point of view. Use this letter structure.

- Dear Sir or Madam, …
- Paragraph 1: Refer to the city's congestion charging scheme and to the recent meeting. State your position for or against it. State why you are writing to the newspaper: it is important for the public to understand this view.
- Paragraph 2: State your opponents' strongest point. Then argue against it.
- Paragraph 3: State another of your opponents' strong points. Then argue against it.
- Paragraph 4: Summarize your strongest arguments for or against the project.

Grammar checkpoint

1 If-sentences type 1 Begleitgrammatik p.200

You are in Bristol and your friend is in Manchester. You want to meet in London and travel to Paris. Email him/her the travel options.
Use If-sentences type 1.

1 If we go by ..., it ... cost ..., and it ... take ...
2 But if we travel by ...
3 On the other hand, ...

TRAVEL INFORMATION

1 Travel between London and Paris

	Cost	Time
Plane	£65 return	(2 hours travel to airport/waiting)
Train	£85 return	1 hr 50 min
Car ferry	£70 return	8 hr 50 min

2 Travellers' opinions

	How flexible	How enjoyable	How reliable
Plane	*	*	**
Train (Eurotunnel)	**	***	***
By car ferry	***	****	*

(* = least; **** = most)

2 If-sentences type 2 Begleitgrammatik p.200

Imagine yourself in these situations. Make statements using If-sentences type 2. You are in London.

1 You need your car for a holiday in France.
 a How would you go?
  If I needed my car for ..., I would go by ...
 b Cost?
  If I went by ..., it ...
2 You have to get to Paris urgently.
 a How would you travel?
 b Time?
3 You have a flight from Paris to Tokyo.
 a How would you go?
 b Cost and time?

3 If-sentences type 3 Begleitgrammatik p.200

Use the pictures and sentence parts to write about a long-distance drive that went very wrong. Use If-sentences type 3. Start like this:

If Mark hadn't woken up late, he would have ... .

1 not wake up late/get up on time

2 have time to plan trip

3 remember check water

4 car not break down

5 not have to push for hours

6 not miss party

4 Comparison of adjectives Begleitgram. p.199

Correct the **five** mistakes in this summary.

With a total journey time of 8 hr 50 min, travel by car ferry is the fastest way of travelling from London to Paris. At £70 return, it is not as expensive as travel by plane, but it is more expensive than by train. Customers feel that it is the most reliable of the three ways of getting from London to Paris. However, they also feel that it is less enjoyable than going by plane or by Eurotunnel.

4 HAVE TO HAVE!

Focus

A **Match the pictures to eight of the retail outlets.**

1 delicatessen
2 department store
3 electrical store
4 boutique
5 fast-food takeaway
6 furniture store
7 jeweller's
8 music store
9 newsagent's
10 shoe shop
11 sports shop
12 supermarket

a

b

c

d

e

f

g

h

B **Have you ever 'gone mad' at shops? Do you have any special weaknesses such as shoes, CDs, ...?**

HOW THEY MAKE YOU BUY

NOTES FROM THE MARKETING EXPERTS

1 Basic essentials ('demand items') are far away, near the back of the shop, and far apart. To reach your milk or eggs, you have to pass many 'semi-demand' and 'impulse' items – things that are nice but not essential. They are also things that make the store big profits.

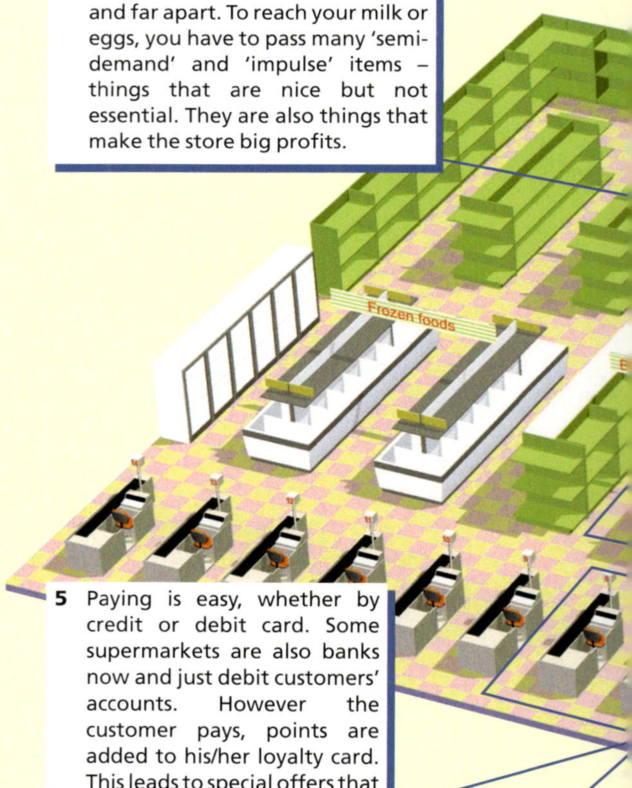

5 Paying is easy, whether by credit or debit card. Some supermarkets are also banks now and just debit customers' accounts. However the customer pays, points are added to his/her loyalty card. This leads to special offers that will bring the customer back soon to shop again.

6 Notice the magazines and sweets at the checkouts – a last chance for further impulse purchases.

A People and business

1.18

What is good and bad about supermarket shopping?

Best Buy Magazine

WATCH OUT when you enter a big supermarket! You won't see them, but the company employs people who make you buy more – and more. Now *Best Buy Magazine* shows you how.

On your way home, you turn into the supermarket. You just want a few basics – coffee, milk, eggs ... . You grab a trolley. Bad mistake! With a basket you would feel the weight of your purchases. With a trolley, you won't. Result: you'll buy more.

Inside, you slow down. You pass beautiful displays of flowers and plants. Ahead are the fresh, natural rainbow colours of fruit and vegetables. They aren't on your list, but those packets of red, green and yellow peppers look delicious. What's more, they're on special offer. Then, further on, that smell of freshly baked bread! How could anyone resist?

The store decor is often green. This gives a 'natural' feel. Bakery, fish and delicatessen counters also offer freshness – and bring back warm memories of traditional shopping.

3 Many large supermarkets (often called hypermarkets) now sell other goods to their captive customers – clothing and electrical goods, for example.

4 Displays of fresh fruit, vegetables and flowers just inside a store are common. They create a feeling of fresh, healthy living before you reach the ordinary canned, bottled and frozen supermarket goods.

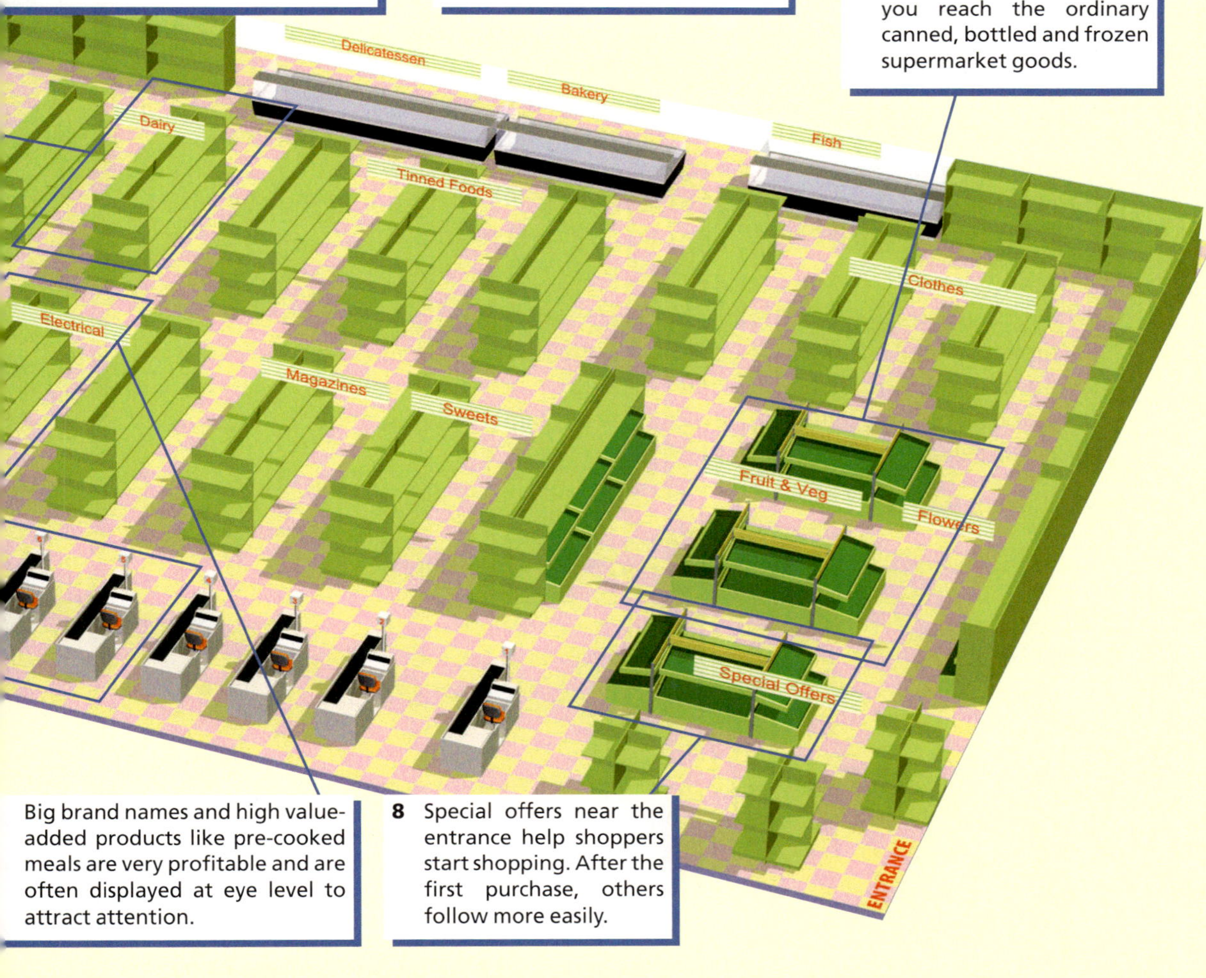

Big brand names and high value-added products like pre-cooked meals are very profitable and are often displayed at eye level to attract attention.

8 Special offers near the entrance help shoppers start shopping. After the first purchase, others follow more easily.

BACKGROUND BRIEFING The retail industry

Household expenditure: percentage of income in 3 EU countries

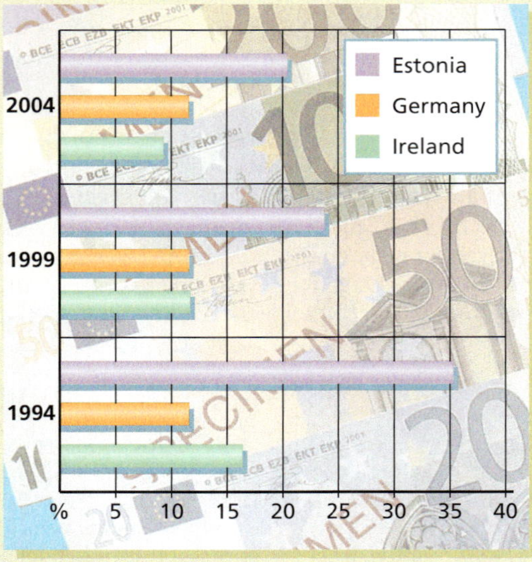

The retail industry includes the following:

- **Retail outlets** that sell to the end consumer. Large out-of-town stores offer competitive prices, easy parking and often also 24-hour shopping. High-street survivors include smaller, more up-market specialists that are often gathered together in shopping centres or malls.
- **Wholesale distributors** that handle products in large quantities ('in bulk') and get them from producers to retailers. Large store chains have their own distribution systems.
- **Home shopping** – traditional mail order shopping from catalogues, TV shopping and online shopping on the Internet. 'E-tail' is growing especially fast, often as part of traditional retailers' operations.

1 Looking at the text

A Answer the questions on the text.

1 How can a supermarket make you feel good to be there?
2 List five ways supermarkets encourage you to buy more goods (and more expensive goods) than you planned.
3 What can supermarkets do to make it easy to pay for all the things you buy?
4 How do they encourage you to return soon and spend more?

B Think about it.

1 Who do you think reads the magazine *Best Buy*?
2 Particular special offers are often sent to individual customers. How does the loyalty card tell a supermarket what interests a particular person?
3 Look at BACKGROUND BRIEFING. How can you explain the different percentages in the countries?

C Say what you think.

2 Working with words

A **Match the words in the two boxes below. (Some can match more than one.)**

a a bag of • a bar of • a bottle of • a box of • a can of • a carton of • a jar of • a loaf of • a packet of • a slice of • a tube of

b bread • eggs • jam • toothpaste • potatoes • chocolate • soup • tea • soap • tomato ketchup • ham

B **Make statements about things you use at home.**

EXAMPLES *At home, we usually use a two-litre bottle of milk every two days.*
In my family, we generally eat two loaves of bread a week.

1.19

3 Listening

a post office
b boutique
c farmer's market
d supermarket

A **Susanne Dittmann is living in England for a year. She has a free afternoon and has gone into town. Listen and match photos a–d to her conversations 1–4.**

B **Listen again and note the following.**

1 Who she is talking to in each conversation.
2 What she is doing.
3 How much she has to pay.

1.19

4 Using language for life

A Being polite. Listen to Susanne again. Say which of these you hear.

1 a Would you like help with packing?
  b Shall I get you some help with packing?
2 a Thanks, but I think I'll be all right.
  b Thanks, but I'm fine.
3 a Can you enter your PIN, please?
  b Could you enter your PIN, please?
4 a I'm sorry, but they're one ninety.
  b I'm afraid they're one ninety.
5 a Would you mind putting it on the scales for me, please?
  b Do you mind putting it on the scales for me, please?
6 a Er … sorry, but do you have this summer jacket in a smaller size?
  b Excuse me, but have you got this summer jacket in a smaller size?
7 a Could I possibly take this other style as well?
  b Would you mind if I took the other style as well?
8 a I wonder if you could tell me if it's made of pure cotton.
  b Perhaps you could tell me: is it made of pure cotton?

CULTURE CHECK Polite expressions

German speakers can sometimes sound too direct, and even rude, to English speakers. On the other hand, English speakers' politeness and indirectness can sound absurd to Germans. However, polite expressions are very important to English speakers – so use them!

please • thank you • certainly • of course • I'm afraid (that) … • I'm sorry, but … • Excuse me, but …

Polite expressions are often used for asking, requesting and offering. Work with a partner. Practise offering and requesting things. Here are some suggestions.

1 You have not got any money for lunch.
2 You are carrying a heavy parcel.
3 The room is very hot.
4 An old lady is standing in a bus.
5 Your boss has given your colleague a lot of work.

May/Can I ask … • If you don't mind me asking … • Perhaps you could tell me … • Could you/I (possibly) … • Would you mind if … • I wonder if you/I could … • Do you think you/I could … • Would you like (me) to … • Shall I … for you?

Do you mind if I …?

! You can't go shopping in England every day, but you can listen to some real English every day. Switch to MTV for news, interviews – and music of course. For sport, try Eurosport. And to find out what's happening in the world, try BBC World or CNN.

B Work with a partner. Choose one of the shopping situations in exercise 3A, adapt it and act it out.

B Business and society

1.20

- Have you ever compared products and prices on the Internet before buying something in the shops? If so, what sort of thing?
- Have you ever bought or sold anything online? What?

Shopping mall or cybermall?

The Internet is part of everyday life for most young Americans: about three-quarters of 18–24-year-olds regularly go online. Many have now added Internet shopping to email and other activities. Since the mid-1990s, shopping online has grown from almost nothing to about five per cent of the whole US retail industry. Sales have been increasing by over 25% per year, and last year goods and services worth $93 billion were bought online.

Many have predicted disaster for traditional shopping, but will this really happen? Are high-street shops and out-of-town superstores about to close? Could millions of sales staff be made redundant?

Well, Internet shopping certainly has big advantages. Travel websites can find the cheapest flights, for example, and fares cost less than they do from a travel agent. In fact, most Internet prices are lower than shop prices. It can also be very convenient to do your shopping from home, day or night. (Internet sales rise rapidly at Christmas because people prefer to avoid the crowded shops.)

However, there are problems. Orders can take around two weeks to arrive and have to be returned at your expense if something is wrong. A lot of people worry about the security of their credit-card numbers. Some also miss the social experience of going shopping with friends.

'E-tail' has brought different levels of success to different types of business. Amazon.com is very successful as a pure e-tailer, but many other dot.coms have failed. They spent too much, sold too little and went bankrupt.

However, traditional retailers have done surprisingly well. For small, specialist shops it can be wonderful. Bill Ross, owner of a farm shop, says, 'Using the Net is like opening shops all over Britain.' Big traditional retailers have been introducing their customers to 'multichannel shopping' even more successfully. Online orders are simply supplied from their stores or warehouses. Walmart, the world's largest supermarket chain also cleverly mixes offline and online services. For example, you can leave your pictures at a store and collect digital images from its website.

Multichannel shopping's biggest winner is often the customer. Take American car-buyers: 75% now research everything from cost to colour on the Internet before they go to the car dealer with the best deal.

So Internet shopping is not going to replace traditional retail. Rather, it is making traditional retail much more imaginative, efficient and competitive. This is great news for the consumer. (409 words)

BACKGROUND BRIEFING Access to the Internet

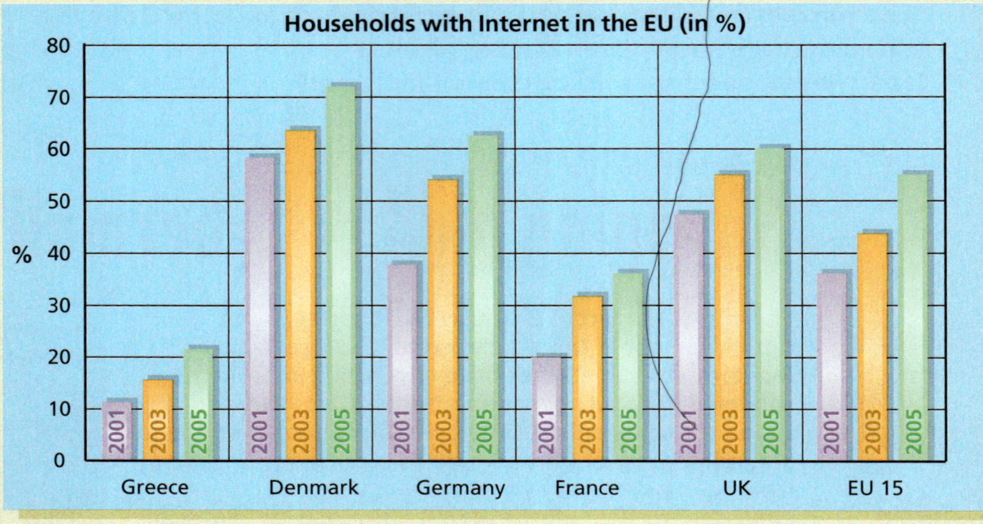

5 Looking at the text

A Say what these numbers in the text and BACKGROUND BRIEFING refer to.

the mid-1990s • $93 billion • millions • two weeks • 75% • 11 • 62 • 55

B Decide who is speaking. Explain why.

1 'They can be ready for you here by 5 p.m. or, if you prefer, we can send them to you by email.'
2 'We've certainly lost sales as the airlines can now sell direct online for about 15% less than we have to charge.'
3 'At first, my little second-hand record store wasn't very successful, but now I've got thousands of customers worldwide, thanks to the Net.'
4 'This year I've decided to try to do all my shopping for the holiday season in the warmth and comfort of my own home.'
5 'Can you match this price I found on the Internet? It's $18,999, complete with a year's insurance.'

C Think about it.

1 Give an example from the text which shows that the Internet is making traditional retailers more competitive and imaginative.
2 Comment on the figures in BACKGROUND BRIEFING? Does anything surprise you?
3 Answer the question in the title: *Shopping mall or cybermall?*

D Say what you think.

What is the most useful thing about the Internet for you?
Use these ideas.

email • games • doing research • downloading music • downloading films • meeting people through chat rooms • online banking • shopping online

6 Working with words

A Find words in the text with similar meanings to the following.

1 hardly anything (paragraph 1)
2 rising (paragraph 1)
3 purchased (paragraph 1)
4 benefits (paragraph 3)
5 quickly (paragraph 3)
6 difficulties (paragraph 4)
7 went out of business (paragraph 5)
8 take the place of (paragraph 8)

B Use words above to replace seven items in this story of eBay.

In September 1995, Pierre Omidyar started a website in California called AuctionWeb that allowed people to compete to buy things online. The name EchoBay.com soon took the place of the first name, but there was a difficulty with the new one because another company already owned it. So then Omidyar changed the name again – this time to eBay.

At the start, there was almost nothing to sell, but business grew quickly as people soon saw the advantages of a website like this. That has continued ever since then. Sales and profits have risen dramatically every year, and there are now well over 100 million eBay users worldwide.

Pierre Omidyar, founder of eBay

7 Writing

A Read this part of the introduction to the Treasurehouse Mail Order Catalogue. Compare mail-order shopping with shopping on the Internet. Make notes about the following:

1 Prices
2 Comfort and convenience
3 Delivery and returning goods
4 Methods of ordering
5 Methods of payment

WELCOME TO MAIL ORDER THE TREASUREHOUSE WAY!

- Enjoy top quality at prices you won't often find in the shops.
- Shop in the comfort of your own home. Relax and take as much time as you want – when you want, day or night.
- Orders are delivered to your door within 14 days.
- Returned goods are accepted without any questions (though we have to ask you to pay the cost of postage).
- You can order by: mail – just complete and send off the pre-addressed, postage-paid form; phone (0845 450 4596); fax (0845 450 4597); email-sales@treasurehouse.co.uk).
- You can pay by: cheque, credit card, direct debit.

B Write a summary with this title: 'Comparison of mail order and shopping online'.

Paragraph 1 *There are several similarities between these two methods of shopping. Like shopping online, mail-order shopping is usually …*

Paragraph 2 *However, there are also differences between the two … With shopping online, you order …, while with catalogue shopping, you …*

Paragraph 3 (Which method you prefer and why.)

C Task options

8 Charts

A **You are part of the important 15–24 youth market. You are probably quite a lot richer than your parents were at your age.**

1 Work out roughly how much money you have had in the last year, and where it has come from, for example:
- allowance
- presents
- earnings from jobs

2 Draw a pie chart to show roughly the percentages.

3 Work out very roughly what percentages you spent last month on:
- Basic necessities (study requirements …)
- Transport (bus fares, petrol …)
- Social expenditure (cinema tickets …)
- Personal expenditure (clothes, CDs …)
- Savings;
- Other (presents …)

4 Draw a bar chart of your monthly expenditure.

B **Write a brief analysis of each chart. Analyze:**
- points that you think are either good or bad;
- any action you think you could take.

EXAMPLE *The pie chart shows that in the last year about … of my money has come from my allowance.*
The bar chart shows that last month I …
It is clear from all this that …
I therefore definitely need to … First of all, I could ask … Secondly, I …

9 Class survey

1 In America, the average individual expenditure in the 15–24 age group is $8,750 a year (see page 41). What is that in euros?

2 Write your own expenditure for the last year on a piece of paper, and pass it to the front of the class. (Figures from exercise 8A, but leave out savings.)

3 When the figures are read out, use your calculator to work out the average. Compare it with the American figure. Try to explain any large difference.

Grammar checkpoint

1 Articles
Begleitgrammatik p.202

Complete the instructions to a new checkout assistant. Add *a/an*, *the* or – (for zero article).

1 Remember: we need …[1] happy customers who will want to come and shop here again. So always be friendly to them, and never forget to give them …[2] pleasant smile.

2 If …[1] customer wants help with …[2] packing, just press …[3] red button here in order to call …[4] assistant.

3 As you're under 18, you're not allowed to sell …[1] alcohol without …[2] permission of …[3] manager in charge of …[4] checkouts. So ring this bell for his or her attention.

4 We prefer …[1] customers to pay …[2] cash or by …[3] credit card because these methods of …[4] payment are quicker than …[5] payment by …[6] cheque. If …[7] customer wants to write …[8] cheque, you must accept it, of course, but always make sure that the card number is written on …[9] back of …[10] cheque, and then check …[11] number carefully against …[12] card number. If there is …[13] mistake, make sure that it is corrected.

5 We divide …[1] products that we sell into …[2] three groups. …[3] first consists of …[4] basic 'demand' items such as …[5] milk and …[6] eggs. Then there is …[7] group which is known as …[8] 'semi-demand' goods. These are important but not quite so basic, and they include …[9] things such as …[10] meat. Finally, we come to …[11] 'impulse' items such as …[12] sweets. They're …[13] sort of …[14] thing …[15] mother might buy if she wants to give …[16] children at home …[17] nice surprise – or indeed if she just wants to give herself …[18] little treat!

2 *some, any, much, many, a few, a little, a lot*
Begleitgrammatik p.198

Complete the first part of the conversation with *some* and *any*.

A I need to do …[1] shopping today.
B Really? What do we need?
A Well, we haven't got …[2] milk, and we also need …[3] tea.
B I thought we still had …[4] teabags.
A No, I've checked, and we don't have …[5].
B What about coffee? Is there …[6] left?
A No, there isn't, so would you like me to get …[7]?

Complete the second part of the conversation with *much, many, a few, a little, a lot*.

B Yes, please. You know I drink …[8] of the stuff!
A Yes, too …[9], I think. You're a coffee addict!
B And what about sugar?
A Well, we've got …[10], but not very …[11], so I'll add that to the list.
B And I don't think we've got …[12] eggs.
A No, just …[13]. I'll put them on my list, too.

3 Articles and *some, any*, etc.
Begleitgram. p.198

Complete the following with appropriate words where necessary.

1 I've only got … things – … coffee and sugar and … cans of coke.
2 And do you have … points card?
3 How much are … eggs, please? – … large ones are one ninety … dozen.
4 You see, they're organic. And … organic produce has to be a bit more expensive than … ordinary food.
5 Fine, well, … dozen, please.
6 And I promise you they're … best eggs in … world. Not like … rubbish they sell you in … supermarket!
7 You can send it letter rate or you can save … money and send it small packet rate.
8 You see, … letters up to two hundred and eighty grams are two fifty-four, and … small packets are just one eighty-eight.
9 Will it take longer? – No, it shouldn't make … difference.
10 Strange! Well, in that case, could you send it as … small packet, please?
11 Excuse me, but have you got this summer jacket in … same colour, but … smaller size?
12 They're only twenty-four ninety-nine, and we've been selling … of them, so unfortunately we don't have … in red now.

5 OUR GLOBAL MARKET

Focus

A **Look at the photos above. What can you say about Jill's life and interests?**

B **The things Jill likes come from all over the world. Name them and match them to the descriptions below. You can check your answers at the bottom of page 73.**

1 Made in China and advertised all over the world by an American sports star.
2 Designed and produced in Sweden for communicating through sound, text and photos.
3 Designed by British and German engineers, made in a German-owned factory in Britain, and sold all over the world.
4 Found underground and sold to health-conscious people everywhere.
5 Designed by American scientists to share information, but now used by over a billion people worldwide.
6 Grown in the tropical Colombian climate, and flown to North America and Europe.
7 Made from natural plants found only in the Amazon jungle.
8 Invented in Germany and developed in America to allow you to keep and play back thousands of hours of music, especially when you are on the move.

C **Do you and your family own similar things? Check the labels when you get home. Talk about what you find out at your next class.**

D **Many producers of goods and services are multinational organizations. Name some multinationals. Say what and where they produce.**

A People and business

1.21

- In an electrical goods store, what German brands might you see?
- What foreign makes might you see? Where are these goods from?

The World Tonight special: the global economy

CHANNEL 4: 7.00–7.30 PM

This 'special' looks at globalization and talks to some of the winners and losers – people like these.

Larry Sleeman, ex-steelworker, Cleveland, Ohio

'The steel mills here used to supply the motor industry in Detroit. But the mills had to compete with foreign products, and that was bad news for us because our prices weren't competitive, they said. These days, they import from cheaper producers abroad to help keep their costs down.

'We steelworkers were happy when the government put import duties on foreign steel. But it was too late. The mills have mostly gone now. I'm lucky to have work as a security guard. But, you know, I'd like my real job back!'

Ranya Patel, software programmer, Siemens, Bangalore, India

'I applied to Siemens before I graduated, and I was lucky. I got my job despite a lot of competition. We work closely with Siemens' Munich team. They send us problems at the end of their working day, and we send back solutions, ready for their next working day.

'Companies like Siemens want to be here because we've got good IT skills and we speak English, and also electronic data transmission costs almost nothing. We also cost much less than German workers. But we're well off by Indian standards.'

Julia Kitale, clerical worker, Kilimanjaro Textile Company, Nairobi, Kenya

'It's hard, badly paid work, and it's getting worse. Our big customer is an American supermarket. They get quotations worldwide, and we have to beat these to get the work. Prices have fallen 30% in three years. And production schedules have been cut from 90 to 60 days. People have to work day and night. When we went on strike for better pay and conditions, we were all fired. Later, they said I could have my job back. I felt terrible for the others, but I have children to feed, so I took it.'

Axel Fischer, production engineer, Porsche, Leipzig, Germany

'I'm from Halle in Saxony-Anhalt. Unemployment reached 20% there, and I became unemployed myself. Then I got work at the brand-new Porsche factory in Leipzig. I do maintenance work on the Cayenne production line. It's all fantastically high-tech.

'Porsche is one company that's decided NOT to move production to China! Instead we're using the most advanced technology in order to be the best. And it's working. We've now raised annual production to 30,000 vehicles. That's 141 per employee, compared with just 46 at Volkswagen. And most are exported, so we're winning the globalization game right here in Germany.' (423 words)

BACKGROUND BRIEFING Globalization

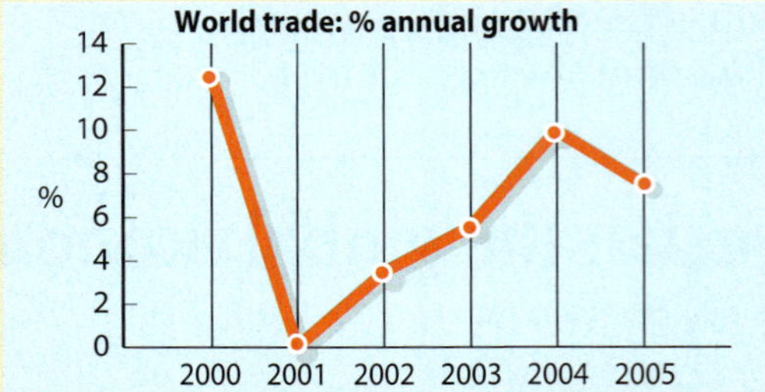

Reasons for globalization

- Cheap data processing plus cheap telecommunications allow rapid global planning and operations.
- Modern transport means people and goods travel further and faster.
- Exporting companies need to set up production in or near important target markets, e.g. Nissan in Britain, VW in the USA.
- Low-cost producers (e.g. China) are hungry to make big profits in high-value markets (e.g. Europe).
- Local producers (e.g. Europe) move production to low-cost countries to survive.

The effects

- Jobs and industries transfer from high-cost to low-cost economies (though high-level skills, such as Research and Development remain).
- Companies compete not just locally, but around the world.
- Whole economic regions – Europe, North America and East Asia – compete for each other's jobs and markets.
- Consumers get wider choice, better quality, and lower prices.

1 Looking at the text

A Answer the questions on the text.

1 Which two people have done best from globalization?
2 How has technology helped their companies to win in the globalized world?
3 Which two groups of people have been hurt by globalization?
4 How have the two speakers been saved from these situations?

B Explain the following. Look carefully at the context.

1 This '**special**' looks at globalization … (introduction)
2 … our prices weren't **competitive**, … (line 7)
3 We also **cost much less** than German workers. (line 38)
4 … we were all **fired**. (line 56)
5 … the globalization **game** … (line 79)

C Think about it.

1 What does Larry think of his present work?
2 Why, perhaps, did Julia get her job back, but not the factory workers?
3 Why does Axel emphasize 'not' in line 72?
4 Whose national economy probably has the brightest future? Why?

D Say what you think about the photos.

2 Working with words

A **Match these words from the text with the dictionary entries below. Which of the definitions is the right one?**

1 mill (line 3)
2 duty (line 13)
3 standard (line 40)
4 quotation (line 49)
5 advanced (line 74)
6 game (line 79)

Many words have several meanings. Before you look up a word in your dictionary, check the context in which you have read it so that you choose the correct definition.

a 1 a building where flour for making bread is produced 2 a small machine for turning things into powder: *a pepper ~* 3 a factory for producing a particular material: *a cotton ~*

b 1 at a higher, more difficult level: *an ~ English* course 2 highly developed technologically

c 1 a phrase or sentence(s) short piece taken and repeated from something that another person has said or written – often a piece of literature 2 the price that somebody says he/she will charge to do a piece of work

d 1 a tax paid to the government, especially for things that are brought into a country 2 something that you have to do because it is part of your job or because you feel it is right to do

e 1 enjoyable activity often played by children 2 a competitive sport or other activity that people taking part try to win 3 something that is not treated seriously: *Love is just a ~ to Peter.*

f 1 a level of quality 2 a moral rule that people should obey

B **Copy and complete the table with words from the text.**

	Verb	Noun (person)	Noun (thing)
1	economize	economist	*economy*
2	lose	…	loss
3	…	competitor	…
4	produce	…	…/…
5	import	importer	…
6	…	applicant	application
7	…	graduate	graduation
8	employ	employer/…	employment

C **Now complete the following with words from the table.**

1 This company's most dangerous … are the Chinese. We have to … with them worldwide.
2 We only started … the new XL100 sportscar six months ago, but we've already increased … to 1,300 per week.
3 I've … for the job in Customer Services, but I've heard there are ten other …, too, so I'm not very hopeful.
4 This department deals with …, and in fact we … products from all over the world.
5 RG Davis Ltd is a very good …, and it makes sure it … people from all ethnic groups.
6 The company makes a … on every product it sells, but if it raises prices, it will … customers. The only answer is to reduce costs.

Key for page 70 (B): 1 h, 2 f, 3 g, 4 e, 5 a, 6 c, 7 d, 8 b

B Business and society

1.22

▶ Have you seen products in the shops with a FAIRTRADE label on them? What do you think it means?

PUTTING FAIRNESS INTO BUSINESS

JANIE HAMILTON REPORTS

The problem

The world is moving towards freer trade, and that is generally good. But while free trade can produce great economic benefits, it can also make poverty much worse.

Nowadays western companies can buy from anywhere, so suppliers have to compete globally and offer the lowest prices. Their only 'freedom' is to force their workers to produce more for less. The effects make depressing reading:

'As a casual worker, I do not get a bonus, paid holiday, or redundancy pay.' (Ragel, who picks fruit in South Africa to be exported to UK supermarkets.)

'We have to do overtime until midnight to earn a proper income. I am afraid of having children because I wouldn't be able to feed them.' (Nong, who sews underwear in Thailand for the US market.)

It is not just the poor workers who suffer. A small coffee farmer in East Africa may suddenly see his crop's value collapse because South American and South East Asian farmers have produced too much coffee.

Today, the poorest 20% of people live on $2 a day or less. Worse, most have no way of improving their own or their children's lives.

The FAIRTRADE solution

Coordinator Dawn Sampson explained how **FAIRTRADE** works. They first visit existing producers to examine their products and their business strengths and weaknesses. 'If all is well, we form an action plan together. We may need to provide design or technical support, so as to get products right for export. Very importantly, we also agree to buy directly for a fair, guaranteed price. This immediately allows workers to start climbing out of poverty, for example by paying for their children's education.

'Later, we provide training in marketing and other skills so that producers can gradually become independent.

'Meanwhile, we sell through our own shops in Britain and an increasing number of other stores. Products range from craft and food products, such as coffee, to fashion clothing. The label is now well known and sales are rising by nearly 50% per year. Consumers realize they are buying a quality product at a competitive price while helping the producer. Instead of increasing the profits of middlemen, their purchases are building a future for some of the world's poorest people.' (367 words)

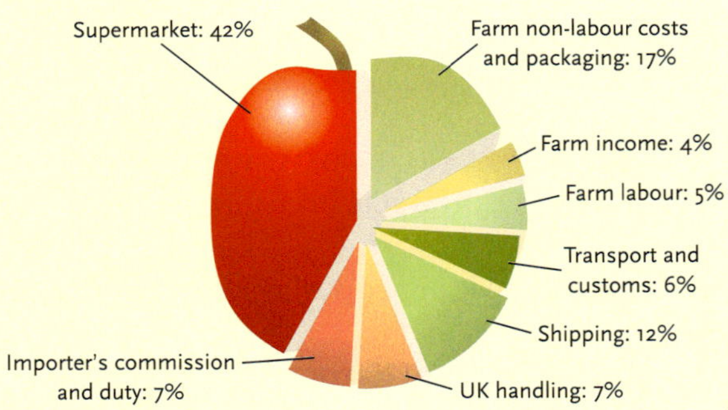

Breakdown of the cost of South African apples in UK supermarket

BACKGROUND BRIEFING The FAIRTRADE Foundation

- In the UK over 100 companies offer FAIRTRADE products. Recent successes include a turnover of over £100m, 18% of the market in fresh coffee, and consumption of 300,000 FAIRTRADE bananas a day.
- Supermarket chains sell them, often as own-brand products.
- Many cities such as Oxford, Cardiff and Edinburgh now tell their council services to use FAIRTRADE products.
- For more information on similar global organizations, see the websites in exercise 8, page 78.

3 Looking at the text

A Say whether the following are true, false or not in the text or BACKGROUND BRIEFING. Correct the false statements.

1 The text refers to people and places in four continents.
2 Paragraph 2 describes the situation of Julia and her employer on page 71.
3 About 20% of the population of the developing world lives on $2 per day or less.
4 According to the diagram, if a South African worker picks apples that sell to the consumer for €100, she will earn €5, and the farm will make a profit of €26.
5 Education is an important key to a better life for poor people.
6 After training by FAIRTRADE, producers must become independent.
7 People buy FAIRTRADE products because they are cheaper than normal supermarket goods.

B Match the words in the text and BACKGROUND BRIEFING (BB) to the definitions.

redundancy (line 13) • overtime (line 16) • income (line 17)
coordinator (line 30) • profit (line 53) • middleman (line 54)
purchase (line 54) • turnover (BB) • own-brand product (BB)

a Money that you earn.
b All the money an organization earns in, for example, a month or a year.
c Person who helps others involved in an activity work together well.
d Situation of losing your job because your work is not needed.
e Thing made just for one retailer to sell and with the name of that retailer on it.
f Thing that you buy.
g Money which is left after all the costs have been paid.
h Extra hours worked for a company.
i Person or organization that buys goods and then sells them to a retailer at a profit.

C Say what you think.

4 Working with words

A Give the opposites of the following. Then look in the text and BACKGROUND BRIEFING (BB) to check your answers.

1 causes (paragraph 2)
2 import (paragraph 3)
3 weaknesses (paragraph 7)
4 dependent (paragraph 8)
5 decreasing (paragraph 9)
6 falling (paragraph 9)
7 failures (BB)
8 exclude (BB)

B Use pairs of words above to complete the following. (You may need to change their forms.)

1 Our quotation ... basic transport costs, but it ... the cost of insurance. The customer has to pay for that.
2 While most African countries have been ... for many years, a lot of them remain very ... on economic aid from the West.
3 Not every project goes well, but we're happy to say that we have had many more ... than ... .
4 Our company is a big manufacturer. It ... raw materials from abroad and ... finished goods to the world.
5 One of Germany's great ... is its high levels of technology, but one of its great ... is its high manufacturing costs.
6 When the Wright brothers' first aeroplane slowly ... into the air in 1903 and then soon ... again to the ground, who could have imagined today's giant air transport industry?
7 The company's situation today is very bad. The basic ... is too little investment in new R&D in the past. And the ... now is expensive, old-fashioned products that cannot compete in today's very competitive market.
8 Due to tough global competition, especially from the Far East, we are seeing ... prices and ... quality in many types of product. This is hard for many traditional western manufacturers, but great news for consumers.

5 Listening

1.23

Janie Hamilton visited Indonesia with Dawn Sampson to write about FAIRTRADE again. Copy her notes from a conversation between Dawn and a local person. Listen and write brief explanations.

Iwan Sukino: partner in ...
2001: ______
Latke: ______
Yogyakarta: ______
Kitchen pans: ______
Sales & prices: ______
Hopes: ______
Kitchen tools: ______

1.23

6 Using language for life

A A formal interview situation. Listen to the conversation again. Say which of these you hear.

1 a So, could you tell me something about yourself first?
  b So, perhaps you could tell me a little about yourself first.
2 a Yes, certainly. You see, …
  b Yes, of course. You see, …
3 a Tell me about your present situation.
  b Can you tell me about your situation at present?
4 a What are you planning to do in the immediate future?
  b What are your plans for the immediate future?
5 a So do you think you'll be able to help?
  b So is it possible you'll be able to help?
6 a Well, yes, I certainly think we can help you.
  b Well, yes, actually, I think we can help you.

B A role-play. **Look at page 193.** **Work with a partner and take a role.**

CULTURE CHECK Body language and personal space

Globalization means more face-to-face contact with people from other parts of the world. But the way people interact varies. It is important to know what is acceptable (✓) and what is not (✗) in business situations in different cultures.

	firm handshake	touching	eye contact	private space 40cm	60cm	80cm
N Europe	✓	✓	✓	✗	✓	✗
USA	✓	✓ (but not M to F)	✓	✗	✓	✗
Latin America, S Europe	✓	✓	✓	✓	✗	✗
East Asian countries	✗	✗	✗	✗	✗	✓

Work with a partner. Use the table to explain what went wrong in these situations.

1 Susan Schriver from New York is talking to Carlos Santos from Mexico City at an international sales conference. Carlos seems amusing, friendly and harmless at first, but Susan starts to feel uncomfortable because he comes very close when talking to her. Carlos is surprised when Susan makes an excuse to leave, and then talks to somebody else.
2 When Nick Crane from Manchester first meets his new Japanese agent, Hiro Honda, their eyes rarely meet while they are talking. Nick thinks that Hiro is pleasant enough, but he wonders if his new 'man in Japan' has the friendly confidence and energy to do a tough selling job. At the same time, Hiro thinks Nick is OK, but finds him uncomfortably pushy.

C Task options

7 Research and spoken presentation

Lernhilfe p.214

A **Visit these websites to explore FAIRTRADE activities around the world.**
International FAIRTRADE Association: www.ifat.org
European FAIRTRADE Association: www.eftafairtrade.org
FAIRTRADE Foundation: www.fairtrade.org.uk

B **Choose a website and find out about one of these topic areas.**
- How the FAIRTRADE system works
- Working with a producer: a case study
- Growth in sales and product range

Prepare a short class presentation. Print out any useful charts or photos.

8 Research and written presentation

Lernhilfe p.211

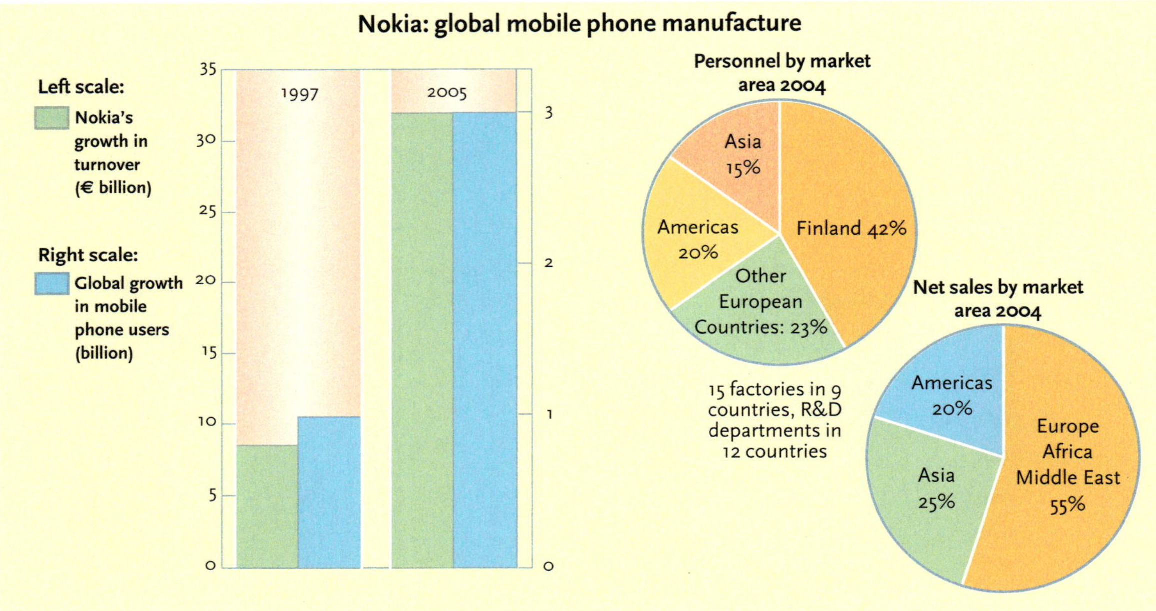

A **Look at the charts and write a brief analysis of the Nokia organization.**
Paragraph 1: The rise of the mobile market and the rise of Nokia
Nokia is the world's largest manufacturer of mobile phones. Between 1997 and …, the number of worldwide mobile phone users grew … At the same time, …
Paragraph 2: Nokia's global spread of personnel, operations and sales
While Nokia still has a strong base in Finland, where it has … of its employees, it now also has … Concerning manufacturing and R&D, there are now … As for sales, these are spread widely around the world, with …

B **Collect similar information about a multinational company in Germany. Produce charts and write an explanation.**

! Try company websites. Or call the public relations department at large companies. (Ask for Abt. Öffentlichkeitsarbeit or PR Abt. Pressestelle.) They may be able to send you an information pack.

Grammar checkpoint

1 Connectors

Two students are talking about their holiday choice. Complete what they say with the connectors.

1 because • so • so as to • so that

A We may never have the money to do anything like this again, …[1] we've decided to go to New Zealand.
B Another thing: we've chosen New Zealand …[2] be able to go skiing in July!
A And also …[3] we've both always really wanted to see New Zealand.

2 as • because of • (in order) to • so that

A I'm going to go online …[1] find cheap flights.
B And I'm going to visit some travel agents …[2] they often have special offers.
A And we're going to borrow some guidebooks from the library …[3] we can find out more about the country.

3 because of • since • so • so as to • so that

A We're going to need lots of winter clothes …[1] the cold.
B We don't have our own skis, …[2] we'll just hire some when we get there.
A Something we will need to take though is lots to read on the plane …[3] it's such a long way!
B My aunt has given me some birthday money early …[4] I can book the holiday early.

2 Indirect speech 1

Begleitgrammatik p.200

Channel 4 is reporting some of the interviews on page 71 in a new booklet. Write part of the report. Use Axel Fischer's words and change them into indirect speech. Choose from these verbs and expressions.

add • believe • explain • feel • finish by saying • go on to say • make the point • say • start by saying • state • tell (our interviewer) • think (that)

He started by saying that he didn't want to take up their time …

3 Indirect speech 2

Begleitgrammatik p.200

Write part of Janie's magazine article reporting Dawn Sampson's discussions in exercise 6. Change what they said into indirect speech. Use this language.

(A)	asked advised asked	(B)	(not) to … if/whether …
	told		that …
	added explained replied said	that …	

1 Dawn Could you tell me something about yourself first?
Dawn asked Iwan to tell her something about himself first.
2 Iwan A group of us got together and started as partners back in 2001.
He told her that … .
3 Dawn Where's your main market?
4 Iwan We mainly sell in Yogyakarta.
5 Dawn Tell me about your present situation.
6 Iwan Things are tough at the moment. Sales are falling.
7 Dawn I'm sorry to hear that because your product quality is very good.
8 Iwan Is it possible you'll be able to help? We badly need to start exporting.
9 Dawn I think we can help. But it may be easier to sell kitchen tools.
10 Iwan We don't know anything about the market.
11 Dawn Don't worry about that. We can send an expert who will be able to help you.
12 Iwan That's fantastic news, and I'm really grateful.

6 THE SERIOUS BUSINESS OF HOLIDAYS

Focus

- **a** an adventure holiday
- **b** a study holiday
- **c** a relaxing holiday
- **d** a safari holiday
- **e** a skiing holiday
- **f** a climbing holiday

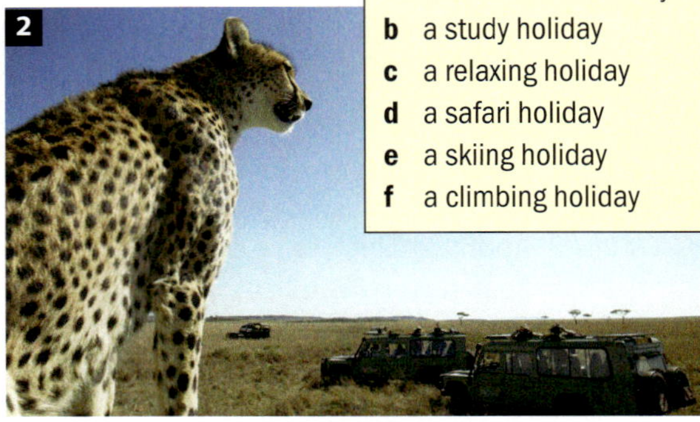

A **You have saved €2,000 from holiday jobs, and you want to spend it on a really good holiday after your final exams.**
Match the holidays **a–f** to the pictures. List any other types of holiday that you would like to try. Then discuss good and bad points about them all. (Think about cost, danger, excitement, fun, new skills, etc.)

B **Decide on a really good holiday with a partner.**

1. Agree on two types of holiday that you think you would both enjoy, and a possible place for each holiday.
2. What would you need to take with you? What could you buy or hire?
3. Compare your ideas with another pair. Together, decide on one holiday for all of you.

A People and business

2.1

- The travel and tourism industry now employs hundreds of thousands of people. Would you like to work in the industry? Why (not)?
- Have you ever wanted to live somewhere that you have been on holiday? If so, where and why?

Sunday Herald | **TRAVEL SECTION** | March 1

Holiday encounter

by Jim Sullivan

We had returned from a wonderful sea trip along the Tenerife coast. It was too early for our final holiday dinner, but a drink and some tapas seemed an excellent idea. Anna and I took a seat outside a harbour café, and I began ordering in my bad Spanish. 'I'll understand quicker if you say it in English,' came the reply.

On finishing preparations for the evening, Danny returned for a chat. It turned out that he was from London, and he had run the Marina Bar for three years. He had worked as a hotel chef one summer in the big Las Americas resort. Afterwards, he had fallen in love with Tenerife while touring the island.

After working and saving hard in Britain for four years, he had returned to set up his own business. I asked him what problems he had had. 'How long have you got?' he laughed.

'When I found this place, it was just a shop, so it needed a complete conversion. I got some quotes, did the figures – and discovered my first problem. Even doing most of the job myself, the costs were about €20,000. I also had to pay a big deposit and three months' rent. Suddenly my savings account didn't look so healthy anymore!

I applied for a loan, but the bank turned me down. They said they'd only lend if the business was already operating and had a positive cash flow. Great!

Then there was the paperwork – which I had to do in Spanish, of course. I needed to get a licence for the business, and that takes ages. But it was already January, so I had to start converting the place and just hope for the best. I knew that if I didn't open in time for the tourist season, I never would. I'd go bankrupt!'

Did he? 'No, not quite. I was down to my last €100, but just before Easter, the Health and Safety people checked and approved everything, my licence arrived – and I was in business!'

I asked if he would ever return to London. He shook his head. 'It's no holiday here, but I'm my own boss, and this is my life now.' Saying that, he hurried away to greet some new customers.

Evening stars and harbour lights were appearing. It was much prettier than the thought of tomorrow's journey home. 'Right now,' Anna said, 'I'd like to make this my life, too!'

(404 words)

BACKGROUND BRIEFING **Travel and tourism**

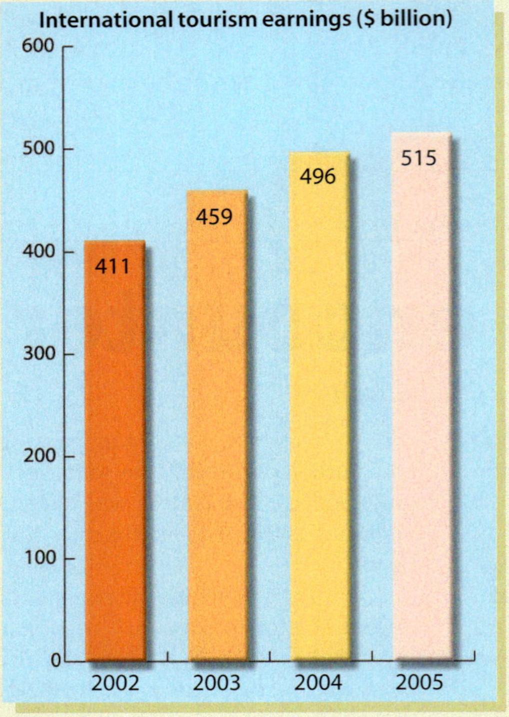

- Tourists made roughly 660 million international trips in 2005.
- Worldwide earnings from tourism were approximately $515 billion in 2005, and that figure is rising by 5–10% per year.
- Western Europe receives almost 50% of the world's tourists – many of them travellers from within western Europe.
- Many west Europeans now also travel east, to the 'transition economies' that were once old Eastern Bloc.

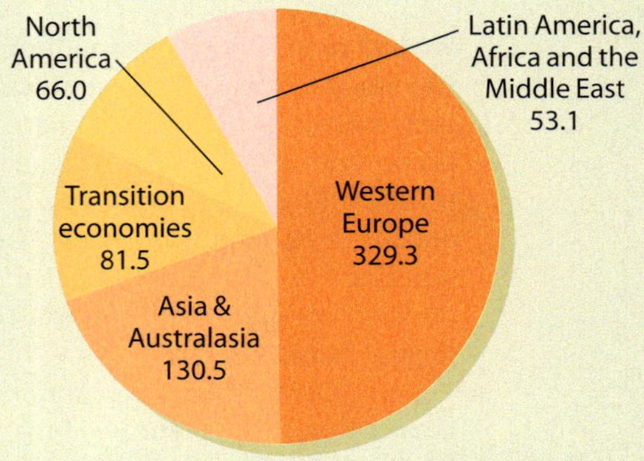

Trips by international tourists 2005 (million)

1 Looking at the text

A Who could have have said the following, and when?

1 'The building materials you want are going to cost about €7,600.'
2 'We'll have three beers and some tapas, please. And by the way, wasn't this place a shop, not a bar, when we were here last Easter?'
3 'We can offer you work from July 15th to September 2nd as assistant chef in our international restaurant on the top floor.'
4 'You can have the keys to the place as soon as your first payment has gone into our bank account.'
5 'But we can help you when the business is running successfully if, for example, you decide that you want to expand.'
6 'It's a wonderful place, and I'm going to work and save till I can go back and set up my own business there.'
7 'Right, everything looks fine in the bar, but now I need to check the kitchen.'

B Interpret the information in BACKGROUND BRIEFING.

1 By roughly what percentage did worldwide earnings from tourism rise between 2002 and 2005?
2 About how many international tourists visited western European destinations in 2005?
3 Approximately what percentage of all international tourism was to North America, Latin America, Africa and the Middle East?

C **Say what you think.**

2 Working with words

A **Add the correct translation of the words in brackets. Be careful of 'false friends'.**

1 There were some free tables in the restaurant, so we went in and … . *(Platz nehmen)*
2 It took me a year to … enough money for this holiday. *(sparen)*
3 You can only open for business when you … your licence. *(bekommen)*
4 The new restaurant owners have … a good job and made a lot of changes. *(machen)*
5 Before I paid for the kitchen equipment, I … that it was all working. *(prüfen)*
6 He's the new …, so he can run the bar just as he wants. *(Chef)*

! **False friends: these are English words which only seem like German words. The German meaning is in fact different.**

B **Check your answers. The correct words are all in the text.**

1: line 5 2: line 18 3: line 25 4: line 37 5: line 49 6: line 53

C **Correct these other 'false friends'. Use your dictionary if necessary.**

1 We stayed in a nice ~~pension~~ on holiday. *(Pension)*
2 Here is a ~~prospect~~ which shows our hotel. *(Prospekt)*
3 All the information you need about the area is in this ~~map~~. *(Mappe)*
4 This is the old price list – the prices are no longer ~~actual~~. *(aktuell)*
5 I've just had a meeting with our bank manager. In his ~~meaning~~, our restaurant business is very risky. *(Meinung)*
6 Before my appointment at the bank, I made ~~notices~~ of all my questions. *(Notizen)*
7 Can an Indian restaurant ever succeed in a traditional ~~land~~ like Bavaria? *(Land)*
8 We ~~wondered~~ at the high cost of starting the business. *(sich wundern)*
9 We had big expenses when we ~~overtook~~ the old restaurant. *(übernehmen)*
10 We put an ~~announcement~~ in the local newspaper for new staff. *(Annonce)*

3 Listening

2.2

Danny opened his first bank account as a student in London. Listen to his conversation at the bank.

1 Note **two** special benefits that Danny's student account offered him.

2 Look at these opposites. Which two words do you not hear?

- to credit ≠ to debit
- to be in credit ≠ to be overdrawn
- to deposit ≠ to withdraw
- in(to) the black ≠ in(to) the red

3 Which two other names for ATM do you hear?

! The words *deposit* and *withdraw* mean the same as *pay in* and *take out*, but they are part of the banking 'register'. Many areas of life have their own registers. Can you think of others?

4 Using language for life

2.2

A **Explaining and checking facts.**
Listen to the conversation again. Say which of these you hear.

1 a The first thing that'll happen is this.
  b First of all, what happens is this.

2 a So I suppose that means I'll be fifty pounds in the black.
  b So that means I'll be fifty pounds in the black, doesn't it?

3 a Now the next thing is this.
  b Now we come to the next point.

4 a I suppose, in other words, people start going into the red.
  b In other words, people start going into the red, I suppose.

5 a But isn't that expensive?
  b But that's expensive, isn't it?

6 a And there's something very important to remember here.
  b And there's a point that's very important not to forget here.

7 a This is how the system works.
  b The system works like this.

8 a Is it true that people don't use them much these days?
  b Am I right that people don't use them much these days?

B **Work with a partner. One of you is an American exchange student. Take turns to explain the following.**

1 How to open a German bank account.

2 How to join a local club or group (sports, drama, music, etc.).

B Business and society

2.3

Think of points for and against mass tourism.

Mass tourism: for and against

a

Sir

I have been following the tourism debate with interest. It seems to me that everyone is partly right.

If we asked our waiter in Bali or our kite-surfing instructor in Tenerife, they would certainly not want us to stay at home. However, perhaps more of us should – and not just because it might be safer. Remember, our own tourist industry needs support, too.

And those continuing to visit far-away destinations really must behave better. Tourists have left a trail of rubbish and damage worldwide. Surely it is mad to destroy the beauty that brings us to these places. Better, surely, to 'Take only photos: leave only footprints'.

Indira Kapoor

b

Sir

I was sad to read that I must now stay at home to save both the world and my life.

Come on! We're all going to die some time, so let's go out and enjoy our wonderful world while we can.

And let's remember something else. When visiting many parts of the world, we bring jobs, money and economic development to places where these things are in short supply.

Who cares if we also cause a few environmental problems? Almost all economic development does. And if the only alternative facing Indonesians is poverty, then they will vote for tourism every time.

Angus McFee

c

Sir

The *Sunday Herald* is a fine newspaper, but articles printed in the travel section often worry me.

I worry about travel diaries describing the last, unknown beach in Thailand and articles telling us to visit Indonesia before the rainforest totally disappears.

This pressure to travel is wrong. It encourages us to visit parts of the world suffering from real environmental damage already. The more people visit, the greater the destruction caused. And all this is before we even start thinking about the harm done by emissions from the long-haul flights required by these 'wonderful' holidays.

Tony Hill

d

Sir

I fully agree that long-haul tourism is bad news – and not just long-haul either. Think of Spanish resorts pulling water from the ground faster than Nature can put it back.

And then consider another danger. In the last few years, there have been terrorist attacks on tourists visiting countries worldwide – including both Indonesia and Spain.

So why not spend next holiday visiting places at home? We have some of the most beautiful tourist spots in the world – and some of the safest!

Lucy Smith

BACKGROUND BRIEFING Air travel

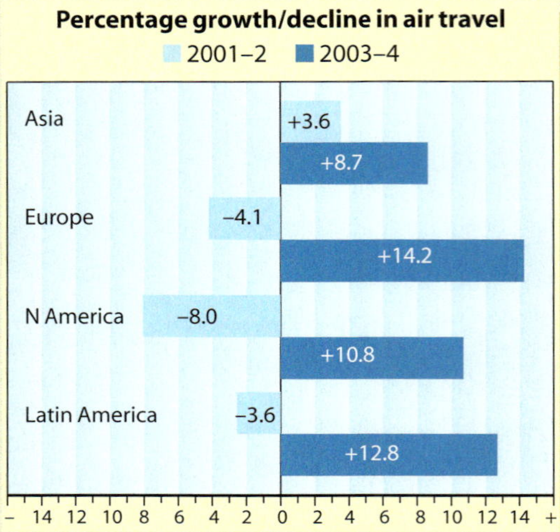

- Air travel declined in 2001–2 because of poor economic conditions and 9/11.
- There was a rapid recovery in 2003–4. Expansion has continued since.
- Budget airlines carry 40% of all passengers in N America. Low-cost European carriers are increasing market share by 20–30% per year.
- Many traditional airlines cannot compete and will go bankrupt. Others, like Singapore Airlines, will do well from their profitable long-haul business.
- In 2004, Airbus production finally overtook Boeing (300 planes to 280). The new Airbus 380 will carry up to 800 passengers, many more than Boeing's 747.

5 Looking at the text

A **Put the letters in the order they were written.**

B **Were the points for and against tourism similar to those you made before you started reading?**

C **Imagine a holiday flight in five years' time:**
- from Germany to Spain;
- from Germany to Singapore.

What will be different? Use information from BACKGROUND BRIEFING.

D **Say what you think.**

CULTURE CHECK National stereotypes

1 What do the cartoons suggest?
2 Do you think there is any truth in these stereotypes?
3 There are also positive national stereotypes. Which nationalities do you associate with the following?

ambitious • determined • dynamic • good-humoured • friendly • hard-working • inventive • loyal • open to new ideas • practical • sociable

6 Working with words

Begleitgrammatik p.202

Complete the following sentences with the correct participle forms.

1 Flying long-haul is … . At the end of a flight, you feel … . *(exhausted/exhausting)*
2 I'm … about our skiing holiday in Canada next month. They say the place has got some of the most … ski runs anywhere in the world. *(excited/exciting)*
3 Flight 753 had to make a … landing in a terrible storm. The … passengers all thought they were going to die. *(terrified/terrifying)*
4 The idea of missing a plane has always been very … to me and, as usual, I'm … about being late for my flight tomorrow. *(worried/worrying)*
5 I watched an … programme about Vietnam a few months ago and since then I've been very … in going there. *(interested/interesting)*
6 After one day on the beach, Tony turned bright red. This was … enough, but he was even more … when a child said he looked like a London bus! *(embarrassed/embarrassing)*
7 I'm glad the holiday is over. We were … to death there. I've never stayed in such a … place! *(bored/boring)*

7 Using language at work

Begleitgrammatik p.202

A **You have to shorten Tony Hill's original letter a little. Change the underlined parts to participles. Then check the printed letter on page 85.**

Sir

The Sunday Herald is a fine newspaper, but articles that are printed[1] in the travel section often worry me.

I worry about travel diaries that describe[2] the last, unknown beach in Thailand and articles that tell[3] us to visit Indonesia before the rainforest totally disappears.

This pressure to travel is wrong. It encourages us to visit parts of the world which suffer[4] from real environmental damage already. The more people visit, the greater the destruction that is caused[5]. And all this is before we even start thinking about the harm which is done[6] by emissions from the long-haul flights that are required[7] by these 'wonderful' holidays.

Tony Hill

8 Writing

Summarize the arguments in the four letters. Write two sentences for each letter. Choose from these reporting verbs and connectors.

add • argue • believe • comment • conclude • (dis)agree • feel • reply • recommend • respond by saying • say • state

… also … • in addition, … • moreover, … • …, too • therefore • by contrast, … • however, … • on the other hand, … • finally, …

Tony Hill stated that articles in the Sunday Herald's travel section often put too much pressure on people to travel. He felt that …

C Task options

9 Discussion and presentation

www.YOURTRAVEL.com

OUTWARD	Friday July 15			
Carrier	Flight No.	Dep.	Arr.	Cost + Taxes
Princess Air	PRA 179	16:25	20:10	€349.00 + €29.00
CostaLine	CSL 2063	19:15	22:30	€285.00 + €29.00
Atlanta Sky	ATS 684	23:45	03:30	€199.00 + €29.00

Hotel Buena Vista
Summer in Tenerife style. Beautiful hotel with 2 pools, 3 restaurants and fitness club. Just metres from the beach, we are also close to the island's liveliest nightlife. Price per person based on twin share room with half board €450 pppw.

Villa Lapas
Experience traditional Tenerife. Family-run bed & breakfast on a quiet street just 5 minutes from the beach and also 5 minutes from the down-town clubs and restaurants. €45 pppn single or €40 twin room.

El Dorado Apartments
Comfortable studio apartment sleeps two, complete with fully-equipped kitchen; 15-min walk from beach, Sky TV, AC, cleaned twice weekly. €400 pw all inclusive. For more information, call 0034 22 657802 or visit: www.eldoradoapart.esp.com.

Work with a partner. You want the best possible two-week holiday in Tenerife. Your maximum budget is €1,700 per person. Follow these steps.

1 Read about the pros and cons of different flights and places to stay. Discuss and make your choices.
2 Work out and add up these further costs.
   - Travel within Germany (include parking, if you drive to the airport)
   - Food per day: self-catering €25; B & B €20; hotel €10
   - Clubbing, sports facilities, transport and day trips, etc.: €30 per day
3 Make your decision.
   - Work out the total cost of your holiday per person. (Remember your budget!)
   - Explain your holiday choices to another pair. Decide whose plans are better.

Grammar checkpoint

Common errors

You often find a great mixture of nationalities on the beach and by the pool in the summer. A lot of their conversations are in English – English that is not always perfect. Read each conversation and correct the errors.

1 Sun tan cream

Kristal The sun's getting very hot now. I need to put some of this stuff on my back. ~~How do you call it~~ in English?

Maria Sun tan cream, I think. And you're right. ~~It's so a hot day~~ now, ~~it'll be too easy~~ to get burned.

Kristal Yes, and the sand is even beginning to burn ~~my feets!~~

2 How long?

Sven ~~I've arrived last night~~. Have you arrived ~~in the last time~~, too?

Stefan No, ~~I'm staying~~ here ~~since twelve days.~~

Sven I'm here on a ~~two- weeks holiday.~~ What about you?

Stefan I'm ~~the same like you~~, so I'm sorry to say I have to leave the day after tomorrow.

3 Things to do

Dieter ~~Gives there~~ much to do in this little place?

Carlo Well, ~~the most peoples~~ stay on the beach, but you can ~~make a lot of water sports also.~~

Dieter And ~~if I would go~~ into town, would there be much to do?

Carlo Oh, yes, it's certainly ~~worth to go~~ into town in the evening. There's always ~~anything to do~~ there.

4 The swimmer

Anita Your little brother is ~~very good in swimming.~~

Barbara Yes, he could already swim ~~with two years.~~ And now he's 11, ~~he trains his swimming~~ at our local sports centre nearly every day. ~~The most time he goes~~ as soon as he finishes ~~the school.~~ ~~He goes always~~ with ~~a friend of him~~, and ~~they stay for at least two hours there.~~ ~~The both boys~~ are very good.

Anita Wow! He's going to be a champion ~~in the next time!~~

5 Till later

Helga (finishing a phone call) That was my mum. She ~~wants that I go back~~ to the hotel for lunch with my family.

Juan Oh, no! ~~Have you to go~~ right now? The sea ~~looks very well~~, so I ~~thought we can go swimming.~~

Helga Sorry, but if I don't go, I'll be in big trouble! We all ~~have to do that what she says!~~ Besides, ~~I have hunger.~~

Juan Now ~~I feel really sadly!~~

Helga Why? ~~We mustn't say~~ goodbye. I don't think lunch will take very long. ~~And if I finish lunch~~, I can come back to the beach again.

Juan Oh, great! What time?

Helga I'm not sure. Listen, give me your ~~handy~~ number, and we can ~~talk to ourselves~~ when ~~I'll be free.~~

Helga OK. ~~We see us~~ back here on the beach ~~today~~ afternoon.

7 ECO-CHOICES

Focus

The most eco-friendly choice is not always clear, as this quiz shows.

1 Answer the questions.

2 Discuss your answers with a partner.

QUIZ

Difficult choices

1 The right car

You know cars are bad for the environment, but you need one. You have an older car which is quite reliable, but you could now afford a new one. Which car is the 'best' choice?

a) An efficient, new saloon car with good fuel economy and a catalytic converter.

b) The car you have now. It's six years old and not very efficient.

c) A new, hybrid petrol-electric car which has excellent fuel economy.

2 On the road

As a driver, which do you or would you regularly do?

a) Drive smoothly because sharp acceleration and braking increase fuel consumption.

b) Walk, cycle or use public transport when possible, instead of using the car.

c) Neither of the above.

3 Clothes shopping

You need new clothes. Which is the first place you look?

a) Low-cost stores, mail-order catalogues or their websites.

b) Outlets – stores, catalogues or websites – for FAIRTRADE goods.

c) Charity shops.

4 On holiday

You need a holiday, but you don't want one which will cause unnecessary environmental damage. So which one do you choose?

a) A cheap, simple package holiday (with flights and hotel included) at a well-established resort with lots of sun and sea.

b) A holiday in your part of the country to get to know it better.

c) A winter-sports holiday in the Alps that just uses what's already there: snow.

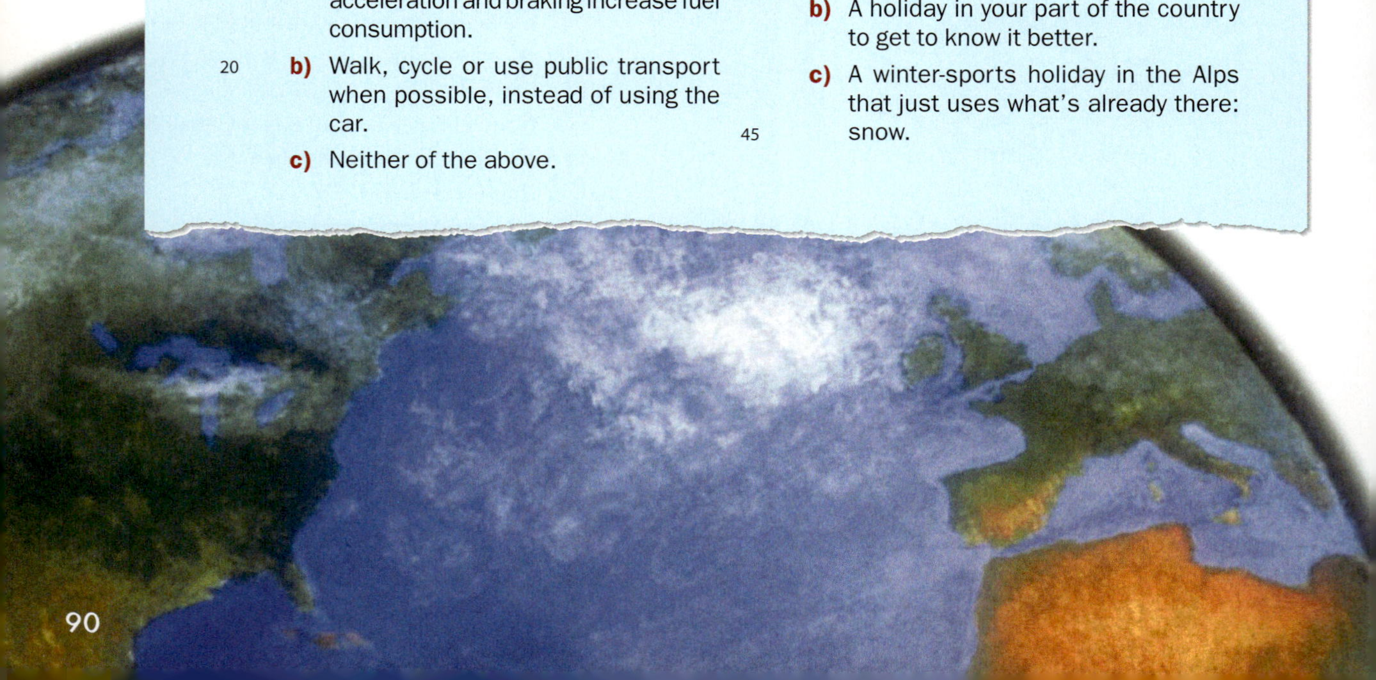

A People and business

- Say what you and your partner (dis)agreed about in the quiz.
- Read the comments below. Be ready for some surprises!

What your answers mean

1 *The right car*

a) 1 point **b)** 3 points **c)** 2 points

Conventional modern cars are now more efficient and less polluting than cars were years ago, but much of the benefit is lost because they are heavier. Hybrid cars offer much better fuel economy than conventional cars, but a new car – conventional or hybrid – uses new resources, and we need to consume less, not more. The best option: keep your older car, look after it well and drive it till it 'dies'.

2 *On the road*

a) 1 point **b)** 2 (+1) points **c)** 0 points

You save fuel if you don't accelerate sharply and when you use your brakes carefully, you also avoid wasting energy in the form of heat.
The best choice is b). Give yourself an extra point if you have done any of the following in the last 24 hours: used public transport, gone by bicycle, or walked a distance most people drive.
Think about public transport: the more we all use it, the more it will be improved and extended. If you chose c), please think again!

fuel economy

3 *Clothes shopping*

a) 0 points **b)** 2 points **c)** 4 points

Clothes from low-cost stores are usually cheap at least partly because the production workers have poor pay and conditions. With Internet and mail-order purchases, there is also the energy cost of delivery by road. On the other hand, if you buy from the shops, catalogues or websites of FAIRTRADE companies such as People Tree, you know that the workers have had a fair deal. Best of all, though, why not bring recycling into your shopping style and visit the local charity shops? That way you re-use expensive resources instead of throwing them away. There's a good chance you'll find a real bargain, too!

4 *On holiday*

a) 0 points **b)** 3 (+1) points **c)** 1 point

A holiday with air flights is worst for the environment. Fuel consumption is high, and emissions in the atmosphere may be much more damaging than pollution at ground level. On top of this, package holiday resorts often bring little benefit to the community and also damage the local environment. You can drive to your winter-sports resort, but with all the heating there, that still means using a lot of fossil-fuel energy. The cost rises further when powerful machines are used to produce artificial snow. The best choice is a local holiday. Have an extra point if you would walk, cycle or use public transport instead of driving.

YOUR SCORES
1–5: Wake up!
6–10: Could do better!
11–14: Your grandchildren will thank you.

(405 words)

BACKGROUND BRIEFING Eco-friendly websites

www.co2.org
www.ecologicalfootprint.com
www.carbonneutral.com

Three automatic carbon 'calculators' for you to find out how much CO_2 you produce and what you can do (e.g. pay for trees) to balance your environmental impact

www.natenergy.org.uk

Lots of information on renewable energy, plus activity kits, e.g. to build your own mini-wind turbine

www.tourismconcern.org.uk

Ideas on how to see the world without destroying it

www.eta.co.uk

New cars checked and rated – from best to worst – for their effects on the environment

1 Looking at the text

Lernhilfe p.211

A **Write a comment about your quiz responses.**

Paragraph 1

Say how good (or bad) a friend to the environment you are according to your quiz score. Give examples of your choices.

Paragraph 2

Say whether you think your quiz score is a fair or an unfair result, and give an example to support your view.

B **Do some practical environmental research.** At home, find out your approximate annual use of energy, as well as how much you use for daily transport and holiday air travel. (See the automatic carbon calculators in BACKGROUND BRIEFING.) Then go to www.futureforests.com to find out how many trees this organization believes you should plant to balance your environmental impact.

C **Say what you think.**

2 Working with words

A **There are several 'word pairs' in the quiz on pages 90 and 91. Match these 'partner' words below, and then check your answers in the texts.**

consumption • flight • package • public • saloon • worker

1 … car	(p. 90, line 7)	4 production …	(p. 91, line 33)
2 fuel …	(p. 90, line 18)	5 air …	(p. 91, line 48)
3 … transport	(p. 90, line 20)	6 … holiday	(p. 91, line 52)

B **Match the following words to words 1–6 above. Collect them in diagrams and use your dictionary to add more words.**

department • economy • equipment • hire • manager • private • pump • rail • road seaside • skiing • sports • stewardess • summer • tax • ticket • travel • used

saloon
used
________ car
____

fuel *consumption*
tax
____
____

Partner words that are often used together can become one word, e.g. ***airline***. Find more examples with ***air***, ***land*** and ***sea*** in your dictionary.

2.4
2.5

3 Listening

A **Ian Marr runs a successful new eco-friendly business. Listen to Parts 1 and 2 and answer the questions.**

1 What was Ian's old job, and what does he do now?
2 What sort of people does he employ?
3 Is his business just in Bristol or all over the UK?

B **Listen to Part 1 again. Note the basic facts of Ian's story.**

2.4

C **Listen to Part 2 again. Note as many facts with numbers as you can.**

4 Using language for life

A **Creating and showing interest. Listen to Part 1 again.**

1 Note expressions which help you make a story interesting.

EXAMPLE *It all happened like this, you see.*

2 Note expressions for showing interest in a story.

EXAMPLE *Wow! That was a big step to take!*

B **Work with a partner. Think of a true story about yourself or someone else.**

1 Prepare to tell your story, using expressions to create interest.
2 Listen to your partner's story, using expressions to show interest from 4A.

B Business and society

- Look at the newspaper headline and the charts in the BACKGROUND BRIEFING. What do you think the newspaper story will be about?
- Do you think any of the electricity you use comes from renewable sources such as hydroelectric, solar or wind?

LARSEN CITY TIMES **March 15**

CLEAN GREEN POWER FOR LARSEN CITY?

Larsen Light & Power Utility Company yesterday announced its planning application for a windfarm along Dawson Ridge, above Lake Larsen.

LL&P hope to start with eight 140-metre wind turbines producing around 10% of the power they supply to their 40,000 customers. If successful, Phase 2 will follow, producing power for a further 4,000 customers.

Larsen City Council has today called a public meeting at City Memorial Hall for Saturday, March 30 to discuss the plans. Says Mayor Helen North: 'All are very welcome. Glenn Brandt, LL&P's Manager, will be there to answer questions.'

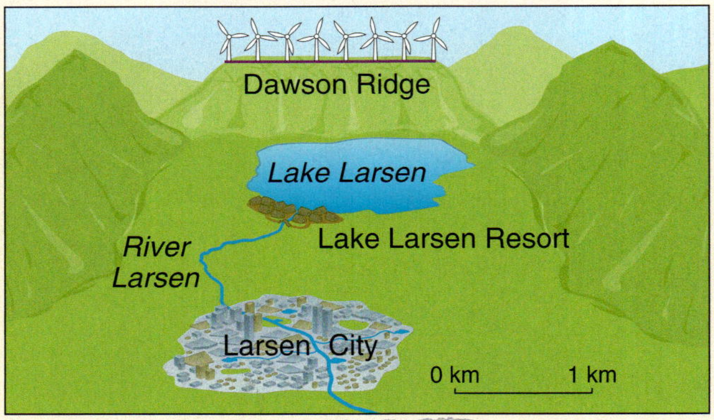

2.6

Public meeting, Larsen City

BRANDT ... To sum up, I believe now is the time to start using clean, renewable energy. Partly, it's because traditional fossil-fuel prices are rising. Much more importantly, though, if people like us don't take action in time, we risk leaving our grandchildren a polluted world facing disastrous climate change.

NORTH Thank you, Glenn Brandt. Let's open the discussion to everyone. OK, Andrew Minsk.

MINSK Thanks. Now, I understand wind energy can be expensive and also unreliable. Will that be the situation here?

Brandt No, it won't. Certainly, wind farms have at times been built in places without enough reliable wind. That's happened in Germany and even in California, America's leading wind energy producer. But we've done our research. First, Montana gets far more wind than California, and secondly, Dawson Ridge is easily the best local site.

Minsk But what about cost?

Brandt Well, fossil-fuel costs are rising. At the same time, efficient, modern technology is reducing wind-power prices. Right now, yes, it's still a bit more expensive, but in five or ten years' time, it won't be.

North Clarke Mason. You next.

Mason I remember the small wind-powered generators pumping water and powering lights on every farm back in the 50s – our own included. They disappeared when LL&P brought power out to us, but they were good, and it'll be great to use free, natural wind power again.

North Susan Radek?

Radek Excuse me! Clarke Mason, are you seriously comparing those little old towers with these modern monsters? Just think! They'll stand 140 metres high above Dawson Ridge, and each rotor will reach up another 100 metres. Now, as some of you know, I run Lake Larsen Resort, right across from Dawson Ridge. People come from everywhere for the peace and natural beauty. What they'll get instead is the sight and sound of these turbines – non-stop. Guess what. We'll lose those visitors, go bankrupt, and over 120 local jobs will be gone. Is that what we want? Glenn Brandt, what do you say to that? ...

(336 words)

BACKGROUND BRIEFING **Global warming and energy**

1. Carbon dioxide (CO_2) is the most important 'greenhouse gas' which, in normal quantities, helps keep the atmosphere at the right temperature for life on Earth.
2. Greenhouse gas levels have been rising fast recently. Global warming is happening at the same time.
3. Most scientists accept that human activities are adding to natural greenhouse gas levels, mainly through use of fossil fuels.
4. If CO_2 levels and global warming continue to rise, violent weather and rising sea levels are expected.
5. The 1997 Kyoto Agreement said that by 2010 industrialized nations – without the USA – would reduce their greenhouse gas emissions to below 1990 levels. Most countries may not reach their targets. Large developing economies (China) were not given targets.
6. To achieve Kyoto targets, better, energy-efficient old technologies, and new, clean energy sources (wind power) are needed.

BACKGROUND BRIEFING Global warming and energy *(continued)*

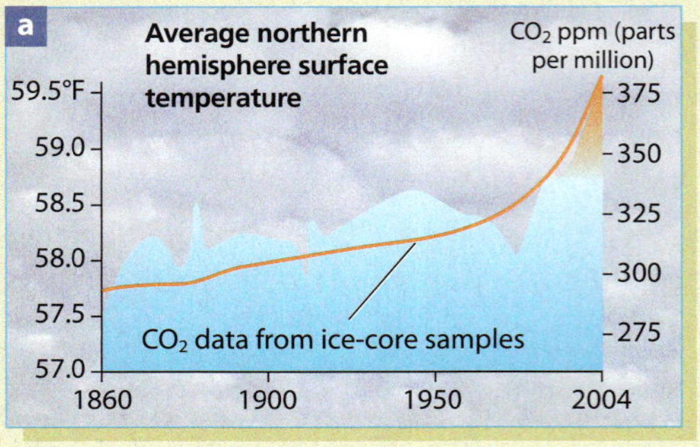

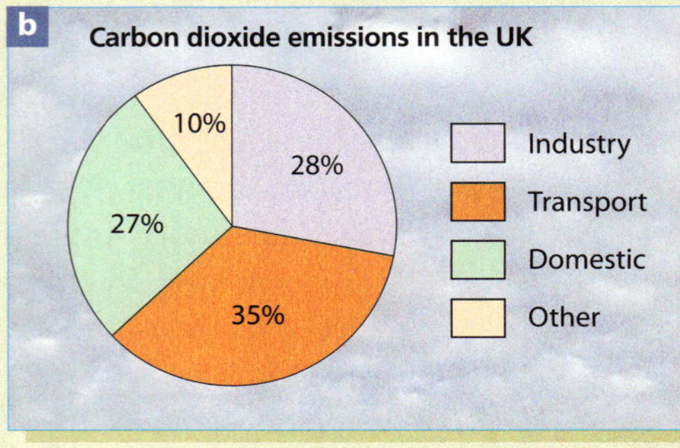

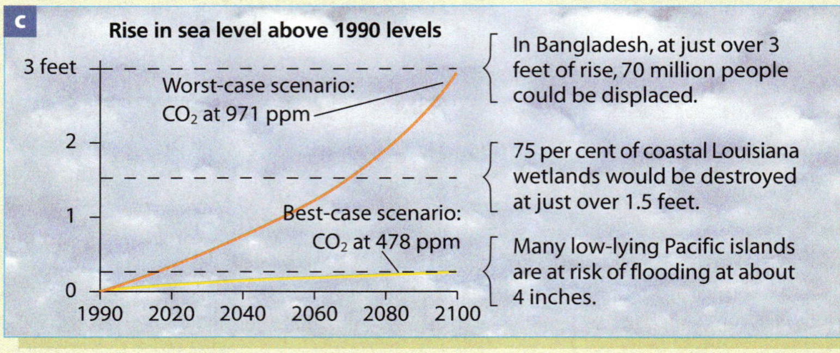

5 Looking at the text

A Say whether the following are true, false or not stated in the text. Correct the false statements.

1 Only members of Larsen City Council are allowed to speak in the discussion.
2 If both Phases 1 and 2 go ahead, about 20% of electricity will be wind powered.
3 Larsen City is in California.
4 Dawson Ridge is the best place in the area for a reliable supply of wind.
5 Brandt believes that wind power will soon be cheaper than energy from fossil fuels.
6 LL&P only supplies electricity to Larsen City itself.
7 LL&P used to supply the farmers' wind-powered generators.
8 The rotors will reach 450 metres at their highest point above the level of the lake.
9 Lake Larsen Resort employs more than 120 local people.

B Use the information in BACKGROUND BRIEFING to do these tasks.

1 Match charts **a–c** to three of points 1–6 on page 95.
2 Then use charts **a–c**, one after another, to help you explain the problems that we now face and the possible effects.

C Say what you think.

6 Working with words

A Match the expressions with *time* to the definitions on the right.

1 now is the time (line 1)
2 in time (line 5)
3 at times (line 13)
4 at the same time (line 19)
5 in five years' time (line 21)

a at a particular point in the future
b before it is too late
c during the same period
d sometimes
e the right time

B Match these other expressions with *time* to the definitions on the right.

1 at all times
2 by the time
3 from time to time
4 on time
5 run out of time

a always
b at the right time – not early and not late
c having no more time available
d sometimes
e up to a point in time

C Use expressions from 6A and B to complete the following.

1 The train arrived exactly ... at 11.23.
2 ... I got to the door, the postman had gone.
3 I usually enjoy the work, but ... I get a bit bored.
4 We've ... for discussion. We have to make a decision right now!
5 The rain has stopped. ... to go out – before it starts raining again.
6 Drive faster, or we'll never get there ... for the wedding.

7 Writing

You are an exchange student at Larsen City High School. Every month you have to write a 'letter from America'. Your letter this month is about the meeting. Write about it in three paragraphs.

1 Say who the meeting was for, where and when it was held, and for what purpose.
2 Summarize briefly what was said.
3 Give your own opinion of the project. Should it go ahead or not? Why?

C Task options

8 Class survey

A **Work with a partner. Use the notes to finish writing this questionnaire.**

You and your environment

1 When you are tired of an old but still-good jacket, what are you most likely to do?

a) Throw it away. b) Keep it anyway. c) Give it to someone who will use it.

2 your family / ever eat ready-prepared meals / supermarket?
a) all / time b) time / time c) almost never
3 if / your room / cold / what / do first?
a) turn up / central heating / all your home b) put on / pullover
c) turn up / heating / your room
4 how / normally go / shopping?
a) use / car / motorbike b) walk / go by bicycle
c) travel / public transport

B **Work with another partner and take turns to use your questionnaire. Note your partner's answers.**

C **Do a class survey. One student stands at the board to collect numbers and asks:**

Who got answer (a)?

How many of us had answer (b)?

Did anybody get answer (c)?

D **Discuss the results. If you have been honest, the survey probably shows you are not all environmentally perfect!**

9 Role-play

A **Imagine a big, new development in your area. For example, a tourist, a retail (shopping centre) or wind farm project. Discuss the advantages and disadvantages of the project.**

B **Work in a group of three. Choose one of your projects and take the roles on page 193:**

the developer • a protester • the local planning officer.

At the end, the planning officer decides for or against the project and explains the decision.

Grammar checkpoint

1 Infinitive or *-ing* form 1 Begleitgrammatik. p. 203

Choose the correct forms of the verbs in brackets to complete the email above.

Dear Sir/Madam

During my recent holiday in Bristol, I very much enjoyed (*to listen / listening*)[1] to Radio Bristol, and I'd like (*to mention / mentioning*)[2] one programme in particular – an interview on *Good Morning, Bristol*. I turned on the radio early one day and I heard an interview between a female reporter and a man who had managed (*to set up / setting up*)[3] a successful business recycling wood. Stupidly, I failed (*to write down / writing down*)[4] his name, but I think it was Ian something.

When I got home to Paderborn, I thought a lot about that interview and wondered whether I could start a similar business. You see, I have recently felt like (*to change / changing*)[5] to some new kind of work, and I have considered (*to try / trying*)[6] various things. This wood recycling idea now seems to me by far the most interesting idea of them all.

However, I've put off (*to make / making*)[7] any decisions so far, because I feel I must find out a lot more first. After all, you always risk (*to fail / failing*)[8] if you set up a new business, and I really must do everything possible to avoid (*to make / making*)[9] unnecessary mistakes.

Could you pass on my email address to Ian? If he could give me some advice, this might really help me (*to change / changing*)[10] my whole life.

2 Infinitive or *-ing* form 2 Begleitgrammatik. p.203

The producer of *Good Morning, Bristol*, Ricky Eastman, is talking to the reporter, Susie Castle. Complete the conversation with the correct forms of the verbs in brackets.

Ricky Oh, Susie, do you remember …[1] (*do*) that interview with the man who runs the wood recycling business?

Susie Yes, of course. Ian Marr. Nice guy. He's trying …[2] (*set up*) a national network of wood recycling businesses.

Ricky Well, this email from Germany is about him. I meant …[3] (*look after*) it yesterday, but I forgot …[4] (*reply*) and today I just can't stop …[5] (*deal with*) it: I'm too busy. So could you answer it for me?

Susie OK, I'll stop …[6] (*work*) on this report.

Ricky Thanks! Well this Alex Hartmann remembers …[7] (*listen*) to you and Ian, and he wants to do something similar in Germany. But first, he wants Ian Marr's advice, so that means …[8] (*put*) them in contact.

Susie OK. Luckily, I decided …[9] (*keep*) Ian's contact details. I'll try his mobile number or I'll try …[10] (*call*) the wood shop.

3 Verb + object + infinitive

Complete Susie's email to Alex with the words above it. Change the verb forms as necessary.

want you / email • ask me / call • encourage him / help • help you / set up

Dear Mr Hartmann

Thank you for your email of 8th Sept. My producer has …[1] Ian Marr concerning your request. As you can imagine, Ian is very busy but I have …[2] you. Unfortunately, he has to be in London for two days, and I am replying for him while he is away. He would be very happy to …[3] your business in any way he can. As a first step, he …[4] him a list of questions which he will try to answer when he gets home from London. His email address is: ianmarr_wrp@aol.com.

I hope this is useful to you, and we wish you every success with your business plans.

8 YOUR WORLD OF WORK

Focus

A **Look at the photos and imagine yourself doing these jobs.**

1 Say what you might like and dislike about each.

2 What other sorts of jobs do you want in the future? Here are some ideas.

> accountant • estate agent • public relations officer • stock controller • (travelling) salesperson • travel agent • hotel receptionist

B **You may not find the job you want. In that case, would you ...**

1 take temporary, low-skilled work, e.g. a factory packing job?

2 accept low-paid work?

3 be ready to work unsocial hours or night shifts?

4 work unusual shifts, e.g. seven days on and seven days off?

5 remain unemployed?

C **If you find the job you want, there may be other problems. Would you be ready to ...**

1 commute for up to four hours a day?

2 accept a part-time job?

3 work a lot of overtime?

4 accept it as a temporary job for a year?

5 accept it as a work placement'? (They offer little pay, but at least they let you 'get a foot in the door'.)

A People and business

2.7

Are you a hard-working and well-organized person? List personal qualities that you think future employers would like.

What every employer wants

Lucy Koenig, Personnel Manager, Office Extra Ltd

We supply office stationery and equipment direct to our customers, usually overnight. Our systems are highly automated, so nearly everyone needs IT skills. But data is only as good as the person who inputs it, so the ability to process information accurately is vital. Numeracy too. It's all about quantities, codes and prices, so everyone has to be good at figures, and mental stamina is very important. And because we deliver overnight, it's essential to work well under pressure to meet tight deadlines. People need to be responsible and pretty well organized, and also highly motivated to get the job done. Our staff need good people skills, too, as we work closely together.

Craig Harris, Project Team Leader, PREview Ltd

We do public relations and various promotional events such as trade shows. Each project is run by a small team, so it's vital to be a good, responsible team player, and to deal well with clients because there's a lot of face-to-face contact, which also means dressing well. Things can change very fast in our world, so it's important for us to be flexible, creative problem solvers who can think on our feet. Our people also have to multi-track, dealing with different things at the same time – and exactly on schedule. So it's vital to be well organized, and to get things right first time. It's all very demanding, and people must really want to give it everything they've got.

Helen Morris, Careers Officer, Witford CFE

I help students find jobs. In fact, even getting a job requires certain qualities. They need to remain determined and optimistic when applications fail – as many do.

The essential qualities most employers want are actually very similar – and similar to qualities necessary here at college, too.

First, students need motivation. Without that sort of enthusiastic commitment, they may not even finish their course. Self-organization is also very important. It means setting realistic goals and taking responsibility for meeting them. Part of that is time management, which includes punctuality and getting work done on time. And work has to be done right, so accuracy and attention to detail are vital. Good interpersonal skills are important too. It's very important to be friendly and helpful, for example when working with others in a project group.

(390 words)

1 Working with the text

A Answer the questions on the text.

1 What do the three employment experts each do?
2 Who probably thinks most about matching people and jobs?
3 Who probably takes part in choosing people for jobs?
4 Which person probably has the most problems if the wrong person gets the job?

B Do these tasks.

1 Which of these qualities should **all** employees have? Find other ways in the text to express **some** of the qualities.

- have good people skills
- have mental stamina
- be able to multi-track
- be accurate
- be creative
- be determined
- be good at figures
- be motivated
- be optimistic
- be organized
- be punctual
- be responsible

2 Copy and complete this diagram. Put the key qualities that the experts all mention in the centre.

3 How many of the key qualities do you have? Do you have other qualities?

C Say what you think.

2 Working with words

A Complete the table of personal qualities with words from the texts.

	Noun	Adjective
1	…	able
2	responsibility	…
3	organization	…
4	flexibility	…
5	creativity	…
6	determination	…
7	…	motivated
8	enthusiasm	…
9	…	committed
10	realism	…
11	…	punctual
12	…	accurate

team work

B Use pairs of words from 2A to complete the following.

1 A sense of … is important when you write a 'jobs-to-do' list. It'll probably be too long, so to be …, cut it in half.
2 In public relations, you must be … to communicate well. The … to communicate with the media is essential.
3 Mark is … to get into advertising, and he just keeps trying. He's really got fantastic … .
4 Susie puts great energy and … into everything she does. Now she's doing IT, and she's very … about that, too.
5 … is vital in modern manufacturing. Product needs change so quickly that the production process has to be very … .
6 At an interview it's vital to be … . Your … is the first thing an interviewer will notice about you, so never be late!

3 Listening

2.8
2.9

BCC File 6
(Job applications)

A Copy the notes. Then listen to the interviews to complete them.

Interview 1 *Interview 2*

Name ____________________ *Name* ____________________

Age _______ *Age* _______

Job both applied for ______________________________

B **Listen again and answer the questions.**

1 What qualifications and experience does each applicant have?
2 What personal qualities – positive or negative – does each applicant have?
3 Listen for examples of the following:
- giving/not giving information freely;
- presenting/not presenting oneself, one's qualifications or experience well;
- showing/not showing enthusiastic commitment.

4 If you were the interviewer, which of the applicants would get the job? Why?

BACKGROUND BRIEFING Job interviews

How to succeed at interviews

1 Find out about the organization, e.g. on the Internet.
2 List questions you may be asked – see below. Prepare good answers.
3 List your own questions to ask – about the organization and the job.
4 Be sure you know where to go, how to get there and how long it takes. You must be punctual on the day.
5 Dress neatly and tidily.
6 When you go in, sit straight and look your interviewer(s) clearly in the eye. Try to look calm (but not too relaxed).
7 Answer questions clearly: say what is necessary and will create interest. Then stop.
8 Only talk about yourself to show what you would bring to the job.
9 Try to show that you would bring useful skills to the organization and that you are a pleasant person.
10 Use chances to ask questions and to show you have thought seriously about the job.

Some questions you may be asked

1 Why are you applying for this job?
2 What skills/experience/personal qualities would you bring to it?
3 What do you know about us/this job?
4 What attracts you to this sort of career?
5 How would you describe yourself?
6 What are your strengths/weaknesses?
7 What are your interests outside work?
8 What achievement in the past are you most pleased with?
9 How do you see yourself and your career in five years' time?
10 What are your long-term aims in life?

2.9

4 Using language for life

A **Interview language. Listen to interview 2 again and note expressions which:**

- present your abilities, qualities and experience

EXAMPLE *People say that I'm a very responsible person.*

- show your enthusiasm for the new job

EXAMPLE *If I got the job, I'd be very committed to making a success of it.*

B **Prepare an interview for the job you chose in Focus. Invent details:**

- school and college courses of study and qualifications;
- skills, including IT and languages;
- career experience and in-job training;
- why you want to move from your present job to the new one;
- what qualities you would bring to the job.

Role-play the interview with a partner.

B Business and society – and you

2.10

At your age, your great-grandparents probably knew what job they would be doing in ten years' time. Why is it much harder for young people now to know?

THE WORKPLACE IS ALWAYS CHANGING

Fields rise, fall, and all but disappear. Look at farming. In 1890, 43% of all US workers were farmers. Today, the figure is 1.6%. At the same time new fields appear, such as computing, and we begin the process all over again.

Companies rise, fall, and often disappear. At the same time new companies arrive, and older companies re-invent themselves, with new strategies, new technology, and new products or services, and so we begin the process all over again.

Jobs also rise, fall and often disappear. Look at the downsizing and other trends in the last few years. At the same time new jobs are born, often in other fields, and we begin the process all over again.

Yes, the workplace is always changing – it always has, and it always will. And new jobs are always being created. Jobs that never existed previously. In the US, over two million jobs are created every year.

That's a lot of new jobs. And you have as much chance as anyone of winning one of these jobs – if you can find them, and if you are qualified to perform them, and if you do well in the job interview.

Write it on your bathroom mirror, sing it, repeat it: there are always jobs out there. There are always jobs out there. (216 words)

CASE STUDY: ONE OF THE NEW JOBS

Stefan Hartman, Events Manager

Stefan used to go to grammar school in Dortmund, but he gradually came to see his schoolwork as pointless. As he became more unhappy and demotivated, his results got worse.

At the age of 16, he started a weekend job as a waiter serving food at a local restaurant. There, he quickly began organizing live music evenings and other special events. Soon, he was building up a network of contacts, including technicians and equipment suppliers. He was also enjoying every minute of it.

At about the same time, he changed school and moved to a business college. He immediately found this kind of study useful and he started doing well at school.

He soon made another decision: he decided to turn his part-time organizing of events into a business. He called it PartyTime, and he began doing events for other bars and restaurants, as well as schools and private parties.

After taking his final exam this year, he will start a two-year apprenticeship as events manager with TOP-Events, a company which was his competitor. But he will be allowed to continue with his own business part-time. In perhaps five years' time, he hopes to return to it full-time and build it into a real company.

For Stefan the future looks very positive. (216 words)

BACKGROUND BRIEFING Inside modern businesses

1 Recent trends in business organization

de-layer	Get rid of unnecessary layers in management, so that the pyramid shape of a company becomes much flatter.
downsize	Reduce the number of employees in a company to make it smaller.
merge	Join companies together for strength in the market, e.g. DaimlerChrysler.
outsource	Pay other companies or individuals to do part of an organization's work.
restructure	Organize a company in a new way so that it can operate more efficiently.

2 Recent trends in the workplace

flexitime	System of work which allows people to work a fixed number of hours while choosing their own start and finish times.
hotdesk	Work at whatever desk and computer is available in an office
jobshare	Divide the responsibilities and pay of one job between two people who work at different times during the day or week.

5 Looking at the the text

A Say what these numbers in the text refer to.

43% • 1.6% • over two million • 16 • two-year

B Answer the questions on the text.

1 What similarity does the author find between fields of work, companies and jobs?
2 In order to get one of the new jobs, what three things do you have to do?
3 Why was the move to business college a good one from Stefan's point of view?
4 What three steps brought Stefan to his apprenticeship as events manager?
5 Why might TOP-Events be disappointed a few years from now?

C Think about it.

1 Name five jobs that did not exist 100 years ago and five traditional jobs that have (almost) disappeared.
2 Name companies that have grown recently and others that have disappeared.
3 BACKGROUND BRIEFING, 2: do you know anyone who works in any of these ways?

D Write a comment.

What's the answer: a 'hire-and-fire' society with lower unemployment, like America? Or a society with more job protection but high unemployment, like Germany?

E Say what you think.

6 Working with words

A Give the opposites. Then check your answers in the text.

1 to rise (line 1)
2 to appear (line 4)
3 to die (line 9)
4 destroyed (line 12)
5 motivated (line 20)
6 excluding (line 24)
7 useless (line 27)
8 full-time (line 29)

B Copy the table of opposites below and add these words to the correct columns. Use your dictionary to help you.

agree • appear • caffeinated • dependent • flexible • legible • logical • patient • practical • punctual • rail • relevant • responsible • usual

> **!**
> il- **before words starting with** l: illegible, illogical
> im- **before words starting with** b, m **or** p: imbalance, immoral, impersonal
> ir- **before words starting with** r: irrational, irresponsible

DE-	(de)motivated	DIS-	(dis)organized	IN-	(in)accurate	IL-	(il)legal
	…		…		…		…
IM-	(im)possible	IR-	(ir)regular	UN-	(un)happy		
	…		…		…		

C Use pairs of opposites from 6B to complete the following.

1 The buses are often late, but people are usually … . But last week there was a woman who got very angry and … .
2 At the start of the exam, Ann's writing was clear and …, but as she ran out of time and started panicking, her writing got more and more … .
3 At first, the bank was very … with Tony's new business, but it soon became very … when he started losing money.
4 It is very dangerous for a small company to be … on just one big company for its sales. If it supplies several customers, it is in a much more … position.
5 The production system is in chaos because the manager is completely … . We need someone in charge who is much more … .
6 We … on the quantity of equipment and the date we will supply you. But we still … on the price, and we can't cut it any more.

7 Writing

Write an essay: 'Your own business: does it make sense?' Use this structure:

Paragraph 1: Describe the difficult employment situation in Germany and state that starting one's own business is an alternative.
Paragraph 2: State the advantages.
Paragraph 3: Explain the risks and problems.
Paragraph 4: Give your personal views. What sort of business would you start? Or why would you prefer normal employment?

C Task options

8 Classified job adverts

Morning Standard — JOBS EXTRA — April 29

Deliver telephone directories in your area and earn up to €15.00 per hour (€0.25 per directory delivered) during June. Must have own transport. Call Liam on 01 878 8542.

Fruit and vegetable pickers urgently needed. Non-English speakers welcome. Day rate up to €75.00, depending on crop and quantities picked. Hours 8.00–4.00. Overtime available. 40 mins by bus from central Dublin. Call Mr Georgi Videnov on 01 493 4209.

Summer holiday relief workers needed at Howth Glass Works during July–Sept to work in Packing & Dispatch. Shifts from 0600–15.30 and 16.00–23.30, four days on, two days off. €90.00 per shift. Free minibus transport from central Dublin (approx 30 mins each way). Call 01 671 2263 or email rohan@houthltd.com for an application form. Return this with a letter of application FAO Mrs R O'Hanlon, Houth Glass Works Ltd, 162–4 Upper Bridge Street, Dublin 3 by 4th May, quoting ref HRW043.

JOBS FOR TEMPS

Public library assistant required by the City Library Service to provide holiday cover for staff. Main duty is to restock shelves with books. Numeracy and reading ability to GCSE level or similar are required. For up to four months during June–September. Hours 9.00–5.00 Mon–Tues and Thu–Fri, 9.00–1.00 Wed and Sat. Pay: €12.50 ph. To apply, write Mrs J McConnell, City Library Services, 21 Margaret Street, Dublin or email jmconnell@jtp.org by 10 May, quoting job ref CLS023.

JOBS FOR TEMPS

Kildare Supermarkets require temporary checkout staff in Dublin during the summer. Experience preferable but not essential. Training & uniform provided. Min employment period 1 month. Flexible hrs & shifts. Basic pay €11.00ph + €4.00 for unsocial hrs; 15% staff shopping discount. Call 01 819 3232 for an application form, or download from www.kildaresupermarco.ie

Please return with a letter of application to Mr S Driscoll, Manpower Services, 43–49 Clare Street, Dublin 3 by May 7th, quoting job ref KS157.

A **Read this information and then the ads. Decide on one job to apply for.**

You plan to fly to Ireland this summer and spend three months in Dublin. You aim to:

- go to English classes in the evening;
- work during the day to help pay for everything, and to practise your English.

Decide on a job to apply for. Think about:

- what skills and personal qualities you have;
- whether it is a suitable job for temporary employment;
- pay and any other benefits;
- what chances there may be to speak English.

B **Work with a partner. Discuss which jobs you would apply for.**

C **Write a letter of application for the job you have chosen. Follow the instructions for applying and invent necessary information.**

BCC File 6 (Job applications)

Grammar checkpoint

1 Prepositional verbs

Begleitgrammatik p. 204

Complete Ann's story with prepositional verbs in the correct tense. Use the verbs in brackets and prepositions from this list.

about • at • for • of • to • with

1 (*look, apply*)
Ann decided to look for [1] work before she finished college and she started ... [2] lots of job adverts. She also started ... [3] various UK companies, and she had soon ... [4] a number of jobs.

2 (*wait, hear, ask*)
While she was ... [1] replies to these applications, she ... [2] an interesting job in New York. She had never ... [3] the company before, so she decided to ... [4] it at the US Embassy. And so the next day, she went there and ... [5] all the information they could give her.

3 (*talk, think, agree*)
Later, Ann ... [1] her best friend, Lisa. They ... [2] this exciting opportunity for a long time, and Lisa advised her to apply. Ann had never even ... [3] working in America before, but the more she ... [4] it, the more she ... [5] Lisa.

4 (*write, reply, invite, agree, provide, congratulate*)
She ... [1] the company, and they ... [2] her letter immediately. They ... her ... [3] an interview, and they ... [4] her request that they should ... her ... [5] air tickets. The interview went very well, and a week later, they phoned to ... her ... [6] getting the job.

2 Adjective + preposition

Begleitgrammatik p. 204

Write statements using the underlined words, the adjectives in brackets and the prepositions.

about • at • for • from • in • of • to • with

1 Mark decided to turn off <u>the business news</u>. (*bored*)
He was bored with the business news.
2 Maria isn't sure whether <u>her job interview</u> went well. (*anxious*)
3 It was a big surprise to us to see <u>the quality of the products</u>. (*amazed*)
4 <u>Working the night shift</u> was hard at first, but I'm all right now. (*used*)
5 The manager actually shouted at <u>his staff</u>. (*angry*)
6 They felt very sad seeing <u>the poor production staff</u> lose their jobs. (*sorry*)
7 Tony is always reading about <u>new business methods</u>. (*interested*)
8 Sally worries a lot about <u>failing her final exam</u>. (*afraid*)
9 I decided to stop <u>storing all my old papers</u> and to throw them away. (*tired*)
10 Sonya's new job is not like <u>the work she used to do</u>. (*different*)

3 Expressions with prepositions

Begleitgram. p. 204

Complete the sentences with the appropriate expressions. Use the nouns in brackets and prepositions from this list.

by • in • on • at • out of • up to

1 Philip didn't damage the copier on purpose. He did it .... (*purpose, mistake*)
2 The train is always exactly ..., and we're late. We'll have to run to get to the station ... to catch it. (*time*)
3 We did most of the journey ..., but when we came to the end of the road, we had to do the last five kilometres .... (*car, foot*)
4 This old computer system is completely .... We're going to get a new one that'll be right .... (*date*)
5 ... of my first day at the factory I was really tired, but I slowly got used to the work and ... I managed just fine. (*the end*)
6 Can I pay ... ? – I'm sorry, sir, but we can only accept payment ... or .... (*credit card, cash, cheque*)
7 Rob Smith started ... in 1988, but he had problems at the start of the 1990s and nearly went .... However, he survived and is now doing well, especially in the EU. As a matter of fact, he's ... in Frankfurt right now. (*business*)

The form and layout of business letters

BodyWorks Limited
a 24 London Road • Brighton • BN6 8KL
Tel +44 (0)1273-4050-0 • **Fax** +44 (0)1273-4050-10
www.bowo.co.uk • e-mail **info@bowo.co.uk**

BodyWorks

b 22 June 20..
— no full-stop after day

c Your ref.:
Our ref.: LD/En/2

d ProVitesse Kosmetika GmbH
Turmstraße 36
50733 Köln
Germany

e **Attn** Ms Karin Feldmann
— = **Attention** (*z. H.*)

f **Wholesale catalogue**
— Nowadays, the subject line is usually placed before *Dear …*, as in DIN form.

g Dear Ms Feldmann
— If possible, start with a name. If this is not possible, then start with *Dear Sir or Madam*.

h Further to our telephone conversation, I enclose two copies of our current catalogue for haircare products. These have been very well received by both the retail trade and the fashion press in the UK and we feel sure that they will also be of interest to you.

We would be delighted to supply you with samples or make you a firm offer.

We look forward to hearing from you.

Yours sincerely
i BodyWorks Limited
— If you started with a name, sign off with *Yours sincerely*. If you started with *Dear Sir or Madam*, sign off with *Yours faithfully*. If you are writing to a company for the first time, give your firm's name and your position in the company.

j Lucy Davis

Lucy Davis
European Sales Manager, Haircare

k **Encs.** Haircare catalogue (2x)
— = **Enclosures** (*Anlagen*)

l **cc** J. K. Cooper, Marketing
— = **carbon copy/ies** or **copy/ies circulated** (*Kopie(n) an …*)

What is a business letter?

Business letters, facsimile messages ('faxes') and emails are written by one firm, organization or individual to another on a business matter. The writer is the **sender**; the receiver is the **addressee**.

Emails are, in effect, spoken messages in written form. However, all the normal rules apply. That means you should not send casual and over-familiar emails to people senior to yourself or to people you don't know well (→ EMAILS, FILE 8).

When you write to a firm for the first time, say **who** you are, **where** you got the firm's address from and **what** you want the addressee to do. If you are writing to a firm you already know, just say **why** you are writing and **what** you want.

How to lay out a business letter

There is no standard layout for business letters in English, so most German companies use the DIN form. However, as a result of globalization, the **American full block form** is becoming increasingly common in international business, and this is the form we have used in this book.

The advantage of the full block form is that it is clear and very easy to use. Below the letterhead, the parts are simply listed in logical order on the left, and without commas in addresses or after *Dear …* or *Yours faithfully/sincerely*. (Commas, though, are still common in business letters.)

Remember that after *Dear …* , the new line begins with a **capital letter**.

Practising language

1 Match parts a–l of the letter with 1–12 below.

1 attention line
2 carbon copy/copy circulated
3 complimentary close
4 date
5 enclosures
6 inside address
7 letterhead
8 body text
9 reference
10 salutation
11 signature block
12 subject line

Always obey the **ABC Rule** when you write a business letter, fax or email:

A Be **accurate**. Make sure that all details – e.g. names, dates, order numbers, prices, etc. – are correct and complete.

B Be **brief**. Say exactly what you want to say and then stop.

C Be **clear**. Use plain, simple English. Write in an easy, natural style without being either too formal or too casual *(salopp)*. Use **long forms** – e.g. *they are, he did not, they would be* – in business letters.

2 a) **Write out these dates and then read them to your partner.**

EXAMPLE 19.11.05

write: 19 November 2005
say: the nineteenth of November, two thousand (and) five

1 07.09.49
2 12.04.61
3 22.11.63
4 20.07.69
5 09.11.89
6 03.10.90
7 11.09.01
8 your date of birth

dd.mm.yy
In modern practice, the six spaces in all-number dates are filled in, if necessary by a zero (0).

b) **In US-style dates, the month comes before the day: mm.dd.yy. Write out the American dates in the European form.**

1 11/03/00 3 November 2000
2 01/05/01
3 08/09/02
4 05.08.03

3 **This enquiry from *Style 4* in London to *Northern Textiles* in Bradford is complete but the parts are in the wrong order. Write out the complete letter.**

Alice Medway	8 Preston Road	Purchasing Assistant
Alice Medway	**Enquiry about denim**	Style 4 Limited
BD3 6TZ	London E2 7TF	Style 4 Limited
Bradford	19 Mile End Road	3 June 20..
Dear Mr Austin	Northern Textiles PLC	Yours sincerely

As I said on the phone, the cloth is intended for our summer range of Pretty Polly children's jeans.

Could you also please let us have details of your discounts for volume orders and conditions of payment?

Further to our telephone conversation today, we would be grateful if you could send us samples of the light denim we discussed.

Thank you for your trouble, and as soon as we have evaluated the samples we will get in touch with you again.

These details will help us to make a final decision, of course.

4 **Turn the email into a more formal business letter by replacing the underlined words and expressions with words from the box.**

advertisement	manufacturer
are	receiving
are particularly interested in	related equipment
could send us	Thank you very much
current	the October edition of
Dear Sir or Madam	will
enclosed image brochure	would be grateful
Incidentally	Yours faithfully

Hello[1]

As you'll[2] see from the attached PDF doc[3], we're[4] a leading German maker[5] of skis and stuff like that[6].

In answer to your advert[7] in last October's[8] *Winter Wonderland*, we'd be glad[9] if you can let us have[10] three copies of your latest[11] catalogue. By the way[12], we're especially keen on[13] your Snow Queen range of snowboards.

Thanks a lot[14] for your trouble and we look forward to getting[15] the catalogues soon.

All the best[16]

Karin Hosenfeld

File 2

Enquiries

Enquiries have up to four parts:

1 **Opening** If you are writing to the firm for the first time, say **where** you obtained their name and address. Otherwise, begin your letter with **2** below.

2 **Reason** Always say **why** you are making the enquiry. In the case of new business, some information about your own company or why you need the product(s) may also help the addressee.

3 **Request** Say exactly **what** you want the addressee to do. If possible, use a list, as in the model enquiry on page 116.

4 **Close** Make a friendly and positive closing comment to motivate the addressee to act promptly.

The situation

Karin Feldmann

Frank Richter

Lucy Davis

Jenna Omono

ProVitesse Kosmetika GmbH, a cosmetics wholesaler in Cologne, supplies drugstores and perfumeries throughout Germany with beauty products. The company is interested in expanding its range of natural cosmetics.

Karin Feldmann is a purchasing manager with ProVitesse. Her assistant is **Frank Richter**.

Lucy Davis is European Sales Manager for haircare products with **BodyWorks Ltd**, a producer of high-quality natural cosmetics in Brighton. Lucy's assistant is **Jenna Omono**.

A couple of weeks ago, Karin Feldmann visited the BodyWorks' stand at the Estetika fair in Brussels. There she met Lucy Davis and they discussed the possibility of doing business.

A Model enquiries

A phone enquiry

2.11

Frank Richter is phoning BodyWorks.

Jenna Hallo. Ms Davis's office. Jenna Omono speaking. Can I help you?
Frank Good morning, Ms Omono. My name's Frank Richter of ProVitesse in Cologne. Ms Davis may have told you …
Jenna Oh, hi, of course – but please call me Jenna, okay?
Frank Sure, thanks, and I'm Frank.
Jenna Hi Frank. Yes, well, Lucy has told me all about ProVitesse. It sounds good. Anyhow, what can I do for you?
Frank Well, Ms Feldmann wanted to know if you can supply in-shop displays for your products. That would be a big help this end, even if we have to translate them into German.
Jenna That won't be a problem – translating into German, I mean. All our display material is international.
Frank Oh, that's good. And you have displays for all your haircare products, do you?
Jenna Yes, and we have extra material for seasonal campaigns.
Frank What, like for sunscreen in early summer?
Jenna Right. Why don't I send you some of our displays? Then you can see if they're suitable for the German market.
Frank Fine, but we're only interested in haircare at the moment, Jenna.

1 You are Jenna. Note the points from the phone call for your boss.

An email enquiry

Datei Bearbeiten Ansicht Einfügen Extras Nachricht Hilfe

Von: Frank Richter <frank.richter@provit.de>
An: Jenna Omono <jenna.omono@bowo.co.uk> **Kopien:** karin.feldmann@provit.de
Betreff: Medexa bottles **Gesendet:** Dienstag, 03. Oktober 20.. 11:06

Hi Jenna

A point came up at the monthly marketing meeting yesterday about your Medexa range of shampoos. At present, these come in glass bottles which could break or damage bathroom surfaces when dropped in the shower, say. Our marketing people think this could harm sales because of safety worries. Have you had any problems with this? Are the shampoos also available in unbreakable plastic bottles?

Hope to hear from you soon,

Frank

2 Answer the questions.

1 When was ProVitesse's monthly marketing meeting?
2 What is the disadvantage of packing shampoos in glass bottles?
3 Why does ProVitesse want to change the packaging?
4 What information does Frank want from Jenna?

An enquiry by letter

In this enquiry, Karin Feldmann asks Lucy Davis for the price of a trial consignment.

ProVitesse Kosmetika GmbH
Turmstraße 36
50733 Köln
Tel +49 (0)221-774422-0 • **Fax** +49 (0)221-774422-11
Mail info@provit.de • **Website** www.provit.de

ProVitesse

BodyWorks Limited
24 London Road
Brighton
BN6 8KL
England

13 September 20..

Enquiry

Dear Ms Davis

Further to my visit to your stand at the Estetika fair in Brussels, we are interested in marketing your range of natural haircare products here in Germany. We would be grateful if you could send us a firm offer for a trial consignment of the following lines:

1 5 (five) cases Adona hair gel, order no. HG1693, 24 boxed tubes/case
2 3 (three) cases FixUp Extra gel, order no. HG1774, 24 boxed tubes/case
3 4 (four) cases Medexa 2 shampoo, order no. SM2091, 12 boxed bottles/case

As agreed in Brussels, please quote DDP our Cologne stores on your usual trade terms. As we are sure that your products could be a big seller here, we look forward to receiving your offer soon.

Yours sincerely
ProVitesse Kosmetika GmbH

Karin Feldmann
Karin Feldmann
Purchasing Manager

3 **Say if the statements are true or false. Correct the false statements.**

1 The letter is a general enquiry about the addressee's products.
2 Karin visited the BodyWorks stand at a fair in Brussels.
3 'Adona' is the brand name of a BodyWorks shampoo.
4 Medexa is packed in boxed bottles.
5 ProVitesse wants BodyWorks to deliver the order to its Cologne stores.

A fax enquiry to a freight company

Dick Page from Bodyworks' logistics department asks Bob Carter of Supertrans Freight Ltd for a quotation for shipping a repeat order to ProVitesse in Cologne.

To	Supertrans Freight Ltd	**Date**	5 November 20..
Fax no.	01273-3366-44	**About**	request for quotation
For	Bob Carter	**Pages**	1

BodyWorks

FAX MESSAGE

BodyWorks Limited
24 London Road • Brighton • BN6 8KL
Tel +44 (0)1273-4050-0 • **Fax** +44 (0)1273-4050-10
www.bowo.co.uk • e-mail **info@bowo.co.uk**

Dear Mr Carter
Please quote for collecting the following consignment from our stores at 12 Dover Road, Brighton and delivering it to ProVitesse Kosmetika GmbH, Turmstraße 36, 50733 Köln (Cologne), Germany:

1 30 (thirty) cases Adona hair gel
2 20 (twenty) cases FixUp Extra gel
3 30 (thirty) cases Medexa 2 shampoo

They will be ready-packed on three europallets with a net weight of 348 kilos.

The goods are protected against impact by expanded polystyrene corner-pieces and against damp by a double layer of heavy-duty polythene sheeting.

The invoiced value of the consignment is £2,782 (€4,173).

We would be grateful for a prompt reply as the consignment must be delivered by Friday, 15 November at the latest.

With best regards

Dick Page
Dick Page

If you have not received the number of pages shown above, please contact us on +44 (0)1273-4050-11 immediately.

4 **Say what roles these names, dates and other details play in the fax.**

EXAMPLE 079-3456-12
This is the fax number of Supertrans Freight Ltd.

1 5 November 20..
2 12 Dover Road
3 FixUp Extra gel
4 348 kilos
5 polythene sheeting
6 4,173
7 15 November
8 Dick Page

B Practising language

5 **Work with a partner. Make the phone calls using products, names, etc. from the Toolbox on page 174. Add any other details, as necessary.**

1 **An enquiry about the availability of products:**

A	B
	meldet sich mit Firma/Namen
meldet sich ebenfalls	
	fragt, worum es geht
interessiert sich für *(Produkt)* und fragt, ob **B** es liefern kann	
	bejaht die Frage; *(Produkt)* ist vorrätig zur sofortigen Lieferung
bedankt und verabschiedet sich	
	verabschiedet sich

2 **A request for a written offer:**

A	B
	meldet sich mit Firma/Namen
meldet sich ebenfalls	
	fragt, worum es geht
bittet um ein schriftliches Angebot für *(Menge/Produkt)* zu üblichen Geschäftsbedingungen	
	ist einverstanden und sagt, dass Lieferung DDP *(Bestimmungsort)* erfolgen wird
sagt, dass dies in Ordnung ist	
	wiederholt die Einzelheiten
bestätigt die Richtigkeit der Einzelheiten	
	bedankt sich und sagt, dass das schriftliche Angebot in den nächsten Tagen rausgehen wird; verabschiedet sich
bedankt und verabschiedet sich	

6 **Complete these sentences with the missing prepositions.**

1 Karin Feldmann is a purchasing manager with[1] ProVitesse Kosmetika …[2] Cologne.
2 Further …[1] her visit …[2] the BodyWorks stand …[3] the Estetika fair …[4] Brussels, Karin sent Lucy Davis an enquiry.
3 ProVitesse is interested …[1] BodyWorks' range …[2] haircare products.
4 The enquiry is …[1] a trial consignment …[2] hair gel and shampoo.
5 Karin asks BodyWorks to quote … their usual trade terms.
6 Karin is looking forward … receiving the offer.

7 **Complete with words from the enquiry by letter on page 116.**

Dear Mr Grant

With reference to our telephone conversation this morning, we are interested in …[1] your …[2] of protective leather clothing for bikers in Germany.

As …[3] on the phone, we would be …[4] if you could send us a … …[5] for a trial …[6] of 20 (twenty) Pegasus AX knee pads and 30 (thirty) Hermes belts on your usual … …[7].

We are sure that your …[8] for bikers could be a big …[9] in Germany, so we look forward to …[10] your offer soon.

Yours …[11]

8 **Work with a partner. Imagine that Dick Page doesn't fax Bob Carter (page 117) his freight enquiry, but phones him. Turn the fax into an enquiry by telephone.**

C Practising writing enquiries

Language you can use: enquiries

Opening

• *Mit Interesse haben wir Ihre Anzeige in* [Name der Zeitung/Zeitschrift] *vom* [Datum] *gelesen/gesehen.*	• We were interested to read/see your advertisement in [*name of paper/magazine*] of [*date*].
• *Als wir Ihre Website besuchten, haben wir mit Interesse gesehen, dass Sie … .*	• When we visited your website, we were interested to see that you … .
• *Wir interessierten uns besonders für …, den/die/das Sie annoncieren.*	• We were especially interested in … you advertise.

Reason

• *Wir sind eine etablierte wachsende/innovative deutsche/… Firma auf diesem Seletor/auf dem … sektor.*	• We are an established/a growing/an innovative German … company in this sector.
• *Als wir Ihren Stand auf der … Messe/Ausstellung besuchten, hörten wir mit Interesse, dass Sie …*	• When we visited your stand at the fair/exhibition, we were interested to hear that you … .
• *Wir suchen nach einem Lieferanten/Händler/Vertreter für … .*	• We are looking for a supplier/dealer/representative of … .

Request

• *Wir wären Ihnen dankbar, wenn Sie uns für … ein Angebot machen könnten.*	• We would be grateful if you could quote us for … .
• *Schicken Sie uns bitte ein (verbindliches) Angebot für folgende Produkte: … .*	• Please send us an (a firm/binding) offer for the following products: … .
• *Könnten Sie uns bitte weitere/detaillierte Informationen zu … schicken?*	• Could you please send us further/detailed information on … .
• *Wir wären dankbar, wenn uns ein/e Außendienstmitarbeiter/in besuchen könnte.*	• We would be grateful if a representative could call on us.

Price (→ FILE 10, GLOSSARY)

• *Alle Preise sollten* [Incoterm + Bestimmungsort] *sein.*	• All prices should be [*Incoterm + place of destination*].

Close

• *Wir freuen uns auf Ihr (baldiges) Angebot.*	• We look forward to receiving your offer/quotation (shortly).

2.12

9 **Listen to Ralf Hansen's enquiry and take notes. You are now Clare King. Write a letter to Ralf Hansen to go with the catalogue and confirm the details you gave him.**

10 **Write an enquiry in letter form based on the following details. Use your own name.**

Situation Sie arbeiten bei der Firma FreiLuft Rhein GmbH (FLR) in Bonn. In der aktuellen Ausgabe der Zeitschrift *Campers' World* lesen Sie eine Anzeige über solarbetriebene Campingleuchten. Der Inserent ist die Firma Apex Leisure Ltd (AL) in Nottingham, England.

Aufgabe Formulieren Sie eine briefliche Anfrage an AL:

- Sagen Sie, woher Sie Name/Anschrift von AL haben.
- Sagen Sie, wer Sie sind.
- Bitten Sie um Zusendung von drei Exemplaren des aktuellen Katalogs und der Preisliste von AL.
- Schließen Sie das Schreiben freundlich/positiv.

11 **Write an enquiry in fax form based on the following details. Use your own name.**

Situation Wie bei Übung 10.

Aufgabe Formulieren Sie eine Fax-Anfrage an Anjali Sen von Apex Leisure Ltd über deren Champion-Serie solarbetriebener Campingleuchten.

- Bedanken Sie sich bei AL für deren Antwort auf Ihre Anfrage.
- Sagen Sie, dass Sie eine Probebestellung für Champion-Campingleuchten aufgeben wollen.
- Verlangen Sie ein Angebot für jeweils 25 Stück Champion 200- und Champion 400-Solarleuchten.
- Sagen Sie, dass die Lieferung DDP an Ihr Bonner Lager gehen soll und Sie den üblichen Handelsrabatt erwarten.
- Betonen Sie, dass alle Benutzerhinweise auf Deutsch sein müssen.
- Schließen Sie freundlich mit dem Hinweis: Es gibt durchaus gute Absatzchancen für AL-Solarleuchten in Deutschland.

12 **Write an enquiry in letter form based on the following details. Use today's date and your own name.**

Situation Sie arbeiten im Materialeinkauf bei Küchenbau Schwarz GmbH in Münster.

Aufgabe Formulieren Sie eine briefliche Anfrage an die Firma Wicklow Industries Ltd, 22–24 Leinster Road, Dublin 3, Irish Republic.

- Sie haben die Adresse der Firma von einem gemeinsamen Kunden *(mutual customer)* in Bochum erhalten.
- Küchenbau Schwarz GmbH ist ein führender Hersteller von hochwertigen Großküchen für die Gastronomie *(large kitchens for the catering industry)*.
- Für einen neuen Geschirrspüler benötigt Schwarz wasserdichte Kabelanschlüsse *(watertight cable connectors)*.
- Wicklow Industries Ltd soll zehn Muster ihres Modells CC12 mit technischen Beschreibungen *(technical descriptions)* schicken.
- Es ist unbedingt erforderlich, dass die Anschlüsse die entsprechenden europäischen Sicherheitsnormen *(safety standards)* erfüllen.
- Schließen Sie das Schreiben in angemessener Form.

Offers and quotations

Offers and quotations are answers to enquiries (→ FILE 2). They tell the buyer on what **terms** the seller is willing to supply the goods or services.

Offers without any special terms are often made by simply filling in a form. The supplier's **terms and conditions of business** *(Geschäftsbedingungen)* are generally printed on the back of the form. Offers or quotations with **special terms** *(Sonderkonditionen)* such as a higher discount or better terms of payment can be made by letter.

Offers or quotations generally have up to **four** parts:

1 **Opening** Refer to the original enquiry, with the date and, if quoted, the writer's reference (Our ref./*Unser Zeichen*).

2 **Details** Give clear and complete details of quantity, product, colour, etc. in tabular form. If the details are different from the original enquiry, point this out and say why (no longer available/blue only).

3 **Terms** To avoid trouble later, it is important to give clear, complete and correct information about discounts, terms of payment and delivery.

4 **Close** Thank the addressee for the enquiry and offer your help if there are any questions. You can add that you would appreciate an order, but don't overdo it.

A Model offers

An introductory offer by letter

In this letter, Lucy Davis of BodyWorks makes Karin Feldmann of ProVitesse Kosmetika an offer in answer to her enquiry (→ FILE 2, A3). *Lucy offers an additional introductory discount of 12.5% below the normal trade price.*

1 Read the letter and link A and B to make true statements.

A 1 We know that BodyWorks wants the business because ...
2 Lucy closes on a positive note by saying ...
3 It's clear that Lucy and Karin have already discussed ...
4 Lucy tells Karin to contact her ...
5 The letter is from BodyWorks in answer to ...
6 The original enquiry ...
7 ProVitesse can have an additional discount ...

B a an enquiry from ProVitesse Kosmetika.
b for payment within 15 days of delivery.
c if she has any queries.
d she's sure the products will sell well in Germany.
e the terms of the offer on the phone.
f they offer an additional discount of 12.5% below trade price.
g was dated 13 September 20.. .

BodyWorks

BodyWorks Limited
24 London Road • Brighton • BN6 8KL
Tel +44 (0)1273-4050-0 • **Fax** +44 (0)1273-4050-10
www.bowo.co.uk • e-mail **info@bowo.co.uk**

17 September 20..

Your ref. KF/A/1
Our ref. LD/PV/Of/1

ProVitesse Kosmetika GmbH
Turmstraße 36
50733 Köln
Germany

Offer

Dear Ms Feldmann

Thank you very much for your enquiry of 13 September. We are pleased to make the following offer:

1	5 (five) cases **Adona** hair gel, HG1693	€216/case	€1080
2	3 (three) cases **FixUp Extra** gel, HG1774	€240/case	€720
3	4 (four) cases **Medexa 2** shampoo, SM2091	€72/case	€288
		Total invoice price	€2088

As requested, all prices are DDP your Cologne premises for immediate delivery.

As agreed on the phone, these prices are 12.5% below normal trade price for a first order. As also agreed, we are willing to allow a cash discount of 2.5% for payment in full within 15 days of delivery.

Thank you again for your enquiry and please get in touch if you have any questions.

We would be delighted to receive an order from you and feel sure that our products will find a ready market in Germany.

Yours sincerely
BodyWorks Limited

Lucy Davis

Lucy Davis
European Sales Manager, Haircare

An offer from a freight company by fax

Supertrans Freight answers BodyWorks' enquiry of 5 November 20.. (→ FILE 2, page 117).

Supertrans Freight Limited
12 Commercial Road • Newhaven • BN14 9XX
Tel +44 (0)1273-3366-0 • Fax +44 (0)1273-3366-44
www.stf.co.uk • email info@stf.co.uk

Supertrans Freight

Fax message

to	BodyWorks Ltd	**date**	6 November 20..
fax no.	01273-4050-10	**about**	quotation
for	Dick Page, Logistics	**pages**	2

Dear Mr Page

Thank you for your fax of 5 November.

We are pleased to quote £283 for collecting your consignment of three europallets from your Dover Road, Brighton stores, and delivering them to the consignee's premises at Turmstraße 36 in Cologne. This price includes loading and unloading as well as insurance.

As delivery must be made by Friday, 15 November, we would collect the pallets two days before that date, on the morning of 13 November.

If you find this quotation satisfactory, please complete and return the attached confirmation of acceptance by fax as soon as possible.

With best regards

Bob Carter

Bob Carter
European Freight Manager

2 Complete the statements with the correct ending.

1 The Supertrans Freight's quotation ...
 a includes loading and unloading, but not insurance.
 b includes loading, unloading and insurance.
2 The freight company plans to collect the goods ...
 a some time before midday on 13 November.
 b very early on 13 November.
3 If BodyWorks accepts the quotation, they should ...
 a fax the confirmation of acceptance to Bob Carter as soon as possible.
 b fax the confirmation of acceptance on delivery.

B Practising language

3 **Work with a partner. Complete the extract from an email with words and expressions from the box.**

cash discount • date of invoice • discounts • introductory discount • payment • quantity discount • refer to • repeat orders • retail price • size of order • standard discounts • trade discount

We ...¹ your telephone call of 23 May about our system of ...².

We give a basic ... ...³ of 10% below ... ...⁴. However, we also offer a ... ...⁵ of between 3% and 6% on orders above €2000, depending on ... ...⁶.

We allow a further ... ...⁷ of 2% for ...⁸ within 15 days of ... ...⁹.

In addition to these ... ...¹⁰, we are willing to negotiate a special ... ...¹¹ on new business, again depending on size of order and on the prospect of ... ...¹².

4 **Say which word is correct.**

Thank you for your (*enquiry / query*¹) of 20 January. We are pleased to (*circulate / submit*²) the following (*estimate / offer*³) for fitness machines:

All prices include (*delivery / distribution*⁴) to your Nuremberg (*location / stores*⁵) at Bahnhofstraße 9 by road.

We (*confirm / ensure*⁶) that these prices are 15% below list price as an introductory (*favour / offer*⁷). We are willing to offer a (*discount / rebate*⁸) of 12.5% on (*duplicate / repeat*⁹) orders up to a (*worth / value*¹⁰) of €10,000 and 15% on orders above that (*amount / extent*¹¹).

The goods will be dispatched immediately on (*receipt / transmission*¹²) of order.

5 **First, complete the phrases with prepositions from the box. Then use six of the phrases to complete the sentences, beginning with the cartoon.**

for • in • of • on • to • with

a depend … sth
b get … touch … sb
c refer … sth
d supply sb … sth
e thank sb … sth
f have pleasure … doing sth
g look forward … doing sth
h take advantage … sth
i be interested … sth
j be satisfied … sth
k be subject … sth
l be valid … a period of time

1 *We are sure you will … the quality of our products.*

2 Our discounts … a number of factors.
3 Please … us if there are any problems.
4 … your prompt reply to our enquiry.
5 This offer … three months.
6 We would like to … your special introductory offer.

2.13

6 **You are Pat King. You work in sales at Wessex Fitness Technology Ltd. Listen to the phone call and fill in the key details.**

Wessex Fitness Technology Ltd
Telephone Message

Call taken by: …[1] **Time/Date:** 11:12, 4 Nov 20..
Call from: …[2]
Caller: …[3]

Subject: …[4] **Ref.:** …[5]
Product: …[6] **Cat. no.:** …[7]
Action agreed: …[8] **Fax no.:** …[9]
Action by: self

Initials: …[10]

C Practising writing offers and quotations

Language you can use: offers and quotations

Opening

• *Wir beziehen uns auf Ihre Anfrage/Ihre E-Mail/Ihr Fax/Ihren Brief vom ....*	• We refer to your enquiry/email/fax/letter of ....
• *Mit Bezug auf Ihren Telefonanruf vom ....*	• With reference to your telephone call of ....
• *... und wir freuen uns, das folgende Angebot zu unterbreiten: ....*	• ... and we have pleasure in submitting the following offer/quotation: ....

Terms

Price

• *Alle Preise sind netto (Kasse).*	• All prices are net (cash).
• *Die Preise sind EXW/FOB Genua/CIF Tilbury/....*	• The prices are EXW/FOB Genoa/CIF Tilbury/....

Delivery

• *Lieferung erfolgt ....*	• Delivery will be made ....
• *Die Sendung/Ware/Bestellung wird ausgeliefert ....*	• The consignment/goods/order will be dispatched ....
• *... sofort bei/nach Auftragseingang per Luftfracht/Bahn/LKW/Seefracht.*	• ... immediately on/after receipt of order by airfreight/rail/road/seafreight.
• *... innerhalb von 7/15/... Tagen nach Auftragseingang.*	• ... within 7/days of/after receipt of order ....

Payment

• *Zahlung sollte ... erfolgen.*	• Payment should be made ....
• *... im Voraus.*	• ... in advance.
• *... bei Eingang des Auftrags/der Sendung/Ware.*	• ... on receipt of (the) order/consignment/goods.
• *... gemäß unseren üblichen Geschäftsbedingungen.*	• ... according to our usual terms and conditions of business.
• *... innerhalb von 15/30/... Tagen nach Lieferung.*	• ... within 15/30/... days of/after delivery.
• *... durch unwiderrufliches und bestätigtes Dokumenten-Akkreditiv.*	• ... by irrevocable and confirmed documentary letter of credit (L/C).

Terms

• *Wir freuen uns/sind bereit, ... einzuräumen/anzubieten.*	• We are pleased/prepared to offer ....
• *... einen Einführungs-/Handels-/Mengenrabatt von ... % auf den Listenpreis.*	• ... an introductory/a trade/quantity discount of ... % off list price.
• *... % Skonto bei Zahlung innerhalb von .... Tagen/zwei Wochen.*	• ... a cash discount of ... % for payment/settlement within ... days/two weeks.

Validity

• *Dieses Angebot ist gültig für ... Wochen/Monate nach dem o.g. Datum.*	• This offer/quotation is valid for .... weeks/months after the above date.
• *Dieses Angebot/... ist verbindlich bis 30. August/....*	• This offer/... is binding/firm until 30 August/....

Close

• *(Nochmals) Vielen Dank für Ihr/e Interesse/Anfrage.*	• Many thanks (again) for your interest/enquiry.
• *Wir hoffen, dass ....*	• We hope/trust (that) ....
• *... Sie von diesem Angebot Gebrauch machen werden.*	• ... you will take advantage of this offer.
• *Sollten Sie weitere Informationen benötigen, setzen Sie sich bitte mit mir/uns in Verbindung.*	• Should you require any further information please contact/get in touch with me/us.
• *Wir freuen uns, mit Ihnen in Geschäftsbeziehungen zu treten.*	• We look forward to doing business with you.

7 **Fax an offer to Humber Computers Ltd based on the following details and handwritten German notes. Use today's date and your own name.**

Situation Sie arbeiten bei der Data-Union GmbH, einem Elektronikhersteller. Firmensitz ist Wiesenstraße 9 in 59558 Lippstadt.
Aufgabe Sie werden gebeten, per Fax ein Angebot für CD-Brenner gemäß folgender Anfrage an Humber Computers Ltd in Hull, England zu schicken.

14/04/20.. 10:47 Fax +4414825588-12 Humber Computers Limited p. 001

FAX MESSAGE
Humber Computers Limited
19–21 Estuary Road • Hull • HU7 9SY
Tel +44 (0)1482 5588-0 • Fax +44 (0)1482 5588-12
www.huco.co.uk • e-mail: info@huco.co.uk

To	Data-Union	**For**	Export
Fax no.	+49-2941-265748	**Date**	14 April 20..
About	enquiry	**Pages**	1

Dear Sir or Madam

Please quote us for:
1 80 (eighty) Superstar CD-burners, order no. 5044, list price €215 each,
2 60 (sixty) TriSonic CD-burners, order no. 7066, list price €375 each.

Could you also give us details of your discounts on orders of this size.

Please let us know when we can expect delivery to our Hull plant.

Thank you in advance, and we look forward to receiving your quotation.

Adam Brown

Auslieferung per Straßentransport (LKW) sofort nach Auftragseingang.

Handelsrabatt 15 %; 3 % Skonto bei Zahlung innerhalb von 15 Tagen; zusätzl. Mengenrabatt 5 % bei Aufträgen über 10.000 Euro

8 **Write an offer in the form of a letter to Sporthuis Noord bv in Dordrecht based on the following details. Use today's date and your own name.**

Situation Sie arbeiten bei der Firma Kahn & Scott Ltd, einem Hersteller von Sportbekleidung in Bradford, England. Vor kurzem erhielt Ihre Firma eine Anfrage von Sporthuis Noord bv, Havenstraat 37, 3311 NC Dordrecht, Holland. Sporthuis Noord interessiert sich für einen größeren Posten Fußballhemden.
Aufgabe Beantworten Sie die Anfrage mithilfe folgender Angaben. Verwenden Sie die *American full block form.*
– Bedanken Sie sich für die Anfrage.
– aktuelle/r Katalog/Preisliste beigefügt
– Muster mit separater Post geschickt
– Handelsrabatt 20 %; Mengenrabatt 5 % für Bestellungen über € 8.000
– Lieferung: per LKW binnen 2 Wochen nach Bestellung
– Bezahlung: ohne Abzug binnen 30 Tagen; 1,5 % Skonto binnen 15 Tagen
– Schließen Sie das Schreiben freundlich/positiv.

9 **Write an offer in the form of a letter based on the following details. Use today's date and your own name.**

Situation Sie arbeiten in der Verkaufsabteilung der Firma Printex GmbH, einem Hersteller von Computerdruckern. Firmensitz ist Querstraße 20 in 44866 Bochum. Die Firma erhält eine Anfrage von Joseph O'Hara (Computers) Ltd, 31 Wicklow Street, Dublin 8, Ireland. Es geht dabei um die Lieferung von Druckern.
Aufgabe Schreiben Sie ein formgerechtes Angebot. Verwenden Sie folgende Angaben:
– Drucker: 300 Tintenstrahldrucker Modell TSD 250 (Listenpreis € 215/Stück) und 200 Laserdrucker Modell LD 400 (Listenpreis € 275/Stück)
– Rabatt/Lieferung: 18 % auf Gesamtpreis; CIF Rosslare
– Zahlung durch unwiderrufliches und bestätigtes Akkreditiv
– Lieferung innerhalb von 15 Tagen nach Auftragseingang
– angemessener Schluss

10 **Write an offer in the form of a fax based on the following details. Use today's date and your own name.**

Situation Sie arbeiten in der Exportabteilung von MGA-Umwelttechnik GmbH, Industriestraße 34, 44225 Dortmund, einem Hersteller von Filteranlagen *(filtration plants)*. Die Firma bekommt eine telefonische Anfrage von einer Firma in England.
Aufgabe Schreiben Sie ein Angebot gemäß folgender Telefonnotizen, die Sie von Ihrem Chef erhalten haben.

- Anrufer: Herr Mike Parks, Sunshine Pools Ltd, 32 Howard Road, Manchester MA9 LL2, England; Fax-Nr. +44 161 89945623
- geht um 150x SBF 90 Filteranlagen für Schwimmbäder
- telefonisch besprochen/vereinbart:
  - Rabatt: 17,5 % auf Listenpreis
  - Lieferung: CIF Liverpool, 4 Wochen nach Auftragsbestätigung
    - Zahlungsbedingung: L/C
- technisches Datenblatt beigelegt
- über Auftrag würden wir uns sehr freuen usw.

Orders, acknowledgements and reminders

Orders by letter have the same parts as offers or quotations (→ FILE 3). For routine orders an order form is often used.

A Part 1 Model order and acknowledgement

An Order

ProVitesse Kosmetika GmbH
Turmstraße 36
50733 Köln
Tel +49 (0)221-774422-0 • **Fax** +49 (0)221-774422-11
Mail info@provit.de • **Website** www.provit.de

BodyWorks Limited
24 London Road
Brighton
BN6 8KL
England

27 September 20..

Trial order

Dear Ms Davis

Thank you for your offer of 17 September. We would like to place a trial order for the following items at the prices you quote:

1	5 (five) cases Adona hair gel, HG1693	€216/case	€1080
2	3 (three) cases FixUp Extra gel, HG1774	€240/case	€720
3	4 (four) cases Medexa 2 shampoo, SM2091	€72/case	€288

We note that all prices are DDP our Cologne stores and are 12.5% below trade price. We also note that you are willing to allow us a further cash discount of 2.5% for payment in full received within 15 days of delivery.

Thank you for dealing with our enquiry so promptly, and we look forward to receiving the consignment soon.

Yours sincerely
ProVitesse Kosmetika GmbH
Karin Feldmann

An acknowledgement of order

Here Lucy Davis acknowledges receipt of the trial order from ProVitesse by fax. She doesn't need to report all the details.

To	ProVitesse Kosmetika	**Date**	29 September 20..
Fax no.	+49-(0) 221-774422-11	**About**	acknowledgement of order
For	Karin Feldmann	**Pages**	1

BodyWorks

FAX MESSAGE

BodyWorks Limited
24 London Road • Brighton • BN6 8KL
Tel +44 (0)1273-4050-0 • **Fax** +44 (0)1273-4050-10
www.bowo.co.uk • e-mail **info@bowo.co.uk**

Dear Ms Feldmann

We acknowledge receipt of your trial order of 27 September on the terms quoted in our offer of 17 September.

Thank you very much for your order, and we are sure that you will be completely satisfied with our products.

Yours sincerely

Lucy Davis

cc Dick Page

B Practising language

1 Replace the underlined words with words from the box.

allow • consignment • dealing with • delivery • information • items • offer • payment • place • promptly • receiving • repeats • ~~satisfied~~

1 Christine is happy[1] with the quotation[2].
2 In the order, Christine copies[1] the most important details[2] from the offer.
3 We would like to submit[1] a trial order for the following articles[2].
4 BodyWorks is willing to give[1] a cash discount for settlement[2] in full within 15 days of receipt[3].
5 Thank you for handling[1] our enquiry so quickly[2] and we look forward to getting[3] the goods[4] soon.

2 Choose the better word for a business letter.

Order

Dear (*Miss / Ms*[1]) Scott

With (*reference / regard*[2]) to your offer of 20 May, we would like to (*place / put*[3]) the following (*order / purchase*[4]) for candles at the prices you (*quote / say*[5]) in your offer:

(list of products)

The (*costs / prices*[6]) are CIF Rostock and are 8% below (*business / trade*[7]) price for a first order. We also (*note / notice*[8]) that you allow a cash (*discount / rebate*[9]) of 2% for (*prompt / quick*[10]) payment.

(*Thanks / Thank you*[11]) for your offer, and we are (*grateful / sure*[12]) that we will be (*able / allowed*[13]) to find a good market for your candles in Germany.

Yours (*faithfully / sincerely*[14])

3 Replace the German words with their English equivalents from the box.

an advice of dispatch • as soon as • business relationship • confirm • receipt • first order • terms of order • in our products • order no. • quotation • would like to • stated • thank you very much

We *möchten*[1] acknowledge *den Empfang*[2] of your *Bestellung Nr.* 3 328/KK of 18 February.

We *bestätigen*[4] that the *Auftragsbedingungen*[5] are as *dargelegt*[6] in our *Angebot*[7] of 27 January.

Sobald[8] we have completed the order, we will send you *eine Versandanzeige*[9] by fax.

Besten Dank[10] for your interest *an unseren Produkten*[11] and we hope that this *erste Bestellung*[12] will be the start of a long and profitable *Geschäftsbeziehung*[13].

We are sure you will find a good market.

C Practising writing orders and acknowledgements

Language you can use: orders and acknowledgements

Opening

• *Wir danken (sehr) für Ihr Angebot vom ....*	• Thank you (very much) for your offer/quotation of ....
• *Vielen Dank für Ihre/n (aktuelle/n) Katalog/Preisliste/Prospekt/Muster.*	• Many thanks for your (current) catalogue/price list/brochure/samples.

Details

• *Wir möchten bestellen/die folgende Bestellung aufgeben: ....*	• We would like to order/to place the following order: ....
• *Auftragsnummer ...: Bitte liefern Sie /die folgenden Produkte:*	• Order number ...: Please supply the following/ the following products:

Terms

Price

• *Wir stellen fest, dass diese Preise einen Einführungs-/Handels-/Mengenrabatt von ... % auf den Listenpreis einschließen.*	• We note that these prices include a/an introductory/trade/volume discount of ...% off list price.
• *Wir entnehmen Ihrem Angebot, dass Sie bereit sind, uns bei Zahlung innerhalb von 14 Tagen ... % Skonto zu gewähren.*	• We understand from your offer/quotation that you are willing to grant/allow us a cash discount of ...% for payment within (14 days).

Payment

• *Zahlung erfolgt ....*	• Payment/Settlement will be made ....
• *... sofort nach Lieferung/Eingang der Sendung/Ware.*	• ... immediately on delivery/receipt of the consignment/goods.
• *... (spätestens) innerhalb von ... Tagen/ Wochen nach Erhalt Ihrer Rechnung.*	• ... (at the latest) within ... days/weeks of receipt of your invoice.
• *... gemäß Ihren/unseren üblichen Geschäftsbedingungen.*	• ... according to your/our usual terms and conditions of business.
• *... entsprechend Ihrem Angebot vom ....*	• ... in accordance with your offer/quotation of ....

Delivery

• *Versand der Sendung am* [Datum] *per Luftfracht/Bahn/LKW/Seefracht an unsere Adresse.*	• Dispatch of the consignment on *[date]* by air/rail/road/sea to our address.
• *Wir gehen davon aus, dass die Sendung/Bestellung von Ihnen sofort/ innerhalb von ... Tagen ausgeliefert wird.*	• We understand that you will dispatch the consignment/order immediately/within ... days.

Close

• *Bestätigen Sie bitte (umgehend) den Eingang dieser Bestellung.*	• Please acknowledge/confirm receipt of this order (by return).
• *Wir bedanken uns im Voraus und freuen uns darauf, die Sendung bis* [Datum]*/in Kürze zu erhalten.*	• Thank you in advance, and we look forward to receiving the consignment by *[date]*/shortly.

Acknowledgements

Opening

• *Vielen Dank/Danke für Ihre Bestellung Nr. … für* [Produkt] *vom* [Datum].	• Many thanks/Thank you for your order no. … for *[product]* of *[date]*.
• *Wir freuen uns, den Erhalt Ihrer Bestellung Nr. … für* [Produkt] *vom* [Datum] *zu bestätigen.*	• We are pleased to acknowledge receipt of your order no. … for *[product]* of *[date]*.

Details

• *Wir bestätigen die Lieferungs- und Zahlungsbedingungen wie im Auftrag angegeben.*	• We confirm the terms of delivery and payment as stated in your order.
• *Ihre Auftragsbedingungen bestätigen wir wie folgt:*	• We confirm the terms of your order as follows:
• *Bitte merken Sie vor, dass die Sendung am* [Datum] *ausgeliefert wird.*	• Please note that the consignment will be dispatched on *[date]*.
• *Wir werden Sie (per Fax/Telefon/E-Mail) benachrichtigen, sobald die Waren unsere Fabrik/unser Lager verlassen haben.*	• We will inform you (by fax/phone/email) as soon as the goods have left our factory/warehouse.

Close

• *Wir danken Ihnen nochmals für Ihre Bestellung/für Ihr Vertrauen in unsere Produkte.*	• We would like to thank you again for your order/for your confidence in our products.
• *Falls es irgendwelche Fragen/Probleme gibt, setzen Sie sich bitte sofort mit mir/uns in Verbindung.*	• If there are any questions/problems, please contact me/us immediately.

4 **Write an order in fax form using German prompts. Use today's date and your own name.**

Situation Stellen Sie sich vor, dass Sie im Materialeinkauf bei der Firma Sportboot Großmann GmbH arbeiten. Sie werden gebeten, Bootslack bei der Firma F. J. Brooks & Sons Ltd, 6 Fisheries Road, Lowestoft, NR26 7HF, England, nachzubestellen.

Aufgabe Schreiben Sie die Bestellung. Verwenden Sie dabei folgende Angaben:

- Nachbestellung *(repeat order):* 80 10-Liter-Kanister ‚Seven Seas' Bootslack *(marine varnish)*
- Bedingungen gemäß ursprünglichem Angebot, 21. März 20..
- baldige Lieferung: Lagerbestände fast aufgebraucht

FAXSCHREIBEN

Sportboot Großmann GmbH
Werftstraße 10
28217 Bremen
Tel +49 (0)421-557812 • Fax +49 (0)421-557822
Mail info@bootgroß.de • Website www.bootgroß.de

An …	Datum …
Fax-Nr. +44 1502-897969	Über …
Für …	Seitenzahl 1

5 **Write an order in letter form using these prompts. Use today's date and your own name.**

Situation Stellen Sie sich vor, dass Sie als Mitarbeiter/in der Einkaufsabteilung der Gebrüder Winter Großhandel GmbH die Auslandsbestellungen bearbeiten.

Aufgabe Sie werden gebeten, bei der Firma Ulster Biochem Ltd, 21 Bay Road, Belfast, BF4 8DH, N. Ireland, eine Bestellung aufzugeben. Verwenden Sie dabei folgende Angaben:

- Dank: Verkaufsprospekte, Proben der Raumsprays *(air fresheners)*, Angebot
- Proben erfolgreich getestet
- Bestellung: je 50 Kartons AF.600 ‚Sea Spray'; AF.603 ‚Meadowlands'; AF.605 ‚Spring Days'
- Preise/Bedingungen wie Angebot, CIF Hamburg
- Lieferung: innerhalb 2 Wochen nach Auftragsbestätigung
- angemessen abschließen

2.14

6 **Write an email acknowledging an order by telephone using these prompts.**

Situation Uta Kemper ist Sachbearbeiterin in der Verkaufsabteilung der Glas Volkmann GmbH in Marsberg. Sie erhält einen Anruf von David Evans, dem Einkaufsleiter der Firma Brecon Table Waters Ltd in Cardiff.

Aufgabe Hören Sie das Telefongespräch und notieren Sie die wichtigsten Informationen. Jetzt übernehmen Sie Utas Rolle, indem Sie eine Auftragsbestätigung per E-Mail an David Evans schreiben. Das Datum ist 10. April 20.. .

Von	Uta Kemper <uta.kemper@glavolk.de>
An	David Evans <david.evans@bretawa.co.uk>
Kopie	Hans Hartung, Versand <h.hartung@glavolk.de>
Gesendet	10.04.20.. 17:47
Betreff	Acknowledgement of order of 10 April 20..

7 **Use the prompts to acknowledge this order. Use your own name and today's date.**

Situation Stellen Sie sich vor, dass Sie bei RheinAudio GmbH in Rastatt arbeiten. Die Firma hat eine Bestellung für Kopfhörer von Duval & Cie, 23, Rue Louis Blériot, 75117 Paris erhalten.

Aufgabe Schreiben Sie eine briefliche Auftragsbestätigung:

- Eingang des Auftrags bestätigen (Datum)
- 120 x AF-3010 Stereokopfhörer m. Hörerpolster (*earpads*), Leder, schwarz
- Listenpreis minus 17,5 % Handelsrabatt und 5 % Mengenrabatt
- Lieferung: EXW Rastatt
- Zahlung: Banküberweisung innerhalb 30 Tagen
- Liefertermin von 2 Wochen bestätigen
- freundlich schließen!

A Part 2 Model reminders

Reminders are requests for payment of overdue invoices. The EU has abolished the old three-stage system of sending out formal reminders. In practice, few companies begin legal proceedings as soon as the agreed period for payment – usually 30 days – is over.

A written reminder

The Customer Accounts department reminds a customer about an overdue invoice.

BodyWorks Limited
24 London Road • Brighton • BN6 8KL
Tel +44 (0)1273-4050-0 • **Fax** +44 (0)1273-4050-10
www.bowo.co.uk • e-mail **info@bowo.co.uk**

BodyWorks

10 March 20..

James Carr & Sons (Chemists) Ltd
4 Station Road
Manchester
M8 7DF

Our invoice no. 3/C/20

Dear Mr Carr

We are sure that the enclosed invoice for £683.34 has been overlooked or perhaps your payment has been misdirected.

As we said in our acknowledgement of order of 10 January, invoices should be paid within 30 days of receipt of goods, unless we have agreed to other terms. In this case, the goods were delivered on 14 January so the invoice should have been paid by 13 February.

As we have already extended the agreed period by a generous margin, we would be grateful if you could arrange for payment within the next few days.

If you have settled the invoice in the meantime, we would like to thank you and ask you to ignore this letter.

Yours sincerely
BodyWorks Limited

Jane Ford

Jane Ford
Customer Accounts

8 **Say if the statements are true, false or the information is not in the letter.**

1 The invoice is for a consignment of shampoo and skin cream.
2 The customer is a chemist's in Manchester.
3 Jane Ford works in Customer Accounts in Brighton.
4 Jane assumes that the customer has simply lost the invoice.
5 If no other terms have been arranged, invoices must be paid within one calendar month of order.
6 In the past, James Carr (Chemists) Ltd has always paid their invoices promptly.
7 Jane gives the customer a few more days to pay without making any threats.
8 If the invoice has been paid in the meantime, the company should return the letter to Jane.

A reminder by telephone

It is now 10 April. As James Carr has not reacted to Jane Ford's written reminder, she decides to speak to him personally.

2.15

9 **Listen to the dialogue and then complete the sentences with the missing information.**

1 At Carr & Sons, the telephone is answered by … .
2 James Carr's sons are called … and … .
3 James Carr retired on … .
4 Jane asks to speak to the Mr … who looks after … .
5 The invoice is for a consignment of … and … .
6 Jane says a … was sent to James Carr … weeks ago and payment is now nearly … weeks overdue.
7 The two sons took over the company on … .
8 Nick promises to pay the outstanding £… immediately.

B Practising language

10 **Give the English equivalents of these German expressions.**

1 eine Rechnung übersehen
2 eine Rechnung verlegen
3 eine Zahlung fehlleiten
4 eine Rechnung begleichen
5 eine Mahnung / Zahlungserinnerung ignorieren
6 eine Zahlung erhalten
7 sich über die Bedingungen einigen
8 eine Sendung liefern
9 sich um die Buchführung kümmern
10 eine Firma übernehmen

The invoice was overlooked.

11 **This reminder is too friendly. Replace the underlined words and expressions with less friendly or more formal ones from the box.**

any reaction on your part • contact us at once • dissatisfied • disturbed at having to write to • legitimate cause • look into the matter • meeting your obligations • must insist that you • outstanding • without further delay

Dear Mr Schneider

We are sorry to trouble[1] you about our unpaid[2] invoice, but we have already phoned you about it without much luck[3].

Perhaps you have a good reason[4] for not paying the bill[5]. If you are unhappy[6] with the consignment of swimwear, please get in touch as soon as possible[7] and we will see what we can do about it[8]. If this is not the case, however, then we would be grateful if you could[9] send us your payment within the next few days[10].

C Practising writing reminders

Language you can use: reminders

Opening	
• *Wir sind sicher, dass Sie unsere Rechnung Nr. … vom … über € … übersehen haben und fügen eine Kopie bei.*	• We are sure that you have overlooked our invoice no. … of … for € … and enclose a copy.
• *Wir beziehen uns auf unsere Rechnung Nr. … vom …/Zahlungserinnerung vom … und … .*	• We refer to our invoice no. … of … /reminder of … and … .
Details	
• *Wie unserer Auftragsbestätigung vom … zu entnehmen ist, sollte die Zahlung bei Lieferung/innerhalb von … Tagen nach Erhalt der Waren erfolgen.*	• As stated in our acknowledgement/confirmation of order dated …, payment was to be made on delivery/within … days of receipt of goods.
• *Da wir keine Reklamation von Ihnen erhalten haben, gehen wir davon aus, dass die Sendung in Ordnung war.*	• As we have received no complaint from you, we take it that the consignment was in order.
Request	
• *Wir wären Ihnen dankbar, wenn Sie unsere Rechnung unverzüglich/in den nächsten Tagen/bis (spätesten) … begleichen würden (um rechtliche Schritte zu vermeiden).*	• We would be grateful if you could settle our invoice without delay/within the next few days/by … (at the latest) (in order to avoid legal proceedings).
Close	
• *Wenn wir irgendetwas/Ihre Zahlung übersehen haben sollten, lassen Sie es uns bitte wissen/setzen Sie sich bitte sofort mit mir/uns in Verbindung.*	• If we should have overlooked something/your payment, please let us know/get in touch with/contact me/us at once.
• *Falls Sie die Rechnung in der Zwischenzeit bezahlt/beglichen haben, sehen Sie bitte diese Erinnerung als gegenstandslos an/möchten wir uns dafür bedanken.*	• If you have paid/settled the invoice in the meantime, please ignore this reminder/please accept our thanks.

12 Write a polite reminder.

Situation Sie arbeiten in der Buchführung der Firma Koch Küchengeräte GmbH in Stuttgart.
Aufgabe Schreiben Sie eine höfliche Zahlungserinnerung an Dream Kitchens Ltd gemäß folgender Rechnung. Das heutige Datum ist der 12. September.

Koch Küchengeräte GmbH
Karl-Benz-Straße 28, 70569 Stuttgart

Dream Kitchens Ltd
56 London Street
Norwich, NR1 8UJ
England

Rechnung-Nr./*Invoice no:* 1278
Datum/*Date:* 23.07.20..
Sachbearbeiter/in/*Responsible:* Ms Jenny Wood

Menge *Quantity*	**Produktbezeichnung** *Product description*	**Stückpreis** *item price*
4	commercial dishwasher, DW360	€ 3.200
8	commercial mixer, M452	€ 830
	zu zahlender Endbetrag *Total amount payable*	**€ 19.440**

Zahlungsbedingungen/ *Terms of payment*:
net, within 30 days of receipt of invoice

13 Write a reminder to a good customer.

Situation Übernehmen Sie die Rolle des Inhabers/der Inhaberin der Firma Grüne Freude Gartenschmuck GmbH, Wiesenhof 9, 52075 Aachen.
Aufgabe Schreiben Sie eine Erinnerung an Le Marché Vert, 32 Rue Monet, 4580 Aubel, Belgien. Richten Sie das Schreiben persönlich an den Besitzer, M. Yves Brisset, mit dem Sie schon zwei Mal in dieser Sache telefoniert haben:

- Ihre Rechnung vom 16. März über € 1.200 ist trotz zweier Telefonate immer noch offen. Im letzten Telefonat mit Herrn Brissett am 30. April wurde die sofortige Zahlung der Rechnung fest zugesagt.
- Trotzdem sind Sie bereit, M. Brisset noch 14 Tage Zeit – also bis zum 28. Mai – zu geben, die Rechnung zu zahlen.
- Da Sie bis jetzt immer gute Erfahrung mit der Firma Le Marché Vert gemacht haben, schließen Sie die Zahlungserinnerung freundlich und positiv.

Dealing with complaints

Most common complaints are about 1) delays in delivery, 2) damage to goods caused by defective packaging, 3) goods of the wrong colour, quantity, size, etc. and 4) faulty goods.

The aim of a complaint is not to hand out blame: it is to get something put right. Always be polite and helpful, and never get 'personal'.

	Complaining	**Dealing with complaints**
Opening	Refer to the consignment received, with all details.	Refer to letter of complaint and apologize.
Details	Give details about what is wrong with consignment.	Give result of investigation into complaint.
Solution	Suggest a solution, such as replacement of goods at supplier's expense.	If you accept the complaint, offer a solution, e.g. replacement of goods or price reduction. If you reject it, say why.
Close	A polite, positive statement.	A polite, positive statement.

A Model complaints

A complaint about a delay in delivery

2.16 **1 Complete the dialogue with these words. Then listen to the CD.**

add • consignment • delivered • delivery schedule • find out • fine • good thing • orders • pressure • stocks • urgent • work

Jenna Hello Frank. How're you?
Frank Hi Jenna. I'm …[1], thanks. How about you?
Jenna Oh, I'm OK, Frank. Too much work, of course, but I suppose that's a …[2], isn't it?
Frank Sure. And I'm afraid I'm about to …[3] to it – the …[4], I mean.
Jenna Oh, dear. Why's that?
Frank Well, the last …[5] hasn't arrived yet. According to the …[6], it should have been …[7] last Thursday, 10 October. That's four days ago.
Jenna I'm sorry to hear that, Frank. Look, let me …[8] what's happened and I'll get back to you as soon as I can. OK?
Frank Fine, Jenna. I don't want to put you under any …[9], but could you treat this as …[10], please? Our …[11] are getting very low and we have an awful lot of …[12] to fill.
Jenna Don't worry, Frank. I'll call you back within an hour or so, OK?

2.17 **2 Listen to Jenna's next call to Frank Richter. Note down the details and then write her email to Frank.**

A complaint about damaged goods and a reply

ProVitesse finds that some items have been damaged in the accident after all. So Frank Richter contacts Jenna Omono.

Dear Jenna

Our order no. HC/472/06 arrived as scheduled, but two 24-bottle cartons of Medexa shampoo were damaged, presumably in the accident at Antwerp.

Do you think you could replace the two cartons as soon as possible?

As this may be an insurance claim, would you like us to return the damaged goods to Brighton?

Best wishes

Frank

Hello Frank

Sorry to hear that part of your order no. HC/472/06 was damaged. I have arranged for the two 24-bottle cartons of Medexa shampoo to be replaced. These have been sent with DHL Express and are scheduled to arrive in Cologne early on Friday morning. At our expense, of course.

Our forwarding agents tell us that the value of the damaged goods is too low to make an insurance claim. Do you think you could dispose of the damaged bottles your end, Frank? That'd be a big help.

Sorry again about this. Please get in touch if there are any further problems.

Best wishes

Jenna

2.18

3 *Lucy Davis, Jenna's boss, wants to know about the problem when she returns from a trip.*

Complete the dialogue with details from the emails. Then listen to the CD to check your answers.

Lucy What's the problem with the ProVitesse order?
Jenna Well, Bob Carter at Supertrans said that the …[1] wasn't damaged in the …[2] at Antwerp but in fact it was. Frank Richter says that two …[3] of Medexa were damaged.
Lucy But they have all been …[4], haven't they?
Jenna Yes. If all goes well, they'll arrive in Cologne on Friday. Everything's at our …[5], of course.
Lucy Sure, but what about …[6]?
Jenna Well, Bob Carter says the value of the …[7] is simply too low.
Lucy I see. Well, thank you for dealing with that for me, Jenna.

A complaint about wrong goods and a reply

Ben Cook, the buyer at BodyWorks, complains to a supplier, Ted Hooper, about a wrong delivery.

FAX MESSAGE

Dear Mr Hooper

Our stores staff had a real surprise when they checked the consignment you delivered on 12 June. Instead of green plastic snap-on caps, they found 5000 screw-on metal caps in assorted colours.

Now we are waiting for our plastic caps – and Obed Williams Pty, Cape Town, are presumably waiting for their metal caps.

Could you please look into this confusion at your end and let us know what you want us to do with the metal caps and when we will get the caps we ordered.

Please treat this matter as urgent because we need the plastic caps for a big order from an important customer in Germany.

We look forward to hearing from you.

Yours sincerely

Ben Cook

Dear Mr Cook

Thank you for your fax. We are very sorry that you were sent the wrong consignment. There was a mix-up of two virtually identical packages in our packing department.

I have instructed our packing department to make up a new shipment of plastic caps immediately. This will be sent to you by express freight tomorrow, 14 June.

Please return the screw-on metal caps intended for Obed Williams Pty by rail at our expense.

We apologize again for this mistake and hope that it has not caused you too much inconvenience.

Best regards

Ted Hooper

---

4 **Say if these statements are true, false or not stated in the texts.**

1 BodyWorks received the wrong consignment of caps on 12 June.
2 BodyWorks ordered plastic caps but was sent metal ones.
3 An inexperienced temporary worker mixed up two very similar packages.
4 The caps sent to BodyWorks were intended for a customer in South Africa.
5 The correct caps are needed quickly to fill several orders from Austria.
6 Ben Cook has already sent the consignment back to the supplier.

A complaint about quality

Karin Feldmann of ProVitesse complains to Lucy Davis of BodyWorks about the quality of printed information on cans of styling mousse.

ProVitesse Kosmetika GmbH
Turmstraße 36
50733 Köln
Tel +49 (0)221-774422-0 • **Fax** +49 (0)221-774422-11
Mail info@provit.de • **Website** www.provit.de

13 September 20..

BodyWorks Limited
24 London Road
Brighton
BN6 8KL
England

Easy Does It Styling Mousse

Dear Ms Davis

Unfortunately, we have received some complaints from our customers about the size of the print on Easy Does It Styling Mousse cans.

The size of print used for the English is larger than the German version, which is so small that it is almost impossible to read without a magnifying glass. This is a real problem because these instructions give essential information about how to use the new product, for example about holding the can.

We are worried about these complaints because this otherwise excellent product is popular among the over-50s who care for their appearance and have money to spend, but who may not understand the English text.

Could you look into this problem with a view to using larger print for the German text or at least providing a clear illustration of how to hold the can?

We look forward to hearing from you.

Yours sincerely

Karin Feldmann
Karin Feldmann
Purchasing Manager, Haircare

5 **Link A to B to make true statements.**

A

1 ProVitesse is getting complaints from customers about …
2 The complaint is not about the product itself …
3 Karin points out that the product is popular …
4 The styling mousse is bought by older people …
5 While the English text is relatively easy to read …
6 This is a problem because the instructions tell buyers …
7 Karin asks if it would be possible …
8 The complaint is important and …

B

a among older people with money to spend.
b BodyWorks' Easy Does It Styling Mousse.
c but about the can.
d how to use the new product.
e it is being dealt with at management level.
f the German version is almost illegible.
g to print the German text in larger letters.
h who may not understand English very well.

Rejecting a complaint about quality

Lucy Davis rejects Karin Feldmann's complaint. She sympathizes with Karin's point, but changing the size of the print would be too expensive.

6 **Read Lucy's letter on the next page and complete her internal memo below to BodyWorks' Product Development Manager about the complaint.**

MEMO

ProVitesse *(complain / German instructions / Styling Mousse can / be printed / small / be / almost impossible / read)*. This is worrying because the instructions *(provide / user / information / how / operate / new system)*.

The English text is easier to read, but ProVitesse *(point out / this fact / not help / German-speaking customer / not understand / English)*. I have looked into using larger print for the German text, but *(packaging designer / say / cost / too high / competitive market)*.

I have pointed out to ProVitesse that *(competition / have / exactly / same problem)*. I also explained that *(legal requirement for / safety warning / be printed / direct / can)*.

However, I sympathize *(complaint / and / feel / should / discuss / problem / you)*.

Lucy Davis

The EU requires detailed information.

BodyWorks Limited
24 London Road • Brighton • BN6 8KL
Tel +44 (0)1273-4050-0 • **Fax** +44 (0)1273-4050-10
www.bowo.co.uk • e-mail **info@bowo.co.uk**

BodyWorks

17 September 20..

Your ref.: KF/dc
Our ref.: LD/hg

ProVitesse Kosmetika GmbH
Turmstraße 36
50733 Köln
Germany

Print size on Easy Does It cans

Dear Ms Feldmann

Thank you for your letter about the size of print used for the German text on Easy Does It Styling Mousse cans.

While I sympathize very much with your request for larger print, I have been told by our packaging designers that this would only be possible if we either increased the size of the can or produced special cans for Germany and other German-speaking countries. Both these solutions would be unacceptably expensive in a highly competitive market.

The problem is caused by EU legislation. This requires more detailed information to be printed directly on to containers, and this is only possible by reducing the size of the print.

In the case of Easy Does It Styling Mousse cans, for example, there is a legal requirement to include safety warnings about keeping the product out of children's reach and about the dangers of the mousse to your eyes.

We are very sorry indeed that we cannot be more helpful. However, an investigation of our competitors' packaging suggests that they have exactly the same problem.

Yours sincerely
BodyWorks Limited

Lucy Davis

Lucy Davis
European Sales Manager, Haircare

B Practising language

7 **Give the English words in this complaint about an incomplete delivery.**

We were very sorry to hear that the *(Sendung)* …[1] of *(Skistiefel)* …[2] that we delivered on 4 September was *(unvollständig)* …[3]. We have now looked into the *(Angelegenheit)* …[4] and the mistake *(wurde verursacht)* …[5] by a mix-up in our *(Logistikabteilung)* …[6].

We have dispatched 30 pairs of ski boots in the *(Größen)* …[7] and colours you require by *(Luftfracht)* …[8] and they will be delivered to your *(Lager)* …[9] on 8 September.

We *(möchten uns nochmals entschuldigen)* …[10] for this mistake and *(sind sicher)* …[11] that you will be *(völlig zufrieden)* …[12] with the consignment this time.

8 **Complete the sentences with a suitable phrase from the box.**

at a reduced price • at our own expense • by a computer failure • by rough handling • by the agreed date • of the teddy bears • our considerable losses • with your insurers

1 We have received a lot of complaints from our own customers due to your failure to deliver the goods … .
2 Please accept our apologies for this mistake, which was caused … .
3 Unfortunately, we must complain about the poor quality … .
4 We accept responsibility for the damage, which was caused … in our stores.
5 We are of course prepared to replace the damaged goods … .
6 We are willing to keep the goods … .
7 We have to ask you for compensation sufficient to cover … .
8 With respect, we suggest that you take up the matter … .

2.19
2.20

9 a) **First, listen to the voice mail. Then fill in the missing information.**

Hi Karl. It's Greg Summers of …[1] Technologies PLC in Birmingham. It's now …[2] our time on 23 September. Karl, can you …[3], please? I'd like to talk to you about your …[4] about faulty valves. I've just got the inspector's …[5], you see. Anyhow, I'm only here till …[6] our time, so here's my mobile number just in case. It's …[7] then …[8]. Bye for now.

b) **You are Karl Eigner. Listen to what Greg Summers says and write a telephone note in German with the most important information.**

TELEFONNOTIZ

Uhrzeit, Datum	12:15, 23.09.20..
Teilnehmer/innen	K. Eigner/G. Summers,
Betreff	Unsere Reklamation, Wasserventile

C Practising dealing with complaints

Language you can use: making and dealing with complaints

Opening

• *Gestern haben wir Ihre Sendung von … erhalten, die wir am … bestellt hatten (Bestellnr. …).*	• Yesterday we received your consignment of … which we had ordered on … (Order no. …).

Saying that something has gone wrong

• *Die geschickten/gelieferten Artikel sind nicht die von uns bestellten/hatten wir nicht bestellt.*	• The goods sent/delivered are not the ones we ordered/had ordered.
• *Die Qualität der Waren entspricht nicht unseren Erwartungen/erfüllt nicht unsere Erwartungen.*	• The quality of the goods does not meet our expectations.

Describing what has gone wrong

• *Sie haben uns 500/200 … statt der 250 geschickt, die wir bestellt hatten.*	• You sent us 500/200 … instead of the 250 which we had ordered.
• *Der Inhalt der Kisten stimmt nicht mit der Packliste/mit dem Lieferschein überein.*	• The contents of the crates do not agree with the packing list/delivery note.
• *Die Artikel entsprechen in Qualität/Farbe/Größe nicht unserer Bestellung/sind fehlerhaft/defekt.*	• The goods do not correspond to the quality/ colour/size we ordered/are faulty/defective.
• *In der Sendung fehlen die/fehlt Artikel Nr. … .*	• Article number(s) … are/is missing from the consignment.
• *Einige Artikel sind verkratzt/zerbrochen/ (leicht/teilweise) beschädigt.*	• Several of the items are scratched/broken/ (slightly/partly) damaged.
• *Die Verpackung/Abpackung der Ware ist unzulänglich./Die Ware scheint schlecht verpackt worden zu sein.*	• The packing/packaging of the goods is inadequate./The goods seem to have been badly packed.

Rejection of goods

• *Aus diesen Gründen können wir die Ware nicht annehmen.*	• For these reasons we cannot accept the goods.
• *Wir müssen Sie bitten, uns so bald wie möglich Ersatz zu schicken.*	• We must ask you to send us (a) replacement(s) as soon as possible.
• *Wir lassen einen Teil der Sendung/die ganze Sendung an Sie zurückgehen.*	• We are returning part of the consignment/the whole consignment.

Solving the problem

• *Wir sind bereit, die Waren (zu einem ermäßigten Stückpreis von …) zu behalten/übernehmen.*	• We are prepared to keep/retain the goods (at a reduced price of … per article/item).
• *Wir sehen uns leider veranlasst, unsere/die Bestellung zu annullieren.*	• Unfortunately we feel prompted to cancel our/the order.
• *Um unsere Verluste zu decken, müssen wir um Entschädigung bitten/auf Entschädigung bestehen.*	• In order to cover our losses we must ask for/ insist on compensation.
• *Wir müssen Sie bitten, uns den Wert der beschädigten Waren gutzuschreiben.*	• We must ask you to credit us with the value of the damaged goods.
• *Dies hat uns beträchtliche Schwierigkeiten mit einigen unserer Kunden bereitet.*	• This has caused us considerable difficulties with some of our customers.

Dealing with complaints

Replying to a complaint

- *Mit Bedauern nehmen wir Ihre Reklamation vom … über … zur Kenntnis.*
- We note with regret your complaint dated … about … .
- *Wir haben Ihre Reklamation/die Angelegenheit überprüft.*
- We have looked into your complaint/the matter.

Accepting a complaint

- *Wir bitten vielmals um Entschuldigung für den Irrtum/Fehler/das Versehen.*
- We offer you our sincere apologies for the error/mistake/oversight.
- *Wir sind bereit, die Ware gegen solche gleicher/ähnlicher Qualität umzutauschen/zu ersetzen.*
- We are prepared to exchange/replace the goods for/by those of the same/a similar quality.
- *Wir werden die Ware auf unsere Kosten ersetzen./Eine Ersatzlieferung ist auf dem Weg.*
- We shall replace the goods at our expense./A replacement delivery is on the way.
- *Wir sind bereit, einen Preisnachlass von … % anzubieten/zu gewähren*
- We are prepared/willing to offer/grant you a price reduction of …%.

Rejecting a complaint

- *Wir haben die Sendung sehr sorgfältig geprüft und können keinen Mangel an der Ware feststellen.*
- We have checked the consignment very carefully and can find no fault with the goods.
- *Wir können keine Verantwortung für den Schaden übernehmen.*
- We cannot accept responsibility for the damage.
- *Wir bedauern (sehr), dass wir die Ware nicht zurücknehmen können.*
- We regret (very much) that we cannot take the goods back.
- *Wir müssen darauf hinweisen, dass die Garantiefrist abgelaufen ist.*
- We must point out that the period of guarantee/warranty has expired.

10 **Write a fax about a late delivery using the following information.**

Situation Sie arbeiten in der Einkaufsabteilung bei Sporting Chance Ltd, 11 Canal Road, Manchester, M24 6LK, England. Eine Lieferung von Alpina Sport GmbH, Stadlweg 23 in 6020 Innsbruck, Österreich, ist überfällig.

Aufgabe Schreiben Sie ein Fax bezüglich folgender Bestellung: Datum 6. Juli 20..; Bestell-Nr. 12/K2 vom 14. Mai; 50 ‚Alpina Star' Snowboards; Lieferung: binnen 2 Wochen nach Auftragserteilung, d. h. bis 28. Mai; Kontaktperson: Bernd Schneekotter, European Sales (Fax-Nr. +43 512 607080).

Erwähnen Sie:

- Bestell-Nr., Datum, Produkt
- bisher kein Wareneingang
- Fälligkeitsdatum
- Frage nach dem Grund, voraussichtliches Lieferdatum
- Dringlichkeit wegen eigener Auftragseingänge

Our stocks are very low.

11 **Write an email.**

Situation Übernehmen Sie die Rolle eines/er Mitarbeiters/in der Gustav Schwab Freizeitmode GmbH. Die Firma hat folgende E-Mail erhalten.
Aufgabe Schreiben Sie eine Antwort:
Bezug auf vorhergehende E-Mail. Prüfung ergab Fehler bei Versand: Richtiger Packzettel wurde falscher Sendung beigelegt. Richtige Sendung bereits per Express abgeschickt, Ankunft voraussichtlich in zwei Tagen. Bitte um Rücksendung der falsch gelieferten Ware. Selbstverständlich werden alle Kosten übernommen. Abschließende Entschuldigung.

> Dear Birgit
>
> We have just unpacked your shipment of swimwear (order no. 4529/LB/06, 6 May). As I couldn't get you on the phone just now, I'm sending you this email.
>
> When we checked the packing list against our order, we found several discrepancies in designs, quantities and sizes. Can you check on this at your end and let us know the result as soon as possible?
>
> We are anxious to complete our range of summer fashions and get it out to customers as soon as possible now as the summer season is nearly upon us.
>
> Hope to hear from you soon.
>
> Wendy

12 **Use the German details to answer a complaint. Use your own name.**

Situation Übernehmen Sie die Rolle eines/er Mitarbeiters/in der Firma Datatechnik Sachsen GmbH in Leipzig. Die Firma hat eine Sendung von 50 Scannern an Pacific Enterprises Inc., 498 Bay Vista, San Francisco, CA 78532, USA, geliefert. Jetzt haben Sie eine Beschwerde erhalten, weil die erforderlichen englischsprachigen Gebrauchsanweisungen *(user instructions)* fehlen.
Aufgabe Schreiben Sie einen Brief an Pacific Enterprises Inc. mit folgendem Inhalt:

– Bezug auf Mängelrüge von Maria Sanchez vom 10. Mai 20.. (Order no. S/NAE/07, FineTime scanner)
– gedruckte Gebrauchsanweisungen werden nicht mehr mitgeliefert
– Mitteilung an Kunden im Rundbrief *(circular)* vom 28. März 20..
– bei einigen Geräten Anweisungen auf CD; für FineTime-Scanner können Anweisungen heruntergeladen werden (www.datasax.de)
– dieser Hinweis ist auf Aufkleber unter Originalabdeckung *(original cover)*
– Bitte um Verständnis. Grund: um günstige Preise halten zu können
– Schließen Sie freundlich/positiv.

13 **Write a letter rejecting a complaint. The technical background is the complaint about water valves in exercise 9 on page 145.**

Situation Übernehmen Sie die Rolle eines/er Mitarbeiters/in der Firma Wassertechnik Ruhr GmbH, Talstraße 10 in 58739 Wickede/Ruhr. Sie bekommen eine Mängelrüge von dem britischen Architektenbüro Johnson & Jacks (Architects) Ltd, 23 Albert Square, London EC1 6TG, über das Ventil, Modell VC-1-MD, das sich angeblich selbstständig schließt. Der Verfasser des Briefes ist Peter Johnson.

Aufgabe Schreiben Sie einen Brief an Peter Johnson, in dem Sie die Mängelrüge als unbegründet ablehnen:

- Nehmen Sie Bezug auf den Brief vom 23.10.20.. .
- Sie nehmen die Mängelrüge sehr ernst, da das Ventil sehr zuverlässig ist.
- Versagen des Ventils ist immer auf falsche Montage zurückzuführen.
- Wie in den Montageanweisungen betont, muss das Ventil so montiert werden, dass der Pfeil in Richtung des Wasserflusses zeigt. Sonst schließt sich das Ventil automatisch.
- Schließen Sie den Brief positiv/freundlich.

14 **Role-play a telephone call about an incomplete delivery with your partner.**

Situation Übernehmen Sie die Rolle eines/er Mitarbeiters/in der Firma Bürogroßhandel Böhm GmbH. Ihre Firma hat von dem niederländischen Lieferanten IRS bv eine unvollständige Sendung Klebstoffe erhalten.

A	B
	Melden Sie sich mit Namen/Firma, fragen Sie, worum es geht.
Begrüßung; geben Sie Grund des Anrufes an: gestern eingetroffene Sendung offenbar unvollständig.	
	Reagieren Sie erstaunt. Fragen Sie nach Auftragsnummer auf dem Lieferschein.
Sie lesen die Nummer vor.	
	Sie möchten Auftrag am Bildschirm einsehen; bitten um Geduld.
Sagen Sie, dass Positionen 2, 4 und 12 nicht geliefert wurden.	
	Sie zeigen sich sehr erstaunt und fragen nach der Anzahl der Pakete.
Drei Pakete sind angekommen.	
	Erklären Sie, dass vor vier Tagen fünf Pakete abgeschickt wurden. Schlagen Sie vor abzuwarten, bis die restlichen Pakete eintreffen.
Erklären Sie sich bereit, höchstens zwei Tage zu warten. Betonen Sie, dass Ihnen bereits Bestellungen vorliegen.	
	…

File 6

Applying for a job

Job applications consist of up to four stages:

1 a **letter of application** enclosing a **CV** (**c**urriculum **v**itae)
2 an **invitation to interview**
3 a **personal interview** or **assessment centre** (with group tasks)
4 a **formal job offer** or **notification of rejection**

An **unsolicited job application** is when you apply in the hope that a company may have vacancies.

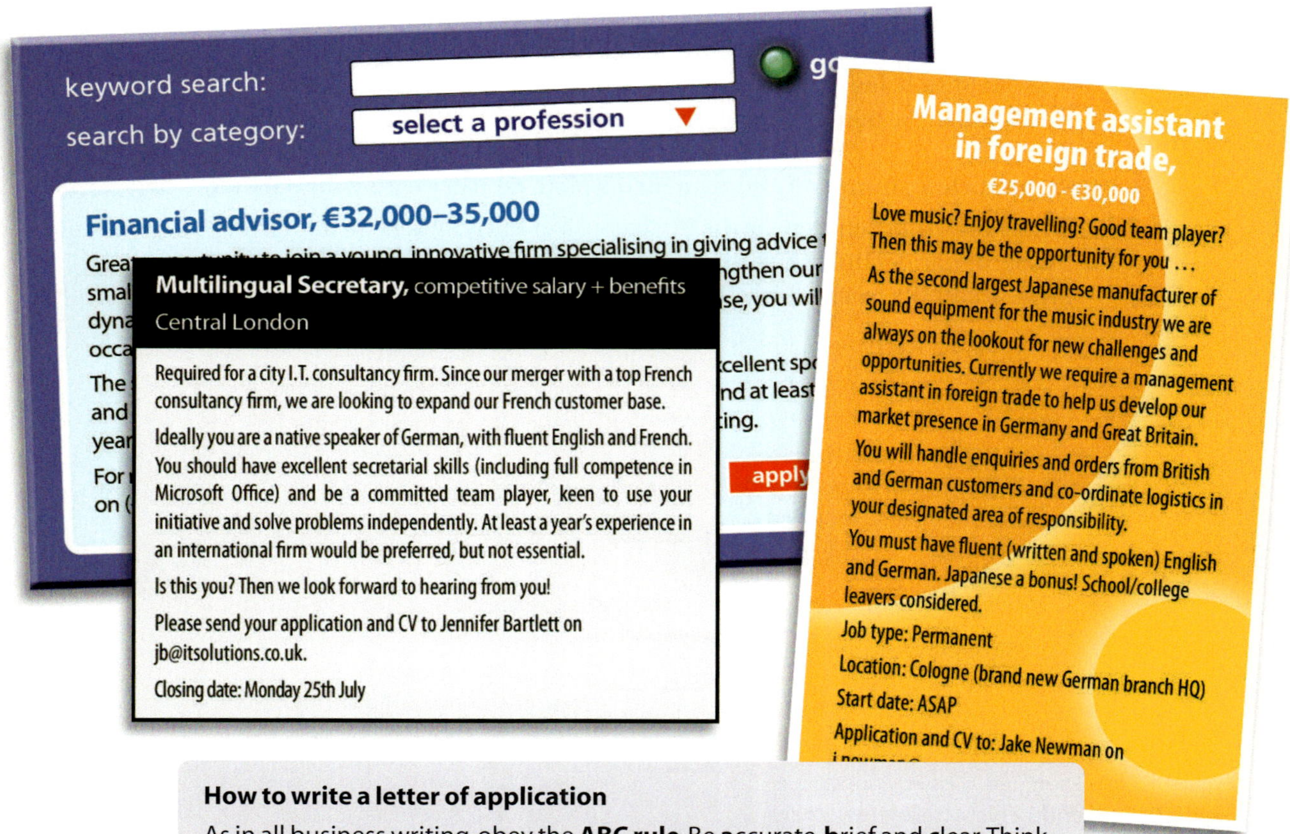

How to write a letter of application

As in all business writing, obey the **ABC rule**. Be **a**ccurate, **b**rief and **c**lear. Think of what the reader needs to know, and provide that information. Then stop. If your letter has more than about 20 lines, it is probably too long.

Divide your letter into four parts, as follows:

Opening	Name the job you are applying for or say where you got the company's name from.
Suitability	Briefly describe your **qualifications**, **skills** and **experience**.
Motivation	Say why you are applying to this particular company and what you hope to achieve in the new post.
Close	Say when you are available for an interview, adding that you would appreciate a positive reply.

A A letter of application and CV

Letter of application

Katja Bergmann applies to BodyWorks in Brighton for an internship. First she writes an unsolicited letter of application enclosing her CV. Note that you do not write your name at the top of English letters.

Beethovenstraße 19
53121 Bonn
Germany

26 April 20..

BodyWorks Limited
24 London Road
Brighton
BN6 8KL
England

Application for an internship

Dear Sir or Madam

As part of my course at the College of Business Studies in Bonn, I am required to have some foreign work experience. I am therefore hoping to find a position as an intern for about five months from October to February next year, and would like to ask you to consider my application for a position in your company.

Your address was given to me by a neighbour who works for your German distributor, ProVitesse, in Cologne. As I want to go into the fashion industry when I qualify, I thought an internship with you would be ideal.

As you see from the enclosed CV, I have a good school-leaving certificate.
I also have IT skills (Word, Excel, PowerPoint) and reasonably fluent English.

If possible, I would like to spend the first semester of the coming academic year and part of my vacation at your firm. However, if the above dates are not possible, please suggest other periods.

Should you have any queries, please do not hesitate to contact me by phone or email. I would like to work in Brighton and look forward to your reply.

Yours faithfully

Katja Bergmann

Katja Bergmann

Enc. CV

1 **Answer the questions.**

1 What are business students at Katja's college expected to do?
2 How long does Katja want to spend in Britain?
3 Where did Katja get BodyWorks' address from?
4 What does Katja want to do after finishing her course?
5 What skills does Katja have that could interest BodyWorks?
6 What should BodyWorks do if they can't agree to Katja's dates?

A CV

Katja Bergmann

Personal details

Name	Katja Bergmann
Address	Beethovenstraße 19, 53121 Bonn, Germany
Date and place of birth	28 May 1987, Bonn
Nationality	German
Daytime phone number	+49-228-189704
Email address	katja.bergmann@web.de

Education

08/2006–present	Mittelrheinische Verwaltungs- und Wirtschafts-Akademie, Bonn (business college); 3-year course in business administration
09/2003–05/2006	Ludwig-Erhard-Berufskolleg, Bonn (vocational school); Abitur (equivalent of A-levels), grade average: 2.6
07/1997–07/2003	Carl-Schurz-Realschule, Bonn (selective secondary school); school-leaving certificate (equivalent of GCSE); grade average: 2.1 on a 6-point scale from 1 (very good) to 6 (very unsatisfactory)

Work experience

2001	Autohaus Bender, Bad Godesberg (office duties)

Paid employment

Summer 2003	vacation job, Andrea Michaelis, lawyer, Bonn (administrative work)
Summer 2004	vacation job, Tourist Information Office, Königswinter
Since 2002	community service, Red Cross, Bonn (volunteer assistant carer in home for the elderly)

Interest and skills

Languages	English, advanced (some knowledge of business English); French, intermediate
IT skills	MS Office (Word, Excel, PowerPoint)
Other	driving licence, EU class C
References	references can be supplied on request

2 **Name the six sections of a CV. A CV is in 'reverse chronological order'. What does that mean?**

3 **Give the English for the following.**

1 *Schulabschlusszeugnis*
2 *Berufspraktikum*
3 *Betriebswirtschaft*
4 *Durchschnittsnote*
5 *entspricht*
6 *berufsbildende Schule*
7 *fortgeschritten*
8 *Sozialdienst*

B Practising language

4 **Complete the letter of application with words from the box.**

business studies • career development • challenging work • continued • current edition • customers and suppliers • for an interview • gained experience • of interest • office procedures • on completing • sales department • to apply for • well-qualified • with reference to

Dear Sir or Madam

...[1] your advertisement in the ...[2] of *Eurotrade News*, I would like ...[3] the position of export assistant.

I believe that I am ...[4] to fill this vacancy. ...[5] my course in ...[6] at Dover College of Further Education, I worked in the ...[7] of a small engineering company. There I ...[8] in dealing with ...[9] at home and abroad.

I am familiar with all routine ...[10] and business software, including MS Office. While at college I ...[11] with French and also learned some basic German.

I am now keen to do more ...[12] in a larger organization that can offer the possibility of ...[13].

I enclose my CV, and am available ...[14] at any time convenient to yourselves.

I hope you will find my application ...[15].

Yours faithfully

Robert Black

5 **Use the expressions to complete the sentences. Add any missing words.**

1 The advertisement on your website for the position of marketing manager caught my attention. (*catch / attention*)
2 As I am interested in the vacancy you advertise ... (*enclose CV / letter*)
3 As a bilingual secretary with ten years' experience ... (*sure / meet requirements*)
4 I believe that I have the drive and team spirit ... (*contribute / success / company*)
5 As my present job involves a lot of computer activity, ... (*familiar / office software*)
6 Having had some experience in a small but busy office, ... (*now / look for / new challenge*)
7 If you feel that I could fit into your team, ... (*be able / attend / interview / your convenience*)
8 Should you require any further information ... (*not hesitate / phone or email*)
9 If necessary I ... (*provide / references*)

6 **Role-play. Interview your partner. List your questions:**

- school qualifications,
- stays abroad (where, for how long),
- knowledge of foreign languages,
- IT-skills (general, specific),
- course at university/college (area of specialization, final qualification),
- job training (where, how long, department, job description).

Use the points above to find out as much as you can about your partner's qualifications, experience and motivation. Put your questions in order, working from past to present.

C Writing letters of application and CVs

Language you can use: applying for a job

Referring to the source of information

• *In der aktuellen Ausgabe der/des* [Name einer Zeitung/Zeitschrift] *schreiben Sie die Stelle einer/eines … aus.*	• In the current issue of [*name of paper/ magazine*] you advertise the position of … .
• *Mit (großem) Interesse habe ich Ihre Anzeige im Internet für eine/einen … gelesen.*	• With (great) interest I read your advertisement for a/an … on the Internet.

Applying for a vacancy

• *Ich möchte mich um die ausgeschriebene Stelle bewerben.*	• I wish to apply for the position you advertise.
• *Nach Abschluss meiner Ausbildung als … suche ich nun nach einer Stellung in … .*	• After having completed my training as a/an …, I am now looking for a position in … .

Giving information

• *Wie Sie dem beiliegenden Lebenslauf entnehmen können, … .*	• As you will see from the enclosed CV … .
• *Zurzeit besuche ich* [Schule], *wo ich einen Kurs in Betriebswirtschaftslehre belegt habe.*	• I am currently attending [*school*] where I have enrolled for a course in business administration.
• *Ich spreche fließend Englisch und habe Grundkenntnisse in Französisch.*	• I speak fluent English and have a basic knowledge of French.
• *Nach meiner Berufsausbildung war ich vier Jahre bei einer ortsansässigen Exportfirma tätig.*	• After my vocational training I worked for a local export firm for four years.
• *Während meines Studiums habe ich zwei Praktika im Ausland gemacht.*	• During my studies I did two internships abroad.

Motivation for the job

• *In dieser Position hoffe ich, meine Kenntnisse in* [Fachgebiet] *anwenden zu können.*	• I hope to be able to use my knowledge of *[field]* in this position.
• *Ich möchte im Ausland arbeiten und meine Sprachkenntnisse anwenden.*	• I wish to work abroad and to make use of my knowledge of languages.

Closing sentences

• *Ich füge diesem Schreiben meinen Lebenslauf als Anlage bei.*	• I enclose my CV with this letter.
• *Für ein Vorstellungsgespräch stehe ich jederzeit zur Verfügung und freue mich auf eine Einladung.*	• I am available for an interview at any time and look forward to an invitation.

7 **Put the sentences in the right order for a letter of application.**

Dear Mr Jackson

a I am available for an interview at any time.
b At the end of June I will have completed my two-year training as an office assistant with Ashton Containers Limited here in Bristol.
c But as my company has no opening for me, I am now looking for other opportunities to use my skills.
d During my training, I also attended evening classes in office management, IT and general secretarial duties.
e While at Ashton Containers, I also gained some experience in the papermaking industry.
f I am confident that my training and the skills I acquired at college qualify me for such a position.
g I found your address at my local job centre and I am very interested in the position of office management assistant that you advertise.
h I hope for a favourable response and look forward to hearing from you in due course.
i If you require any additional information, please do not hesitate to contact me.
j In my new job I hope to gain further experience in office procedures and to make a positive contribution to your company's business.

Yours sincerely

8 **Write a letter of application enclosing your CV for one of the following office jobs. Refer to a telephone conversation you had with somebody at the temping agency.**

Positions
Legal assistant
Bilingual secretary
Receptionist

Requirements
at least one year's office experience
MS Office skills
foreign languages
friendly personality
good communicative skills
able to work under pressure

9 **Write a letter of application and CV based on your own personal profile (school career, work experience, activities, skills, interests) for a 3-month work placement in any country or field of your choice.**

working under pressure

File 7

Telephoning: making contacts and arranging appointments

Telephoning in business

In business, telephoning is the most important means of communication – both **internal calls** within the same company and **external calls** with customers and suppliers. In an increasingly global economy, a large number of external calls are in English.

face-to-face

video link

chat room

voice mail

letter and parcel post

1 **Copy and complete the 'word spider' with the means of communication from the box.**

answerphone • chat room • email • ~~face-to-face~~ • fax • landline • ~~letter and parcel post~~ • mobile phone • multimedia messaging • text messaging • video link • ~~voice mail~~

means of communication

audio (voice)
voice mail
…
…
…

audio-visual
face-to-face
…

visual (print/image)
letter and parcel post
…
…
…
…
…

2 **Which means of communication have you used in the last 24 hours? Which ones have you never used? Compare your answers in class. Which seems to be the most popular means of communication?**

A Making contact calls

The situation

Sean Kavanagh is head of **Connemara Outdoor,** an Irish manufacturer of outdoor clothing. His assistant is **Kate Connors**. Sean plans to market his Stormy Weather range in Germany. He wants to get in touch with **UB Consult**, a fashion consultancy in Dusseldorf that helps foreign companies to enter the German market. UB Consult is run by **Udo** and **Ulla Bach**. Their assisant is **Lisa Kraft**.

Taking notes

In this dialogue, Sean Kavanagh is calling Ulla Bach of UB Consult for the first time. Ulla is not there, so Lisa Kraft asks if she can take a message.

2.21

3 **You are Lisa. Listen to the phone call, add the missing information and write the message in German.**

UB Consult GmbH - Rheinweg 24 - 40489 Düsseldorf

TELEFONNOTIZ

Anruf für *Frau* ... **(1)** Datum *22.11.*

Anruf von *Herrn* ... **(3)** Uhrzeit *ca. 9:20*

Firma ... **(4)** Angenommen von ... **(2)**

Telefonnr. ... **(5)**

Nachricht

(6)

4 **Listen again. Note the English for these German sentences.**

1 Haben Sie etwas dagegen, wenn ich ...
2 Wer ist am Apparat, bitte?
3 Bleiben Sie bitte am Apparat.
4 Ich stelle Sie durch.
5 Kann ich ihr irgendetwas ausrichten?
6 Das habe ich notiert.
7 Bitte schön.
8 Könnten Sie das für mich buchstabieren?

5 **Listen again. Who or what do the pronouns refer to?**

EXAMPLE Do you mind if I speak English? *'You' is Lisa, and 'I' is Sean.*

1 Could you spell that for me, please?
2 Yes, that's right, but we don't pronounce them.
3 She had to go out, I'm afraid.
4 Can you ask her to ring me, please?
5 Could you tell her it's quite urgent?
6 I'll make sure she has your message as soon as she gets back.

Making contact calls

2.22

6 **Listen to the telephone language. Complete this list.**

1 **Phoning somebody**
- My name's Ben Dexter. Can I speak to Ms Adams, please?
- May I speak to whoever is in charge of marketing, please?
- …

2 **Answering the phone**
- Good morning. United Digital Limited. Can I help you?
- …

3 **Putting a caller through**
- Could you hold the line, please? I'll put you through to accounts.
- …

4 **Saying somebody is not available**
- I'm sorry, but Ms Adams is not available at the moment.
- I'm sorry, but Ms Adams is out of the office today.
- I'm sorry, but Ms Adams is speaking on another line at present.
- …

5 **Offering help**
- Can I give Ms Adams a message?
- Would you like to call back, or should Ms Adams call you?
- I'll ask Ms Adams to call you back as soon as possible.
- …

6 **Asking for information**
- Who's calling, please?
- Can you spell that for me, please?
- Could you give me your phone number, please?
- …

7 **Getting out of trouble**
- I'm afraid I didn't understand that. Could you say it again, please?
- I'll put you through to somebody who can speak English.
- …

8 **Saying goodbye**
- Thank you for your call. Goodbye.
- …

In business, use **Mr** for men and **Ms** [məz] for women.

good morning
guten Morgen
00:00 to 12:00

good afternoon
guten Tag
12:00 to 18:00

good evening
guten Abend
18:00 to 24:00

"Speak English, please!"

Using telephone language

7 **Role-play this dialogue with a partner. Choose more names from the box.**

Mr Hidvegi	Mr Ogunyemi
Ms Kepuska	Ms Piatkowski
Mr Laroussi	Mr Rozendaal
Ms Müller	Ms Kästner

You Can you tell me your surname, please?
Partner Of course. It's Lüders.
You Could you spell that for me, please?
Partner Sure. It's L – U UMLAUT – D – E – R – S.
You Sorry, is that U for uniform with two dots above it?
Partner That's right. U with an umlaut.
You Thanks, Mr/Ms Lüders.

Saying phone numbers
694400: six – nine – double four (four – four) – double oh (zero – zero)
180723: one – eight – oh (zero) – seven – two – three
- Say the numbers one after the other. Say **0** as the letter **oh** (common in British English) or **zero** (common in American and international English).
- Never use tens, e.g. 'fifty-seven' for 'five – seven'.
- With double numbers say either 'double three, double seven' and so in or 'three – three, seven-seven'.

2.23

8 **Work with a partner. Listen to the answerphone messages and complete the statements with the missing information.**

1 Katrin Drexler from Cologne wants …¹ to call her on 0221 - …² before …³ to tell her whether he can pick her up at …⁴ station next …⁵.
2 Odile Dubois from …¹ wants Ms …² to ask … …³ to call her on 0172 - …⁴ about the new … …⁵.
3 Ruud van Laar asks …¹ to fax the offer for …² to him at his …³ in Venlo by …⁴ o'clock Dutch time on …⁵. It's quite urgent because he needs it for an important …⁶.

2.24

9 **First, read the information on the right and listen to the examples. Then dictate the email and website addresses to your partner. Swap roles at least once.**

1 info@bahn.de
2 odile_dubois@net-online.fr
3 www.bbc.co.uk/radio four/today/
4 http://www.birds.net/owls
5 info@ifabs.co.uk
6 o_duval@wanadoo.fr
7 markus.erdmann@web.de
8 www.itv.co.uk/anglia-news

.	dot
@	at
_	underscore
-	hyphen
/	slash
//	double slash
\	backslash
:	colon
www	double u – double u – double u

The international aviation alphabet

A Alpha	G Golf	M Mike	S Sierra	Y Yankee
B Bravo	H Hotel	N November	T Tango	Z Zulu
C Charlie	I India	O Oscar	U Uniform	
D Delta	J Juliette	P Papa	V Victor	
E Echo	K Kilo	Q Quebec	W Whisky	
F Foxtrot	L Lima	R Romeo	X X-Ray	

2.25

10 **Work with a partner. Read the dialogue and fill in as many gaps as you can. Then listen and check your answers.**

Jane Good afternoon. Carr & Sons Limited. …[1]?
Ben Good afternoon. …[2] through to Ms King's office, please?
Jane Certainly. …[3], please?
Ben …[4] Ben Todd.
Jane …[5], please, Mr Todd.

Ann Good afternoon. Ms King's office. Ann Johnson …[6].
Ben Good afternoon. It's Ben Todd here. …[7] Ms King, please?
Ann I'm sorry. I'm …[8] Ms King is in a …[9] at the moment.
Ben Oh, dear. Do you know when she'll be available? I'll …[10] later.
Ann Well, I can't really say, but can I give her …[11] perhaps?
Ben Oh, no. I'd rather not …[12]. It's private, you see.

11 **Work with a partner. Role-play this conversation back to back. Make notes first, think of names, polite forms, etc.**

A	B
	Telefon klingelt. **B** meldet sich mit Namen der Firma und dem eigenen Namen. **B** fragt was er/sie für A tun kann.
A sagt, dass er/sie [Namen] sprechen möchte.	
	B fragt wer anruft.
A sagt **B** seinen/ihren Namen.	
	B bittet **A** mit Namen am Apparat zu bleiben. Er/Sie stellt ihn/sie durch.
	B teilt **A** mit, dass [Name] momentan leider nicht im Büro ist.
A sagt, dass er/sie in etwa einer Stunde nochmals anrufen wird.	
	B sagt, dass er/sie [Namen] Bescheid geben wird (let sb know sth).
A bedankt und verabschiedet sich.	
	B verabschiedet sich.

12 **Work with a partner. Read this note to Kate West from her assistant, Mark Hobbs. What was the original call?**

Kate: Bob Carter (Apex Software) called about Friday (meeting, Leeds). Will try again tomorrow, Thursday. If he misses you, BC will meet you and Mike Carr in hotel lobby (Crown Plaza), 9:30 a.m. Any problems, his mobile no. is 0173-1894554. He's looking forward to seeing you.
Mark.

B Arranging appointments

Taking notes

Sean Kavanagh's secretary, Kate Connors, calls Lisa Kraft to arrange an appointment for her boss to meet the Bachs in Munich.

2.26

13 Listen to the phone conversation and complete Lisa's email to Kate with the missing details.

Datei Bearbeiten Ansicht Einfügen Extras Nachricht Hilfe

Von: Lisa Kraft <lisa.kraft@ubconsult.de>
An: Kate Connors <k.connors@connemara_outdoor.ie> **Kopie:** <udo.bach@ubconsult.de>
Betreff: Arrangements for meeting **Gesendet:** Dienstag, 18 Januar 05, 11:17:49

Hi Kate

This is just to *confirm*[1] the arrangements we made for Mr Kavanagh's …[2] with Mr and Mrs Bach at the ispo …[3] in Munich next …[4], as follows:

Time/date …[5] a.m. on …, …[6]
Place Room …[7], first …[8], small … …[9], near …[10] entrance

All the best

Lisa

2.26

14 Complete the sentences with the missing verbs. Be careful about tenses. Then listen to the phone conversation again and check your answers.

1 Kate wants to … a date and time for a meeting.
2 Mr Bach … Lisa some possible dates and times.
3 Did he … anything about where the meeting …?
4 Mr Bach … a room for Saturday morning.
5 Please … Mr Kavanagh … to Room 8 on the first floor.
6 There … any problems because everything is … in English.
7 Let me just … the details, Lisa.
8 … Kate. I … the details by email.

*'We **confirm** departure of the flight to Sydney.'*

15 Link the German and the English sentences.

1 Nun, ich rufe nur an, um …
2 Wie wäre es mit …?
3 Oh, das ist sehr gut, …
4 Sicher. Er hat schon … gebucht.
5 Das sollte kein Problem sein.
6 Alles ist sehr gut ausgeschildert.
7 Lass mich das eben überprüfen.
8 Also, mach's gut, Lisa!

a Everything's very well signposted.
b Oh, that's just fine …
c Let me just check …
d Well, how about …?
e Sure. He has already booked …
f Well, I'm just calling to …
g That shouldn't be a problem.
h Well, take care, Lisa.

Arranging appointments

16 **Add the correct headings to the telephone language below.**

Accepting and rejecting suggestions
Asking for an appointment
Closing
Fixing a time and date

I'm afraid Mr Carter is on a business trip.

1 ______
- I'd like to make an appointment to see Ms Brown, please.
- Would it be possible for me to see Mr Carter, please?

2 ______
- Do you have any particular date in mind?
- How/What about 10 o'clock next Tuesday?
- Would 10.30 on 6 June be all right/convenient?

3 ______
- No problem. 3.30 next Wednesday will suit me fine/very well.
- Yes, I can make it by 11o'clock on 21 October.
- I'm afraid Ms Brown has a meeting/another appointment then.
- Unfortunately, Mr Carter is not here/on a business trip/on holiday then.

4 ______
- Fine. I'll look forward to seeing you on Monday, 28 September then.
- Good. We'll expect you at 2.30 on Friday.

On the phone

17 **Work with a partner. Think of dates and your partner writes them down. Change roles.**

Dates

Written:	10 May 2006	May 10, 2006	May 10th, 2006
Spoken:	**the** tenth **of** May, two thousand and six	May ten, two thousand six	May tenth, two thousand six
	more usual in BE	usual in AE	

All-number dates

BE day – month – year 10.5.06; 10/5/06; 10-5-06

AE month – day – year 5.10.06; 5/10/06; 5-10-06

- Never use all-number dates in external correspondence. It can cause big misunderstandings!

18 **What would you say in English in these situations? Put in any missing names or dates yourself.**

Sie möchten jemanden fragen bzw. jemandem sagen,

1 … ob Sie einen Termin haben können, um (*Name*) zu besuchen.
2 … wie es mit (*Uhrzeit*) am nächsten (*Tag*)/am (*Datum*) wäre.
3 … ob die Person, die Sie besuchen wollen, einen Termin selbst vorschlagen möchte.
4 … dass (*Name*) am (*Tag*) verreist ist.
5 … dass die andere Person Anfang nächster Woche nochmals anrufen soll.
6 … dass Sie am (*Tag*) schon voll ausgebucht sind.

2.27

19 **Helen Brown wants to arrange an appointment to see John Hill. When she calls his office, she gets his assistant, Chris Jones.**

You are Chris Jones. Listen to the telephone call, noting down names, dates, times, places, etc. Then write a memo to John Hill telling him about the arrangements you have made.

20 **Work with a partner. Role-play this conversation back to back. Make notes first, think of names, polite forms, etc.**

A calls **B** to arrange an appointment. **A** wants to talk to **B** about his/her firm's improved guarantee conditions.

A	B
	Telefon klingelt. **B** meldet sich mit Namen der Firma.
A meldet sich mit Namen und Firma. Er/sie fragt, ob er/sie einen Termin bei Herrn Hansen haben könnte.	
	B fragt freundlich, worum es geht.
A sagt, dass es sich um die neuen Garantiebedingungen seiner/ihrer Firma handelt.	
	B fragt, ob **A** schon eine bestimmte Terminvorstellung hat.
A bejaht diese Frage und schlägt den 11. Mai, 10.30 Uhr vor.	
	B antwortet, dass er/sie zuerst in Herrn Hansens Terminkalender nachsehen muss. Nach einer kurzen Pause sagt **B**, dass der Termin in Ordnung geht.
A bedankt sich und verabschiedet sich.	
	B bedankt sich für den Anruf und verabschiedet sich ebenfalls.

File 8

Emailing: making appointments, travel arrangements

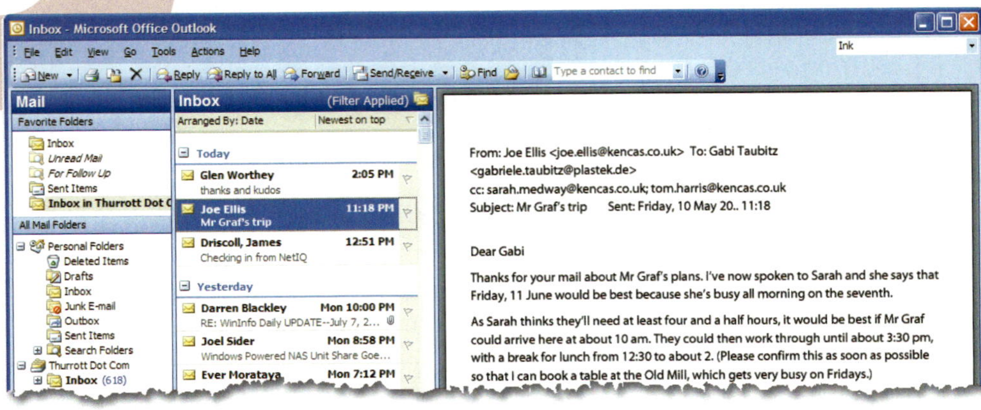

Emails use spoken language, particularly short forms (*it's, don't, hasn't, we'd* etc) and an informal style. A good tip before you send an email is to simply write down what you would say to the other person on the phone.

How to write emails

subject box	Be brief but precise: *Meeting, Bonn, 23 May* or *Arrangements: Brussels fashion fair.*
opening	*Dear (Jane)* = standard *Hello/Hi Ben/...* = less formal, particularly *Hi*
topic	Say what the email is about, for example, *I'm writing about ...* or *This is to let you know that ....*
aim	Say what you want. Often, you will either ask the addressee to do something or give him or her some information.
close	Close with a friendly sentence like *Thanks a lot for your trouble.*
signing off	*Yours sincerely/faithfully* sounds too formal in emails. Write *Best regards/Best wishes, All the best* or simply *Yours.* Sometimes these are shortened to *Best/bw* and *ab/atb.*

The situation

Kent Casings Limited is a manufacturer of clear plastic cases for CDs and DVDs in Ashford, Kent, not far from the Channel Tunnel. **Sarah Medway** is head of purchasing and **Joe Ellis** is her personal assistant or 'PA'.

PlasTek GmbH in Leverkusen supplies Kent Casings with plastics for many of its products.

Bernd Graf is the export manager at PlasTek. So he and his secretary, **Gabi Taubitz**, have a lot of contact with Sarah and Joe.

A Appointments

Making appointments

Gabi Taubitz and Joe Ellis arrange for Bernd Graf to visit Sarah Medway in Ashford.

Von: Gabi Taubitz <gabriele.taubitz@plastek.de>
An: Joe Ellis <joe.ellis@kencas.co.uk> **Kopie:**
Betreff: Mr Graf's trip to UK **Gesendet:** Mittwoch, 8. Mai 20.. 14:56

Dear Joe

Mr Graf asked me to get in touch with you about fixing a date for his visit to you next month.

Mr Graf will be travelling to the UK by car through the Channel Tunnel on Sunday, 6 June, so his first full day in England will be Monday, 7 June. Before returning home early on Saturday, 12 June, he also has appointments in Nottingham, Liverpool and Oxford.

As you're only about 20 kilometres from the tunnel, it would probably be best if Mr Graf could visit you at the beginning or the end of his trip, i.e. on either Monday, 7 June or Friday, 11 June. Is one of these dates convenient for you?

Could you also let me know if there are any points that Ms Medway would particularly like to discuss at the meeting?

Best wishes

Gabi

From: Joe Ellis <joe.ellis@kencas.co.uk> **To:** Gabi Taubitz <gabriele.taubitz@plastek.de>
cc: sarah.medway@kencas.co.uk; tom.harris@kencas.co.uk
Subject: Mr Graf's trip **Sent:** Friday, 10 May 20.. 11:18

Dear Gabi

Thanks for your mail about Mr Graf's plans. I've now spoken to Sarah and she says that Friday, 11 June would be best because she's busy all morning on the seventh.

It would be best if Mr Graf could arrive here at about 10 a.m. They could then work through until about 3.30 p.m., with a break for lunch. (Please confirm this as soon as possible so that I can book a table at the Old Mill, which gets very busy on Fridays.)

As far as the agenda goes, Sarah would like to discuss two points:

1 The delivery schedule for next year
2 PlasTek's new scratch-resistant and impact-resistant plastic

By the way, Tom Harris from production planning would like to join them when they discuss the delivery schedule.

Well, that's about it, Gabi. I hope Mr Graf is happy with this programme. Could you please let me know as soon as possible?

Best wishes

Joe

PS Can we help with a hotel for Friday night?

1 **Answer the questions.**

1 How is Bernd Graf travelling to England?
2 Why does Mr Graf want to visit Ashford on either his first or last day in England?
3 Apart from fixing a date, what other information do the senders ask for?

2 **Say if the information below is true, false or not in the email.**

1 Sarah Medway is busy all afternoon on 7 June.
2 She tells Joe that Mr Graf can come at any time he wants on 11 June.
3 She suggests that Mr Graf comes at about 10 a.m.
4 Joe is joining Sarah and Mr Graf for lunch at the Old Mill.
5 One thing Sarah wants to discuss is a new plastic.

Confirming appointments

Gabi Taubitz confirms the arrangements for Bernd Graf's visit.

Hi Joe

Thanks for your email about Mr Graf's visit to Ashford. 10 o'clock on Friday, 11 June would be fine.

And now to the agenda. As well as Ms Medway's two points, Mr Graf would like to present our new discounts for volume orders.

We would definitely like to take advantage of your offer to find a hotel for Mr Graf for Friday night. Let me know the details when you are able to do so.

Well, I think that's all for now. Please get in touch with me if there are any problems.

All the best

Gabi

3 **You are Gabi. Write Bernd Graf a note in German telling him what arrangements you have made.**

PlasTek GmbH

Interne Notiz

An: Herrn Graf Datum: 10. Mai 20..

Von: Gabi Taubitz Über: Besuch bei Kent Casings Ltd

Hinsichtlich des o.g. Besuches habe ich folgende Vereinbarungen getroffen:

Language you can use: appointments

Making appointments

• *… würde gerne einen Termin vereinbaren um Herrn/Frau … zu besuchen.*	• … would like to make an appointment to see Mr/Ms … .
• *Sollte dieser Vorschlag ungünstig sein, schlagen Sie bitte ein anderes Datum vor.*	• Should this proposal be inconvenient, please suggest another date.
• *Da Herr/Frau … am (19 April) in (Scotland) sein wird, … .*	• As Mr/Ms … will be in (Scotland) on (19 April), … .
• *… würde er/sie gerne die Gelegenheit nutzen um … zu besuchen.*	• … he/she would like the opportunity to visit … .

Changing appointments

• *Können wir den Termin mit Herrn/Frau … ändern?*	• Can we change the appointment with Mr/Ms …?
• *Ist es möglich den Termin mit Herrn/Frau … auf (15 Uhr) zu verschieben?*	• Is it possible to postpone the appointment with Mr/Ms … until (3 p.m.).
• *Leider kann ich nicht vor (11.30 Uhr) ankommen.*	• I'm afraid I can't arrive before (11.30 a.m.).
• *Leider müssen wir wegen organisatorischer Schwierigkeiten unseren Termin absagen/verschieben.*	• Unfortunately we must cancel/postpone our appointment because of organizational difficulties.

B Hotel reservations

Making and confirming hotel reservations

Joe Ellis confirms a telephone reservation for Bernd Graf.

From: Joe Ellis <joe.ellis@kencas.co.uk>
To: The Garden House <reception@garden-marsham.co.uk> **cc:**
Sent: Tuesday, 14 May 20.. 10:43 **Subject:** Confirmation of reservation

Good morning!

Further to our telephone conversation earlier this morning, I would like to confirm my reservation of a single room with en suite bathroom for Mr Bernd Graf for one night from Friday, 11 June 20.. to Saturday, 12 June, including full breakfast. Mr Graf will be arriving during the early evening and will require off-road parking.

As agreed, please send the invoice to me at Kent Casings Ltd.

Thank you for your assistance. Please get in touch if you have any questions.

Kind regards

Joe Ellis

4 Link the sentence halves to make true statements.

A	B
1 Joe Ellis sent an email to …	a room for one night for Bernd Graf.
2 The purpose of the email was …	b The Garden House on 14 May.
3 The reservation was for a single …	c to be included in the price of the room.
4 Joe asked for a full breakfast …	d to confirm a telephone reservation.
5 He agreed with the hotel that the invoice …	e would be sent to him at Kent Casings.

Informing others about hotel reservations

From: Joe Ellis <joe.ellis@kencas.co.uk> **To:** Gabi Taubitz <gabriele.taubitz@plastek.de>
cc: sarah.medway@kencas.co.uk
Subject: Hotel reservation **Sent:** Tuesday, 14 May 20.. 12:04

Hi Gabi

This is to let you know that I've booked a room with English breakfast for Mr Graf at our expense for the night of 11 June. I've also arranged off-road parking.

The hotel is pleasantly situated in a quiet village about five kilometres south of Ashford, just off the main road to the tunnel terminal. Here are the details:

The Garden House
The Street
Marsham, Kent Tel: (01580) 675529

I hope this is okay. Please get in touch if you have any questions.

All the best

Joe

5 Who is speaking?

Bernd Graf • accountant • Gabi Taubitz • Joe Ellis • hotel receptionist • Sarah Medway

1 'Have you emailed PlasTek about Bernd Graf's room?'
2 'Vielleicht könnte ich Sarah zum Abendessen einladen.'
3 'Joe sagt, dass das Hotel in einem ruhigen Dorf liegt.'
4 'Oh, and I managed to get him off-road parking, too.'
5 'We're only about 20 minutes from the tunnel.'
6 'Why are we paying for the hotel? We're *their* customer, aren't we?'

Language you can use: hotel reservations

Asking about and booking rooms

• *Ich hätte/Wir hätten gerne … Einzel- und … Doppelzimmer mit Bad.*	• I/We would like … single and … double room(s) with en suite facilities.
• *Ich würde/Wir würden gerne … Zimmer mit englischem/kontinentalem Frühstück vom … bis … reservieren.*	• I'd/We'd like to reserve … room(s) from … to … with English/continental breakfast.

Booking parking, conference facilities

• *Ich benötige/Wir benötigen ebenfalls einen Konferenzraum für … Personen.*	• I/We will also require a conference room for … people.
• *Das Konferenzzimmer sollte mit einem Beamer ausgestattet sein.*	• The conference room should be equipped with a data projector.

Confirming and arranging payment

• *Bestätigen Sie bitte diese Reservierung schriftlich.*	• Please confirm this reservation in writing.
• *Schicken Sie bitte die Rechnung an* [Firma] *zu Händen von ….*	• Please send the invoice to *[name of company]* for the attention of ….
• *… wird alle Kosten übernehmen außer den Kosten für Bar/Minibar/Telefon.*	• … will meet all costs except for those for the bar/minibar/phone calls.

C Travel arrangements

Asking a travel agent for an itinerary

Sarah Medway is going on a business trip to the Netherlands and Germany. She asks Joe Ellis to make the travel arrangements. Joe emails Geeta Sen, Kent Casing's travel agent.

From: Joe Ellis <joe.ellis@kencas.co.uk>
To: Geeta Sen <geeta.sen@pegtrav.co.uk> **cc:**
Subject: Travel arrangements **Sent:** Wednesday, 24 August 20.. 12:03

Hello Geeta

Sarah Medway has appointments in Utrecht at 11.30 on Tuesday, 6 September, and in Leverkusen at 9.30 on Wednesday, 7 September. She has to be back in Ashford for a meeting at 14.30 on Thursday, 8 September.

Sarah would like to fly from Gatwick to Amsterdam Schiphol Airport on the Tuesday morning, drive a hire car to Utrecht – the driving time's about an hour, by the way – and then drive on to Leverkusen during the late afternoon.

After spending Wednesday night in Leverkusen, she'd like to fly back to Gatwick from Düsseldorf on Thursday, returning the car there.

As I've already said, she has an important meeting in Ashford at 14.30 on the Thursday, so I suppose she'll have to land in Gatwick by 12.30 at the latest.

Geeta, could you work out an itinerary for Sarah and email it to me as soon as possible, please?

Thanks a lot and please get in touch if there are any problems.

Best wishes

Joe

PS Sarah wants to fly business class as she'll have to work on the plane.

6 Answer the questions.

1 Why does Joe email Geeta Sen?
2 Which four continental towns are mentioned?
3 Which two means of transport does Sarah want to use?
4 Why must Sarah be back in Ashford by 14.30 on 8 September?
5 What two things does Joe ask Geeta to do?
6 Why does Sarah want to travel business class?

Confirming an itinerary

Sarah thinks the itinerary that Geeta has worked out is fine, so she asks Joe to tell Pegasus to make the reservations.

Hi Geeta

Thanks for getting back to me so promptly.

I've now spoken to Sarah and she says the itinerary is fine. Could you make the necessary reservations and send the e-ticket, please?

As far as the car and hotel go, a Group B car's okay – and our German business partner in Leverkusen is arranging the hotel. No problem.

All the best

Joe

From PEGASUS TRAVEL (AGENTID00887429) [mailto:emailserverpop3.amadeus.net]
Sent Monday 29 August 20.. 11:13
To JOE.ELLIS@KENVAS.CO.UK
Subject MEDWAY/SARAH 06SEPT LGW AMS

MEDWAY/SARAH 06SEPT LGW AMS

ELECTRONIC TICKET
PASSENGER ITINERARY RECEIPT

PEGASUS TRAVEL DATE: 29 AUGUST 20..
AGENT: 9745 NAME. MEDWAY/SARAH

ISSUING AIRLINE BRITISH AIRWAYS
48642

Language you can use: travel arrangements

Fixing the details

• *Um welche Uhrzeit wollen Sie/will* [Name] *in … abreisen/ankommen?*	• At what time do you want/does *[name]* want to leave …/arrive in …?
• *Ich/*[Name] *muss spätestens um (15.30 Uhr) in … ankommen.*	• I/*[name]* must arrive in … by … (3.30 p.m./ 15.30 hrs) at the latest.
• *Wie möchten Sie/möchte* [Name] *von … nach … reisen?*	• How would you/*[name]* like to travel from … to …?
• *Ich/*[Name] *will in der ersten/zweiten Klasse/ Businessklasse/Economyklasse fahren/fliegen.*	• I want/*[name]* wants to travel/fly first/second/ business/economy class.
• *Ich/Er/Sie/Herr …/Frau … möchte einen Gangplatz/Fensterplatz haben.*	• I/He/She/Mr … /Ms … would like to have an aisle/a window seat.
• *Ich/*[Name] *will einen direkten Flug/eine direkte Verbindung.*	• I want/*[name]* would like a direct flight/service.

Giving instructions

• *Reservieren Sie bitte einen (Hin- und Rück-)Flug für mich/*[Name] *nach … um … am ….*	• Please reserve a (return) flight for me/*[name]* to … at … on ….
• *Sie können/*[Name] *kann die Tickets am Lufthansa-Schalter abholen.*	• You/*[name]* can pick up the tickets at the Lufthansa desk.
• *Sie müssen mindestens 60 Minuten vor Abflug einchecken.*	• You must check in at least 60 minutes before departure.
• *Ich möchte ein Auto (mit Automatikgetriebe) für … Tage mieten.*	• I'd like to hire a car (with automatic transmission) for … days.
• *Ich benötige das Auto/einen Kombi von … am … bis … am ….*	• I need the car/an estate car from … on … until … on ….

D Practising language

7 **Complete the email about changing a room reservation with words or expressions from the box.**

confirm • please mark • departing • does not get in • get in touch • has left • made • must change • will be taken • will need

Good morning

I'm afraid we ...[1] the reservation we ...[2] for Ms Sigrid Meier, who ...[3] the company. Ms Maier's place at the Halifax Textile Fair ...[4] by Mr Klaus Schmitz, who ...[5] her room for one further night, ...[6] on 12 October.

Just one last point: ...[7] Mr Schmitz's reservation 'late arrival' as his train ...[8] until 11.30 p.m. on 9 October.

Could you ...[9] that these new arrangements are okay. Please ...[10] if there are any questions.

Best wishes

8 **This email confirming a room reservation is complete, but the parts are mixed up. Write the email.**

a Best regards

b Good afternoon

c Guest Ms Birgit Klein
Arrival 06 June 20..
Departure 08 June 20..

d I also wish to book a space in the hotel garage. Ms Klein's car is a VW Passat, registration number MS-UU 107.

e I'd like to reserve a single room with en suite facilities for two nights, as follows:

f Please note that Ms Klein won't arrive at the hotel before about 10.30 p.m. on 6 June.

g Thank you for your trouble, and please get in touch with me if you have any questions.

h This is to confirm the phone reservation I made this morning.

2.28

9 *Sarah Medway wants to take a short holiday in Scotland. She plans to fly to Aberdeen, pick up a hire car, tour the Highlands and then return the car to Glasgow Airport before flying home. Sarah asks Joe to find out about hiring cars at Aberdeen Dyce Airport.*

Listen to Joe's phone conversation with Kim Cameron of Star Car Hire at Dyce, and then complete Joe's email to Sarah.

Hi Sarah

I've looked into a hire car for you. The price may seem a bit high, but I've compared prices and …[1] seems to offer the best deal.

Here are the details:

Car	Group C, …[2]
Pick up	…[3] a.m. on Monday, …[4] at …[5] Airport
Drop off	…[6] p.m. on …[7], 20 March at …[8]
Price	£…[9], including …[10] and unlimited mileage.

The car will have a full tank of …[11], but you must give it back with a full tank as well. (If you don't, there's a £…[12] surcharge on top of the cost of Star Car Hire filling the tank.)

I told them that I'd check with you before making a firm …[13]. What do you think? Should I go ahead? (They're open until …[14], by the way.)

E Writing emails

10 **Work with a partner (A and B). Write the emails below. Think of names, details, polite forms, etc. yourselves.**

Email 1: A will **B** in seinem/ihrem Büro in *(Ort)* besuchen. **A** schlägt Montag, den 2. Juni, um *(Zeit)* vor, wenn er/sie sowieso in *(Ort)* sein wird. Er/Sie hofft, dass dieser Vorschlag in Ordnung ist.

Email 2: B fragt, ob **A** zwei Stunden später kommen könnte, da er/sie vorher eine Sitzung hat.

Email 3: A erwidert, dass der spätere Termin in Ordnung sei.

11 **Work with a partner and write the emails.**

Email 1: A writes an email to York Hotel based on the note on the next page.

Email 2: B confirms the reservation.

I can email anyone in the world – but I don't know anyone outside my town!

Vergiss bitte nicht, das York Hotel anzumailen: Einzelzimmer mit Bad/Frühstück, 8.–10. Aug. (mit Garagenplatz). Auch Tisch für 4 Pers. am 9. reservieren. Sage bitte unbedingt, dass ich am 8. voraussichtlich sehr spät ankomme (etwa um Mitternacht). Danke.

12 **Work with a partner. A is a personal assistant, B works as a receptionist. Exchange emails using the prompts.**

Email 1: A will ein Einzelzimmer für *(Zahl)* Nächte vom *(Datum)* bis zum *(Datum)* für *(Name)* reservieren. Er/Sie fügt hinzu, dass *(Name)* auch einen ruhigen Hund mitbringen will.
Email 2: B bestätigt die Reservierung mit dem Hinweis, dass a) nur kleine bis mittelgroße *(medium-sized)* Hunde erlaubt sind, b) es einen Preisaufschlag *(surcharge)* von £ 5 pro Tag gibt und c) Hunde nicht in den Frühstücksraum mitgenommen werden dürfen.

13 **Read the following note and write the two emails.**

3.2

Bitte E-Mail an Mr Carlos L. Gonzales schicken. Sagen Sie ihm, dass unser Treffen morgen in Ordnung geht. Ich komme um ca. 9 Uhr an und werde im Foyer seines Hotels auf ihn warten. (Ich trage einen schwarzen Mantel und einen roten Schal!) Wir werden etwa vier Stunden benötigen. Anschließend würde ich ihn gerne zum Mittagessen im Caledonian Grill einladen. Bitte sagen Sie ihm, dass ich spätestens um 15.30 Uhr weg muss (Flug). Danke!

PS Bitte auch per E-Mail einen Tisch reservieren!

I'm just phoning to say I've sent you an email.

Toolbox for business communication

When you are role-playing phone calls or writing letters or emails in English, it is often difficult to think up authentic names, addresses and products.

The lists below help you to solve this problem, but don't forget the Internet. You can get a lot of help there.

1 English names

Here are some fairly common and easy English names. The short form has also been given when this is widely used. Never use nicknames unless you know the person well.

Female

Alison – Ann – Barbara – Carol – Chelsea – Christine/Tina – Clare – Denise – Elizabeth/Liz – Ellen/Elli – Emma – Fiona – Helen – Judith/Judy – Julia/Julie – Lisa – Lucy – Maria – Marsha – Mary – Michelle – Rebecca/Becky – Sharon – Susan/Sue – Suzanne/Susie – Wendy – Yvonne

Male

Alan – Andrew/Andy– Anthony/Tony – Benjamin/Ben – Daniel/Dan – David – Dominic – Edward/Ted – Harold/Harry – James/Jim – John – Joshua/Josh – Lee – Michael/Mike – Nicholas/Nick – Peter/Pete – Richard/Dick – Robert/Bob – Roger – Simon – Thomas/Tom – William/Bill

Last names

Anderson – Atkins – Barton – Brown – Carr – Carter – Clark – Davis – Dixon – Edwards – Fox – Gardner – Green – Harper – Hudson – Hunter – Johnson – Kent – King – Moore – Morris – Owen – Parker – Peters – Philips – Price – Richards – Webb – Wood

2 Company names and addresses

Here is a selection of companies and addresses from the English-speaking world. At least two of the names in each list do not specify the particular product or industry. (Remember that in American full block form you don't include commas in letters.)

Universal Postal Union

The **Universal Postal Union** is a division of the United Nations. You can find out how to write addresses in over 180 member countries by visiting its website at **www.upu.int**.

UK and Ireland

Apex Advertising Ltd, 24 Wicklow Road, Dublin 3, Ireland
Carr & Co Ltd, 14 Albert Road, King's Lynn, NR22 6TH, England
C. Davis & Sons Ltd, 3 Valley Road, Cardiff, CD3 6TF, Wales
Galway Enterprises Ltd, 16 Arran Street, Galway, Ireland

Pegasus Travel PLC, 42 Burns Road, Edinburgh, ED1 9DS, Scotland
Wessex Electronics Ltd, 13 Avon Street, Bristol, BR2 8UH, England

USA, Canada
Able and Willing Inc., Suite 231, 380 Island Avenue, Vancouver BC V8P 2T6, Canada
CompuLink Media Inc., 578 Pacific Heights, Santa Barbara, CA 17893, USA
Dawson Mining Inc., 23 Alaska Highway, Dawson YT D3T 4H2, Canada
Delta Electronics Inc., Building 10, 47 East Portway, New Orleans, LA 31265, USA
John Moore & Partners, 43 Kennedy Road, Buffalo, NY 86321, USA
Richmond Engineering Inc., 22 Monroe Drive, Richmond, VA 84931, USA

Australia, New Zealand
Australian Automotive Pty Ltd, 5 North Road, BRISBANE QLD 4000, AUSTRALIA
James Barton & Sons Pty Ltd, 237 Mount Street, WELLINGTON 6002, NEW ZEALAND
Myra Freeman Lifestyles, 17 Beach Street, NORTH SYDNEY NSW 2080, AUSTRALIA
Nelson Ecology Co, PO Box 324, AUCKLAND 2121, NEW ZEALAND

Africa, Asia
AWP Products Ltd, Lodhi Road, NEW DELHI-110045, INDIA
Cape Industrial Pty, PO Box 176, ALRODE, 1451, SOUTH AFRICA
Asian Star Shipping Ltd, 16 Portside, SINGAPORE 546090, REP. OF SINGAPORE
Hong Kong Export Pty Co, 121 Kennedy Road, NORTH POINT, HONG KONG

3 Some products

When you write business letters, you always need the names of products. Here are some products you can choose from.

Automotive

Alarmanlage	*alarm system*	Kindersitz	*child's safety seat*
Anhängerkupplung	*tow bar*	Leichtmetallfelge	*aluminium wheel*
Autoradio	*car radio*	Radkappe	*hubcap*
Batterie	*battery*	Reifen	*tyre (AE: tire)*
Bremse	*brake*	Scheibenwischerblatt	*windscreen wiper blade*
Bremslicht	*brake light*	Scheinwerfer	*headlight*
Bremsscheibe	*brake disc*	Schlusslicht	*tail-light*
Frostschutzmittel	*antifreeze*	Sicherheitsgurt	*seat belt*
		Zündkerze	*spark plug*

Fashion accessories

Armband	*bracelet*	Modeschmuck	*costume jewellery*
Brosche	*brooch*	Mütze	*cap*
Gürtel	*belt*	Nagellack	*nail varnish*
Haarspange	*hair slide*	Ohrring	*earring*
Halskette	*necklace*	Ring	*ring*
Handschuhe	*gloves*	Rücksack	*backpack*
Krawattenhalter	*tie clip*	Schal	*scarf*
Lippenstift	*lipstick*	Stiefel	*boots*
		Tasche	*bag*

Kitchen and household equipment

Dampfbügeleisen	*steam iron*	Kaffeemaschine	*coffee maker*
Dunstabzugshaube	*extractor hood*	Küchenmaschine	*food processor*
Entsafter	*juice extractor*	Mikro(wellenherd)	*microwave (oven)*
Föhn	*hairdryer*	Mixer	*blender*
Fritteuse	*deep fryer*	Staubsauger	*vacuum cleaner*
Gefrierschrank	*upright freezer*	Waschmaschine	*washing machine*
Gefriertruhe	*chest freezer*	Wäschetrockner	*tumble dryer*
Geschirrspülmaschine	*dishwasher*	Wasserkocher	*electric kettle*
Heizlüfter	*fan heater*		

Office furniture and equipment

Aktenschrank	*filing cabinet*	Laserdrucker	*laser printer*
Anrufbeantworter	*answerphone*	Regale	*shelves*
Beamer	*data projector*	Reißwolf	*shredder*
Drucker	*printer*	schnurloses Telefon	*cordless phone*
Farbdrucker	*colour printer*	Schrank	*cupboard*
Fax(gerät)	*fax (machine)*	Taschenrechner	*calculator*
Handy	*mobile (phone)*	Tintenstrahldrucker	*inkjet printer*
	(AE: cell phone)	Tonerpatrone	*toner (cartridge)*
Kopierer	*photocopier*		

Services

Architektur	*architecture*	Reinigungsbetrieb	*contract cleaners*
Bankwesen	*banking*	Reisebüro	*travel agency*
Bauwesen	*building/construction*	Sicherheitsdienst	*security service*
Druckgewerbe	*printing industry*	Stellenvermittlungs-agentur	*employment agency*
Einzelhandel	*retailing*		
Gastronomie	*catering*	Übersetzungsbüro	*translation agency*
Großhandel	*wholesaling*	Verlagswesen	*publishing*
Immobilienmakler	*estate agency*	Versicherung	*insurance*
	(AE: real-estate agency)	Werbung	*advertising*

4 Packaging

Here is a list of the most common types of packaging used when transporting goods. Note that there are sometimes more names in German than in English.

Ballen	*bale*	Kiste	*box*	Seecontainer	*sea container*
Beutel	*bag (small)*	Kiste	*crate*	Tasche	*bag (big)*
Dose	*can*	Korb	*basket*	Tasche	*pouch (small)*
Dose	*tin*	Paket	*carton*	Tonne	*barrel*
Fass	*barrel*	Paket	*packet*	Tonne	*drum*
Flasche	*bottle*	Rolle	*roll*	Tube	*tube*
Karton	*carton*	Sack	*sack*	Umschlag	*envelope*
Kasten	*box*	Schachtel	*box*		

Glossary of business terms

1 Types of business organization

In the **EU**, there are two basic types of company, the **private limited company** (GB: Ltd; German: *GmbH*) and the **public limited company** (GB: PLC; German: *AG*). In the **USA and Canada** there are three types of company, as follows:

Incorporated company (Inc.) There is no exact equivalent of an incorporated company in the EU. 'Incorporated' simply means 'registered as a company'. It does not say anything about ownership or liability, or capitalization.

Close corporation (Corp.) This is the North American equivalent of the British Ltd and German *GmbH*. Close corporations have a small number of shareholders (here: *Gesellschafter/in*) and do not offer their shares on the stock market *(Börse)*.

Open corporation (Corp.) The North American equivalent of the British PLC and German *AG*. Open corporations usually have numerous shareholders (here: *Aktienbesitzer/in*), often other corporations, and sell their shares on the stock market.

In **Australia**, **New Zealand** and **South Africa**, the equivalent of both the British Ltd and PLC is the **proprietary company** or Pty.

2 Terms of delivery

International trade was once a risky business. This was not only because of storms at sea, piracy, local wars and other disasters. Losses were also caused by buyers not paying for the goods in full and on time, and by disagreements about who paid for transport and insurance, for example.

These disagreements were often just misunderstandings caused by an ignorance of foreign languages and cultures. For example, Asian languages did not have a word for 'insurance' because paying somebody to take over your risk was seen as morally wrong.

For this reason, the International Chamber of Commerce in Paris developed standard commercial terms (Incoterms) which everybody could easily understand. These terms apply all over the world and have done a lot to take the risk out of international trade and to encourage the growth of global markets.

Incoterms

CFR
cost freight
Kosten und Fracht
The seller takes over only transport costs. The buyer is responsible for arranging and paying for insurance.

DEQ
delivered ex quay, duty paid
geliefert ab Kai, verzollt
From the buyer's point of view, DEQ is more attractive than DES because the seller pays customs duties.

CIF
cost insurance freight
Kosten, Versicherung und Fracht
The seller takes over all transport and insurance costs. CIF is popular among buyers because insurance can be expensive.

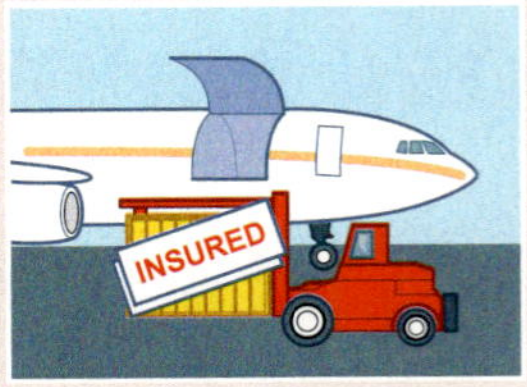

CIP
carriage and insurance paid to
frachtfrei versichert bis
The seller takes over all transport and insurance costs until the goods have reached an agreed point, often a carrier in the buyer's country.

CPT
carriage paid to
frachtfrei bis
The seller takes over all transport costs until the goods have reached an agreed point, often a carrier in the buyer's country. The buyer is responsible for insurance and customs duties.

DAF
delivered at frontier
geliefert Grenze
The seller is responsible for all transport and insurance costs to the customs border of a named country, usually the seller's own country.

DDP
delivered duty paid
geliefert verzollt
DDP is the opposite of EXW because the seller meets all delivery costs, including insurance and customs duties, to the buyer's premises.

DDU
delivered duty unpaid
geliefert unverzollt
DDU is quite common because the buyer can usually deal with customs formalities and local taxes more easily than a foreign seller

DES
delivered ex ship
geliefert ab Schiff
Importers like DES because the seller pays all the costs of transporting goods to a named port, e.g. DES Rotterdam.

EXW
ex works
ab Werk
The buyer takes over all delivery costs, including insurance and customs duties, from the seller's premises onwards.

FAS
free alongside ship
frei Längsseite Schiff
The buyer takes over all costs and risks immediately before the goods are loaded onto a ship.

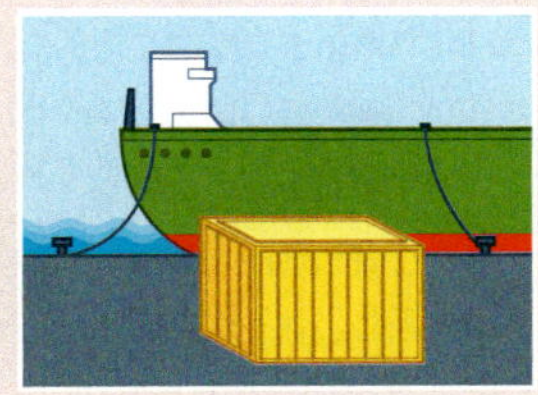

FCA
free carrier
frei Frachtführer
The seller hands over the goods to a carrier who is then responsible for them.

FOB
free on board
frei an Bord
The buyer takes over all costs and risks once the goods have been safely loaded onto a ship. The difference between FAS and FOB is important because goods are sometimes damaged during loading.

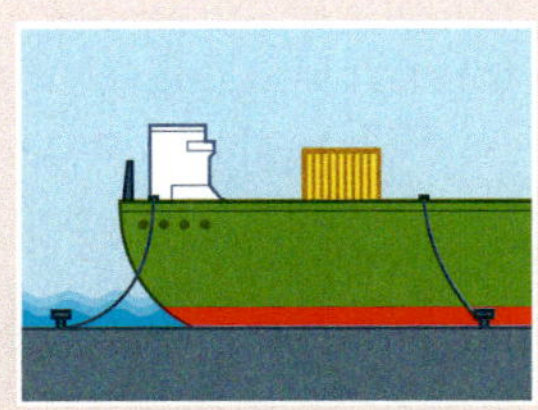

3 Shipping documents

airfreight *Luftfracht*
air waybill (AWB) *Luftfrachtbrief*
approval: on approval *zur Ansicht, auf Probe*
bill of lading (B/L) *Seefrachtbrief, Konnossement*
bonded warehouse *Zollverschlusslager*
cargo *Ladung, Fracht*
cargo liner *Frachtschiff*
cargo space *Frachtraum*
certificate of origin (C/O) *Ursprungszeugnis*
chamber of (industry and) commerce *(Industrie- und) Handelskammer*
combined transport waybill *kombinierter Warenbegleitschein*
commercial invoice *Handelsrechnung*
consignment note [road or rail] *Frachtbrief [Straßen- oder Bahn-]*
consignee *Empfänger/in*
consignor *Absender/in, Versender/in*
consular invoice *Konsularrechnung, Konsultatsfaktura*
contract of carriage *Beförderungsvertrag*
customs clearance *Zollabfertigung*
customs declaration *Zollinhaltserklärung*
customs invoice *Zollrechnung, Zollfaktura*
dangerous goods certificate *Gefahrgut-bescheinigung*
delivery note *Lieferschein, Versandanzeige*
destination; port of destination *Bestimmungsort; Bestimmungshafen*
export licence *Exportlizenz*
forwarder's certificate of receipt (FCR) *Spediteurübernahmebescheinigung*
freight *Fracht*
freight rates *Frachttarife*
import licence *Exportlizenz*
to take out insurance *eine Versicherung abschließen*
insurance certificate (IC) *Versicherungsschein, -police*
to insure goods against a risk *Ware gegen ein Risiko versichern*
to issue *ausstellen, ausfertigen*
loss; total or partial loss *Verlust; Gesamt- oder Teilverlust*
packing list *Packliste*
pro forma invoice (P/I) *Proforma-Rechnung*
rail consignment note *Bahnfrachtbrief*
receipt *Erhalt; Empfangsbescheinigung*
ro-ro (roll on-roll off) ferry/vessel *von Straßenfahrzeugen befahrbare/s Fähre/Schiff*
shipping note (S/N) *Schiffszettel, Versandanzeige, Warenbegleitschein*
single administrative document *Einheitspapier*
warehouse *Lager*
waybill (WB) *Frachtbrief*

Air waybill An airline issues an air waybill to the consignor of a cargo as both a receipt and as a contract of carriage. A copy accompanies the cargo to its destination.
Bill of lading A shipping line issues a bill of lading to the consignor. It confirms receipt of the cargo, records its condition and promises to deliver it to the consignee complete and undamaged. Unlike an air waybill, the consignee's copy confirms that he or she can take possession of the goods.
Certificate of origin A certificate of origin shows where the goods were produced. It is issued by a chamber of commerce or the customs in the exporting country.
Combined transport waybill Containers transported by road are popular because goods are delivered door-to-door without unloading and repacking them. Very often, however, this involves more than one means of transport, for example road–sea–road. A combined waybill makes life easier because it covers all means of transport in just one document.
Commercial invoice (→ Pro forma invoice)
Insurance certificate An insurance certificate says to what value goods have been insured, by whom and against which risks.
Packing list The packing list is put both inside the container with the goods and on the outside of the container. It says exactly what is in the container.

Pro forma invoice Another name for a 'commercial invoice'. When goods are paid for by letter of credit (→ 4 Terms of payment), the pro forma invoice shows the amount and terms of the credit required. Also used as a provisional invoice for goods sent on approval.

Rail consignment note Both a receipt and a contract of carriage. A copy accompanies the goods to their destination.

Shipping note A document signed by the ship's cargo officer when goods are taken on board.

Shipping notes This is all the documentation used when exporting goods (insurance certificates, certificates of origin, etc).

Single administrative document This is a unified document that is used within the EU. It has made the transport of goods between EU member countries faster, easier and cheaper. Important in creating a single market.

4 Terms of payment

bill of exchange (B/E) *Wechsel*
cash against documents (CAD) *Kasse gegen Dokumente*
(2%) cash discount *(2 %) Skonto / Barzahlungsrabatt*
cash in advance (CIA) *Vorkasse*
cash on delivery (COD) *Barzahlung bei Lieferung / gegen Nachnahme*
cash with order (CWO) *Zahlung bei Auftrags-erteilung/Bestellung*
(3 months') credit *(3 Monate) Zahlungsziel*
credit note (C/N) *Gutschrift, Gutschriftsanzeige*
credit status *Kreditwürdigkeit*
debit note (D/N) *Lastschrift, Lastschriftanzeige*
deposit *Anzahlung, Kaution*
documents against acceptance (D/A) *Dokumente gegen Wechselakzept*
documents against payment (D/P) *Dokumente gegen Zahlung*
to honour a cheque/bill *(AE: honor)* *einen Scheck/Wechsel einlösen*
(not) negotiable *(nicht) negoziierbar/mit Rechten übertragbar/begebbar*
net cash *netto Kasse*
payment by cheque *(BE)* *Zahlung durch Scheck*
payment by credit transfer *Zahlung durch Überweisung*
payment by irrevocable and confirmed letter of credit (L/C) *Zahlung durch unwiderrufliches und bestätigtes Akkreditiv*
payment in cash *Zahlung in bar*
payment in national currency *Zahlung in Landeswährung*
payment in instalments *Ratenzahlung, Teilzahlung*
payment on receipt of goods *Zahlung bei Erhalt der Ware / bei Wareneingang*
payment on receipt of invoice *Zahlung bei Rechnungserhalt*
payment within ... days/weeks/months *Zahlung innerhalb von ... Tagen/Wochen/Monaten*
from date of invoice *nach Rechnungsdatum*

Payments in foreign trade

International business is taking place in an increasingly well-regulated global market. This has had an effect on how buyers pay for goods. It is now much easier to get up-to-date information about a buyer's credit status. This is the result of advances in information technology, the spread of multinational companies and greater openness among banks to stop money laundering.

Today, most payments in foreign trade are made by either **credit transfer**, **cheque** or – above all in the case of new customers that the seller does not know – by **letter of credit**. The **bill of exchange**, which in practice is not much better than a **cheque**, has become very much less common.

Payment by letter of credit

The trouble with credit transfers and cheques is that the buyer's bank may refuse to honour them. The problem with bills of exchange is that the buyer may refuse to pay them when they are due.

For these reasons, the **documentary credit**, i.e. the **confirmed and irrevocable letter of credit** (**L/C**), is now by far the most popular method of payment in more risky foreign business. 'Confirmed' means that the seller's bank guarantees payment for the goods; 'irrevocable' means that the buyer cannot cancel the letter of credit or change its terms.

A business transaction by confirmed and irrevocable letter of credit

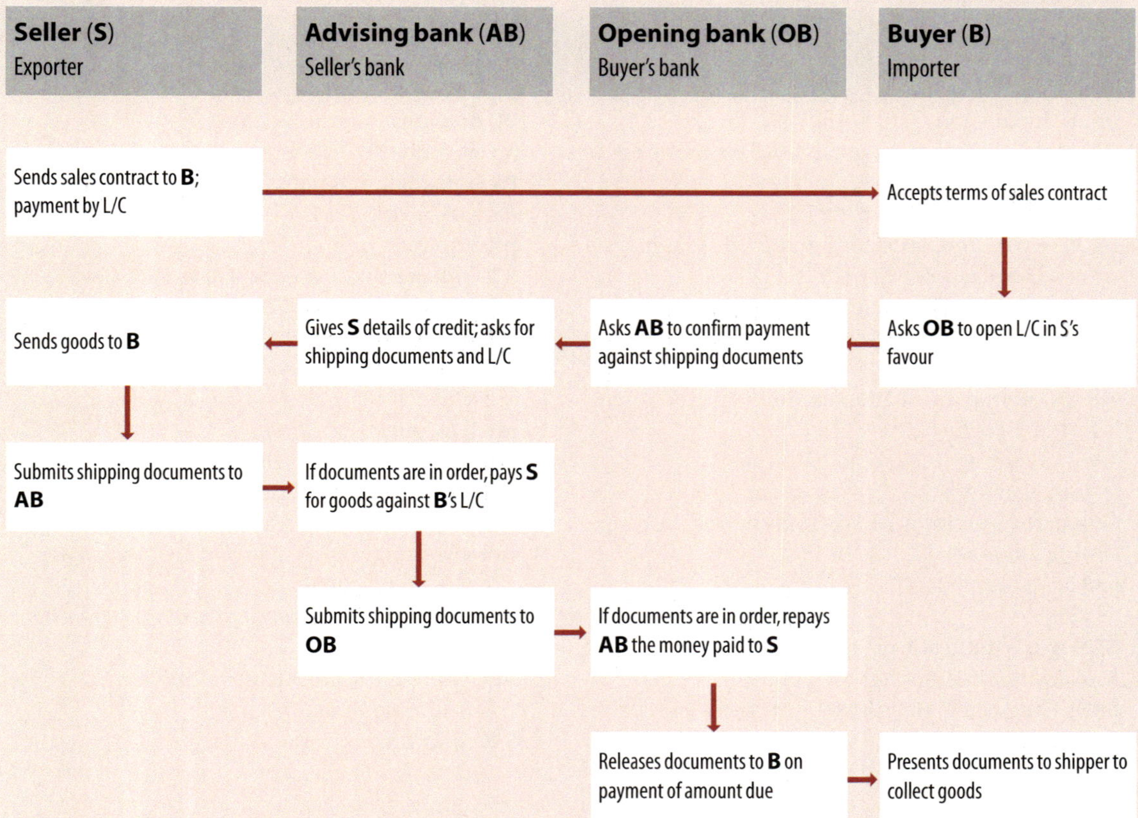

5 Common abbreviations

a/c account *Konto*
a.m. *vormittags* (→ **p.m.**)
AOB any other business *Sonstiges, Verschiedenes [Tagesordnung]*
approx approximate(ly) *ungefähr*
arr. arrival *Ankunft*
asap as soon as possible *so bald wie möglich*
attn attention *zu Händen (von) (z. Hd.)*
Ave. *(BE)* **Av.** *(AE)* Avenue *Allee*
AWB air waybill *Luftfrachtbrief*
bal balance *Kontostand, Saldo*
B/E bill of exchange *Wechsel*
B/L bill of lading *Seefrachtbrief, Konnossement*
bn billion *Billion (GB); Milliarde (USA)*
BOP balance of payment *Zahlungsbilanz*
Bros brothers *Gebrüder*
BST British Summer Time *britische Sommerzeit*
CAD cash against documents *Zahlung gegen Dokumente*
CBD cash before delivery *Zahlung vor Lieferung*
cc carbon copy *Kopie, Durchschrift*
CC Chamber of Commerce *Handelskammer*
CEO Chief Executive Officer *Vorstandsvorsitzende/r*
cf. *vergleiche (vgl.)*
chq cheque *Scheck*
CIA cash in advance *Vorkasse, Vorauszahlung*

c/o care of *bei [Adresse], zu Händen (von)*
C/O certificate of origin *Ursprungszeugnis*
COD cash on delivery *Zahlung bei Lieferung*
cr credit *Haben; Kredit* (➜ **deb**)
CWO cash with order *Zahlung bei Auftragserteilung/Bestellung*
d/a days after acceptance *Tage nach Wechselakzept*
D/A documents against acceptance *Dokumente gegen Wechselakzept*
DAD documents against disposition *Dokumente gegen Verfügung über Ladung*
deb debit *Soll, Debet* (➜ **cr**)
dep. departure *Abreise, Abfahrt, Abflug*
Dept department *Abteilung*
D/P documents against payment *Dokumente gegen Zahlung*
enc(s). enclosure(s) *Anlage(n)*
E&OE errors and omissions excepted *Irrtümer und Auslassungen vorbehalten*
est. established; estimated *gegründet; geschätzt*
ETA estimated time of arrival *voraussichtliche Ankunftzeit*
etd estimated time of departure *voraussichtliche Abfahrt-/Abflugzeit*
excl. excluding *ausschließlich, ohne*
ft foot, feet [length] *Fuß [30,48 cm]*
FYI(O) for your information (only) *(nur) zu Ihrer Information*
gal(s). gallon(s) *Gallone(n) [GB: 4,546 l, USA: 3,785 l]*
GDP gross domestic product *Bruttoinlandsprodukt*
GMT Greenwich Mean Time *Greenwicher Zeit*
GNP gross national product *Bruttosozialprodukt*
HGV heavy goods vehicle *(Schwer-)Lastfahrzeug*
h.p. horsepower *Pferdestärke(n) (PS) [Kfz]*
IC insurance certificate *Versicherungsschein*
i.e. *das heißt (d. h.)*
incl. including *einschließlich, mit*
IOU I Owe You *Schuldanerkenntnis, Schuldschein*
K thousand *tausend*
lb(s) pound(s) [weight] *Pfund [0,454 kg]*
L/C (also l/c or l.c.) letter of credit *Akkreditiv*
m million(s) *Million(en)*
max maximum *Höchst-*
MD Managing Director *Geschäftsführer*
min. minimum *Mindest-*
misc miscellaneous *Verschiedenes*
mpg miles per gallon *Meilen pro Gallone*
mph miles per hour *Meilen pro Stunde*
mtg(s) meeting(s) *Treffen, Konferenz(en)*
n/a non-applicable; not available *nicht zutreffend; nicht verfügbar*
no. (nos) number(s) *Nummer(n), Nr.*
nwt net weight *Nettogewicht*
oz ounce(s) [weight] *Unze(n) [28,35 g]*
p.a. *pro Jahr*
PA personal assistant
P/A power of attorney *Vertretungsvollmacht*
pd paid *bezahlt*
pls please *bitte*
p.m. *nachmittags* (➜ **a.m.**)
PO Box post office box *Postfach*
pp on behalf of *im Auftrag (i. A.)*
P&P postage and packing *Porto und Verpackung*
PS postscript *Postskriptum, Nachsatz*
pt(s) part(s) *Teil(e)*
PTO please turn over *bitte wenden (b. w.)*
qtly quarterly *vierteljährlich*
Rd Road *Straße (Str.)*
R&D research and development *Forschung und Entwicklung*
recd received *erhalten*
ref. reference *Bezug, Bezugszeichen*
reg(d). registered *eingetragen; eingeschrieben [Post]*
rep representative *Vertreter/in*
ro-ro roll-on roll-off *von Straßenfahrzeugen befahrbar [Schiff]*
RRP recommended retail price *unverbindliche Preisempfehlung*
sae stamped addressed envelope *frankierter und adressierter Rückumschlag*
S/N shipping note(s) *Schiffszettel, Warenbegleitschein(e)*
sq square *Quadrat(-)*
Sq. Square *Platz*
St Street *Straße*
SWIFT Society for Worldwide Interbank Financial Telecommunication *Gesellschaft für internationalen Bankverkehr*
TM trademark *(eingetragenes) Warenzeichen*
VAT value added tax *Mehrwertsteuer (MwSt.)*
via by way of [named place] *über [Ortsangabe]*
vol. volume *Volumen; Band [Buch]*
WB waybill *Frachtbrief*
wk(s) week(s) *Woche(n)*
yd(s) **yard(s)** [length] *Yard(s) [91,4 cm]*

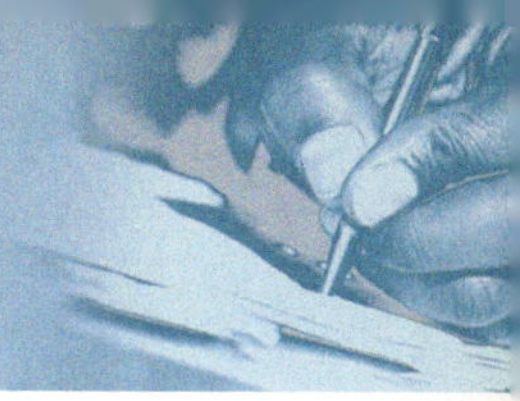

Exam practice

1 Reading

THE PERFECT MARKET PLACE

When Peter Omidyar set up eBay in 1995, he intended it to be a 'perfect market place' which would allow anyone to buy and sell almost anything by auction online. The market price would be decided purely by the highest bid that competing buyers were willing to make.

This is exactly what has happened. The system Omidyar created is just as available to the individual who wants to sell unwanted presents as it is to a company like IBM when it needs to get rid of excess stock.

Today, eBay is a global market place, or rather a series of over 30 different regional market places. Together, the 135 million members registered globally are trading around 35 million items at any one time. In Britain, eBay's third biggest market after the US and Germany, there are now well over 10,000 people who make their full-time living through eBay. The most successful of these are known as 'powersellers' by eBay staff, and some of them sell goods worth well over £1 million per year.

It seems hard to believe that the system works as well as it does. After all, it requires users to trust that people who they have never seen will send both goods and payments correctly and honestly. In the early days, Omidyar himself wrote about this to members. He said: 'Some people are dishonest. But we'll drive them away ... This grand hope depends on your active participation ... Use our feedback forum. Give praise where it is due; make complaints where appropriate.'

There *are* risks of fraud, but generally this feedback forum is very effective. Members rate everyone they trade with, whether as buyers or sellers. They state publicly for all to see whether their experience was positive, negative or neutral and can then add other relevant comments. This works well for someone like Ray Bolton, one of those 10,000 Britons who make their living on eBay. His 99.5% positive feedback ratings plus excellent reviews by over 2,000 satisfied customers mean that he can be sure of new customers who are willing to trust him and the sports equipment he sells. (349 words)

Annotations 35 fraud *Betrug* 36 to rate *beurteien, einstufen* 45 review *Rezension, Kritik*

A Comprehension

1 What differences are there between a traditional auction of expensive old pictures and auctions on eBay?
2 What is a 'powerseller' (line 22)?
3 What are you supposed to do after both selling and buying something on eBay? What sort of things are people supposed to say when they do this?
4 What effect is this meant have on people who behave dishonestly? And on people who are honest?

B Meaning from context

Explain the following in your own words:

the highest bid (line 5)
unwanted present (line 10)
make their full-time living (line 20)
give praise where it is due (line 33)
satisfied customers (line 45)

C Summary

Summarize the text in approximately 100 words.

D Comment

'The true value of anything is the maximum amount that people will pay for it.'
Write what you think. Give your comment a title.

2 Business letter: writing a complaint (wrong delivery of goods)

Situation:

Sie sind Einkäufer/in beim Versandhaus Techno Innovations, Breite Str. 7, 52076 Aachen, und haben vor einiger Zeit unter Bestellnummer BX 1056 beim japanischen Hersteller Konocam, 43 Toranomon, Tokyo 103, Fax 03-356789, sechstausend Fotodrucker bestellt, und zwar: 3.000 Stück Modell Easy-Digicam und 3.000 Stück Modell Pro-Digicam. Die Sendung traf gestern ein, geliefert wurden 6.000 Pro-Digicams.

Ihre Aufgabe:

- Schreiben Sie unter dem heutigen Datum einen unterschriftsreifen Brief (Diktatzeichen nach eigener Wahl) an den Exportleiter von Konocam, Mr M. Sasaki, persönlich; Fax-Kopie des Briefes vorab (Vorwahl Japan: 0081).
- Beziehen Sie sich auf den Auftrag und fügen Sie Kopie der Auftragsbestätigung als Anlage bei.
- Schildern Sie die Situation und betonen Sie, dass beide Modelle im aktuellen Versandkatalog angeboten werden, und dass Sie sich gerade vom billigeren Easy-Digicam gute Geschäfte versprechen.
- Fordern Sie Konocam höflich aber unmissverständlich auf, sofort die fehlenden Easy-Digicams per Luftfracht kostenfrei abzusenden, da Ihnen andernfalls erhebliche Verluste drohen.
- Versanddaten der Ersatzlieferung bitte umgehend per Fax oder E-Mail mitteilen.
- Bitten Sie um Auskunft darüber, ob die überzähligen 3.000 Pro-Digicams zu Lasten Konocams zurückgesandt werden sollen oder ob dafür ein substanzieller Preisnachlass gewährt werden kann.
- Weisen Sie abschließend nochmals auf die Dringlichkeit der Angelegenheit hin und bitten Sie um sofortige Erledigung.

3 Mediation

You work for a small company, Classic Models GmbH, that makes high-quality 1:20 scale models of classic cars. CM has never exported before, but this situation may soon change. Today, Mr Mori, an interested buyer from the up-market Shinsei Japanese department store chain is visiting the company. You have to show Mr Mori round and translate. He speaks English, but some of CM's senior staff do not. Write your part of these two conversations.

Conversation with Sales Manager, Frau Hohner (1)

FRAU HOHNER	Bitte sagen Sie Herrn Mori, dass wir ihn sehr gern in unserem Haus begrüßen und alles tun werden um ihn zu unterstützen.
YOU	*Mr Mori, Frau Hohner wants me to tell you* ________________
MR MORI	Well, could you first of all thank Frau Hohner for being so helpful. And please also say that all of us in Shinsei Sales and Marketing find the Klassiker Wagen products very attractive. If the price is right, they should sell very well through Shinsei, which has department stores in all the major cities of Japan.
YOU	*Herr Mori möchten Ihnen danken für* ________________

MR MORI	And now concerning an initial trial order, I'd like Frau Hohner to quote us for a mixed selection of 5,000 Mercedes, Bugatti, Rolls Royce and Cadillac classics, CIF Yokohama, along with the earliest possible delivery date.
YOU	______________

Conversation with Production Manager, Herr Blek (2)

HERR BLEK	Bitte sagen Sie Herrn Mori, dass ich alle seine Fragen nach der Arbeit hier in unserem Werk sehr gern beantworten werde.
YOU	*Herr Blek says that* ______________
MR MORI	Please first of all thank him for finding time to see me. And could you also say that everyone at Shinsei loves the close attention to detail and the high quality of production that you manage to achieve here at Classic Models.
YOU	______________
MR MORI	Could you ask Herr Blek whether the company carries out the complete production process here at this factory, or whether parts are bought in from outside suppliers? I'd also like to ask him if the models are assembled by hand, or whether the whole production process is automated.
YOU	______________

EXAM B

1 Business letter: writing a complaint (poor quality of goods)

Situation:

Sie arbeiten für die Sportspro GmbH in Düsseldorf. Alle Mitarbeiter haben persönliche E-Mail-Adressen. Ihr Vorgesetzter, Einkaufsleiter Bernd Gehler (gehler.b@sportspro.de), teilt Ihnen mit, dass soeben eine Sendung Skateboards aus den USA eingetroffen ist, die fehlerhafte Stücke enthält. Sie sollen mit Lagerleiter Alex Pesch die Einzelheiten klären und bei Susan Carter (s.carter@mountmaistro.co) per E-Mail eine Ersatzlieferung anfordern. Kopien an Gehler und Pesch.

Ihre Aufgabe:

Aus Ihrem Gespräch mit dem Lagerleiter ergibt sich, dass in Lieferung NC-105DRLT2 des Herstellers Mount Maistro von 600 Boards 152 Stück wegen Qualitätsmängeln (Kratzern) unverkäuflich sind. Die Verpackungen weisen keine Beschädigungen auf.

An:	…
Cc:	…
Betreff:	…

- Übernehmen Sie das E-Mail-Formular und schreiben Sie an Susan Carter.
- Susan Carter ist Ihnen persönlich bekannt. Wählen Sie eine entsprechende Anrede.
- Beziehen Sie sich auf die Lieferung und erklären Sie den Sachverhalt.
- Fordern Sie, weil die Sommersaison bevorsteht und Ihnen zahlreiche Bestellungen vorliegen, eine dringende Ersatzlieferung per Luftfracht Flughafen Düsseldorf an. Flugdaten bitte per E-Mail mitteilen.
- Die fehlerhaften Skateboards werden demnächst per Seefracht unfrei an Mount Maistro zurückgeschickt.
- Bitten Sie im Interesse zukünftiger Geschäftsbeziehungen um Maßnahmen, die eine Wiederholung solcher Vorfälle von vornherein ausschließen.
- Bedanken Sie sich im Voraus für die umgehende Bearbeitung der Angelegenheit.
- Wählen Sie eine angemessene Grußformel.

2 Listening: Kevin Costello's job

Kevin Costello is being interviewed about his job.

2.29
2.30

A **Listen to Part 1.**
Write short answers to these questions. Then listen again and check your answers.

1 What is Kevin's present job title?
2 What sort of company is ValueDirect?
3 What sort of goods does it sell?
4 What qualification did Kevin get after he left school?
5 Before he joined ValueDirect, where was Kevin's main work experience?

B **Listen to Part 2.**
Write short answers to these questions. Then listen again and check your answers.

1 What connection is there between the BBC and ValueDirect?
2 What does Kevin do at ValueDirect?
3 Describe what a ValueDirect co-branded website is. What is its purpose?
4 What are the two main attractions of the website to the target audience?

Annotations staff *Mitarbeiter* set up with BT *mit BT zusammengeschlossen* access *Zugang*

3 Mediation

You work in the sales team at ValueDirect's new company in Germany, and you are at a trade fair. Your boss is meeting clients, and the only senior person with you is Kevin Costello. (He is there to help set up the new German company.) Herr Kline of Mediavision, a large media company, comes to the stand and is very interested in doing business. Neither he nor Kevin speaks the other's language, so you have to translate. Write your part of the conversation.

HERR KLINE Bitte fragen Sie Herrn Costello, ob ValueDirect daran interessiert ist mit Mediavision Geschäfte zu machen.

YOU Herr Kline would like to know if ____________________

K COSTELLO Well, please tell Herr Kline that we'd be very interested in working with his organization. Could you ask him whether Mediavision has ever offered its staff anything like this before?

YOU Er sagt, dass er sehr daran interessiert wäre, ____________________

HERR KLINE Bitte sagen Sie ihm, dass das etwas Neues für uns wäre. Deshalb wäre es wichtig für ValueDirect, herzukommen und uns das Konzept persönlich vorzustellen.

YOU Herr Kline says that ____________________

K COSTELLO Yes, naturally, we'd be very happy to do that at any time. Please apologize to Herr Kline for the fact that our German manager is in meeting at the moment. Ask him if he would like him to visit Mediavision. Ask him to suggest a date.

YOU ____________________

HERR KLINE Eine kurze Präsentation in unserer Zentrale wäre die beste Idee. Wenn möglich, am Ende unserer nächsten Konferenz der Unternehmensleitung am 3. April.

YOU ____________________

K COSTELLO Right, Monday 3rd April. Please ask what time that will be, and how long we will have.

YOU ____________________

HERR KLINE	Wir sollten die Konferenz gegen 16 Uhr beendet haben. Sagen wir, von 16 bis 17 Uhr.
YOU	______________
K COSTELLO	OK. Please tell Herr Kline that I'll pass these details on to our German manager, as soon as he comes back. If he could leave contact details, I'm sure he'll call him immediately.
YOU	______________

EXAM C

1 Reading

JOBS TOMORROW

ACROSS AMERICA, Europe and Japan, millions of workers fear losing their jobs as these are either automated or outsourced – and very often sent offshore to parts of the world where the work can be done more cheaply. This applies not only to factory jobs, but also to skilled jobs in areas such as IT.

The numbers are large, too. A recent survey by the University of California estimates that 14 million Americans – 11% of the workforce – are in jobs that are at risk.

Is this a new fear though? Perhaps the speed and scale of change are, but not the fear itself. Since English workers first destroyed machines in factories two centuries ago during the early Industrial Revolution, people have faced and often fought the uncertainty and danger of change.

However, the fear is often worse than it needs to be. People always forget that job-destroying changes open the way to new jobs that never existed before. Machines and/or foreign workers do the old work more cheaply, costs and prices fall, and this frees us to answer new needs and demands with fresh goods and services that require new skills and create new jobs.

To prove the point, economist William Nordhaus has shown that over 70% of goods and services that were consumed at the start of this century were completely unrelated to those that were in demand a century earlier. Would any tough pioneer farmer in late 19th-century America even have dreamed that his country would need 104,000 flower designers just over 100 years later? Or that the number of people in his own industry would shrink from 43% of the national workforce to well under 2%?

People back then could hardly imagine modern communications, transport or medicine – and the jobs they would create. And it is the same today, although, if we look carefully, we can already see much of the shape of things to come. We can see, for example, that the Internet is creating new businesses daily. And it is clear that the problems of global warming and climate change are also great opportunities for new technologies – and new jobs. (353 words)

A Comprehension

1 How does the author show that the fear of job losses through industrial change is not new?
2 Why is the fear unnecessary?
3 What is surprising about the difference between consumption in 1900 and in 2000?
4 Looking to the future, where will new job creation come from?

B Meaning from context

Explain the following in your own words:

automated (line 3)
outsourced (line 3)
jobs that are at risk (line 11)
shrink from (line 35)
the shape of things to come (line 41)

C Summary

Summarize the text in approximately 100 words.

D **Comment**

'The law should stop German businesses from moving offshore.'
Write what you think. Give your comment a title.

E **Dictation**

Check your work carefully in this order: overall meaning, grammatical forms, spelling, punctuation and capital letters. (Dictation text on page 215)

2 Business letter: answering a complaint about quality

Situation:

Übernehmen Sie die Rolle von Susan Carter aus *Exam practice B1*. Ms Carter (s.carter@mountmaistro.co) hat den Sachverhalt bezüglich der Lieferung von 152 fehlerhaften Skateboards in Sendung NC-105DRLT2 geprüft und schickt als Antwort eine E-Mail an Bernd Gehler, den Einkaufsleiter der Firma in Düsseldorf (gehler.b@sportspro.de). Kopie für den Produktionsleiter bei Mount Maistro, Mario Silvestrini.

Ihre Aufgabe:

To:	...
Cc:	...
From:	...

- Übernehmen Sie das E-Mail-Formular.
- Susan Carter und Bernd Gehler kennen sich seit längerem. Wählen Sie eine entsprechende Anrede.
- Ms Carter hat den Sachverhalt sofort geprüft und entschuldigt sich für die Unannehmlichkeiten.
- Sie hat umgehend in ihrer Produktionsabteilung 200 Skateboards bestellt, die einer besonderen Qualitätskontrolle zugeführt werden.
- Diese Menge wird sobald wie überhaupt möglich per Luftfracht-Express ausgeliefert. Flugdaten und Ankunftszeit folgen per E-Mail, Versandkosten entstehen Sportspro selbstverständlich nicht.
- Für den Fall, dass Sportspro noch weitere fehlerhafte Skateboards finden sollte, wurde die Ersatzlieferung vorsorglich auf 200 Einheiten erhöht.
- Die Qualitätsmängel in der ursprünglichen Lieferung wurden durch einen Produktionsfehler verursacht, der inzwischen behoben worden ist.
- Susan Carter bringt nochmals ihr Bedauern über den Vorfall zum Ausdruck und versichert, dass sie alles tun wird um die Ersatzlieferung zu beschleunigen.
- Wählen Sie eine angemessene Grußformel.

1 Reading

TOURISM AND DEVELOPMENT

As we continue to travel abroad in ever-greater numbers, international tourism has become a huge world industry. The World Travel and Tourism Council reports that tourism and related activities now employ 200 million people and produce over 10% of the world's income. As for tourists themselves, numbers are predicted to rise from 700 million in 2004 to 1,400 million by 2020.

Moreover, people are travelling much farther now. Sri Lanka, Mexico and Gambia are no longer just for the rich or the brave young backpacker. Thanks to the dramatic fall in the cost of flying, nearly everyone can get there. In many such places, visitor numbers have multiplied in the last decade.

These locations are often in poorer parts of the world. Of the top 20 long-haul destinations, 14 are in developing countries. For places like these, tourism offers the possibility of employment, infrastructure development and economic growth that could hardly be created in any other way.

However, the news is often not all good. Benefits can be quickly lost by negative effects on the local environment. Fragile coastal ecosystems may for instance be destroyed by over-development along the beaches, and tourist hotels may take vital water resources from local farmers.

Local people may lose out in other ways, too. Today's travel companies often own every part of the holiday service – from the travel agent to the airline to the hotel and even to the local transport company that gets visitors there. This provides low-paid local employment, but it prevents local business from developing and winning more of the tourist euro, dollar or pound for the community.

Some people believe that we ought simply to stop taking long, environmentally damaging flights to exotic locations. (A single passenger on a return flight from London to East Africa causes more global warming through CO_2 emissions than the average driver does in a year.) Others are less hardline, saying that when we travel, we should at least try to create benefits. This means choosing tour operators with a responsible travel policy aimed at avoiding damage to the local environment and community. Ideally the company should also provide financial support for local conservation and community projects, and work with local businesses to help spread the economic advantages of tourism.

As consumers of tourism, we all have choices, and responsible tourism is surely the choice that we should make. (394 words)

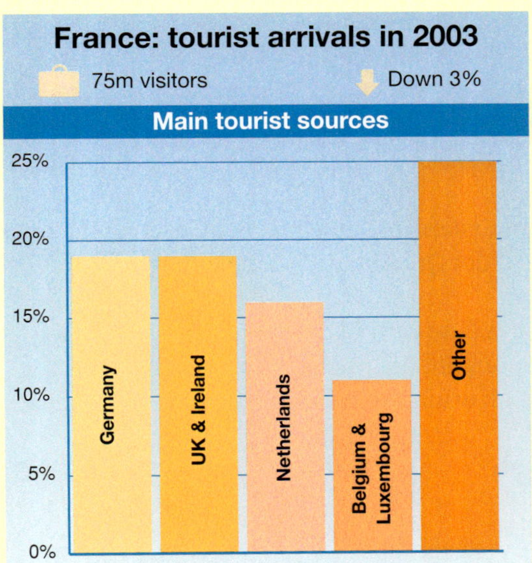

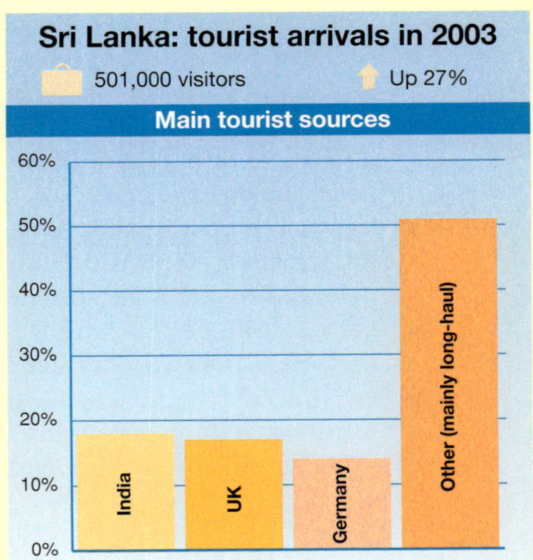

Annotations 8 to predict *vorhersagen* 18 long-haul *Langstrecken(-Ziele)*

A Comprehension

1 In what two important ways has international tourism been changing in recent years?
2 Which of these two trends is supported by the charts? Explain.
3 What benefits can tourism bring to poorer economies?
4 What environmental problems can long-haul tourism cause?
5 What questions could you ask your tour operator to find out whether they have a responsible policy?

B Meaning from context

Explain the following in your own words:

in ever-greater numbers (line 1)
infrastructure (line 21)
exotic locations (line 42)
hardline (line 46)
consumers of tourism (line 55)

C Summary

Summarize the text in approximately 100 words.

D Comment

'Forget holidays abroad! We've got our own wonderful country to explore.' Write what you think. Give your comment a title.

2 Business letter: delay in payment

Situation:

Sie arbeiten als Finanzbuchhalter/in für die System AG, 51145 Köln, Bonner Str. 123. Ihr Unternehmen hat im März mit Rechnung SP1534/1NM erstmals Büromöbel an die Firma Office Impact Ltd, 17-19 Clifton Street, Bristol, BR3 7DH, geliefert. Der Rechnungsbetrag von € 4.947,00 war am 07. April fällig, ging aber nicht ein. Am 2. Mai schickten Sie der Einkaufsleiterin bei Office Impact, Ms A. Parkes, eine Zahlungserinnerung per E-Mail und erfuhren, die Zahlung sei auf dem Weg. Heute ist der 15. Mai, und der Betrag steht immer noch aus.

Ihre Aufgabe:

- Schreiben Sie unter dem Datum des 15. Mai einen unterschriftsreifen Brief (Diktatzeichen nach eigener Wahl) zu Händen von Ms A. Parkes.
- Beziehen Sie sich auf den Vorgang, schildern Sie den Stand der Dinge und fügen Sie als Anlage eine Kopie der Rechnung bei.
- Erinnern Sie Frau Parkes an ihre Antwort auf die E-Mail und bringen Sie Ihre Enttäuschung darüber zum Ausdruck, dass der Rechnungsbetrag bis heute nicht eingegangen ist.
- Vielmehr hatten Sie gehofft, dass dem Erstauftrag eine längere Geschäftsbeziehung folgen würde, zumal Office Impact mit der Qualität der Möbel offenbar zufrieden ist, denn Beschwerden liegen keine vor.
- Setzen Sie für den Eingang des Betrages eine Frist bis zum Ende des Monats, andernfalls sehen Sie sich leider gezwungen, rechtliche Schritte einzuleiten.
- Falls die Zahlung zwischenzeitlich doch erfolgt sein sollte, betrachte man dieses Schreiben bitte als gegenstandslos.
- Schließen Sie den Brief angemessen ab.

Anhang

Partner pages

Unit 1, exercise 4, p.34

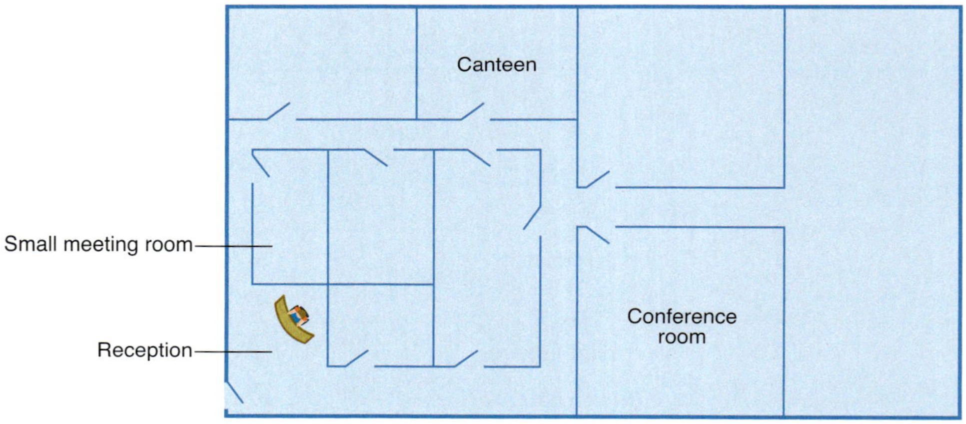

Unit 3, exercise 9, p.58

The commuter

- You know public transport services are very bad. (Quote figures from the Factsheet on page 58.)
- Add that if the Council had invested properly during the last 50 years, Manchester would not be in such a mess.
- You want big improvements to present transport services before you talk about congestion charging.
- You especially want the tram system to be extended. It covers only a small part of the city at the moment.
- Without these improvements, public transport could not cope with all the extra commuters if the city introduced congestion charging. A cut in road traffic would double the numbers of people using public transport.
- If public transport is improved, congestion charging might not be necessary.

The businessperson

- You want big improvements to present transport services before you talk about congestion charging.
- Car parking in Manchester is already very expensive. Congestion charging on top of this would destroy many businesses. (Quote figures for London from BACKGROUND BRIEFING, page 52.)
- Business would suffer more than in London because people would spend their money in the many other towns near Manchester, such as Trafford. Manchester would become an economic desert. (This would of course answer the traffic congestion problem!)

The Ministry of Transport official

- You accept that congestion charging creates some problems. (See BACKGROUND BRIEFING, page 52.)
- But you believe that fast action is necessary, and that congestion charging must be part of the solution to the problem (even if it hurts some people for a few years).
- Your Ministry will give Manchester most of the money necessary to extend the tram system (about £90m at present estimates), but *only* if Manchester first introduces congestion charging.

The city councillor (chairperson)

- You are the chairperson and must allow everybody to speak in turn.
- You know something must be done, but you are not yet sure what.
- You basically support congestion charging, but you worry that it could cause even greater problems than Manchester already has.
- In particular, you understand the danger to businesses. So if you introduce congestion charging, it must cover the whole area within the M60 – a big technical challenge, because this is much larger than the London zone.
- You badly want the money from the Ministry of Transport.
- You have to help the meeting find a compromise that everyone can agree to.

Unit 5, exercise 7, page 77

A You are yourself. You are having a short interview at a temping agency, FastFind, for a part-time or a temporary holiday job.

1. Be ready to give personal and contact details: name, address, date of birth, mobile and/or landline numbers, email address and when you can be contacted.
2. Be ready to explain your present situation, and when you can work, e.g. for six weeks during the summer, on Saturday mornings.
3. Think of jobs you would be happy to do, e.g. shop assistant, waiter/waitress, office assistant, factory worker. Ask if the agency can help.

B You work at FastFind, a temping agency which specialises in part-time and holiday jobs.

1. Request and write down personal and contact details.
2. Ask when **A** can work.
3. Ask what sort of work **A** would be happy to do.
4. Tell **A** that you think the agency certainly can help. Invent and give details of particular jobs to fit **A**'s interests and available time.

Unit 7, exercise 9, p.98

The developer

Don't say this, but your company has had a bad year, and you must get this project or many people will lose their jobs – you included!

Use real information from your own knowledge to support the development. Explain the social and/or economic benefits of the project, e.g. better infrastructure, improvement to the local economy, new jobs, a better life for ordinary people.

Accept that there are negative aspects – there always are in any project – but emphasize that the benefits are much more important.

A protester

Use real information from your own knowledge to attack the development. Explain the social, economic and/or environmental problems with the project, e.g. no real economic or social benefits to the community, pressure on infrastructure through overdevelopment, damage to wildlife.

Accept that there are certain advantages, but show that the problems are much bigger than these.

The local planning officer (chairperson)

Use real information from your own knowledge to question both the developer and the protester carefully.

At the end, you must decide whether to allow the development or not. Be ready to explain the reasons for your decision and to defend it.

Begleitgrammatik

Übersicht

1 Das simple present

Form

- Mit Ausnahme der **3. Person Singular** ist die Form des **simple present** immer dieselbe. Sie gleicht dem Infinitiv (Grundform). Bei Vollverben endet die **3. Person Singular** immer auf *-s*. Die **Schreibregeln** für das Anhängen von *-s* entsprechen denen der Pluralbildung:
  – Alison **works** in Glasgow. She normally **finishes** work at 5.
- Ist kein anderes Hilfsverb bzw. eine Form von *be* im Satz vorhanden, dann bilden wir die **Verneinung** und **Fragen** mit *do/does*:
  – Ted **can't attend** the meeting today.
  – **Would you like** a cup of coffee?
  – I'm sorry. We **do not accept** cheques.
  – **Does** the firm **pay** a Christmas bonus?

Gebrauch

- Wir verwenden das **simple present**, um **andauernde Situationen** und **ständig wiederkehrende Ereignisse** auszudrücken:
  – ASM **develops** software for industry.
  – We often **work** on Saturdays.
- Daher kommen die folgenden **Zeitadverbien** mit dem **simple present** häufig vor:
  always, often, normally, generally, usually, regularly, sometimes, occasionally, now and then, seldom, never, every day/week/month/…, on Mondays/…

2 Das present progressive

Form

- Wir bilden das **present progressive** mit *am/is/are* und der *-ing*-Form des Vollverbs:
  – Mary is lucky. She**'s working** for her uncle in the USA.
  – Some volunteers **are cleaning** parks in London.
- Die **Verneinung** wird mit *not/n't* und **Fragen** werden durch Umstellung gebildet:
  – This product **isn't selling** well.
  – **Are** you **enjoying** your new job?

Gebrauch

- Wir verwenden das **present progressive** um zu sagen, was **im Moment des Sprechens** oder Schreibens tatsächlich passiert (‚Gleichzeitigkeit'):

- Wendy **is writing** a letter **at the moment**.
- **At present**, we **are looking for** staff.

■ Daher kommt das **present progressive** mit den folgenden **Zeitadverbien** häufig vor: *at present, at the moment, currently* (gegenwärtig), *now*

■ Wir verwenden das **present progressive** auch für **zeitweilige Ausnahmen**:
- We normally **close** at Christmas, but we **are staying** open this year.

! **Beachten Sie**:
Folgende Verben haben **keine progressive form**:
believe, hate, know, like, love, mean (bedeuten), *notice, see, seem, think* (= meinen), *understand, want, wish*

3 Das simple past

Form

■ Alle Personen des **simple past** der regelmäßigen Verben enden auf *-ed*:
- ASM **developed** this computer program specially for us.

■ Viele gängige Verben sind **unregelmäßig**. Diese Verben müssen einfach auswendig gelernt werden (➜ **Unregelmäßige Verben**, s. Seite 263):
- The boss **spoke** to Ted last week because he **went** home early.

■ Gibt es kein anderes Hilfsverb im Satz, bilden wir die **Verneinung** und **Fragen** mit *did*:
- They **did not deliver** the goods on time.
- **Did** Jane **get** the job?

Gebrauch

■ Wir verwenden das **simple past**, um **abgeschlossene** Handlungen in der Vergangenheit zu schildern:
- Simon **worked** as a waiter in Italy **last year**.
- Odile **took** a job in London **in 2004**.

■ Daher gebrauchen wir oft eine **Zeitangabe** wie: *yesterday, the day before yesterday, last week/month/Christmas, two/three months/years ago, in 1999, when she was a girl* … usw.

4 Das past progressive

Form

■ Wir bilden das **past progressive** mit *was/were* und der *-ing*-Form des Vollverbs:
- We **were playing** computer games when the boss came in.

■ Die **Verneinung** wird mit *not/n't* und **Fragen** werden durch Umstellung gebildet:
- I **wasn't** just **helping**. I was doing everything.
- **Were** they **working** when you saw them?

Gebrauch

■ Wir verwenden das **past progressive**, wenn wir ausdrücken wollen, dass eine (oder mehrere) Handlung(en) zu einem bestimmten **Zeitpunkt**:
- Odile **was working** in London on her birthday.

oder während eines bestimmten **Zeitraumes**:
- Ann and Jim **were attending** a computer course all last month.

in der Vergangenheit im Gange war(en).

■ Wir verwenden das **past progressive** auch um auszudrücken, dass eine Handlung im Gange war, als ein neues Ereignis (plötzlich) eintrat:
- When the visitors arrived, nobody **was waiting** to welcome them.

5 Das present perfect

Form

■ Das **present perfect** bilden wir mit *have/has* und der **3. Form** (Partizip Perfekt) des Vollverbs:
- ASM **has received** a big order for software from China.
- We **have sold** our old machines to Pakistan.

■ Die **Verneinung** und **Fragen** werden wie folgt gebildet:
- Alison **hasn't finished** the report yet.
- **Have** you **found** a new assistant yet?

Gebrauch

■ Wir verwenden das **present perfect** für **nicht abgeschlossene Handlungen**, die in der Vergangenheit angefangen haben, aber noch andauern:
- VW **has invested** millions in Seat and Skoda **for years**. (*for* + Zeitdauer)
- We **have taken** on 11 new workers **since May**. (*since* + Zeitpunkt)

■ Möchten wir ausdrücken, dass irgendetwas geschehen ist, **ohne den genauen Zeitpunkt des Ereignisses** zu nennen, verwenden wir auch das **present perfect**:

– European companies **have lost** a lot of market share to the Chinese.

- Wollen wir ausdrücken, dass etwas **gerade passiert** und noch aktuell ist, gebrauchen wir ebenfalls das **present perfect**:
  – Ted can't come to work this week. He **has broken** his leg.

6 Das present perfect progressive

Form

- Das **present perfect progressive** bilden wir mit *have/has + been + -ing*-Form des Vollverbs.
  – I **have been waiting** for you since 5 o'clock.
- Wir bilden die **Verneinung** durch das Einfügen von *not* unmittelbar nach *have/has*.
  – They **have not been working** all the time.
- Wollen wir **Fragen** bilden, tauschen wir *have/has* und das Subjekt einfach aus.
  – **Have** you **been waiting** long?

Gebrauch

- Wir verwenden das *present perfect progressive* für **länger andauernde** Handlungen und Situationen, die zum Zeitpunkt des Sprechens noch andauern.

Tipp: Im Deutschen verwenden wir in solchen Fällen meist das Präsens mit ‚schon', um zu verdeutlichen, dass die Handlung bzw. Situation bereits länger andauert:

– Mark **has been working** for nearly ten hours.
Mark arbeitet schon seit fast zehn Stunden.

– Clare and Joe **have been writing** reports the whole time.
Clare und Joe schreiben schon die ganze Zeit Berichte.

7 Das will future

Form

- Das **will future** bilden wir mit *will* und dem Infinitiv des Vollverbs. Es hat dieselbe Form für alle Personen.
- Die **Verneinung** wird mit *will not/won't* und **Fragen** werden durch Umstellung gebildet:
  – The boss **will not/won't pay** us more money.
  – **Will** you **be** at the party on Friday, Christine?

! **Beachten Sie**:
Die **Kurzform** von *will not* ist *won't*.

Gebrauch

Wir verwenden das **will future** für

- zukünftige Situationen und Ereignisse, die unausweichlich eintreten werden:
  – The firm **will be** 100 years old on 10 September next year.
- Vermutungen, Hoffnungen und Erwartungen:
  – Of course we hope that we **will get** the order.
  – I expect I **will see** you again before I leave for Japan.
- spontane, unüberlegte Entscheidungen:
  – I've got a great idea. **I'll ask** Thomas to help me.

8 Das going to future

Form

- Das **going to future** bilden wir mit *am/is/are + going to +* Infinitiv des Vollverbs:
  – We **are going to invest** in a new factory in Poland.
  – I think it **is going to rain** in a minute.
- Die **Verneinung** wird mit *not* und **Fragen** werden durch Umstellung gebildet:
  – We **aren't going to move** after all.
  – **Are** you **going to apply** for the job?

Gebrauch

- Wir verwenden das **going to future** für Pläne und Absichten:
  – Alex **is going to use** Jeff's garage in York Street.

  Ereignisse, die in der nahen Zukunft unmittelbar bevorstehen:
  – Business is so bad that some workers **are going to lose** their jobs.

! **Beachten Sie**:
Der Gebrauch von *will* und *going to* hängt in gewissem Maße von der Absicht bzw. Sichtweise des Sprechers ab. Dies gilt insbesondere für *going to*. Daher ist es im Zweifelsfall ratsam, das neutralere *will* zu verwenden.

9 Das present progressive mit zukünftiger Bedeutung

- Häufig verwenden wir das **present progressive** mit einem **Adverb der zukünftigen Zeit**, um über **schon entschiedene** Pläne, Verabredungen und Vorkehrungen zu sprechen:
  – I **am starting** my new job **next Monday**.
  – Christine **is flying** to Spain **in a few days**.

10 Das simple present mit zukünftiger Bedeutung

- Wie im Deutschen verwenden wir auch im Englischen das **simple present** für **fest terminierte** Vorgänge und Ereignisse (Fahrpläne, Kinoprogramme usw.):
  - I'll be late **tonight**. The only bus **leaves at 8 p.m.**

11 Das past perfect

Form

- Wir bilden das **past perfect** bei allen Personen mit *had* und der **3. Form** (Partizip Perfekt) des Vollverbs:
  - We couldn't start until the visitors **had arrived**.
  - The company did well after it **had introduced** its new models.
- Die **Verneinung** wird mit *not* und **Fragen** werden durch Umstellung gebildet:
  - I **hadn't been** here long before I got a raise.
  - **Had** Helen already **left** when you arrived?

Gebrauch

- Wir verwenden das **past perfect**, wenn wir verdeutlichen wollen, dass irgendetwas in der Vergangenheit bereits abgeschlossen war, als ein neues Ereignis eintrat:
  - When we **checked** the delivery, we found they **had sent** faulty goods.
  - After Sally **had finished** the letters, she **typed** some invoices.

12 Übersicht der modalen Hilfsverben

! Beachten Sie:
In vollständigen Sätzen steht im Englischen ein Hilfsverb nie ohne Vollverb:
- Mark **can speak** French. *Mark kann Französisch.*
- Sally **must leave** at 3. *Sally muss um 3 weg.*
- **May** I **go** home now? *Darf ich jetzt nach Hause?*

Notwendigkeit: must, have to

- Der Gebrauch von *must* entspricht dem des deutschen Modalverbs ‚müssen'. Da aber *must* nur im Präsens vorkommen, verwenden wir *have to* als ‚Ersatzverb' zur Bildung aller anderen Zeitformen:
  - The staff **must work** harder for less money. (Präsens)
  - Alex **had to borrow** a lot of money to buy cars. (Vergangenheit)
  - Alex **will have to pay** somebody to repair the cars. (Futur)

Keine Notwendigkeit: needn't, not have to

- Das Modalverb *needn't* entspricht dem deutschen ‚nicht müssen'. Wie bei *must* kommt auch *needn't* nur im Präsens vor. Zur Bildung anderer Zeiten gebrauchen wir *not have to*:
  - Alex **needn't get** an office. (Präsens)
  - I **didn't have to borrow** any money from the bank. (Vergangenheit)
  - Alex **won't have to employ** an office worker. (Futur)

Verbot: mustn't, not be allowed to

- Das Modalverb *mustn't* bedeutet ‚nicht dürfen'. Es drückt ein **Verbot** aus. Als Ersatzverb verwenden wir *not be allowed to*:
  - Firms **mustn't employ** illegal immigrants. (Präsens)
  - Tom **wasn't allowed to go** home early yesterday. (Vergangenheit)
  - I **won't be allowed to leave** my job immediately. (Futur)

Fähigkeit: can/could, be able to

- Ebenso wie ‚können' im Deutschen verwenden wir *can* im Englischen, um eine **Fähigkeit** auszudrücken. Genau wie *must* kann auch *can* nicht alle Zeiten bilden. Mit Ausnahme von *could* verwenden wir zur Bildung anderer Zeiten eine Form von *be able to*:
  - Simon **can speak** good Italian now.
  - He **couldn't speak** any Italian a year ago.
  - Birgit **will be able to join** Living World after 14 July.

Erlaubnis: can, may, be allowed to

- Die Modalverben *can* und *may* drücken auch eine **Erlaubnis** aus. Diese Bedeutung hat ebenfalls das Ersatzverb *be allowed to*:
  - You **can/may go** home now.
  - We **were allowed to go** home early yesterday.
  - Benny **will allow us to go** home early next Saturday.

Empfehlung: should, ought to

- Die Modalverben *should* und *ought to* haben die gleiche Bedeutung. Wie das deutsche Modalverben ‚sollten' drücken sie eine **Empfehlung** aus:
  - You **should/ought to stop** smoking, Brenda.
  - Jack **shouldn't/ought not to be** so rude to customers.

13 Zählbare und nicht zählbare Substantive

- Substantive mit einer Pluralform sind **zählbar**. Sie können mit Zahlen und dem unbestimmten Artikel *a/an* verwendet werden:
  - **Firms** are taking on more **workers** now.
- Substantive ohne eine Pluralform dagegen sind **nicht zählbar**. Sie können also nicht mit Zahlen und *a/an* verwendet werden:
  - Wholemeal **bread**, **muesli** and **yoghurt** are good for you.
- Möchten wir ein **nicht zählbares Substantiv** zählbar machen, dann müssen wir eine geeignete Mengenangabe hinzufügen:
  - I'll buy **two loaves of bread**, **a packet of muesli** and **a jar of honey**.
- Weitere geläufige **Mengenangaben** sind: *a bag of ..., a bar of ..., a bottle of ..., a box of ..., a can of ..., a cup of ..., a glass of ..., a pair of ..., a piece of ..., a slice of ..., a tin of ..., a tube of ..., a kilo of ..., a litre of ..., a pint of ..., a pound of ..., a tonne of ...*
- *Advice, information, news, progress* und *research* sind ebenfalls nicht zählbar und daher steht das Verb immer im Singular. Um diese Substantive zählbar zu machen, verwenden wir *a piece of ...* (formell) bzw. *a bit of ...* (weniger formell):
  - Please sit down. I'm afraid the **news is** not good.
  - We heard two interesting **bits/pieces of information** at the meeting.

14 Some/any und ihre Zusammensetzungen

- Wir verwenden *some* in **bejahten Aussagen** und *any* in **verneinten Aussagen** und **‚echten' Fragen**:
  - **Some American reseach** shows that organic food is very popular.
  - Organic farmers do not use **any chemical pesticides**.
  - Have you got **any brown eggs**, please?
- Drückt die Frage eine höfliche **Bitte** bzw. ein **Angebot** aus, auf die eine positive Antwort erwartet wird, verwenden wir ebenfalls *some*:

  A Can I have **some bread**, please?
  B Yes, of course.
  A Can I get you **some more coffee**, Ann?
  B Yes, please.

- Wir verwenden die Zusammensetzungen von *some* und *any* – also *somebody/someone, something, somewhere, anybody/anyone, anything* und *anywhere* – in genau derselben Art und Weise:
  - Ask **somebody/someone** what 'organic food' is and they'll tell you it's **something** that grows naturally.
  - Organic food is good for you. What can **anybody/anyone** have against that?
  - I can't find that letter **anywhere**.

15 Much, many, a lot of (lots of), plenty of/loads of

- Wir verwenden *many* mit **zählbaren** und *much* mit **nicht zählbaren** Substantiven in **verneinten Aussagen** und in **Fragen**:
  - We haven't got **many bananas**.
  - How **many eggs** did you buy?
  - We don't have **much food** because we ate so much last night.
  - How **much mineral water** have we got?
- In **bejahten Aussagen** verwenden wir *a lot of* bzw. *lots of* (weniger formell) mit **zählbaren** sowie **nicht zählbaren** Substantiven:
  - **A lot of/lots of supermarkets** sell organic food now.
- Möchten wir ‚mehr als genug' ausdrücken, verwenden wir *plenty of* bzw. *loads of* (weniger formell) mit **zählbaren** sowie mit **nicht zählbaren** Substantiven:
  - **Plenty of consumers** are happy to change to organic food.
  - Don't buy any bread. We've got **loads of rolls**.

16 Adjektive und Adverbien der Art und Weise

Wir verwenden **Adjektive**, um Personen und Sachen – also **Substantive** – näher zu beschreiben.
Wir stellen **Adjektive**

- vor ein **Substantiv**:
  - The **new government** wants to create **good jobs** for **young people**.
- nach einer Form von *be, become, get* (= werden) und *seem*, die *be* ersetzen können:
  - Susan **is absent** (*abwesend*) today because she **is ill**.
  - Don't ask Jack about his work. He immediately **becomes/gets angry**.

- nach *feel, look* (= aussehen), *taste, smell* und *sound*, die ein Gefühl bzw. eine Wahrnehmung ausdrücken:
  – A lot of Europeans **feel doubtful** about working in the service sector.
  – The office isn't a disco. You **look awful**.

Adverbien verwenden wir, um folgende Wortarten näher zu beschreiben:

- **Verben**
  – The new trainees **are working hard** for their exams at the moment.
- **Adjektive**
  – We will not accept the consignment unless it's **absolutely satisfactory**.
- **andere Adverbien**
  – Wages are rising **fairly steeply** in the USA because of a shortage of labour.
  – Last year, unemployment was **well over** 10% of the workforce.

17 Die Bildung von Adverbien

- In der Regel haben im Englischen Adjektive und Adverbien unterschiedliche Formen. Weitaus die meisten Adverbien werden durch das Anhängen von *-ly* an das entsprechende Adjektiv gebildet:
  – We **normally** work 38.5 hours a week.
  – The company is **unusually** busy just now.
  – Have you serviced the machine **regularly**?
- Die Adverbien *hard* und *fast* haben dieselbe Form wie das Adjektiv:
  – Only people who work **hard** get on in life.
  – We must work **fast** to finish the order today.
- Bei Adjektiven auf *-ly* – am wichtigsten *friendly, lively, lovely, silly* – verwenden wir die Umschreibung *in a(n) … way*, um das entsprechende Adverb zu bilden:
  – Answer the phone **in a friendly way**.
  – Don't behave **in** such **a silly way**.

! **Beachten Sie**:
Das Adverb von *good* ist *well*:
– Did you do **well** in the job interview?

18 Die Steigerung von Adjektiven und Adverbien

- **Einsilbige** Adjektive, **zweisilbige** Adjektive, die auf *-y* enden, und Adverbien, die **dieselbe Form** wie das entsprechende Adjektiv haben, werden auf *-er, -est* gesteigert:
  – Most consumers want **lower prices**. Discount shops are popular because they have the **lowest prices**.
  – Ben is so **lazy**. He's **lazier** than anybody else in the department. But he's also the **happiest**.
- **Mehrsilbige** Adjektive und Adverbien, die auf *-ly* enden, werden mit *more/most* gesteigert:
  – Continental Europeans find it **more difficult** to accept the service economy than the British do. What they find **most difficult** to accept is the low pay.
  – Carol works **more carefully** than Ben, but Alan works **most carefully** of all.

! **Beachten Sie** diese **unregelmäßigen** Steigerungen:

well	–	**better**	–	**best**
badly	–	**worse**	–	**worst**

19 Relativsätze mit *who/that, which/that*

- Wir verwenden **Relativsätze**, um den Hauptsatz durch zusätzliche Informationen genauer zu bestimmen:
  – The man **who spoke to me** is my boss**.**
  – The computer **which we ordered** has still not arrived.
- Für **Sachen** verwenden wir das Relativpronomen *which* bzw. *that* und für **Personen** *who* bzw. *that*:
  – The **boy who/that** got the job is my nephew.
  – The car **which/that** was stolen is an Audi.
- Um **Besitz** bzw. **Zugehörigkeit** anzuzeigen, setzen wir *whose* unmittelbar vor das Substantiv bei **Personen** sowie **Sachen**:
  – **Ted** is the manager **whose** job is at risk.
  – Is this the **computer whose** CD-drive is broken?

! **Beachten Sie:**
In folgenden Sätzen wird die Präposition ans Satzende gesetzt:
– He's **the man who/that** I had a drink **with**.
– Where's **the street which/that** we parked **in**?

20 Contact clauses

- Steht das Relativpronomen für das **Objekt** des Hauptsatzes, dann können wir es weglassen. Wir nennen solche Relativsätze **contact clauses**:
  – The person **who/that** dealt with you has left us.
  – The person (-)you dealt with has left us.

- The computer **that/which** failed cost €10,000.
- The computer (-) we bought cost €10,000.

21 Das Passiv

Form

- Das Passiv bilden wir mit einer Zeitform von *be* und der **3. Form** (Partizip Perfekt) des Vollverbs:
  - Export licences **are issued** by the government. (simple present)
  - New rules **are being introduced** about equal pay. (present progressive)
  - This computer **was imported** from the USA. (simple past)
  - The hotel we stayed in **was** still **being built**. (past progressive)
  - The machine **has been repaired** twice this week. (present perfect)
  - The machine **had been repaired** when we got to work. (past perfect)
  - The consignment **will be delivered** on Friday. (will future)
  - Some workers **are going to be sacked** on 31 May. (going to future)
- Mit **modalen Hilfsverben** ist das Muster:
  - Tickets **can be bought** on the train.
  - **Can** tickets **be bought** on the train?

Gebrauch

- Ist der **Verursacher** einer Handlung **unbekannt** oder **zweitrangig**, verwenden wir das **Passiv**. Das **Ergebnis** des Vorganges steht eindeutig im Vordergrund:
  - Fifty mobile phones were stolen last week.
  - Our new offices will be finished soon.
- Möchten wir den **Verursacher** doch angeben, verwenden wir *by*. Auch in solchen Passivsätzen steht die **Handlung** im Vordergrund:
  - The report was typed and sent out **by Carol** before she went home.
  - The new factory will be opened **by Prince Charles** at the end of May.

22 Bedingungssätze

Form

- Ein **Bedingungssatz** besteht aus **zwei** Teilen: dem ***if*-Teil** und dem **Hauptteil**. Der ***if*-Teil** drückt eine **Bedingung** aus, der **Hauptteil** eine **Folge**:

Bedingung	Folge
– If we get the order,	we will take on more staff.
– If business was better,	we would invest more in new machinery.

- Der ***if*-Teil** kann vor oder nach dem **Hauptteil** stehen. Steht er an erster Stelle, trennen wir die beiden Teile durch ein Komma:
  - If you don't work harder**,** you will lose your job.
  - You will lose your job if you don't work harder.
- Die **drei Typen** von Bedingungssätzen unterscheiden sich durch folgende **Zeitmuster**:

  I If + simple present + will future:
  - If we **invest** in new technology, we **will do** better.

  II If + simple past + *would* + Infinitiv:
  - If we **invested** in new technology, we **would do** better.

  III If + past perfect + *would have* + 3. Form (Partizip Perfekt):
  - If we **had invested** in new technology, we **would have done** better.

Gebrauch

- Wir verwenden **Bedingungssätze** gemäß der **Wahrscheinlichkeit** der zu erwartenden Folge:

  I Folge (fast) sicher:
  - If we invest in new technology, a lot of people will lose their jobs.

  II Folge theoretisch möglich, aber kaum wahrscheinlich:
  - If we invested in new technology, a lot of people would lose their jobs.

  III Folge unmöglich, da Ergebnis schon bekannt:
  - If we had invested in new technology, a lot of people would have lost their jobs.

23 Die indirekte Rede

Aussagesätze

- Wenn wir einem Dritten berichten möchten, was während eines Gespräches gesagt wurde, verwenden wir die **indirekte Rede**:
  - Diana said, 'My plane lands at Düsseldorf tomorrow at 3 o'clock.'
  - Diana said (that) her plane landed at Düsseldorf the next day at 3 o'clock.
- Wir verwenden hierfür ein **einleitendes Verb**, wie *answer, claim, mention, remind, say, think* usw., um zu verdeutlichen, dass wir berichten:
  - Jack **claimed** (that) he went home because he felt ill.
  - Diana **reminded us** (that) she would be a little late. (**remind** + Objekt!)

– Ted **answered** (that) he had emailed the firm four times.

- Steht das einleitende Verb **in der Vergangenheit** – also *said, answered, mentioned* usw. – dann **verschieben sich die Zeiten** wie folgt:

Die Zeitverschiebung

direkte Rede	→ indirekte Rede
simple present she works hard	→ simple past she worked hard
present progressive she is working hard	→ past progressive she was working hard
simple past she worked hard	→ past perfect she had worked hard
past progressive she was working hard	→ past perfect progressive she had been working hard
present perfect she has worked hard	→ past perfect she had worked hard
present perfect progressive she has been working hard	→ past perfect progressive she had been working hard
past perfect she had worked hard	→ (keine Verschiebung) —
will she will work hard	→ would she would work hard
is going to she is going to work hard	→ was going to she was going to work hard
would she would work hard	→ would have she would have worked hard

Modalverben direkte Rede	→ indirekte Rede	Bedeutung
can	could, was/were able to	Fähigkeit
can	was/were allowed to	Erlaubnis
may	might	Möglichkeit
may	was/were allowed to	Erlaubnis
must	had to	Pflicht
mustn't	was/were not allowed to	Verbot
needn't	did not/didn't have to	freie Wahl

Verschiebung der Zeit- und Ortsangaben

- Außer wenn wir über ein Gespräch, das am selben Tag stattgefunden hat, berichten, müssen fast alle **Zeit-** und einige **Ortsangaben** ebenfalls entsprechend geändert werden:

direkte Rede	→ indirekte Rede
today	that day
tomorrow	the next day
yesterday	the day before
the day after tomorrow	two days later
the day before yesterday	two days before
last Friday/week/summer/Easter/...	the Friday/week/summer/Easter/... before
next day/Friday/month/Christmas/...	the following day/Friday/month/Christmas/...
two years/centuries/weeks/... ago	two years/centuries/weeks/... before
now, at present	then
at the moment	at that moment
at this time	at that time
here	there
in this place	in that place
this	that
these	those

Fragesätze

- Bei indirekten Fragen unterscheiden wir zwischen **Fragen mit** und **Fragen ohne Fragewort**:
  – **Ann** **Why** is Tim late again?
  – **Ben** Have you seen Mary anywhere?
- Bei **indirekten Fragen mit Fragewort** wird das Fragewort übernommen:
  – Ann asked **why** Tim was late again.
- Bei **indirekten Fragen ohne Fragewort** verwenden wir *if* bzw. *whether* (= ‚ob'), um zu verdeutlichen, dass es sich um eine Frage handelt:
  – Ben asked **if/whether** I had seen Mary anywhere.

Bitten, Aufforderungen und Befehle

- **Indirekte Bitten** werden meist durch *asked* eingeleitet:
  – **Ann** Do you mind closing the window, please.
  → Ann **asked** Tim if he minded closing the window.
  – **Pat** Do you mind **not** smoking, Ann?
  → Pat **asked** Ann if she minded **not** smoking.
- **Indirekte Aufforderungen** und **Befehle** werden meist durch *told* eingeleitet. Bei **positiven Sätzen** erscheint das Verb als *to* + Infinitiv:
  – **Ann** Write this letter at once, please, Tim.
  → Ann told Tim **to write** the letter at once.

  Bei **negativen Aufforderungen** und **Befehlen** setzen wir *not* unmittelbar vor *to*:

– **Pat** **Don't smoke** in my office, please, Ann.
→ Pat told Ann **not to smoke** in her office.

! **Beachten Sie:**
Die Verben *asked* und *told* stehen immer mit einem Objekt, das die angesprochene Person erwähnt:
Jim Ann, can you tell Carol to type this report?
→ He asked Ann to tell Carol to type the report.

24 Das Partizip

- Das **Partizip** hat zwei Formen: das **Partizip Perfekt** (die 3. Form) und das **Partizip Präsens** (die *-ing*-Form):
  – trainees **interviewed** today were all good.
  – After **phoning** Jane, Tom went home.
- Ist das **Subjekt des Hauptsatzes** auch das **Subjekt des Nebensatzes**, können wir das **Partizip** verwenden, um Sätze zu **verkürzen**. Bei **Aktivsätzen** verwenden wir das **Partizip Präsens** (*-ing*-Form) und bei **Passivsätzen** das **Partizip Perfekt** (3. Form). Vergleichen Sie:
  – We are a firm that **is using** computers to reduce costs.
  → We are a firm **using** computers to reduce costs.
  – Skoda is the Czech firm that **was bought** by VW.
  → Skoda is the Czech firm **bought** by VW.

Adverbialsätze

- **Adverbialsätze** können mit einem Partizip wie folgt verkürzt werden:
  1 **We agreed** on terms. Then **we** signed the contract.
  → **After we had agreed** on terms, we signed the contract.
  → **After agreeing** on terms, we signed the contract.
  2 **Cars** must be **driven** sensibly. Then **they** are safe.
  → **When they are driven sensibly**, cars are safe.
  → **When driven** sensibly, cars are safe.

Verkürzung von Relativsätzen

- **Relativsätze** können wie folgt verkürzt werden:
  1 The **goods that were delivered** today were late.
  → The **goods delivered** today were late.
  (Passivsatz mit gleichem Subjekt)
  2 The **man who is standing** at the bar is my boss.
  → The **man standing** at the bar is my boss.
  (Aktivsatz mit gleichem Subjekt)

25 Der bestimmte und unbestimmte Artikel

Der bestimmte Artikel

- Hat ein Substantiv eine **allgemeine,** uneingeschränkte Bedeutung, dann steht es **ohne** Artikel:
  – **Companies** report that business is improving.
  – **Faulty goods** are sent back.
- Ist die Bedeutung eines Substantives auf bestimmte Fälle **eingeschränkt**, verwenden wir den Artikel:
  – **The companies we spoke to** said sales are rising.
  – **The faulty goods we found** came from the same firm.
- Ferner wird der **bestimmte Artikel** in den folgenden Fällen und Wendungen im Englischen – anders übrigens als im Deutschen – **nicht** gebraucht:
  bei **most** in der Bedeutung ‚die meisten'
  – **Most people** enjoy going to work.
  bei **öffentlichen Gebäuden** im allgemeinen Sinn
  – Jack is **in hospital** at the moment.
  bei **Mahlzeiten**
  – I never read my emails **before lunch**.
  bei **Verkehrsmitteln**
  – I usually come to work **by train**.
  bei **Straßennamen**
  – Helen lives **in Oak Lane**.
  bei **Wochentagen**, **Monaten** und **Jahreszeiten** im allgemeinen Sinn
  – I'll see you **on Monday**.
  – The firms closes down **in July**.

! **Beachten Sie:**
Im Englischen wird der bestimmte Artikel nach *all* und *half* verwendet:
– Please finish **all the** letters today.
– You've only typed **half the** letters, Carol.

Der unbestimmte Artikel

Anders als im Deutschen verwenden wir im Englischen den **unbestimmten Artikel** *(a/an)* in folgenden Fällen:

- bei **Berufsangaben**
  – Jane is **a secretary**.
- bei Angaben über **Nationalität**, **Religion** und **Politik**
  – Is Mike **a Scot**?
  – In spite of his name, Ali is **a Christian**.
  – Abraham Lincoln was **a Republican**.

- bei **Maß-**, **Verpackungs-** und **Zeitangaben**
  - How much does petrol cost **a litre**?
  - This whisky costs £45 **a bottle**.
  - Modern trains can travel at 250 kilometres **an hour**.
  - We have planning meetings four times **a month**.
- bei den folgenden **Wendungen**

to be in a hurry	*in Eile sein, es eilig haben*
to come to an end	*enden*
to have a bath/ shower/…	*sich baden/duschen/…*
to have a go	*es ausprobieren*
to have a turn at (+ -*ing*-Form)	*an der Reihe sein, etwas zu tun*
to make a noise	*Lärm machen*
to take a seat	*Platz nehmen*
for a change	*zur Abwechslung*
for a long/short time	*lange/kurze Zeit*
in a loud/quiet voice	*mit lauter/ruhiger Stimme*
What a pity!	*Wie schade!*
without a break	*ohne Pause*

! Beachten Sie:
Bei *half, quite, rather* und *such* wird der unbestimmte Artikel nachgestellt:
- The meeting starts in **half an** hour.
- We had **quite a** successful year in 2005.
- Jack can be **rather an** idiot sometimes.
- We've never had **such a** big order.

26 Infinitiv oder -*ing*-Form

- Nach einigen Verben folgt immer der **Infinitiv**:
  - We can't **afford to buy** a new computer this year.
  - Helen has **decided to accept** the job in Paris.

  Die wichtigsten Verben dieser Gruppe sind: *afford, choose, decide, expect, hope, mean, promise, refuse, want.*
- Nach einigen Verben folgt immer die **-*ing*-Form**:
  - John still hasn't **finished writing** the report.
  - Do you **mind not smoking** here, please?

  Am wichtigsten sind: *admit, avoid, consider, deny, enjoy, finish, imagine, mention, mind* (etwas dagegen haben), *miss, practise, risk, suggest.*

! Beachten Sie:
Nach den Verben *begin, continue, intend* und *start* kann wahlweise der Infinitiv oder die -*ing*-Form verwendet werden:
- When did you begin to learn/learning French?
- The company continued to sell/selling this model in spite of the faults.

27 Infinitiv oder -*ing*-Form: Verben mit unterschiedlicher Bedeutung

Einige Verben werden je nach Bedeutung entweder mit dem **Infinitiv** oder mit der **-*ing*-Form** verwendet.

- *like, dislike, love, hate, prefer*

  Wenn von einer **allgemein gültigen Situation** die Rede ist, folgt auf diese Verben die **-*ing*-Form**. Handelt es sich aber um eine **Ausnahme**, dann verwenden wir den **Infinitiv**:
  - I **normally like attending** trade fairs, but **this year** I'd **prefer not to go**.
- *advise, allow, encourage, forbid, permit, recommend*

  Handelt es sich um **einen konkreten Einzelfall**, verwenden wir **ein Objekt + Infinitiv**:
  - I strongly **advise you to be** more polite to people.
  - Her boss **encouraged Helen to apply** for the job.
  - The law **forbade companies to employ** illegal immigrants.

  Wenn es sich aber um eine **allgemeine Situation** handelt, dann verwenden wir die **-*ing*-Form**:
  - **As a rule**, we **recommend talking** to the unions about our plans.
  - **Increasingly**, American firms do not **permit smoking** at work.
- *forget, remember*

  Die Struktur *forget/remember* + -*ing*-Form bezieht sich auf die **Vergangenheit**:
  - I'll never **forget winning** my first big order **as a young man**.
  - Do you **remember meeting** the Russian delegation **in 2005**?

  Die Struktur *forget/remember* + Infinitiv bezieht sich auf die **Zukunft**:
  - **Don't forget to pick up** Jane from the airport.
  - Please **remember to post** the letters on your way home.

- *regret*
  Die Struktur *regret* + *-ing*-Form drückt Bedauern über eine vergangene Situation aus.
  – A lot of young people **regret leaving** school without qualifications.
  Die Struktur *regret* + Infinitiv drückt eine schlechte Nachricht aus:
  – We **regret to inform** you that our prices will increase from 1 January.
- *stop*
  Bedeutet *stop* ‚aufhören, etwas zu tun', steht das nachfolgende Verb in der ***-ing*-Form**. Bedeutet aber *stop* ‚kurz anhalten, um etwas anderes zu tun', folgt ein Verb im **Infinitiv**:
  – For heaven's sake **stop shouting** at the the staff.
  – I'm a little late because I **stopped to give** somebody a lift.
- *try*
  Bedeutet **try** ‚irgendetwas ausprobieren', steht das nachfolgende Verb in der ***-ing*-Form**. Bedeutet aber **try** ‚sich anstrengen, irgendetwas zu tun', folgt ein Verb im **Infinitiv**:
  – I **tried phoning** Jane, but there was no answer.
  – We can't promise, but we'll certainly **try to deliver** the machine today.

28 Präpositionen

Der Gebrauch von Präpositionen kann nicht in allgemein gültigen Regeln zusammengefasst werden. Aus diesem Grund sollten Sie mögliche Präpositionen immer mit dem **entsprechenden Wort** lernen, z.B. *to be **interested in** sb/sth, to be **keen on*** usw. Hier eine Liste von häufig verwendeten Wörtern mit den dazugehörigen Präpositionen.

Adjektiv + Präposition

afraid of	*Angst haben, sich fürchten*
amazed at	*erstaunt sein*
angry with	*böse sein mit/auf*
anxious about	*sich Sorgen machen um*
bad for	*schlecht für*
bored with	*langweilen*
committed to	*festlegen auf*
different from/to	*anders als*
keen on	*begeistert sein*
pleased with	*zufrieden sein*
proud of	*stolz auf*
ready for	*bereit sein*
responsible for	*verantwortlich für*
similar to	*ähnlich wie*
sorry for	*bemitleiden*
tired of	*leid sein, satt haben*
used to	*gewöhnt/gewohnt an*
worried about	*besorgt sein, sich sorgen*

Verb + Präposition oder Partikel

to agree to	*sich bereit erklären zu*
to agree with	*übereinstimmen/ einverstanden sein mit*
to apply for	*sich bewerben um*
to apply to	*anwenden auf, gelten für*
to ask about	*fragen nach*
to ask for	*jdn. verlangen*
to build up	*aufbauen*
to call off	*absagen*
to carry out	*durchführen*
to congratulate on	*beglückwünschen zu*
to get on with	*sich vertragen*
to give in	*nachgeben*
to give up	*aufgeben*
to go on	*weitermachen*
to hear about	*hören von*
to invite to	*einladen zu*
to look after	*sich kümmern um*
to look at	*anschauen*
to look for	*suchen*
to look up	*nachschlagen*
to look forward to	*sich freuen auf*
to pick up	*abholen*
to point out	*hinweisen auf*
to provide with	*versorgen mit*
to put up (price)	*erhöhen*
to reply to	*antworten auf*
to set off	*aufbrechen*
to talk to/with	*sprechen mit*
to think about	*nachdenken über*
to think of	*denken an*
to think up	*sich ausdenken*
to turn out	*sich herausstellen (als)*
to turn up	*aufkreuzen*
to wait for	*warten auf*
to work for	*arbeiten bei*
to work on	*arbeiten an*
to work out	*ausrechnen, verstehen*
write to	*schreiben an*

Präpositionen der Zeit

at Christmas/Easter/…	*zu Weihnachten/Ostern/…*
at 25/… (years of age)	*mit 25 (Jahren)*
at breakfast/lunch/…	*beim Frühstück/Mittagessen/…*
at night	*bei Nacht*
at the end	*am Ende*
at the weekend/ at weekends	*am Wochenende*
at the moment	*im Moment*
at present	*zur Zeit, gegenwärtig*
at once	*sofort*

in January	*im Januar*
in spring	*im Frühling*
in 1999	*1999*
in time	*rechtzeitig*
in the morning/ evening	*am Morgen/Abend*
in a minute/moment/ second	*gleich*
on Monday	*am Montag*
on the third of May	*am dritten Mai*
on time	*planmäßig, pünktlich*
on the hour	*zur vollen Stunde*
out of date	*überholt, altmodisch*
up to date	*auf dem neuesten Stand, modern*

! Beachten Sie:
Im Englischen werden *last* und *next* ohne einleitende Präpositionen verwendet:
- We had an appointment **last** Tuesday.
- **Next** month I'll be in New York.

Präpositionen des Ortes

at the airport/ station/...	*am Flughafen/Bahnhof/...*
at the stationer's/ baker's/...	*beim Schreibwarenhändler/ Bäcker/...*
at home	*zu Hause*
at work	*bei der Arbeit*
at a meeting	*bei einer Sitzung*
at the office	*im Büro*
at Joan's party	*auf Joans Party*
at the company's reception	*auf dem Firmenempfang*
in the street	*auf der Straße*
in the country	*auf dem Land*
in the city/town	*in der Stadt*
in the picture/photo	*auf dem Bild/Foto*
in the world	*auf der Welt*
in the middle	*in der Mitte*
on the board of directors	*im Vorstand*
on the supervisory board	*im Aufsichtsrat*
on the bus/plane	*im Bus/Flugzeug*
on the first/second/ ... floor	*im ersten/zweiten/... Stock*
on the left/right	*links/rechts*

Sonstige Präpositionen

at last	*endlich*
at least	*mindestens*
not at all	*überhaupt nicht*
at any rate	*zumindest*
by bike/bus/car	*mit dem Rad/Bus/Auto*
by cheque/credit card	*mit Scheck-/Kreditkarte*
by means of	*durch, mit Hilfe von*
by mistake	*aus Versehen*
by Mozart	*von Mozart*
in accordance with	*laut, gemäß*
in my opinion/view	*meiner Meinung nach*
in other words	*mit anderen Worten*
in German/French	*auf Deutsch/Französisch*
in the end	*schließlich*
in addition to	*zusätzlich zu*
in any case	*auf jeden Fall*
in business	*geschäftlich tätig*
in comparison with	*im Vergleich mit*
in contrast to	*im Gegensatz zu*
in conclusion	*zum Schluss*
in cash	*bar*
in a hurry	*in Eile*
on business	*geschäftlich unterwegs*
on the phone	*am Telefon*
on holiday/vacation	*im Urlaub*
on sick leave	*krankgeschrieben*
on the contrary	*im Gegenteil*
on foot	*zu Fuß*
on purpose	*absichtlich*
out of business	*aus dem Geschäft*
out of money/time	*kein Geld/keine Zeit*
out of work	*arbeitslos*

Lernhilfen

A Lesen

1 Intensives Lesen zum Detailverständnis

Focus on Business enthält eine ganze Reihe von Texten. Bei der intensiven Bearbeitung des jeweiligen Themas werden neue Vokabeln eingeführt. Viele dieser Texte dienen auch der gezielten Wiederholung und Vertiefung grammatikalischer Strukturen. Eines ist sicher: Details zu verstehen, ist eine unentbehrliche Fertigkeit, um mit vielen Textsorten überhaupt arbeiten zu können.

Hier sind einige praktische Tipps für das Lesen schwieriger Texte:

- Lesen Sie zuerst die **Überschrift**. Überlegen Sie, wovon der Text handelt oder handeln könnte.
- Folgt der Überschrift eine **Einleitung**, lesen Sie auch diese. Einleitungen sind meist einfacher als der Text selbst gehalten und sollen den Zugang zum Text erleichtern.
- Kommen **Abbildungen** (ggf. mit Unterschriften) im Text vor, sehen Sie sich diese genau an. Wie Einleitungen werden nämlich Abbildungen oft als visuelle Hilfe eingesetzt, um das Verständnis zu erleichtern.
- Lesen Sie nun den Text zügig durch. Konzentrieren Sie sich auf **Schlüsselwörter** (Substantive und Verben, manchmal durch Adjektive bzw. Adverbien näher bestimmt), um den Sinn des Textes allgemein zu erfassen.
- Lesen Sie die **Fragen zum Inhalt**. Anhand der Fragen können Sie erkennen, worauf Sie bei der Bearbeitung des Textes achten müssen.
- Lesen Sie nun den Text langsam Satz für Satz **im Detail**. Markieren Sie oder notieren Sie dabei die Ihnen unbekannten Wörter.
- Sollten Sie einen Satz in seiner Gesamtheit nicht verstehen, dann lesen Sie einfach weiter. Oft schließen sich Verständnislücken von selbst.
- Enthält der Text viele **unbekannte Wörter**, bleiben Sie gelassen. Die Bedeutung einiger dieser Wörter wird sich Ihnen erschließen und manch andere sind letztlich für das Verständnis nicht relevant.
- Schlagen Sie im **Wörterbuch** die Wörter nach, die Sie wirklich kennen müssen und deren Bedeutung Sie nur so ermitteln können.
- Nachdem Sie die Bedeutung der sinntragenden unbekannten Wörter geklärt haben, lesen Sie den ganzen Text ein drittes Mal ohne Pause durch.

Nützliche Grundfertigkeiten

Wie man die Bedeutung eines Wortes erschließt

Wenn Sie Wörter oder Ausdrücke nicht verstehen, greifen Sie nicht gleich zum Wörterbuch. Bedienen Sie sich stattdessen folgender Methoden, um die Bedeutung unbekannter Wörter zu ermitteln:

- Wird das Wort in einer Wortliste am Ende des Textes erklärt? (Es könnte sein, dass Sie Glück haben!)
- Kommt das Wort in einer Bildunterschrift oder in einem Diagramm vor?

- Ist das Wort u. U. der Name einer Person, eines Ortes oder einer Organisation?
- Gibt es ein **ähnliches Wort** im Deutschen oder ggf. in Ihrer zweiten Fremdsprache?
- Kennen Sie ein anderes Wort der **Wortfamilie**, z. B. *describe* (Verb), *description* (Substantive), *descriptive* (Adjektiv)?
- Könnte die **Wortbildung** hilfreich sein, indem Sie Vor- oder Nachsilben abtrennen und die Teile zusammengesetzter Wörter einzeln betrachten?
- Können Sie die wahrscheinliche Bedeutung des Wortes aus dem **Kontext** erschließen?
- Kommt ein **Synonym** des Wortes in demselben oder in einem der nachfolgenden Sätze vor?

2 Extensives Lesen zum Globalverständnis

Globales Textverständnis, also sinnerschließendes Lesen, heißt den Text zu überfliegen, ohne dabei auf jedes Wort zu achten. So lesen wir auch einen Roman oder eine Zeitung in unserer Muttersprache. Hier dazu einige Tipps:

- Lesen Sie zunächst nur die Überschrift und ggf. die Einleitung, um sich mit der Thematik vertraut zu machen.
- Sinnerschließende Aufgabenstellungen – wie *Read the text and say what each part is about* – werden dem Text oft vorausgestellt. Lesen Sie diese sorgfältig, bevor Sie sich mit dem Text befassen.
- Konzentrieren Sie sich beim Lesen auf **Schlüsselwörter**. Diese, meist Verben und Substantive, sind die sinntragenden Elemente eines Textes. Setzen Sie Methoden zur Bedeutungsklärung von Wörtern ohne Wörterbuch ein.
- Sollten Sie ein Schlüsselwort nicht verstehen, **lesen Sie weiter**. Die Bedeutung vieler Wörter wird oft aus dem Kontext deutlich oder vielleicht durch ein Synonym einige Zeilen später erklärt.

Nützliche Grundfertigkeiten

Wie man ein Wörterbuch verwendet

- Machen Sie sich zunächst mit Ihrem Wörterbuch vertraut. Nehmen Sie sich die Zeit, die einleitenden **Benutzerhinweise** sorgfältig durchzulesen.
- Neben der Bedeutung des Stichwortes in verschiedenen Kontexten enthalten gute Wörterbücher eine Fülle an zusätzlichen Informationen wie beispielsweise:
  - Wortart
  - Silbentrennung
  - Aussprache und Betonung
  - Formen (Plural, Steigerung usw.)
  - Synonyme
  - Stilebene (förmlich, umgangssprachlich usw.)
  - (ggf.) britisches oder amerikanisches Englisch
- Lesen Sie immer **alle** Informationen zu dem jeweiligen Stichwort. Viele Wörter haben abhängig vom Kontext mehrere Bedeutungen und die erste Bedeutung, auf die Sie stoßen, ist oft nicht die, die Sie brauchen.
- Wörterbücher vermitteln auch nützliche grammatikalische Informationen, z. B. über unregelmäßige Verbformen und ob Verben transitiv, intransitiv oder, je nach Bedeutung, beides sind. Denken Sie daran, dass solche Informationen Ihnen helfen, Fehler zu vermeiden.

3 Texte ‚scannen'

Einen Text gezielt auf Informationen zu durchforsten, also zu ‚scannen', ist eine Lesetechnik, die wir besonders in der Muttersprache häufig anwenden. Wenn wir beispielsweise ein Fernsehprogramm überfliegen um herauszufinden, wann eine bestimmte Sendung beginnt, blenden wir alle anderen Informationen aus.

Diese Technik bietet sich insbesondere bei Aufgabenstellungen wie z.B. den folgenden an:

- *What role do the figures 23%, 597, 3.5% and 45,981 play in the report?*
- *What effect has globalization had on Levi Strauss & Co?*

Um solche gezielten Fragen zu beantworten, muss man möglicherweise über den gesamten Text verstreute Informationen durch ‚Scannen' finden und zusammenstellen.

B Schreiben

1 Wie man Inhaltsfragen beantwortet

Inhaltsfragen werden üblicherweise in Prüfungen eingesetzt, um das Leseverständnis zu überprüfen. Gehen Sie schrittweise wie folgt vor, um Inhaltsfragen systematisch zu beantworten:

- Beantworten Sie die Fragen erst dann, wenn Sie den **ganzen** Text gelesen und gut verstanden haben.
- Lesen Sie **alle Fragen** gründlich durch, bevor Sie sich mit der ersten befassen. Ansonsten kann es passieren, dass Sie bei der Beantwortung einer Frage Informationen verwenden, die eigentlich zu einer anderen Frage gehören.
- Achten Sie auf folgende Punkte bei der Beantwortung:
  - Inhaltsfragen beziehen sich ausschließlich auf den tatsächlichen Inhalt eines Textes. **Bringen Sie auf keinen Fall Ihre eigene Meinung ein.**
  - Zur Beantwortung richtig gestellter Inhaltsfragen werden Informationen gebraucht, die an verschiedenen Textstellen zu finden sind.
  - Verwenden Sie **die gleiche Zeitform**, die in der Fragestellung vorkommt.
  - Verwenden Sie nur die Inhalte, die nötig sind, um eine klare und präzise Antwort zu geben. Bauschen Sie Ihre Antwort nicht unnötig auf, nur um eine höhere Wortzahl zu erzielen!
- Der erste Satz ist immer der schwierigste. Greifen Sie daher für den Beginn Ihrer Antwort den **Wortlaut der Frage** auf.
- Bloßes Abschreiben führt immer zu einem Punkteverlust. Daher ist es unbedingt notwendig, **eigene Formulierungen** zu verwenden.
- Vergessen Sie nicht, Ihre Antworten auf eventuelle **Rechtschreib- und Sprachfehler** zu überprüfen. Dies gilt vor allem für die Wortstellung.

Nützliche Grundfertigkeiten

Wie man Textabschnitte miteinander verbindet

Verwenden Sie folgende sprachliche Mittel, um Ihren Text leicht lesbar zu machen:

- **Strukturieren von Texten**
  First(ly) / Second(ly) / Third(ly), …
  First of all, … / To begin with, … / To start with, …
  Following on from that, … / The next point (I'd like to mention) is, …
  Summing up what has been said so far, …
  Finally, … / In conclusion, …
- **Ergänzende Informationen**
  Furthermore, … / Moreover, …
  In addition to that, …
  What is more, …
  Let's not forget that … / We should remember that …
- **Ausdrücken eines Gegensatzes**
  However, …
  Nevertheless, …
  For all that, …
  In spite of … / Despite this, …
  On the one hand …, but on the other (hand) …
  But (the fact is that) …
  In comparison … / By contrast to that …

2 Zusammenfassungen

Während Ihres Kurses könnten Sie gebeten werden, einen ganzen Text oder einen längeren Abschnitt eines Textes zusammenzufassen, indem Sie diesen etwa auf ein Drittel des Originaltextes verkürzen. In der Abschlussprüfung wird von Ihnen definitiv erwartet, dass Sie **‚summarizing questions'** bewältigen, d. h. Fragen beantworten, die nur durch das Zusammenfassen von im Text verstreuten Informationen beantwortet werden können.

Diese Tipps gelten für beide Arten des Zusammenfassens.

- Notieren Sie **Schlüsselwörter**, die auf die Hauptinformationen des Textes verweisen. (Die sechs Fragewörter **wer?**, **was?**, **wo?**, **wann?**, **wie?** und **warum?** können Ihnen helfen, Schlüsselwörter zu erkennen.)
- **Strukturieren** Sie Ihre Zusammenfassung, indem Sie eine Einleitung, einen Hauptteil und einen Schlussteil schreiben.
- Verwenden Sie **Aufzählungen** und **Konjunktionen** *(connectors)* um Sätze und Absätze miteinander zu verbinden, wie:

  firstly/secondly/…, to begin with, finally, although, moreover, however, on the one hand …, but on the other (hand) …, despite/in spite of this, … .
- Halten Sie Ihre Zusammenfassung kurz und einfach; sie soll nur die **Hauptaussagen** des Textes enthalten. Lassen Sie Folgendes aus:
  - **Beispiele**, die durch *for example, e.g., for instance, such as, as in the case of, as, when* etc. eingeleitet sein können;
  - **Anekdoten** und **Nebensächlichkeiten**, die beispielsweise durch *by the way, incidentally, in passing, that reminds me* etc. eingeleitet werden;

- **Wiederholungen** zur Hervorhebung einer Aussage, eingeleitet durch Wendungen wie *in other words, put another way, as I was saying, as I have already said, to repeat* etc;
- **Stilmittel**, inbesondere Vergleiche mit *like*, Listen von Beispielen und natürlich Wiederholungen;
- **Zitate** und ‚Expertenmeinungen', die der Stützung eines Arguments oder der Erläuterung einer Aussage dienen.

■ Schreiben Sie nicht vom Originaltext ab. Formulieren Sie mit eigenen Worten.

3 Notizen

Es ist sinnvoll, sich beim Lesen eines Textes Notizen zu machen *(take notes)*. Obwohl dies eigentlich nicht schwierig ist, da man das Arbeitstempo selbst bestimmen kann, fällt es vielen schwer, wirklich kurze, sinnvolle Stichpunkte zu notieren. Oft führt die Sorge, etwas Wichtiges auszulassen, dazu, dass ganze Sätze des Originaltextes abgeschrieben werden.

Hier einige Tipps, damit Sie diese Falle umgehen:

■ Gehen Sie den Text durch und filtern Sie die **wesentlichen Unterthemen** heraus, die Sie als Überschriften verwenden können. Die Einteilung der Absätze wird Ihnen dabei helfen. Denken Sie daran, unter den Überschriften genug Platz für Ihre Stichpunkte zu lassen.

■ Konkret ergeben Ihre Stichpunkte eine Liste von Schlüsselwörtern, in der Regel Substantive und Verben, die auch durch Adjektive näher bestimmt sein können.

■ Halten Sie Ausschau nach Signalen wie Hervorhebungen, Wiederholungen und bedeutungstragenden Adjektiven wie *huge, incredible, devastating* etc. Diese sagen Ihnen, was der Verfasser für wichtig hält.

■ Kontrollieren Sie, ob Sie alle notwendigen Informationen zusammengetragen haben. Vergessen Sie nicht, dass sie oft über den gesamten Text verstreut sind.

Nützliche Grundfertigkeiten

Networks, topic webs und mind maps

■ *Networks* – die Sie als *word spiders* oder eventuell *word webs* kennen – sind ein effektiver Weg, um **Wortfelder** zu erstellen und zu kategorisieren. Auf Seite 32 finden Sie ein Beispiel für ein Netzwerk.

■ *Topic webs* und *mind maps* sind ähnlich wie *networks*, aber sie konzentrieren sich mehr auf den Inhalt als auf die Vokabeln. Wir setzen *topic webs* ein, um objektive Fakten und Informationen zu einem bestimmten Thema in Beziehung zueinander zu bringen.

■ Eine *mind map* wird dagegen erstellt, um die individuellen Gedanken, Gefühle und Meinungen zu einem Thema zu sammeln und einzuordnen. *Mind maps* haben also eher einen persönlichen Charakter und sind daher oft sehr subjektiv.

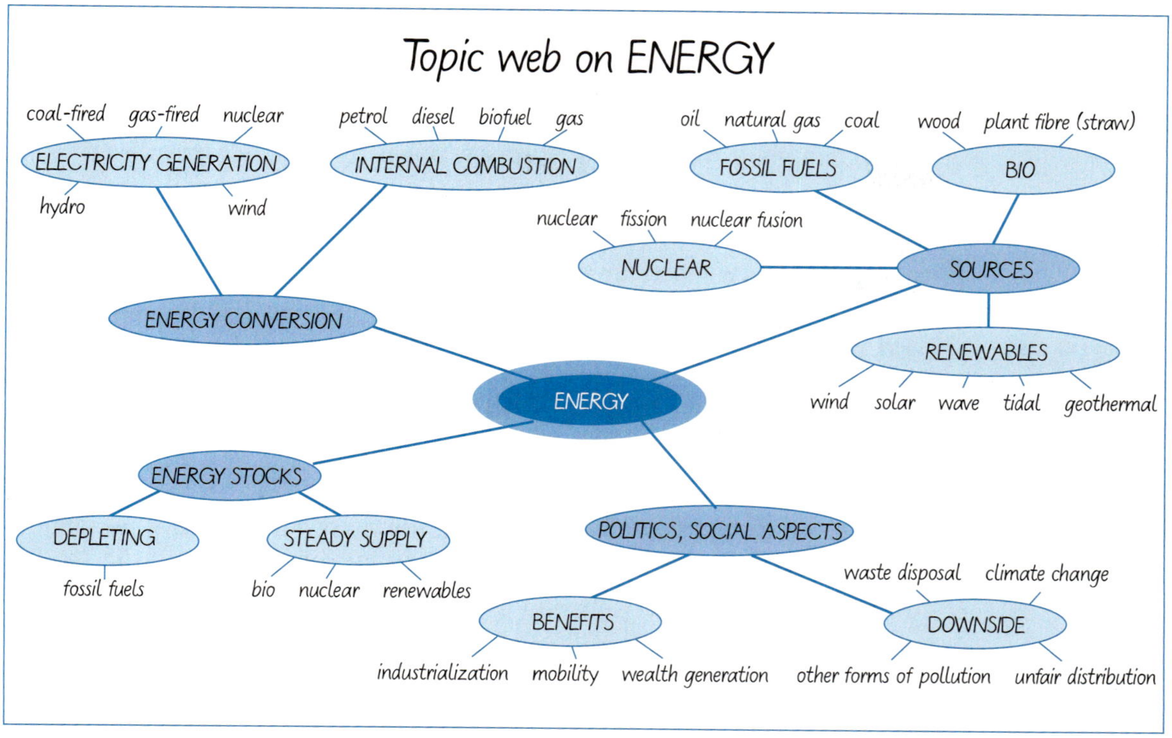

4 Wie man einen Kommentar schreibt

Ein Kommentar ist eine Kombination von a) einer knappen Zusammenfassung eines Textes oder eines Gespräches und b) Ihrer eigenen Meinung zu diesem Thema.

Vergewissern Sie sich daher immer – nachdem Sie die im Text enthaltenen wichtigen Argumente knapp zusammengefasst haben – dass Sie:

- Argumente für und gegen einen Vorschlag oder das Für und Wider einer Situation dargestellt haben,
- Ihre Meinung durch relevante Expertenmeinungen, Statistiken, sachliche Informationen und Beispiele gestützt haben,
- einen Schlussteil verfassen, in dem Sie Ihren eigenen Standpunkt kurz wiederholen,
- ggf. eine Empfehlung aussprechen, insbesondere dazu, wie eine Situation verbessert werden könnte.

5 Wie man einen Bericht schreibt

Ein Bericht fasst die Hauptinformationen einer Präsentation, einer Sitzung, eines Geschäftsvorhabens oder über ein wichtiges Ereignis wie einen Streik, einen Unfall oder die Folgen einer Naturkatastrophe zusammen.

- Ein Bericht ist die **objektive Darstellung** eines Vorgangs oder einer Situation. Daher enthalten Berichte oft Antworten auf folgende Fragen:
  - ***What*** *event took place? /* ***What*** *situation came about?*
  - ***Where*** *and* ***when*** *did it take place?*
  - ***Who*** *was involved in the event or situation?*
  - ***Why*** *and* ***how*** *did the event take place or the situation arise?*

- Berichte haben einen **förmlicheren Stil**. Eine objektive Haltung wird durch den Gebrauch des **Passivs**, insbesondere des **unpersönlichen Passivs** *(It was suggested that ..., The sales department was reported to have ...)* und durch eine wertfreie Darstellungsweise zum Ausdruck gebracht.
- Beginnen Sie immer mit einer knappen Einleitung, in der Sie das **Ziel** Ihres Berichts aufzeigen.
- Lassen Sie alles Unwesentliche weg! Beziehen Sie nur so viele Informationen ein, wie der Leser braucht, um zu verstehen, was Sie ihm sagen wollen.
- Verwenden Sie Überschriften, um Ihren Bericht klar zu strukturieren.

6 Wie man eine Stellungnahme schreibt

Viele Aufgaben verlangen, dass Sie eine persönliche Stellungnahme zu einem strittigen Thema verfassen. Hier dazu einige Tipps:

- Lesen Sie sich die **Aufgabenstellung** sorgfältig durch. Ist sie nur auf bestimmte Aspekte des Themas beschränkt, achten Sie streng auf eben nur diese Aspekte.
- Sammeln Sie zunächst Argumente für und gegen die dargestellte Kontroverse. Diese Argumente beruhen auf Texten, die Sie im Unterricht gelesen haben, und natürlich auf Ihren eigenen Ideen und Überzeugungen. In dieser Phase des ‚brainstormings' kann eine *mind map* nützlich sein.
- Strukturieren Sie Ihre Stellungnahme folgendermaßen:

Einleitung	Darstellung des Problems und Ihres eigenen Standpunktes
Mittelteil	Argumente dafür/dagegen, gestützt von relevanten Fakten und Beweisen
Schlussteil	Hauptargument für Ihren Standpunkt und kurze Schlussfolgerung.

C Hören

Taking notes

Wir notieren Stichpunkte, wenn wir einem gesprochenen Text wie beispielsweise einem Vortrag oder einem Interview zuhören. In Ihrem Fall wird gesprochener Text meist von einer CD vorgespielt.

Die meisten Menschen finden es ungleich schwerer, sich im Vergleich zu geschriebenem Text Stichpunkte zu gesprochenem Text zu notieren. Das kommt daher, weil man oft nicht Schritt halten kann und dann wichtige Punkte überhört. Hier dazu einige Tipps:

- Hören Sie sich den gesamten Hörtext zunächst in Ruhe an, um grob zu verstehen, worum es geht. Machen Sie in dieser Phase keine Notizen.
- Bevor Sie sich Notizen machen, lesen Sie die gesamte Aufgabenstellung sorgfältig durch. Achten Sie bei einem zweiten Hören nur auf die für die Aufgabe relevanten Informationen.
- Notieren Sie Informationen nur **stichpunktartig**, niemals in ganzen Sätzen. Dabei kann ein Gitter (s. u.) sehr hilfreich sein.

In diesem Beispiel handelt es sich um die veränderte Rolle von Männern und Frauen in der Gesellschaft:

	changed role	reasons	consequences
men			
women			

- Verwenden Sie Zeichen, Abkürzungen und Wortverkürzungen, um beim Notieren Zeit zu sparen:
  - **Zeichen** (‚=' für *is the same as*, ‚+' für *and* usw.)
  - **Abkürzungen** (‚e.g.' für *for example*, ‚km' für *kilometres* usw.)
  - **Wortverkürzungen** (‚dev' für *development*, ‚env prot' für *environmental protection*, ‚govt' für *government* usw.)
- Formulieren Sie Ihre Stichpunkte so schnell wie möglich aus, denn vielleicht können Sie später Ihre Aufzeichnungen nicht mehr lesen und/oder Ihre Wortverkürzungen nicht mehr verstehen.

D Sprechen

Nützliche Grundfertigkeiten

Wie man ein Handout produziert

Ein Handout ist eine **kurze Zusammenfassung** eines Gespräches oder einer Präsentation. Zweck eines Handouts ist es, Zuhörer durch beispielsweise eine Präsentation zu führen und ihnen eine geschriebene Aufzeichnung darüber zum späteren Gebrauch an die Hand zu geben.

Hier dazu einige Tipps:

- Halten Sie Handouts so kurz wie möglich. Sie sind **keine** Niederschrift einer gesamten Präsentation.
- Lenken Sie den Leser nicht ab, indem Sie mehr als drei Schriftarten und Schriftgrößen pro Seite verwenden. Gehen Sie ebenfalls sparsam mit Fett- und Kursivdruck um.
- Helfen Sie dem Leser, indem Sie Unterüberschriften, Aufzählungszeichen (•, ■, →) und Leerzeilen einsetzen. Verwenden Sie für jeden Punkt bzw. Aspekt einen gesonderten Absatz oder eine gesonderte Zeile. Nummerieren Sie die Seiten so: *1 of 2*.
- Beziehen Sie Kopien von Overheadfolien, Schaubildern, Abbildungen etc. in der Reihenfolge, in der sie eingesetzt wurden, mit ein.
- Nennen Sie am Ende des Handouts Ihre Quellen und geben Sie eventuell Empfehlungen für das weitere Lesen. Es kann auch nützlich sein, Platz für Notizen zu lassen.

1 Wie man eine Präsentation gibt

Die Fähigkeit, eine effektive Präsentation zu geben, ist wichtig im Geschäftsleben und zunehmend auch in der Schule. Präsentationen unterscheiden sich von einfachen Vorträgen dadurch, dass sie strenger strukturiert sind und mehr Gebrauch von Anschauungsmaterial machen, allgemein in Form von Overheadfolien. Hier dazu einige Tipps:

- Es mag banal klingen, aber versichern Sie sich, dass ein Overheadprojektor verfügbar und betriebsbereit ist.

> **!** Legen Sie Ihre Präsentationsseiten niemals an die Abzugsseite des Ventilators. Sie könnten vom Tisch auf den Boden geweht werden.

- Beginnen Sie immer, indem Sie das Publikum willkommen heißen, sich selbst vorstellen und das Thema vorstellen, über das Sie sprechen werden.
- Geben Sie einen knappen Überblick über den Inhalt Ihrer Präsentation.
- Wenn möglich, verwenden Sie Anschauungsmaterial, praktische Beispiele und persönliche Erfahrungen, um Ihre Präsentation interessant zu gestalten.
- Seien Sie immer offen für Fragen. Sie können andere auffordern, Sie während der Präsentation zu unterbrechen, oder vorschlagen, Fragen nach Abschluss vorzubringen.
- Achten Sie auf Ihre Körpersprache. Nehmen Sie eine entspannte Haltung ein. Vermeiden Sie ‚abwehrende' Haltungen wie vor der Brust verschränkte Arme. Kehren Sie dem Publikum niemals den Rücken zu.
- Lesen Sie Ihre Präsentation niemals vom Blatt ab oder tragen Sie sie auswendig vor. Schreiben Sie Stichpunkte und wesentliche Einzelheiten auf einen Spickzettel.
- Verwenden Sie kurze und einfache Sätze. Reden Sie so, als würden Sie zu einem Kreis interessierter Menschen in angenehmer Umgebung sprechen.
- Fixieren Sie nicht bestimmte Mitglieder des Publikums, vermeiden Sie aber auch nicht jeglichen Augenkontakt. Gute Sprecher lassen ihren Blick durch den Raum von einer zur anderen Seite und von vorne nach hinten schweifen.
- Versuchen Sie, mit einer positiven Anmerkung zu schließen. Fassen Sie kurz die Hauptaspekte noch einmal zusammen.
- Bedanken Sie sich bei Ihrem Publikum dafür, dass es Ihnen seine Aufmerksamkeit geschenkt hat und bitten Sie um Fragen und Kommentare.

Nützliche Grundfertigkeiten

Wie man einen Spickzettel *(prompt card)* **anfertigt**

Spickzettel haben zwei Funktionen: a) sie erinnern die Sprecher an die wichtigsten Informationen, die sie präsentieren wollen, und b) sie zeigen dem Sprecher die Reihenfolge der zu präsentierenden Informationen an.

- Verwenden Sie nur Stichpunkte, am besten in großer Schrift.
- Markieren Sie die genaue Platzierung von Anschauungsmaterialien im Aufbau Ihrer Präsentation, vorzugsweise in einer anderen Farbe.
- Schreiben Sie niemals ganze Absätze auf einen Spickzettel.

2 Wie man ein Interview führt

Interviewer

May I start/end by asking you your views on …?
Can/May I go on to ask you about …?
Do you mind if we turn to … now?

I (quite) see what you mean.
That's interesting. I didn't know / wasn't aware that …
Yes, I was just about to turn to the question of …
It's funny/interesting you say that because I wanted to ask you …

So what you are getting at is …
Am I correct/right in thinking that …?

Tell me more.
Yes, but I'm sure you'd agree that …

Sorry to break in / interrupt you, but …
If I may just go back (for a moment) to …

Interviewee

What I mean is …
What I'm getting at / trying to say is …
In other words, …

Take … for instance. In my opinion/view, …
To give you an example of this / of what I'm getting at, …

From my point of view, the fact is that …
It seems to me that …

Ein Interview ist eine Unterhaltung zwischen Ebenbürtigen, das heißt der Person, die Fragen stellt *(the interviewer)* und der, die sie beantwortet *(the interviewee)*. Es ist kein Verhör. Die Wendungen oben werden Ihnen helfen, nicht in diese Falle zu tappen.

- Beginnen Sie, indem Sie sich bei dem zu Befragenden dafür bedanken, dass er/sie sich die Zeit genommen hat, Ihre Fragen beantworten zu wollen.
- Machen Sie sich im Voraus ein Konzept zur Reihenfolge Ihrer Fragen, aber bleiben Sie flexibel. Seien Sie darauf vorbereitet, Fragen zu vertauschen oder wegzulassen, je nach den Antworten des Befragten. Wenn Sie zu unnachgiebig sind, könnte sich Ihr Interview in ein Quiz verwandeln!
- Seien Sie niemals aggressiv oder aufdringlich. Wenn der Befragte eine Frage nicht beantworten möchte, bringen Sie Ihre Frage anders zum Ausdruck. Wenn er/sie immer noch nicht bereit ist zu antworten, fahren Sie fort.
- Beenden Sie das Interview mit einer positiven Anmerkung, beispielsweise indem Sie sagen, wie interessant Sie es fanden. Vergessen Sie nicht, sich bei dem Befragten nochmals dafür zu bedanken, dass er/sie sich die Zeit genommen hat.

Dictation from Exam practice C, page 188

In 1988, it was officially predicted that there would be strong future demand for travel agents in the USA. But we now see that the rapid rise of online travel booking means that employment in high-street travel agencies is in fact in sharp decline.

On the other hand, there is increasing demand in other areas – fields which are difficult or impossible to automate. These are often jobs that require a human mind to think and respond quickly and appropriately to a wide variety of different situations. They are also often jobs that require contact and communication between people. Typically, they are jobs in services rather than in the production of goods.

Such types of work naturally include jobs like nursing and business management, which require much training, long experience and good people skills. However, they also include the poorly paid and so-called 'semi-skilled' work of a restaurant waiter or waitress. Such jobs are actually very highly skilled and remain far beyond the abilities of even the most advanced robot. (169 words)

Hörverständnistexte

Main course

Unit 1 Ex 3 Part 1

1.8

Marita: Hi! It's Carla Pertini and Ricky North, isn't it?
Carla: Yes, and you're Marita Schneider?
Marita: That's right. Welcome to Mediscan.
Carla/Ricky: Thanks.
Marita: I hear that you're both doing the course that I did at Oxford CFE.
Ricky: Yes, we started two weeks ago.
Marita: How's it going?
Carla: It's good, but there's a lot to learn.
Marita: Including the structure of a company, and that's why they've asked me to show you round Mediscan.
Ricky: It's good of you to give us the time.
Marita: You're very welcome. I'm glad to be able to do it. So … let's make a start.

Unit 1 Ex 3 Part 2

1.9

Marita: Well, as you can see, we're in Reception. All company visitors come here first and our receptionist here calls the person they've come to see. Right, let's go this way, past the meeting room on our left and through the double doors … And now … this is the Personnel Department on our right.
Carla: What exactly does Personnel do?
Marita: Several things. It deals with staff pay and conditions, and it also helps with staff training. Mediscan is quite small, so here the Personnel Manager is the person who looks after pay and conditions. She does that part of the work herself.
Ricky: What about staff training?
Marita: The staff development officers are the ones who do staff training.
Ricky: How many of them are there?
Marita: Just two. I told you Mediscan is small, and it really is! Now, on our left, opposite Personnel, we have Finance.
Carla: I suppose that's the department that looks after the money side of things.
Marita: That's right. It's the accountants in Finance that watch the money coming in and the money going out. Next on our right, we have the canteen.
Ricky: What's the food like?
Marita: Very good, actually, and not too expensive. And straight ahead of us now, at the end of the corridor, we have Research and Development. Or R & D for short. The product designers in here are the ones who design the company's new products. Now, let's turn right along the corridor and next we come to Production on our left, and as you'd expect in a manufacturing company, it's by far the biggest department.
Carla: So I suppose most of the people here are the production workers who actually make the company's products.
Marita: That's right, and there are also some quality controllers. They're very important. They're the people who check that all the products are perfect.
Ricky: And what's this room on the right?
Marita: That's the conference room. We usually use it when there are large groups of visitors, or when we have a big sales conference … and now we turn right again.
Carla: But where does this double door on the left go?
Marita: Oh, that's the entrance to Distribution. Finished goods go through there from Production, and it's the distribution staff who get the products to the customers. … So let's go straight down the corridor now. On our right, there's just another door into the conference room, and then on the left we have Marketing.
Ricky: Is that just another word for Sales?
Marita: No, no, that's quite different. In Marketing, we have marketing research staff who find out what the market wants. They do lots of research with surveys, questionnaires and so on.
Marita: And talking of Sales, that's the next door on our right. It's also my own department, and I'm in Export Sales. I'm one of the sales staff and as you'd expect, we're the people who actually sell the company's products.
Ricky: What about advertising? Does that come under Sales?
Marita: Absolutely right. Over there is the publicity section. And as you say, the publicity staff are the ones who arrange the company's advertising.
Carla: So now we've seen every department.
Marita: That's right, so let's go to the canteen, get a coffee and talk a bit more about our work.
Ricky: Great idea!
Marita: Ah, but wait, here's my boss, the head of Sales. Er … Ms Brant?
Ms Brant: Hi, there!
Marita: Can I introduce the students that you asked me to show round. This is Carla Pertini, and this is Ricky North.
Ms Brant: Very pleased to meet you. I hope you're finding the visit useful.
Carla: Yes, it's really useful, thank you.
Ricky: It's good to see how the different parts of a company all fit together.
Ms Brant: Well, I'm glad we're able to help you. I have to rush now, but Marita, do bring our visitors to my office a bit later, and we'll talk a little more.

Unit 2 Ex 7B

1.13

1

Zara: Hi, Terry! How are you?
Terry: Fine, thanks, Zara. How did you get on with your trip to Germany?
Zara: Very well, thanks. I think you'll have to produce several contracts for new clients over there very soon.

Terry Great. And talking of contracts, I received signed copies of the Starlight contract a few days ago, and everything is going ahead on that project now.
Zara Good. And did you sort out the schedule of payments with the client? There were some problems, weren't there?
Terry That's all fine now. They've agreed to twenty per cent immediately, and the rest in three stages – just as we wanted.

2
Pierre Ah, Mr Green, come in, sit down. How do you do? It's nice to meet you.
David How do you do, Monsieur Dubois? It's good to meet you, too, at last.
Pierre Yes, I was sorry that we couldn't meet when your team first came and pitched for the work and presented the Starlight campaign concept.
David Me too, but I was very busy with other clients at that time. I was only able to take over this project quite recently.
Pierre Well, now that the Starlight contract is signed, we can really get on with things.
David Yes, and I've brought you some first roughs for the poster campaign. Here they are. We'd very much like your opinion before the creative team develop the idea further.
Pierre Let's have a look. Ah, yes … rather interesting, but I wonder whether the background colour is right. You see …

3
David Oh, hi, Petra. How's everything?
Petra Not too bad, thanks. Yourself?
David Fine, fine. Listen, I've just come back from the Starlight people, and I'm on my way to see Alex and Sameera and look at the poster designs again. But I wanted to have a word with you about the campaign schedule.
Petra Right. Just a moment. Let me get the right schedule planner up on screen. Then we can have a look. … Here we are. Of course, none of the dates are fixed yet.
David That's right, which is a good thing because now the client wants to move everything forward by two weeks. They know there's a competitor coming out, and they want to be on the market first.
Petra So that would mean a TV launch on April the first, not April the fifteenth.
David That's right. And then there are the magazine and poster campaigns to change as well.

Unit 2 Ex 10A
1.14
Zara … and so we move on now to a very basic sort of advertising – something we often see in magazines. It follows a well-known formula and it tries to get you to buy immediately. The formula is known as AIDA, A-I-D-A, which stands for *attract attention* – that's A; *raise interest* – that's I; *create desire* – that's D; and *encourage action* – that's A again. So, there we have it: AIDA.
It's easiest to show how it works if we use a real-life example. Take this ad from a typical teenage magazine. It's aimed at mobile phone users, and it *attracts attention* simply through the name of the company's website up at the top: CheapTones.com. After all, everyone wants something that's cheap. (Of course, though, when you look at the smaller print and see that it costs 60p per minute, you see that it isn't really so cheap!)
But let's not worry about that. Let's go on to the next point. How does it *raise interest*? Well, the ad has a whole series of sub-headings – 'Music Ringtones', 'Logos', 'Pictures', 'Colour Backgrounds' and, as the magazine is out just before Christmas, 'Christmas Specials', too! So there's something here to interest just about any kid with a mobile.
And what about *creating desire*? Well, that depends on your interest. If it's a musical ringtone, then just look down the list of bands and singers and songs. If it's colour backgrounds for your mobile screen, then just look at the pictures and choose the one you like best. Same thing with Christmas specials. Just look at these lovable pictures and pick out the one you love most. Then, finally, we come to *action*. And we go back to near the top of the ad, to the heading which says: 'How do I order?' And it's simple, isn't it? 'Just call the Order Line …' and then type in the digit code. And that's it. Your order comes straight to your mobile – and of course the cost goes straight to your phone account.

Unit 3 Ex 7
1.19
David Here with me in the studio are Tessa Parr, Government Transport Secretary, and Simon Way, head of FOR – Free Our Roads campaign group. Tessa Parr, if I could start with you, the last time we spoke here in this studio, you said, and here I quote, 'We need new answers. People who have to drive must be able to drive efficiently. We must also cut environmental and health damage.'
Tessa That's right, and now we in the government have presented the best way forward. It's called 'road pricing'. I really believe this is the right answer.
David Simon Way, how do you feel about road pricing?
Simon Well, first, I have to say this. If all our governments ever since World War Two had planned transport properly, we wouldn't have got into the awful mess we're in today. And so, yes, of course, I agree that there's a serious problem with traffic congestion. In fact, here in Britain we have the worst traffic congestion in the whole of Europe. But I'm afraid I can't really agree with the proposal that Tessa Parr has put forward.
David Could you explain your problem with the proposal?
Simon It's simply this. This plan does a lot to destroy our right to keep our lives private. It takes us a long way towards the nightmare world of 'Big Brother' in George Orwell's novel, 1984. I don't want the government or the police or anybody else to know where I've been on the roads.
Tessa I'm sorry, but I simply can't accept that argument. As I've said before, if you've nothing to hide from the police, what's the problem?
Simon The problem is that it takes away an important freedom, and I just can't accept that.

David Well, let's move on. Simon Way, I believe you have another problem with road pricing.

Simon I have several. Here's an important economic one. A lot of businesses need to be able to use the roads freely at any time of the day. Take road hauliers, for example. Road pricing will destroy their businesses, and we need them to move goods around the country day and night. Will the government allow essential road users like them not to pay?

Tessa No, we won't. But don't forget that we plan to do other things, too. We also plan to cut all fuel and road taxes. For truck drivers that will be an enormous saving, so I'm sure everything will be all right for businesses like that. They even save money, provided they avoid rush hour on the busiest roads.

Simon But that's exactly my point. People like them have to use the roads at certain times of day …

Unit 4 Ex 3

1.19

1 *(CA = checkout assistant)*

CA Hello.

Susanne Hi.

CA Would you like help with packing?

Susanne Thanks, but I'm fine. I've only got a few things – some coffee and sugar and some cans of coke.

CA Right … That's five seventy-three.

Susanne Here's my card.

CA Thanks. And do you have a points card?

Susanne Oh, yes, here you are.

CA Could you enter your PIN, please?

Susanne Sure.

CA Thank you. Here are your cards.

Susanne Thanks. Bye.

CA Bye.

2

Susanne How much are the eggs, please?

Farmer The large ones are one ninety a dozen.

Susanne Er … one nineteen, did you say?

Farmer No, sorry. I'm afraid they're one ninety. You see, they're organic. And organic produce is always a bit more expensive than ordinary food.

Susanne I see. And the medium?

Farmer One eighty.

Susanne Fine, well, I'll take a dozen, please.

Farmer Right. One carton of medium-size eggs. Here you are, Miss.

Susanne I'm sorry, but I don't seem to have any small change. Can you take a note?

Farmer No problem. And I promise you they're the best eggs in the world. Not like the rubbish they sell you in the supermarket!

3 *(PO = Post Office Assistant)*

PO Next, please.

Susanne This has to go to Germany.

PO Fine, dear. Would you mind putting it on the scales for me, please?

Susanne Right.

PO That's two hundred and sixty-four grams. And it's within the EU, you say?

Susanne That's right.

PO You can send it letter rate or you can save a little money and send it small packet rate, which is a bit cheaper. You see, letters up to two hundred and eighty grams are two fifty-four, and small packets are just one eighty-eight.

Susanne Will it take longer?

PO No, it shouldn't make any difference.

Susanne Strange! Well, in that case, could you send it as a small packet, please?

PO Certainly, dear.

4 *(SA = sales assistant)*

Susanne Excuse me, but have you got this summer jacket in a smaller size?

SA Red? Yes, I'm sure we have. You're a size twelve, aren't you? … And it's red you want. Here's one. Would you like to try it on? The changing rooms are just over there.

Susanne Thank you, and could I possibly take this other style as well?

SA Yes, of course, and look, they've been reduced. They're only twenty-four ninety-nine, and we've been selling a lot of them. So unfortunately we don't have any in red now.

Susanne That's OK. This green one is nice. I'll be back soon.

…

SA How did you get on?

Susanne Well, the red one's a bit loose at the waist and a little long in the sleeve. But the green one is just right.

SA Good!

Susanne Perhaps you could tell me: is it made of pure cotton?

SA Well, no, not quite. I think this one is 80% cotton and 20% synthetic.

Susanne Well, it looks fine. I'll take it.

Unit 5 Ex 6

1.23

Dawn Janie, this is Iwan Sukino. Iwan, Janie Hamilton. Janie's a friend of mine. Is it all right if she records our discussion? She's a journalist, and she's writing about FAIRTRADE and how the system works.

Iwan That's fine. Hi, Janie!

Janie Hi, Iwan. Thanks for letting me do this.

Dawn So, could you tell me something about yourself first? And your business and partners.

Iwan Yes, of course. You see, I've always been a metal worker – just like my partners. A group of us got together and started as partners back in 2001.

Dawn Was that here in Latke?

Iwan That's right – here in the same workshop that we're sitting in now.

Dawn And where's your main market at the moment?

Iwan We mainly sell in the city of Yogyakarta, which is the nearest big city.

Dawn And your main products are kitchen pans, aren't they?

Iwan That's right.

Dawn Tell me about your present situation. How's everything going at the moment?

Iwan Things are tough at the moment. The local economy is weak, sales are falling, and the middlemen also keep forcing down prices.

Dawn What are your plans for the immediate future – here in Indonesia, I mean?

Iwan — Well, we just have to keep going, but it's hard and getting harder.
Dawn — I'm sorry to hear that because the quality of your products is very good.
Iwan — Thank you. That's good to hear. So is it possible you'll be able to help? We badly need to start exporting.
Dawn — Well, yes, I certainly think we can help you. But it may be easier to sell kitchen tools. We know there's a demand for quality products in that area.
Iwan — But we don't know anything about the market for that sort of thing.
Dawn — Don't worry about that. We can send an expert designer who will be able to help you.
Iwan — That's fantastic news, and I'm really grateful.

Unit 6 Ex 3
2.2
Adviser — So now you've decided to open a student account with us, various things follow. The first thing that'll happen is this. We'll put fifty pounds into your new account. That's our way of saying thank you.
Danny — So that means I'll be fifty pounds in the black, doesn't it?
Adviser — That's right.
Danny — And then there's my own money to pay in, of course. I'm feeling quite rich!
Adviser — Ah, but now we come to the next point. You'll be in credit for a while, but you'll have a lot of expenses, and most students have money problems towards the end of term. They find that they need to spend money they haven't got.
Danny — In other words, people start going into the red, I suppose.
Adviser — Yes, and that's why we offer an overdraft facility. We allow students to be overdrawn by up to a thousand pounds.
Danny — But isn't that expensive? I mean, don't you charge a high rate of interest?
Adviser — No. Because you're a student, it's interest free.
Danny — That's really useful.
Adviser — Now, in the next few days, you're going to get some things in the post. There'll be a cheque book and a debit card. Then, separately, you'll get your secret PIN.
Danny — PIN? Sorry, but what's that?
Adviser — Your Personal Identification Number. P-I-N. You use it with your debit card, and it's the secret key to your account. That means you'll need to learn it, and then destroy our letter to you with the number. And there's something very important to remember here. You must never give the number to anyone else.
Danny — Right, so can I use it to take out money?
Adviser — Yes, that and your debit card – at an ATM – an automated teller machine.
Danny — Isn't that the same as a cashpoint – the sort of machine in the wall outside the bank?
Adviser — Yes, or cash machines, some people call them. Anyway, the system works like this. You put your card into the machine, you key in your PIN, and you key in the amount of money of money you want to withdraw. Then, out comes your card and the money, and the machine automatically debits your account by the same amount
Danny — But what if I'm overdrawn, and I'm almost on my credit limit?
Adviser — Ah, well, in that case, the ATM may not let you have any money.
Danny — I see, and can I use the card to buy things?
Adviser — Sure. The most common way to use it is very similar to the ATM method. You go to the supermarket checkout with your purchases. The card goes into the checkout system, you key in your PIN and your account is debited.
Danny — OK, now what about the chequebook? Am I right that people don't use them much these days?
Adviser — Yes, people are using cheques much less than they used to. Electronic payment methods are so much easier for everybody – including the bank.

Unit 7 Ex 3
2.4
Part 1
Hostess — Ian, come and say hello to Susie Castle. She's a reporter with Radio Bristol, and she's always looking for a good story like yours.
Ian — Well, OK …
Hostess — Susie, this is Ian Marr, who runs the Bristol Wood Recycling Project.
Susie — Hi, Ian, nice to meet you.
Ian — And the same.
Susie — I've heard of your project. Tell me a bit about it.
Ian — Well, I don't think we really want to talk about work at a party like this.
Susie — But it's not just ordinary work, is it? I mean, it's something really unusual, isn't it? Tell me, how did you get started?
Ian — Well, all right then. It all happened like this, you see. After I finished college, I became a travelling pharmaceuticals salesman – you know, nice car, good pay, and all that. But after I'd been doing it for several years, I needed a change, and I finally decided to take a year off to think about life.
Susie — Wow! That was a big step to take!
Ian — Well, just after that my five-year-old daughter asked for a playhouse. Now, I'd saved some money for my year off, of course, but that didn't include things like a playhouse.
Susie — So what did you do?
Ian — I decided to build it myself. And while I was looking for some good second-hand wood, I found a local company that imports expensive machine tools from Germany. They have to be carefully packed in huge wooden crates, and so they had a great big pile of wood that looked brand new. When I asked if I could take some, do you know what they said? They said, 'Help yourself. We're only going to landfill it.'
Susie — Really!
Ian — I know! I couldn't believe it either, so after I'd chosen the wood I needed, I told them I'd get the local wood recyclers to collect it. But guess what! When I went home and phoned around and checked the Internet, I found no one was recycling wood, locally or nationally.
Susie — Really! That's amazing!
Ian — And I suddenly saw that it was a completely new business opportunity – and the chance to do something really useful. I decided then and there to set up my own wood-recycling company.

Susie And then what happened?
Ian I contacted the local newspaper and explained what I was doing. And they wrote a really good article. You wouldn't believe the response it produced! There were loads of calls. Unemployed people said they'd help, builders offered me wood, and people called and asked for wood. And guess what. Another builder gave me an old lorry.
Susie So you really got off to a great start!

Unit 7 Ex 3
2.5
Part 2
Susie So how long has the project been going now?
Ian For six years, and we're really well established now. I mean, we turn over about three hundred thousand pounds a year now.
Susie Three hundred thousand pounds in one year! That's not bad!
Ian And I reckon we've recycled around 4,000 tonnes of wood that would otherwise have been landfilled.
Susie 4,000 tonnes! So, you must have had some help.
Ian Yes, I employ three full-time people now. Plus six part-time people. They were all long-term unemployed before.
Susie Right, so there are good social as well as environmental effects. But tell me, how does the business actually work? Do people just give you wood and you just sell it to other people?
Ian Well, it's not as simple as that. About fifteen per cent of all the wood we get has chemicals in it, so we have to throw it out.
Susie What about the rest?
Ian We divide it into three grades. About ten per cent is good stuff – Grade One – and we sell it in our shop to builders and DIY people.
Susie So ten per cent is simply resaleable. Excellent.
Ian And then, another twenty per cent is Grade Two: it's good, but the pieces are too small to sell just as they are. So in our workshop we turn them into useful items – things like compost bins for garden waste.
Susie That's twenty percent reusable wood then. And Grade Three?
Ian That's the other seventy per cent. It's all sorts of broken bits and pieces, and most of that is recycled into wood-based products – things like chipboard.
Susie Well, if there's all this wood just here in Bristol, I wonder how much wood is wasted all over the country!
Ian Oh, I've worked it out. You know what? I believe the amount of wood that we throw out up and down the country must be around ten million tonnes every year.
Susie Ten million! That's awful! Listen, how would you like to do an interview with me for Radio Bristol?
Ian Sounds like a great idea. It ought to be very useful publicity …

Unit 8 Ex 3
2.8
1
David Please come in and take a seat, Ms Parker. Ann Parker, isn't it?
Ann Yup.
David Well, er … did you have a problem finding us?
Ann Yeah, sorry, I'm a bit late. The traffic was really bad.
David Well, I'm afraid it means this interview will have to be rather short, so let's begin. Now, from your CV, I see that you're twenty-eight.
Ann That's right.
David And you have a degree in business studies. It was a four-year course, wasn't it?
Ann Right.
David Would you like to talk about it?
Ann Well, it was just an ordinary university degree. There's not a lot to say.
David What about your third year – the practical experience year?
Ann That wasn't much good. I worked for an import-export company in Amsterdam. I just did data inputting all day long.
David Hm, I see. Well, let's talk about your career so far. You joined Tesbury Supermarket management training programme, and you finished the programme, but then you only spent another six months there. Why was that?
Ann I didn't really like being part of such a big organization.
David And you've spent the last four years as a travelling sales representative for DeutschePharma based in West London. Now that's the right job title, but it's quite a big jump from pharmaceuticals to our field of alternative energy technology, isn't it?
Ann Sort of, but selling one thing is pretty much like selling anything else, I think.
David Well, we like to think our products are pretty special, actually. Anyway, why are you applying for this particular job?
Ann It's just that my fiancé's got a job move to Bristol, so I need to move, too.
David Ms Parker, I'm looking for some enthusiasm for us and our products. I expect you've studied them, haven't you?
Ann I haven't been able to find out much about them, to tell the truth.
David Have you at least visited our website?
Ann Er … well … I had a quick look.

Unit 8 Ex 3
2.9
2
David Please come in and take a seat, Mr Day. Peter Day, isn't it?
Peter Yes, Mr Ross.
David Well, I'm glad you managed to find us all right. So, let's begin. Now, from your CV, I see that you're twenty-three.
Peter That's correct.
David Now that is quite young for the job of regional sales representative for the whole of South-West England, isn't it?
Peter That's true, but people say that I'm a very responsible person. And I want to do well, so I'm very determined to get on as fast as possible. If I got the job, I'd be totally committed to making it a success.
David Well, it's good to be ambitious. Now, let's move on to other things. You did a two-year diploma in business studies at Witford CFE, didn't you?

Peter That's right. I specialized in sales and marketing. I knew immediately that I wanted to work in selling.

David And tell me about any other skills and qualifications.

Peter Well, I've taken several evening courses in IT – in Word, Excel and PowerPoint. I've found PowerPoint especially useful for sales presentations with my present employer.

David Ah, yes, Geotherma, isn't it? Tell me about your work for them.

Peter Certainly. It's my job to turn sales leads into firm sales. As you know, we sell a system for taking heat from under the ground and using it to heat homes and other buildings. My Powerpoint presentations show how this system deep underground works. Our customers always get very enthusiastic!

David Perhaps they're catching some of your enthusiasm! But tell me, as you clearly enjoy your work, why do you want to change jobs?

Peter There are several reasons. First of all, Geotherma is a one-product company, and I feel I've done all I can do there. I really need a new challenge. And as you sell various alternative energy systems that are all really excellent, I feel this job would offer lots of challenges. I also feel ready for this big, new responsibility. I really want the chance to look after a whole region.

Business communication course

File 2 Ex 9

2.12

Clare Good morning. Clare King, Export. Can I help you?

Ralf Good morning. My name's Ralf Hansen of Sportversand Lohmann in Hanover.

Clare Oh, hello. And what can I do for you, Mr Hansen?

Ralf Well, I've read about your company in the International Buyer's Guide for 2001/2002. Is that still up to date?

Clare Oh, yes. The details are the same in the current edition.

Ralf Fine. Well, we're interested in placing an order for a large quantity of footballs in various sizes and colours – providing the price is right, of course.

Clare Well, I'm sure we'll be able to help you there. Our prices are among the most competitive in the industry.

Ralf I see. Now, you offer indoor and outdoor footballs, right?

Clare That's right – and in all sizes and weights, by the way.

Ralf And colours?

Clare Our standard colours are white, orange, white and black, red and black and yellow and silver, but we also offer other colours and print designs according to customers' requirements, of course.

Ralf That sounds fine. And what about prices?

Clare Well, prices range from 10 euros for indoor training balls through to 60 euros for professional outdoor match balls. It all depends, of course.

Ralf And trade discounts?

Clare We offer discounts of between 15 and 28% depending on size of order. We also offer a cash discount of 2.5% and a special discount of 5% on first orders above 1000 euros.

Ralf That sounds interesting. Well, Ms … er …

Clare King. Clare King.

Ralf Well, Ms King, could you send us your latest catalogue and export price list?

Clare Yes, of course. Would you like our comprehensive catalogue at a nominal charge of 8 euros, or just our ball games catalogue? That's free.

Ralf Just ball games at the moment, please.

Clare Good. I'll make sure they go out today, Mr Hansen. Now, could you just give me …

File 3 Ex 6

2.13

Pat Good morning. Wessex Fitness Technology. Pat King speaking.

Jo Hi. It's Top Fit Studios in Southport here. I'm calling about our enquiry for digital-

Pat Er, excuse me could you speak more slowly? Who's speaking, please?

Jo Oh, sorry. My name's Jo Clarke. That's Jo without an 'e', and Clarke with one.

Pat And you're calling from?

Jo Top Fit Studios, Southport.

Pat OK. I've got that. And you're ringing about an enquiry?

Jo Right. I'm calling about our enquiry for digital timers.

Pat Can you give me the details, please? The date, reference number, if any, and if possible the catalogue number.

Jo Sure. The date's 21 October. The reference number's J – C slash 2 – 1 – 1 – O slash P – C, and the catalogue number is D – P – C hyphen 4 – X.

Pat OK. I've got that. Now, what's the trouble exactly?

Jo Well, we are still waiting for your offer. And things are getting urgent this end. We already have several orders.

Pat Oh, dear. Then something may have gone wrong here. Could you hold on a moment, please?

Jo Yes, of course.

…

Pat Hello. Well, I can't understand it. This offer went out by post on the twenty-fifth of October. You should have got it, well, a week ago.

Jo Oh, the post again! Great. Could you fax us a copy then?

Pat Of course. What's your number?

Jo It's oh – one – seven – one – four for Southport, then double nine – double six – oh – three, okay?

Pat Fine. Oh – one – seven – one – four, then double nine – double six – oh – three, right?

Jo That's right. And I could you do that as soon as possible?

Pat Don't worry. I'll do it immediately.

Jo Great. Bye now.

File 4 Part 1 Ex 6

2.13

Uta Guten Tag. Glas Volkmann. Uta Kemper am Apparat.

David Good morning. Can I speak English, please?

Uta Of course. How can I help you?

David Well, my name's David Evans of Brecon Table Waters in Wales. We got your offer for mineral water glasses some weeks ago. Now, I …

Uta	One moment, please, Mr Evans. Sorry to interrupt. I dealt with that offer, so I'll just call it up, Mr Evans. OK, I've got our offer on the screen now. Are there any problems?
David	Oh, no. The opposite, in fact. We'd now like to place an order.
Uta	Fine. So that's for 3,000 0.1-litre glasses and 2,000 0.2-litre glasses. Is that right?
David	That's right, but with one addition. We'd like all the glasses to be printed with our logo if that's possible.
Uta	No problem, Mr Evans. We do that often. Just let us have your logo and we'll take it from there.
David	And the cost?
Uta	Well, on first orders printing costs 10 euro cents per glass.
David	I see, so on 5,000 glasses that's 500 euros, are we?
Uta	Right, but that's just on first orders. On repeat orders printing costs 5 cents per glass.
David	Fine. Then I'd like to place the order at a net price of 11,200 euros. That's after deducting 20% discount from list, of course.
Uta	Okay, but then there's the additional 500 euros for printing.
David	Sure. So the total price is 11,700 euros, right?
Uta	Right. And delivery, Mr Evans? CIF Cardiff Docks, as in our offer?
David	That's right. The docks are just down the road from us. Can we still expect delivery in three weeks? I mean, you need time to do the printing …
Uta	Well, if you send us your logo by the end of the week, we can certainly deliver in three weeks. No problem.
David	That's good news. Now, do you need all that in writing, Ms Kemper?
Uta	Oh, no, that won't be necessary, Mr Evans. I'll email you an acknowledgement of your order immediately and you can confirm by return mail …

File 4 Part 2 Ex 9

2.15

Ellen	Good morning. James Carr & Sons. Ellen Brown speaking. Can I help you?
Jane	Good morning. This is Jane Ford of BodyWorks in Brighton. I'd like to speak to Mr Carr, please.
Ellen	Which Mr Carr would you like to speak to, Ms Ford? Mr Nick or Mr Charles Carr?
Jane	Well, Mr James Carr, actually.
Ellen	Oh, I'm afraid he no longer works here. He retired on 31 March, you see.
Jane	I see. Can I speak to the Mr Carr who looks after payments then, please?
Ellen	That's Nick Carr. Hold on. I'll put you through.
Nick	Hello, Nick Carr speaking.
Jane	Hello Mr Carr. My name's Jane Ford of BodyWorks in Brighton.
Nick	Oh, yes. What can I do for you, Ms Ford?
Jane	Well, I'm phoning about our invoice for the last consignment of shampoo and skin cream. I sent Mr James Carr a reminder four weeks ago. Payment is nearly nine weeks overdue now and we can't wait forever.
Nick	No, of course you can't. The thing is, my brother and I took over the company from my father on 1 April and … well, Dad's a brilliant chemist but frankly he was not very good at the paperwork. Look, give me the details and I'll make sure the invoice is paid immediately. OK?
Jane	Oh, I would be grateful, Mr Carr. Now, it's invoice number 3/C/20, dated …
Nick	3/C/20, was it?
Jane	That's right. Invoice 3/C/20 for £683.34. Dated 14 January.
Nick	Good heavens, 14 January? You really have been very patient. I'll get straight on to it.
Jane	Thank you very much, Mr Carr. Goodbye.
Nick	Goodbye, Ms Ford.

File 5 Ex 1

2.16

Jenna	Hello Frank. How're you?
Frank	Hi Jenna. I'm fine, thanks. How about you?
Jenna	Oh, I'm OK, Frank. Too much work, of course, but I suppose that's a good thing, isn't it?
Frank	Sure. And I'm afraid I'm about to add to it – the work, I mean.
Jenna	Oh, dear. Why's that?
Frank	Well, the last consignment hasn't arrived yet. According to the delivery schedule, it should have been delivered last Thursday, 10 October. That's four days ago.
Jenna	I'm sorry to hear that, Frank. Look, let me find out what's happened and I'll get back to you as soon as I can. OK?
Frank	Fine, Jenna. I don't want to put you under any pressure, but could you treat this as urgent, please? Our stocks are getting very low and we have an awful lot of orders to fill.
Jenna	Don't worry, Frank. I'll do it immediately and call you back within an hour or so, OK?
Frank	That'd be great, Jenna. Thanks a lot…

File 5 Ex 2

2.17

Jenna	Hi Frank. It's Jenna again.
Frank	Hi Jenna. That was quick. What have you found out?
Jenna	Well, the consignment left our stores on time last Monday afternoon. I've been in touch with our carriers and they told me that the truck was on schedule until it was involved in a bad accident on the motorway near Antwerp in Belgium on Wednesday.
Frank	Oh, that's bad. Was our consignment damaged in the accident?
Jenna	Well, the carriers say no, it wasn't. It's being transferred to another truck today, and it should arrive in Cologne at about 11 o'clock your time tomorrow morning, 15 October.
Frank	Good heavens. What took so long?
Jenna	I'm afraid it's the old story, Frank. As far as I can see, on the continent the weekend starts about Friday midday. Anyhow, I'll confirm all this by email, OK?
Frank	Fine, Jenna. I'd appreciate that.
Jenna	Well, I'm very sorry about this, Frank, but I suppose it could have been worse, couldn't it?
Frank	True. Well, goodbye, Jenna. And thanks a lot for your help.

File 5 Ex 3

2.18

Lucy	What's the problem with the ProVitesse order?
Jenna	Well, Bob Carter at Supertrans said that the consignment wasn't damaged in the accident at Antwerp but in fact it was. Frank Richter says that two cases of Medexa were damaged.
Lucy	But they have all been replaced, haven't they?
Jenna	Yes. If all goes well, they'll arrive in Cologne on Friday. Everything's at our expense, of course.
Lucy	Sure, but what about insurance?
Jenna	Well, Bob Carter says the value of the damaged goods is simply too low.
Lucy	I see. Well, thank you for dealing with that for me, Jenna.

File 5 Ex 9 a

2.19 Hi Karl. It's Greg Summers of Water Technologies PLC in Birmingham. It's now 10.30 our time on 23 September. Karl, can you give me a call, please? I'd like to talk to you about your complaint about faulty valves. I've just got the inspector's report, you see. Anyhow, I'm only here till 12.00 our time, so here's my mobile number just in case. It's 0044-173 then 1889032. Bye for now.

File 5 Ex 9 b

2.20

Greg	Hello. Greg Summers.
Karl	Hello Greg. It's Karl Eigner here. I got your message.
Greg	Oh, hello Karl. Thanks for calling back. Look, as I said in my voice mail, our quality assurance inspectors have looked into your complaint about faulty valves.
Karl	Yes?
Greg	Well, I'll fax you a copy of the report, of course, but it's very short – three lines, in fact.
Karl	Good heavens, that really is short.
Greg	Sure. Anyhow, of the 216 VC-1-M valves that we inspected on site, the 87 valves you complained about were all perfect. They'd been fitted the wrong way round, that's all.
Karl	What? But how's that possible?
Greg	I don't know, Karl. But it says clearly in the fitting instructions that the arrow on the valve must point in the direction of water flow.
Karl	I see, so it was the construction company's fault, was it?
Greg	That's right. They have no claim against either ourselves as the manufacturer or you as the supplier. It's entirely their fault or more likely the fault of one of their sub-contractors. As far as we're concerned, that's the end of the matter. File closed.
Karl	Oh, come on, Greg. We like to be a little more helpful than that. I mean, this mistake was really caused by people not understanding the instructions, wasn't it? Perhaps we ought to think about making the instructions clearer – using big illustrations, for example, and more languages. German construction companies are employing a lot of people from Poland and Hungary who might not understand either English or German.
Greg	Yes, that's a point, Karl. We'll certainly look into that. Or we could simply tell people to fit the new VC-15-BD valve, of course. BD stands for 'bi-directional'. It's a bit more expensive than the VC-1-M, but it doesn't matter which way round you fit it. Anyhow, Karl, I'll get somebody to fax the …

File 7 Ex 3

2.21

Lisa	Guten Morgen. UB Consult. Mein Name ist Lisa Kraft. Was kann ich für Sie tun?
Sean	Oh, good morning. I'm calling from Ireland. Do you mind if I speak English, please?
Lisa	Not at all. Go ahead.
Sean	Thanks. Can I speak to Ms Bach, please?
Lisa	Of course. Who's calling, please?
Sean	My name's Kavanagh, Sean Kavanagh of Connemara Outdoor Limited.
Lisa	Oh … Could you spell your name for me, please?
Sean	Sure. It's K – A – V – A – N – A – G – H.
Lisa	Sorry, is that G for Golf and H for Hotel?
Sean	Yes, that's right, but we don't pronounce them. We just say 'Kavana'.
Lisa	OK, I've got that. Could you hold the line, Mr Kavanagh? I'll put you through.
Sean	Thanks a lot.
Lisa	Hello? Mr Kavanagh?
Sean	Yes?
Lisa	I'm sorry but Ms Bach's not in her office at the moment. She had to go out. I'm afraid. Can I give her a message?
Sean	Yes. Can you ask her to ring me, please? The number's 00353 for Ireland, then 91 for Galway, then 572231.
Lisa	I've got that. International code 00353, then 91, then 572231. Right?
Sean	That's right. Oh, and could you tell Ms Bach it's quite urgent, please? I'm away for the rest of the week.
Lisa	I'll make sure she has your message as soon as she gets back.
Sean	Thanks very much. Goodbye.
Lisa	You're welcome. Bye now, Mr Kavanagh.

File 7 Ex 6

2.22

a Can I put you through to her assistant?
b Can I speak to somebody in sales, please?
c Good afternoon. Jane Adams speaking.
d Goodbye and thanks for your help.
e I'm afraid Ms Adams is in a meeting at the moment.
f I'm sorry, but could you speak more slowly, please?
g Just one moment, please. I'll see if Ms Adams is free.
h May I have your email address, please?

File 7 Ex 8

2.23

1. Hello. It's Katrin Drexler from Cologne here. Will you be able to collect me from Waterloo station next Wednesday, Ben? Perhaps you could give me a call on 0221, then 645368 before 5.30 our time this afternoon. Thanks. See you.
2. Hi. This is Odile Dubois in Paris. Can you ask Jack Sutton to call me about the new shoe catalogue, please, Ms Brown? I'm out of the office at the moment, but my cellphone number's 0172, then 8996754. Thank you very much. Goodbye.
3. Hi. This is Ruud van Laar. It's 3 o'clock on Tuesday afternoon. Nina, can you please fax the offer for webcams to me at my hotel by 9 o'clock our time tomorrow morning? I need it for an important meeting. The fax number's 0031 for the Netherlands, then 182 for Venlo, then 330061. Thanks a lot. Bye.

File 7 Ex 9

2.24
1 info at bahn dot d e
2 odile underscore dubois at net hyphen online dot f r
3 double u – double u – double u dot b b c dot co dot u k slash radio four slash today slash
4 h t t p colon double slash double u – double u – double u dot birds dot net slash owls

File 7 Ex 10

2.25
Jane Good afternoon. Carr & Sons Limited. Can I help you?
Ben Good afternoon. Could you put me through to Ms King's office, please?
Jane Certainly. Who's calling, please?
Ben My name's Ben Todd.
Jane Hold the line, please, Mr Todd.

Ann Good afternoon. Ms King's office. Ann Johnson speaking.
Ben Good afternoon. It's Ben Todd here. May I speak to Ms King, please?
Ann I'm sorry. I'm afraid Ms King is in a meeting at the moment.
Ben Oh, dear. Do you know when she'll be available? I'll call again later.
Ann Well, I can't really say, but can I give her a message perhaps?
Ben Oh, no. I'd rather not leave a message. It's private, you see.

File 7 Ex 13

2.26
Lisa Guten Tag. UB Consult.
Kate Lisa? It's Kate Connors here.
Lisa Oh, hello Kate. How are you?
Kate Fine, thanks, Lisa. And you?
Lisa I'm fine, too, thanks. Now, what can I do for you?
Kate Well, I'm just calling to arrange a date and time for Sean's meeting with Mr and Mrs Bach at the ispo fair next month.
Lisa Oh, yes. Just a moment, Kate. Mr Bach gave me some dates and times yesterday.
...
Lisa Kate?
Kate Yes?
Lisa Well, how about Saturday, the first, at 9.30? That's on the first day of the fair.
Kate Oh, that's just fine, Lisa. Sean's free then. Now, did Mr Bach say anything about where the meeting should take place?
Lisa Sure. He has already booked a room for Saturday morning. Could you ask Mr Kavanagh to go to Room 8 on the first floor of the small conference centre near the Theresienhöhe entrance to the exhibition ground?
Kate Oh, dear. Can you spell that for me, Lisa?
Lisa Sure. It's T – H – E – R – E – S – I – E – N, then H – O with an umlaut – H – E. Theresienhöhe.
Kate Fine. I've got that. Now, you were saying, Lisa?
Lisa Well, the small conference centre is just inside the Theresienhöhe entrance to the exhibition ground. But that shouldn't be a problem. Everything's very well signposted in German and English.
Kate Fine, I've got that, I think, but let me just check the details – 9.30 1 February in Room 8 on the first floor of the conference centre at the ... uhm ... Theresienhöhe entrance to the exhibition ground, right?
Lisa That's right, but don't worry. I'll confirm by email anyhow. Well, thanks for calling, Kate, and please tell Mr Kavanagh that Mr and Mrs Bach are looking forward to meeting him.
Kate I'll certainly do that. Well, take care, Lisa. Goodbye.
Lisa Bye now, Kate.

File 7 Ex 19

2.27
Chris Good afternoon. John Hill's office. Chris Jones speaking.
Helen Oh, hello Chris. It's Helen Brown here.
Chris Oh, hello Helen. What can I do for you?
Helen Well, I'm in Oxford next Tuesday, so I was wondering if I could visit John while I'm there. It could save a lot of time.
Chris Sure. Did you say next Tuesday?
Helen That's right. I'm tied up during the morning, but I'm free all afternoon.
Chris Hang on a moment, Helen. I'll just look in John's diary. ... Helen?
Helen Yes.
Chris Well, Tuesday afternoon is already full, I'm afraid. John has a meeting at 2.30, and then another visitor after that.
Helen Oh, dear. Well, how about a lunch appointment, then? We could meet at that pub in Lion Street, couldn't we?
Chris Well, yes, I suppose so. Look, Helen, ... uhm, I'll tell you what ... uhm, why don't we pencil in 12.30 at the Black Dog in Lion Street, OK? I'll speak to John and confirm per email first thing tomorrow.
Helen That sounds fine. Thanks a lot, Chris. Bye now.
Chris Bye, Helen.

File 8 Ex 9

2.28
Kim Good morning. Star Car Hire. I'm Kim Cameron. Can I help you?
Joe Hi. My name's Joe Ellis. I've a question first. Is it possible to hire a car at Aberdeen Dyce Airport and return it at Glasgow Airport?
Kim No problem, sir. There's a Star office at all Scottish airports.
Joe Fine. In that case, what would a car cost for five days, please?
Kim That depends on what class of car you're thinking of, sir.
Joe Well, the car's not for me, actually. It's for my boss. She certainly doesn't want anything luxurious, though.
Kim That sounds like Group C, then, sir. What about an Audi A4 or a Peugeot 307, for example?
Joe The Peugeot sounds good. She drives a Peugeot herself. How much is the 307, then?
Kim That depends on the day of the week, sir. Weekends are much cheaper, particularly at this time of year.
Joe Well, she wants to pick up the car at 9 a.m. on Monday, 16 March at Dyce and drop it off at 6 p.m. on Friday, the 20th at Glasgow Airport.
Kim Thanks. So that's Group C for four days and nine

hours during the week. Just a moment, please. Er … that's £211.99.

Joe: Good heavens. That's a lot, isn't it? Does that price include a full tank of petrol?

Kim: No, it doesn't, sir. The tank's full when you pick up the car, of course, but you have to give it back with a full tank as well. If you don't, you have to pay a £10 surcharge in addition to the cost of our filling the tank, I'm afraid.

Joe: I see. Are there any other extras?

Kim: No. Petrol is the only extra. The price includes full insurance and unlimited mileage.

Joe: Ah, so there's no mileage surcharge?

Kim: No, sir – and that's important if you're touring.

Joe: OK, then. Look, can I get back to you later? I have to check with my boss before making a firm reservation.

Kim: Sure. No problem, sir. We're open at Dyce until 10 p.m., by the way.

Joe: Fine. Well, thanks for your help. Bye now.

Kim: You're welcome. Goodbye, sir.

Exam practice

2.29 *Part 1*

Interviewer: Thanks for agreeing to appear on Which Career?

Kevin: No problem. I'm glad to do anything that helps young people decide what they're going to do in life. It certainly took me a long time to make up my mind!

Interviewer: Right, well, you're now Sales Manager at a company called ValueDirect, aren't you?

Kevin: That's right.

Interviewer: And can you tell me a bit about the company? What sort of company is it?

Kevin: Yes, well, it's a 'dot.com' business, which means that we work on the Internet.

Interviewer: And what does ValueDirect actually do? From the name, it sounds as if you sell something.

Kevin: That's right. We sell electrical goods for the home – everything from fridges to cookers to TVs.

Interviewer: Right. Now you said that it took a long time for you to decide what to do in life. Can you tell us how you got the job you're doing now?

Kevin: Sure. Well, I left school at the age of 16, and I went to the local college of further education.

Interviewer: What did you do there?

Kevin: I did a two-year business course, and I got a Diploma in Business and Finance.

Interviewer: And what did you do after that?

Kevin: I decided to go into car sales, so I joined a BMW dealer in Manchester and worked as a junior sales executive there for three years.

Interviewer: And then?

Kevin: Well, then I worked for a small public relations firm for 18 months. I enjoyed it, but in the end I wanted to get back into selling. So I went back to car sales – this time with Lexus.

Interviewer: And how long did you stay there?

Kevin: For another four years, and then I saw an advert for this interesting job with ValueDirect … and so here I am now!

2.30 *Part 2*

Interviewer: How exactly does ValueDirect reach its customers?

Kevin: Well, only ten to twenty per cent of our sales are actually direct sales to the public. Our unique selling point is our 'partnership scheme'.

Interviewer: Partnership scheme? Perhaps you could explain.

Kevin: Yes, of course. It means that we work with other companies and organizations, and we sell through them to their staff.

Interviewer: What sort of companies are we talking about?

Kevin: The BBC, for example, and British Telecom. Then there's 'Which' consumer magazine and the Royal Bank of Scotland – to name but a few. Their huge staff numbers are a great market for us.

Interviewer: And how do you personally fit in? What's your role in running these partnership schemes?

Kevin: It's my job first to find partners. And then I have to look after them.

Interviewer: I see, and how do you actually reach the staff of these organizations?

Kevin: Our main tool is always a co-branded website, that's to say a website with both the partner's logo and our own logo. For example, we recently set up with BT. Now, as you know, British Telecom is an enormous organization with people all over the country. But all one hundred and twenty thousand of them have access to the organization's internal intranet - and there on the intranet is our website.

Interviewer: OK, so you have your target audience of BT staff up and down the country. What's the attraction to them compared with any other website or going to their local electrical superstore?

Kevin: There are two things. First, they immediately trust the website because it's supported by their employer. After all, it's got BT's name on it. That's the first thing. And the second is simply this: we're very competitive. We offer a range of 5,600 quality products at extremely attractive prices - prices which they probably won't find anywhere else.

Grundwortschatz

Diese Liste enthält ca. 950 Grundwörter, die in *Focus on Business The New Edition* als bekannt vorausgesetzt werden. Nicht aufgeführt, jedoch vorausgesetzt sind einige sehr elementare Wörter wie einfache Präpositionen, Pronomen, Farben, Zahlen, Tage, Jahreszeiten, Staaten und genaue Entsprechungen, wie z. B. *hotel, restaurant.*

able: to be ~ to können
about um, über, ungefähr
above über, oben, oberhalb
above: ~ all vor allem
abroad im/ins Ausland
absolutely absolut, völlig
to accept akzeptieren, annehmen
accident Unfall
across (hin)über; quer durch
active aktiv
activity Tätigkeit, Beschäftigung
actual(ly) eigentlich, tatsächlich
to add hinzufügen
address auch Anrede, anreden
advice Rat(schlag)
aeroplane Flugzeug
afraid: I'm ~ leider
after nach
afternoon Nachmittag
afterwards nachher, danach
again wieder
against gegen
age Alter, Zeitalter
agent Vertreter/in; Handelnde/r
ago vor
to agree zustimmen, sich einigen, vereinbaren
ahead voraus, vorn
air Luft
airline Fluggesellschaft
airport Flughafen
all alle
to allow erlauben, gestatten
to allow: to be ~ed to etw dürfen
almost fast, beinah
alone allein(e)
along entlang, weiter, vorwärts
already schon, bereits
also auch, außerdem
although obwohl
always immer
amazing erstaunlich
ambulance Krankenwagen
among unter, zwischen
amusing lustig
angry böse, zornig, ärgerlich
animal Tier
another noch eine/r/s, ein/e andere/r/s
to answer; answer (be)antworten; Antwort, Lösung
any irgendetwas, irgendwelche
anybody (irgend)jemand, jeder
anymore: not ~ nicht mehr
anyone jede/r
anything (irgend)etwas
anyway trotzdem, sowieso
anywhere irgendwo
apartment Wohnung
apple Apfel

to argue sich streiten; argumentieren
around ungefähr, zirka; um (... herum)
to arrive ankommen, eintreffen
as well (as) ebenso (wie)
to ask fragen, bitten
at least zumindest, wenigstens
to attack; attack angreifen; Angriff
to attend teilnehmen, besuchen
aunt Tante
away weg, entfernt

back Rücken; zurück
bad(ly) schlecht
bag Tasche, Tüte
to bake backen
band Band
bar Bar; Barren, Riegel
basic Grund-, Haupt-, grundsätzlich
basically im Prinzip, im Grunde
bathroom Badezimmer
beach Strand
beautiful(ly) schön, herrlich
because weil, da
to become werden
bed Bett
beer Bier
before vor, vorher, zuvor, bevor
to begin anfangen, beginnen
behind hinter, hinten
to believe glauben, meinen
below unter(halb), unten
between zwischen
beyond darüber hinaus
bicycle Fahrrad
big groß
bike (Fahr-, Motor-)Rad
biking Fahrradfahren
birthday Geburtstag
bit: a ~ ein wenig, etwas
block Block
body Körper
to book; book buchen; Buch
bored: to be/get bored sich langweilen
boring langweilig
born geboren
boss Chef
both beide
bottle Flasche
box Kiste, Kasten, Karton
boy Junge
boyfriend Freund
bread Brot
breakfast Frühstück
bright hell, strahlend, glänzend
brilliant glänzend, genial
to bring bringen, mitbringen
brother Bruder

to build (auf)bauen
building Gebäude
to burn (ver)brennen
business Geschäft(e), Unternehmen
busy beschäftigt; verkehrsreich
but aber, sondern
to buy kaufen

calculator Taschenrechner
calendar Kalender
to call; call (an)rufen; Anruf
to call: to be ~ed heißen
can können; Dose
car Auto
card Karte
careful(ly) vorsichtig, sorgfältig
to carry tragen, befördern
cash Bargeld, kasse; in bar
to catch fangen; packen; erreichen
to cause; cause hervorrufen, verursachen; Ursache, Grund
central Zentral-
centre Mitte, Mittelpunkt, Zentrum
certain(ly) sicher(lich), gewiss, bestimmt
chance Gelegenheit, Chance
to change; change wechseln, (sich ver)ändern; Veränderung
to chat; chat (mit jdm) plaudern; Schwätzchen
cheap billig, preiswert
to check (über)prüfen, kontrollieren
child, children Kind, Kinder
chocolate Schokolade, Praline
choice Wahl, Auswahl
to choose wählen, aussuchen
Christmas Weihnachten
cinema Kino
city Stadt
class Klasse, Kurs, Unterricht
to clean; clean putzen, säubern; sauber
clear(ly) klar, deutlich
clever(ly) klug, gescheit, raffiniert
to climb klettern, steigen
to close schließen, zumachen
clothes Kleidung, Kleider
coast Küste
cold Kälte; kalt
to collect (ein)sammeln; abholen
college Hochschule, Berufsschule, Universität
colour Farbe
colourful bunt, farbenfroh
to comb kämmen
to come kommen

comfort Komfort, Bequemlichkeit
comfortable bequem
common üblich, verbreitet
common: to have sth in ~ with etw mit jdm gemeinsam haben
communication Kommunikation
to complete; complete(ly) abschließen, ausfüllen, vervollständigen; völlig, vollständig, komplett
context Zusammenhang, Kontext
to continue weitergehen, fortsetzen, anhalten
contract Vertrag
conversation Gespräch, Unterhaltung
to cook kochen
cool kühl, cool
to copy; copy kopieren, abschreiben; Kopie, Exemplar
to correct; correct(ly) berichtigen; richtig, genau
corridor Gang, Flur
to cost; cost kosten; Kosten
to count zählen
country Land, Staat
countryside Land(schaft), Natur
couple (Ehe-)Paar
couple: a ~ ein paar, einige
course Kurs, Studiengang
course: of ~ natürlich, selbstverständlich
cousin Cousin, Cousine
cow Kuh
crazy verrückt
cream Creme
creative kreativ, schöpferisch
crowd Menge
cupboard Schrank
customer Kunde/Kundin
to cut schneiden
to cycle radeln

daily täglich
to dance; dance tanzen; Tanz
danger Gefahr
dangerous gefährlich
darling Schatz, Liebling
date Datum, Verabredung
daughter Tochter
day Tag
day: one ~ eines Tages
dear liebe/r
to decide (sich) entscheiden, beschließen, sich entschließen
decision Entscheidung, Beschluss
deep tief

to demonstrate demonstrieren
dentist Zahnarzt/-ärztin
to describe beschreiben
desert Wüste
detail Einzelheit, Detail, Angabe(n)
to develop (sich) entwickeln
development Entwicklung
dialogue Dialog
diary Tagebuch, Terminkalender
dictionary Wörterbuch
to die sterben
difference Unterschied
different(ly) verschieden, unterschiedlich
difficult schwierig, schwer
difficulty Schwierigkeit
dinner Abendessen
direction Richtung
direction: to give ~s den Weg beschreiben
to discuss diskutieren, besprechen, erörtern
to do tun, machen
doctor Arzt/Ärztin
dog Hund
door Tür
double doppelt, Doppel-
down her-/hinunter, runter
to dress sich kleiden
to drink; drink trinken; Getränk
to drive fahren
driver Fahrer/in
during während

each jede/r/s, jeweils
each: ~ other einander
early früh
to earn verdienen
Easter Ostern
eas(il)y einfach, leicht
to eat essen
edition Ausgabe
effect Auswirkung
egg Ei
either: ~ ... or entweder ... oder
either: not ... ~ auch nicht, auch kein/e
else sonst (noch), andere/r/s
empty leer
to end; end (be)enden; Ende, Schluss
engine Motor
to enjoy genießen, gefallen
enough genug, ausreichend
even sogar, noch
event Ereignis, Veranstaltung
ever je(mals)
every jede/r/s
everybody jede/r
everyone jede/r
everything alles
everywhere überall(hin)
exact(ly) genau, exakt
exam Prüfung
example Beispiel
example: for ~ zum Beispiel
excellent ausgezeichnet, hervorragend
except außer
excited (freudig) aufgeregt
exciting aufregend

to excuse; excuse entschuldigen; Ausrede
to exercise; exercise üben, trainieren; Übung, Training
to expect erwarten
expensive teuer
to explain erklären
expression Ausdruck
extreme(ly) äußerst, extrem
eye Auge

fact Tatsache
factory Fabrik
fair Messe; fair, gerecht
fairly ziemlich
to fall; fall sinken, fallen; Rückgang
false falsch
family Familie
famous berühmt
fantastic fantastisch, großartig
far weit
farm Bauernhof
farmer Bauer/Bäuerin
fascinating faszinierend
fast schnell
fat dick
father Vater
favourite Lieblings-
to feel (sich) fühlen, glauben
feeling Gefühl
few wenige
few: a ~ einige, ein paar
field Feld
to fight; fight (be)kämpfen; Kampf
to file; file ablegen; Ordner, Akte
to fill (aus-, be-)füllen; übernehmen; erledigen
to fill: ~ in ausfüllen
final letzte/r/s, End-
finally endlich, schließlich, zuletzt
financial(ly) finanziell
to find (out) (heraus)finden
fine gut, schön, in Ordnung
finger Finger
to finish; finish zu Ende bringen, (be-, ab)schließen; Schluss
fire Feuer, Brand
first name Vorname
fish Fisch
fit: to keep ~ in Form bleiben
flat Wohnung; flach
floor Etage
flower Blume, Blüte
to fly fliegen
following folgende/r/s
food Essen, Lebensmittel
foot Fuß
to forget vergessen
forward vorwärts, nach vorn
free frei, umsonst
freedom Freiheit
fresh frisch
friend Freund/in
friendly freundlich
front: in ~ vorne, davor
front: in ~ of vor
fruit Obst, Frucht
full(y) voll, völlig
fun Spaß

funny lustig, seltsam
furniture Möbel, Einrichtung
further weiter/e/s
future Zukunft, zukünftige/r/s

game Spiel
garden Garten
gate Tor; Flugsteig
general(ly) allgemein, generell
to get bekommen, werden
to get on vorankommen
to get up aufstehen
giant Riese; riesig
girl Mädchen
girlfriend Freundin
to give geben, schenken
to give up aufgeben, aufhören mit
glad froh
glass Glas
to go gehen, fahren
to go on weitermachen, fortfahren
good gut
goodbye auf Wiedersehen
grammar Grammatik
grandchildren Enkelkinder
great groß, großartig, toll
group Gruppe
to grow (an)wachsen
to grow up aufwachsen
guest Gast
gun Pistole

hair Haar, Haare
hairdresser Friseur/in
half Hälfte, halb
ham Schinken
hand Hand
hand: on the one ~, on the other ~ einerseits, andererseits
to happen passieren, geschehen
happy glücklich, zufrieden
hard hart, schwer, schwierig
harmless harmlos
to have to müssen
head Kopf
health Gesundheit(szustand)
healthy gesund
to hear hören
heart Herz, Zentrum
heavy schwer
to help; help helfen; Hilfe
helpful hilfreich, hilfsbereit
here hier
high hoch
hill Hügel
to hold halten
holiday Ferien, Urlaub, Feiertag
home zu/nach Hause, Zuhause
homework Hausaufgaben
to hope; hope hoffen; Hoffnung
hour Stunde
house Haus
how wie
however doch, jedoch, aber; egal wie
hungry hungrig

idea Idee, Gedanke, Vorstellung
if wenn, falls
ill krank

immediate(ly) unmittelbar, umgehend, sofort
important wichtig
to improve (sich) verbessern
indoors drinnen
to inform informieren
inside in, innen, hinein
to interest; interest interessieren; Interesse
interested: to be ~ in interessiert sein an, sich interessieren für
interesting interessant
to introduce einführen, vorstellen
introduction Einleitung, Einführung
to invite einladen
island Insel

jacket Jacke, Jackett
jam Marmelade, Konfitüre
job Arbeit, Stelle, Arbeitsplatz
to join verbinden, beitreten, sich anschließen
journey Fahrt, Reise
just einfach, gerade

to keep bleiben, halten, behalten, aufbewahren, etw weiter tun
kids Kinder
kind Sorte; freundlich
kitchen Küche
to know wissen, kennen
knowledge Wissen, Kenntnis

lady Dame
lake See
to land; land landen; Land
language Sprache
large groß, bedeutend
last: at ~ endlich
to last; last dauern; letzte/r/s
late späte
to lead führen
to learn lernen
to leave (ver-, hinter-, da)lassen, weggehen
to lend leihen
less weniger
to let lassen
letter Brief, Buchstabe
to lie liegen
life Leben
lift Aufzug
light hell, leicht; Licht
to like; like mögen, gern haben; (ähnlich) wie
line Linie, Zeile, Leitung
lion Löwe
to list; list auflisten; Liste
to listen (to) (zu-, an)hören
little klein, wenig
little: a ~ ein bisschen
to live leben
lonely einsam
long lang, lang
to look ansehen, aussehen
to look after sich kümmern um
look: take a ~ at sich etw anschauen
lorry Lastwagen

to lose verlieren
lot: a ~ (of) viel, viele
lots of viel, viele
to love; love lieben, sehr gern mögen; Liebe
lovely hübsch, nett
low niedrig
luck Glück
luckily glücklicherweise
lucky glücklich
lucky: to be ~ Glück haben
lunch Mittagessen
lunch break Mittagspause
madam gnädige Frau
magazine Magazin
main Haupt-, hauptsächliche/r/s
to make machen
to make contact Kontakt aufnehmen
man, men Mann
many viele
map Stadtplan, Landkarte
to market; market vermarkten; Markt
married verheiratet
mate Freund/in, Kumpel
may dürfen, können
maybe vielleicht
to mean bedeuten, heißen, meinen
meaning Bedeutung, Sinn
meat Fleisch
to meet treffen, kennen lernen
meeting Sitzung, Besprechung, Konferenz
member Mitglied
message Nachricht, Botschaft
midday Mittag
middle mittlere/r/s
midnight Mitternach
might könnte
mile Meile
milk Milch
minute Minute
mirror Spiegel
to miss vermissen, verpassen
missing fehlend
mistake Fehler
to mix; mix mischen; Mischung
model Modell, Beispiel
moment Moment, Augenblick
moment: at the ~ im Augenblick
money Geld
month Monat
more mehr
morning Morgen
most der/die/das meiste, die meisten
mostly größtenteils
mother Mutter
motorbike Motorrad
motorcycling Motorradfahren
mountain Berg
to move (sich) bewegen, umziehen, verlegen, versetzen
much viel
mum Mutti
must müssen
must not nicht dürfen
to name; name (be)nennen; Name
nature Nature
near nahe, in der Nähe von
nearly beinahe, fast
necessary notwendig, nötig
to need; need brauchen, benötigen; Bedarf, Bedürfnis
neighbour Nachbar/in
neither keines (von beiden), auch nicht
never nie(mals)
new neu
news Neuigkeit(en), Nachricht(en)
newsagent Zeitungshändler
newspaper Zeitung
next nächste/r/s, danach
nice schön, nett
night Nacht
nobody niemand
none keine/r/s
normal(ly) normal(erweise)
north (nach) Norden, Nord-
to note; note notieren, zur Kenntnis nehmen; Notiz
nothing nichts
to notice beachten, bemerken
now nun, jetzt
nowhere nirgends
number Zahl, (Telefon-) / Nummer
obvious(ly) offensichtlich
occasional(ly) gelegentlich
to offer; offer (an)bieten; Angebot
office Büro, Amt
often oft, häufig
oil Öl
old alt
once einmal
only nur
to open; open (sich) öffnen, eröffnen; offen
opinion Meinung
opportunity Gelegenheit
opposite Gegenteil; gegenüber(liegend)
or oder
order: in ~ to um ... zu
to order; order bestellen; Bestellung, Auftrag, Reihenfolge
ordinary gewöhnlich, normal
other andere/r/s, weitere/r/s
otherwise sonst, ansonsten
ought to sollte
outside Außenseite; außerhalb von, draußen
over über, vorüber
to own; own besitzen; eigene/r/s
page Seite
paint Farbe
pair Paar
paragraph Absatz, Abschnitt
parents Eltern
part Teil
particular bestimmt, besondere/r/s
particularly besonders, vor allem, insbesondere
partner Partner, Gesellschafter/in
past Vergangenheit; vorbei (an), hinter
path Weg, Pfad
to pay; pay (be)zahlen; Bezahlung, Gehalt
people Leute, Menschen
per cent Prozent
perfect vollkommen, perfekt
perhaps vielleicht
period Zeit(raum), Frist
permanent(ly) dauerhaft, bleibend
person Person
to phone; phone telefonieren, anrufen; Telefon
photo Foto
phrase Ausdruck, Redewendung
to pick up abholen
picture Bild
piece Stück, Teil
place Stelle, Platz, Ort
to plan; plan planen; Plan
plane Flugzeug
planet Planet
to play spielen
pleasant angenehm, freundlich
please bitte
pleased zufrieden, froh
pleasure Vergnügen
pocket Tasche,
to point; point zeigen, richten; Punkt, Argumente, Seite
police Polizei
pool Schwimmbad, Pool
poor arm, schlecht
popular beliebt, populär
possible möglich, denkbar
possibly möglicherweise
post Post
potato Kartoffel
pound Pfund
practice Praxis, übliche Verfahrensweise
to practise üben, trainieren
to prefer vorziehen, lieber mögen
to prepare (sich) vorbereiten
present Geschenk
pretty hübsch; ziemlich
price Preis
private privat
probably wahrscheinlich
programme Programm, Plan, Sendung
to promise; promise versprechen; Versprechen
proper(ly) richtig, ordnungsgemäß
to protect schützen
pub Kneipe
to pull ziehen
pupil Schüler/in
to put setzen, stellen, legen
to put on anziehen
quality Qualität, Eigenschaft
queen Königin
question Frage
quick(ly) schnell
quiet(ly) still, ruhig, leise
quite ziemlich, ganz
to race rennen, um die Wette laufen
to rain; rain regnen; Regen
rather ziemlich
to reach; reach erreichen; Reichweite
to read lesen, vorlesen
ready bereit
real(ly) echt, wirklich, sehr
to receive erhalten, empfangen
recent jüngst, aktuell
recently neulich, kürzlich, in letzter Zeit
regularly regelmäßig
to relax sich entspannen
to remember sich an etw erinnern, daran denken
to rent mieten
to reply; reply antworten; Antwort
to report; report berichten; Bericht
to reserve reservieren, buchen
rest Rest
result Folge, Ergebnis
to return zurückkehren, zurückgeben, -senden
rich reich, wohlhabend
right richtig; rechts; Recht
to risk; risk riskieren; Risiko
river Fluss
road Straße
role Rolle
room Zimmer, Raum
round rund; (um/in ...) herum
rule Regel, Vorschrift
to run laufen, rennen
sad traurig
safe sicher
safety Sicherheit
to sail; sail segeln; Segel
salad Salat
salt Salz
same gleiche/r/s, der-, die-, dasselbe
to say sagen
school Schule
sea Meer, See
season Saison
seat Sitz, Platz
second-hand gebraucht, aus zweiter Hand
secretary Sektretär/in
to see sehen
to seem scheinen
to sell verkaufen
to send senden schicken
sentence Satz
serious(ly) ernst(haft)
several etliche, einige, mehrere
shelf Regal
shirt Hemd
shoe Schuh
to shop; shop einkaufen; Laden, Geschäft
short kurz
should sollte
shoulder Schulter
to show zeigen
sightseeing Besichtigungen
to sign; sign unterschrieben; Zeichen, Schild
silly albern, doof
simple (simply) einfach, schlicht
since seit, seitdem
to sing singen

sir mein Herr
to sit sitzen
to sit down sich setzen
size Größe
slow(ly) langsam
small klein
to smell; smell riechen; Duft, Geruch
to smile lächeln
to smoke; smoke rauchen; Rauch
snow Schnee
so so, also
soap Seife
some etwas, einige, irgendein
somebody jemand
something etwas
sometimes manchmal
somewhere irgendwo(hin)
son Sohn
song Lied
soon bald
(I'm) sorry es tut mir leid
sort Sorte, Art
sort: What ~ of ...? Was für ...?
to sound; sound klingen; Klang
soup Suppe
to speak sprechen
special besondere/r/s, Sonder-
to spend verbringen, ausgeben
sport Sport(art)
stairs Treppe
to stand stehen
star Stern, Star
to start; start beginnen, eröffnen; Anfang
station Bahnhof
to stay bleiben, wohnen
still noch immer
to stop aufhören, anhalten
storm Sturm, Gewitter, Unwetter
story Geschichte
straight direkt, gerade
strange seltsam
stranger Fremde/r
street Straße
strong stark
to study lernen, studieren
subject Thema; (Schul-)Fach; Betreff
success Erfolg
successful(ly) erfolgreich
such solche/r/s
sudden(ly) plötzlich
sugar Zucker
summer Sommer
sun Sonne
to suppose glauben, annehmen, vermuten
sure sicher, freilich
to surprise; surprise überraschen; Überraschung
sweet süß
sweets Süßigkeiten
to swim schwimmen
table Tisch; Tabelle
to take (an-, ein-, mit)nehmen, dauern
to talk reden, sprechen
tall groß, hoch
task Aufgabe
tea Tee
to tell sagen
tent Zelt
terrible furchtbar, schrecklich
than als
to thank danken
thanks danke
that dies; der, die, das; dass; jene/r/s
(the) movies Kino
then dann
there da, dort, dorthin
therefore deshalb
these diese
thief Dieb
thing Sache, Ding
to think (of) denken (an), halten von
this dies, diese/r/s
those jene
though obwohl, doch
through durch, hindurch
to tidy (up) aufräumen
time Zeit, Mal
title Titel, Anrede, Bezeichnung
today heute
together zusammen
tomato Tomate
tomorrow morgen
tonight heute Abend
too zu, auch
toothpaste Zahncreme
top Spitze, Anfang; Spitzen-, oberste/r/s
top: on ~ of zusätzlich zu
total(ly) völlig, total
to tour; tour (be)reisen; Rundreise, Tour
towards gegen, auf ... zu, (in) Richtung
town Stadt
toy Spielzeug
traffic Verkehr
train Zug
trainee Auszubildende/r
to translate übersetzen
to travel; travel reisen, fahren; Reisen
tree Baum
trip Reise, Ausflug
trouble Problem(e), Schwierigkeiten, Mühe(n)
truck Lastwagen
true wahr
to try versuchen, probieren
twice zweimal
twin Zwilling, Zwillings-
to type; type tippen; Sorte, Typ
ugly häßlich
under unter
to understand verstehen, begreifen
unfortunately leider
unfriendly unfreundlich
unhappy unglücklich
unhealthy ungesund
unit Einheit, Lektion
university Universität
unless wenn nicht; es sei denn, dass
unnecessary unnötig
until bis
unusual ungewöhnlich, unüblich
uphill bergauf
to use; use gebrauchen, benutzen; Verwendung, Gebrauch
useful nützlich
usual(ly) normal(erweise), gewöhnlich
vegetable Gemüse
very sehr
via über
village Dorf
to visit; visit besuchen, besichtigen; Besuch, Besichtigung
visitor Besucher/in
to wait warten
waiter, waitress Kellner/in
to wake up aufwachen
to walk; walk (zu Fuß) gehen; Spaziergang, Fußweg
wall Wand
to want wollen, mögen
warm warm
to warn warnen
to watch zusehen, beobachten, anschauen
way Weg, Methode
way: this ~ hier entlang
weak schwach
to wear tragen
week Woche
weekday Wochentag
weekend Wochenende
weight Gewicht
to welcome; welcome willkommen heißen; willkommen
well also; gut
what was, welche/r/s
whatever was auch immer
wheel Rad
when wenn, als, wann
where wo, wohin
whether ob
which welche/r/s
while während, solange
while: a ~ eine Weile
who wer, die, der
whoever wer auch immer
whole ganze/r/s
why warum, weshalb
why: that's ~ deshalb, darum
will will, wollen, werden
to win gewinnen, siegen
to wish; wish wünschen; Wunsch
with mit, bei
within innerhalb, binnen, in
without ohne
woman, women Frau
to wonder (about); wonder sich (etw) fragen; Wunder
wonderful wunderbar
word Wort
to work; work arbeiten, funktionieren; Arbeit
world Welt
to worry; worry sich Sorgen machen; Sorge
to write (down) (auf-, ab)schreiben
wrong falsch
year Jahr
yesterday gestern
yet schon, bereits
young jung

Chronologisches Wörterverzeichnis

Dieses Wörterverzeichnis enthält alle Wörter (mit Ausnahme des Grundwortschatzes) in der Reihenfolge ihres Auftretens. Das Vokabular des *Main Course* (S. 30–109) wird für den *Business Communication Course* (S. 110–182) nicht als bekannt vorausgesetzt; daher werden im *Business Communication Course* Wörter auch dann aufgeführt, wenn sie bereits im *Main Course* vorhanden sind. Wörter, die in den Hörverständnisübungen vorkommen, sind mit einem blauen Balken gekennzeichnet.

Refresher Course

7	**edition** [ɪ'dɪʃn]	Ausgabe
	in charge of [ɪn 'tʃɑːdʒ əv]	verantwortlich für
	agony ['ægəni]	Qual
	to look after [lʊk 'ɑːftə]	sich kümmern um, betreuen
	contact page ['kɒntækt peɪdʒ]	*etwa:* Kontaktvermittlungs-Seite
	lifestyle ['laɪfstaɪl]	Lebensstil, Lifestyle

Unit A Making contact

8	**leisure** ['leʒə]	Freizeit, Freizeit-
	kite-surfing ['kaɪt sɜːfɪŋ]	Kitesurfen
	dream partner ['driːm pɑːtnə]	Traumpartner/in
	mad (about) ['mæd əbaʊt]	verrückt (nach)
	to switch off [ˌswɪtʃ 'ɒf]	ausschalten
	anyhow ['enihaʊ]	jedenfalls, sowieso
	to pass a test [ˌpɑːs ə 'test]	eine Prüfung bestehen
	instead [ɪn'sted]	stattdessen, anstatt
9	**to link** [lɪŋk]	verbinden
	request [rɪ'kwest]	Bitte, Anfrage
	to match [mætʃ]	zuordnen
	cross-country skiing [krɒsˌkʌntri 'skiːɪŋ]	Skilanglauf
	downhill [ˌdaʊn'hɪl]	Abfahrt(slauf)
	evening class ['iːvnɪŋ klɑːs]	Abendkurs, VHS-Kurs
	chess [tʃes]	Schach
	seldom ['seldəm]	selten
10	**alcohol** ['ælkəhɒl]	Alkohol
	to go clubbing [gəʊ 'klʌbɪŋ]	in die Disko gehen
	currently ['kʌrəntli]	momentan, zurzeit
	form [fɔːm]	Form
	job applicant ['dʒɒb æplɪkənt]	Stellenbewerber/in
	company ['kʌmpəni]	Unternehmen, Firma, Gesellschaft
	invoice ['ɪnvɔɪs]	Rechnung
	client ['klaɪənt]	Kunde, Kundin
11	**to file** [faɪl]	ablegen, zu den Akten legen
	rubber plant ['rʌbə plɑːnt]	Gummibaum
	fingernail ['fɪŋgəneɪl]	Fingernagel
	to water plants [ˌwɔːtə 'plɑːnts]	Blumen gießen
12	**to cancel** ['kænsl]	stornieren, absagen
	flight [flaɪt]	Flug
	motor caravan [ˌməʊtə 'kærəvæn]	Wohnmobil
	connected [kə'nektɪd]	angeschlossen, verbunden
	for ages [fər 'eɪdʒɪz]	eine Ewigkeit

Unit B News and views: Work experience

13	**view** [vjuː]	Ansicht
	work experience ['wɜːk ɪkspɪəriəns]	Berufs-, Arbeitserfahrung
	electronics [ˌɪlek'trɒnɪks]	Elektronik
	retailer ['riːteɪlə]	(Einzel-)Händler
	law firm ['lɔː fɜːm]	Anwaltskanzlei
	store [stɔː]	Laden, Geschäft
	shelf-filling ['ʃelf fɪlɪŋ]	Regalbestückung, -auffüllung
	to get bored [get 'bɔːd]	sich langweilen
	filing ['faɪlɪŋ]	Ablage
	appointment [ə'pɔɪntmənt]	Termin, Verabredung
	lawyer ['lɔːjə]	(Rechts-)Anwalt/Anwältin
	to take dictations [teɪk dɪk'teɪʃnz]	Diktate aufnehmen
14	**statement** ['steɪtmənt]	Aussage, Behauptung
	(not) to be allowed to do sth [bi ə'laʊd tə duː]	etw (nicht) tun dürfen
	to replace [rɪ'pleɪs]	ersetzen, austauschen
	italics [ɪ'tælɪks]	Kursivschrift
	similar ['sɪmələ]	ähnlich
	to arrange [ə'reɪndʒ]	arrangieren, vereinbaren
	apprentice [ə'prentɪs]	Auszubildende/r
15	**attitude** ['ætɪtjuːd]	Einstellung, Haltung
	to carry on [ˌkæri 'ɒn]	weitermachen, fortfahren
	to allow [ə'laʊ]	erlauben, gestatten
	rude [ruːd]	unhöflich, ungezogen, rücksichtslos
	virtually ['vɜːtʃuəli]	praktisch, nahezu
	liar ['laɪə]	Lügner/in
16	**circumstance** ['sɜːkəmstəns]	Umstand, Bedingung
	court [kɔːt]	Gericht(shof)
	schedule ['ʃedjuːl]	Terminplan, Fahrplan
17	**to demonstrate** ['demənstreɪt]	demonstrieren
	stationery ['steɪʃənri]	Briefpapier, Büromaterial
	closing time ['kləʊzɪŋ taɪm]	Geschäftsschluss, Ladenschlusszeit
	mask [mɑːsk]	Maske
	to catch hold of sb [ˌkætʃ 'həʊld əv]	jdn packen
	tight [taɪt]	fest; knapp
	till [tɪl]	(Laden-)Kasse
	to get hurt [get 'hɜːt]	(sich) verletzen, (sich) wehtun

Unit C Time out

18	**to get in touch** [get ɪn 'tʌtʃ]	(sich) in Verbindung setzen
	to take time out [teɪk ˌtaɪm 'aʊt]	Pause machen, Auszeit nehmen
	exotic [ɪg'zɒtɪk]	exotisch
	destination [ˌdestɪ'neɪʃn]	(Reise-)Ziel
	financial(ly) [faɪ'nænʃl]	finanziell
	suitable ['su:təbl]	geeignet, angemessen
	especially [ɪ'speʃəli]	besonders, insbesondere
	nasty ['nɑ:sti]	unangenehm
	to get real [get 'ri:əl]	etw endlich begreifen
	temporary job [ˌtemprəri 'dʒɒb]	Aushilfstätigkeit
	to survive [sə'vaɪv]	überleben
	to combine [kəm'baɪn]	verbinden, kombinieren
	to search [sɜ:tʃ]	suchen
19	**package holiday** ['pækɪdʒ hɒlədeɪ]	Pauschalreise
	touring holiday [ˌtʊərɪŋ 'hɒlədeɪ]	Rundreise
	to integrate ['ɪntɪgreɪt]	integrieren, einbauen
	school-leaver [ˌsku:l'li:və]	Schulabgänger/in
21	**summer camp** ['sʌmə kæmp]	Sommer(ferien)lager
	weather forecast ['weðə fɔ:kɑ:st]	Wettervorhersage

Unit D You are what you eat

22	**fatty** ['fæti]	fettreich, fettig
	body mass index (BMI) [ˌbɒdi mæs 'ɪndeks]	Körpermassenzahl
	guide [gaɪd]	Richtlinie
	to divide [dɪ'vaɪd]	teilen
	square [skweə]	Quadrat
	height [haɪt]	Höhe, Größe
	to weigh [weɪ]	wiegen
	according to [ə'kɔ:dɪŋ tə]	zufolge, nach, gemäß
	classification [ˌklæsɪfɪ'keɪʃn]	Klassifizierung, Einstufung
	underweight [ˌʌndə'weɪt]	untergewichtig
	overweight [ˌəʊvə'weɪt]	übergewichtig
	obese [əʊ'bi:s]	fettleibig
	extreme [ɪk'stri:m]	äußerst, außerordentlich
	propaganda [ˌprɒpə'gændə]	Propaganda
	to annoy [ə'nɔɪ]	ärgern
	honest ['ɒnɪst]	ehrlich, anständig
	to apply [ə'plaɪ]	gelten, zutreffen
	definitely ['defɪnətli]	bestimmt, sicher, auf jeden Fall
	out of breath [aʊt əf 'breθ]	außer Atem
	to kid oneself ['kɪd wʌnself]	sich etwas vormachen
	diet ['daɪət]	Diät, Ernährung
	physical ['fɪzɪkl]	körperlich
	to realize ['rɪəlaɪz]	sich klar werden, (be)merken
	gym [dʒɪm]	Fitnessstudio
	athletics [æθ'letɪks]	Leichtathletik
	burger ['bɜ:gə]	Hamburger
	fries [fraɪz]	Pommes frites
	balanced ['bælənst]	ausgeglichen, ausgewogen
23	**fanatic** [fə'nætɪk]	Fanatiker
	issue ['ɪʃu:]	Frage, Angelegenheit, Thema, Problem
	to advise [əd'vaɪz]	(be-)raten, empfehlen
	careless ['keələs]	leichtsinnig, unvorsichtig
	medical ['medɪkl]	medizinisch, ärztlich
	public ['pʌblɪk]	öffentlich
	obesity [əʊ'bi:səti]	Fettleibigkeit
	to cause [kɔ:z]	verursachen, verschulden
	irresponsible [ˌɪrɪ'spɒnsəbl]	unverantwortlich
	to injure ['ɪndʒə]	verletzen
24	**energetic** [ˌenə'dʒetɪk]	energisch, tatkräftig
	equipment [ɪ'kwɪpmənt]	Ausrüstung, Ausstattung, Geräte
	to lose weight [ˌlu:z 'weɪt]	abnehmen
	youth [ju:θ]	Jugend
	to take up [ˌteɪk 'ʌp]	anfangen, etw zu tun
25	**to adjust** [ə'dʒʌst]	anpassen, einstellen
	organize ['ɔ:gənaɪz]	organisieren, arrangieren
	campsite ['kæmpsaɪt]	Campingplatz
	arrangements [ə'reɪndʒmənts]	Vorbereitungen, Pläne, Abmachungen
	suggestion [sə'dʒestʃən]	Vorschlag
	first aid kit [ˌfɜ:st 'eɪd kɪt]	Verbandskasten
	to fix [fɪks]	festsetzen, ausmachen
	in brackets [ɪn 'brækɪts]	in Klammern
	It's a pity. [ɪts ə 'pɪti]	Schade.
	ban [bæn]	Verbot

Unit E Getting about

26	**to get about** [ˌget ə'baʊt]	herumkommen, sich fortbewegen
	scooter ['sku:tə]	Motorroller
	ahead of [ə'hed əv]	vor
	fashionable ['fæʃnəbl]	modisch
	clothing ['kləʊðɪŋ]	Kleidung, Kleider
	the latest [ðə 'leɪtɪst]	das Allerneueste
	electronic [ˌɪlek'trɒnɪk]	elektronisch
	gadget ['gædʒɪt]	Gerät
	fatal ['feɪtl]	tödlich
	injury ['ɪndʒəri]	Verletzung
	avoidable [ə'vɔɪdəbl]	vermeidbar
	highway patrol ['haɪweɪ pətrəʊl]	Verkehrspolizei
	government ['gʌvənmənt]	Regierung
	probationary period [prəˌbeɪʃnri 'pɪəriəd]	Probezeit
	law [lɔ:]	Gesetz
	automatically [ˌɔ:tə'mætɪkli]	automatisch
	licence ['laɪsns]	Führerschein
	to retake (a test) [ˌri:'teɪk]	(eine Prüfung) nochmals machen
	far fewer [ˌfɑ: 'fju:ə]	weit weniger
	resident ['rezɪdənt]	Einwohner, Bewohner
	to limit ['lɪmɪt]	beschränken, begrenzen
	ownership ['əʊnəʃɪp]	Besitz, Eigentum
	gridlock ['grɪdlɒk]	Verkehrsinfarkt

environmental [ɪn,vaɪrən'mentl] Umwelt-, umweltbezogen
climate ['klaɪmət] Klima
climate change ['klaɪmət tʃeɪndʒ] Klimawandel
limit ['lɪmɪt] Beschränkung, Begrenzung
maximum ['mæksɪməm] Maximum, Höchst-
household ['haʊshəʊld] Haushalt
psychologist [saɪ'kɒlədʒɪst] Psychologe/in
particularly [pə'tɪkjələli] besonders, bestimmt
personality [,pɜ:sə'næləti] Persönlichkeit
petrol ['petrəl] Benzin
nowadays ['naʊədeɪz] heutzutage
27 **caption** ['kæpʃn] Bildunterschrift
to illustrate ['ɪləstreɪt] illustrieren, veranschaulichen
aspect ['æspekt] Aspekt, Seite
personal ['pɜ:sənl] persönlich, privat
mobility [məʊ'bɪləti] Beweglichkeit, Mobilität
set [set] Satz
wheel [wi:l] Rad
local ['ləʊkl] örtlich, einheimisch
gap [gæp] Lücke
cartoon [kɑ:'tu:n] Karikatur
single household ['sɪŋgl haʊshəʊld] Einpersonenhaushalt
28 **to oversleep** [,əʊvə'sli:p] verschlafen
29 **speed camera** ['spi:d kæmərə] Radargerät, Blitzer
traffic lights ['træfɪk laɪts] (Verkehrs-)Ampel
to increase [ɪn'kri:s] zunehmen, steigen, erhöhen
to repair [rɪ'peə] reparieren
speed [spi:d] Geschwindigkeit
speed limit ['spi:d lɪmɪt] Geschwindigkeits-begrenzung
to scare [skeə] Angst machen
doubt [daʊt] Zweifel
likely ['laɪkli] wahrscheinlich

Main Course

Unit 1 Europe at work

30 **check-in** ['tʃekɪn] Abfertigung, Check-In
clerk [klɑ:k] Angestellte/r
booking ['bʊkɪŋ] Buchung, Reservierung
sales assistant ['seɪlz əsɪstənt] Verkäufer/in
flight attendant [,flaɪt ə'tendənt] Flugbegleiter/in
florist ['flɒrɪst] Blumenhändler/in
challenging ['tʃælɪndʒɪŋ] herausfordernd, anstrengend
secure [sɪ'kjuə] sicher
stressful ['stresfl] sehr anstrengend, stressig
varied ['veərid] vielfältig, abwechslungsreich
repetitive [rɪ'petətɪv] (sich dauernd) wiederholend, monoton
well-paid [,wel'peɪd] gut bezahlt
badly-paid [,bædli'peɪd] schlecht bezahlt
independent [,ɪndɪ'pendənt] unabhängig
career [kə'rɪə] Karriere, (beruflicher) Werdegang
to deal with ['di:l wɪð] umgehen mit, bearbeiten, erledigen
salary ['sæləri] Gehalt, Lohn
benefits ['benɪfɪts] Vergünstigungen
to work … hours [wɜ:k 'aʊəz] … Arbeitszeiten haben
irregular [ɪ'regjələ] unregelmäßig
31 **stock control** ['stɒk kəntrəʊl] Lagerhaltung, Inventur
ICT [,aɪ si: ti:] Informations- und Kommunikationstechnologie
dead-end job [,dedend 'dʒɒb] Stelle ohne Aufstiegschancen
production [prə'dʌkʃn] Produktion, Herstellung, Fertigung
redundant [rɪ'dʌndənt] überflüssig, arbeitslos
huge [hju:dʒ] riesig
out of work [aʊt əv 'wɜ:k] arbeitslos
push [pʊʃ] Stoß, Anstoß
access ['ækses] Zugang, Zugriff
further education [,fɜ:ðə edʒu'keɪʃn] *etwa:* höhere Schulbildung
college of further education (CFE) [,kɒlɪdʒ əv ,fɜ:ðər ,edʒu'keɪʃn] berufsbildende Schule,
information technology [ɪnfə,meɪʃn tek'nɒlədʒi] Informationstechnologie
redundancy pay [rɪ'dʌndənsi peɪ] Arbeitslosengeld, Abfindung
to cover ['kʌvə] (be-, zu-, ab)decken
living expenses ['lɪvɪŋ ɪkspensɪz] Lebenshaltungskosten
part-time [,pɑ:t'taɪm] halbtags-, Teilzeit
to work out well [,wɜ:k aʊt 'wel] gut klappen, gut funktionieren
to expand [ɪk'spænd] sich ausdehnen, (sich) erweitern
to apply for [ə'plaɪ] sich bewerben um
full-time [,fʊl 'taɪm] ganztags, Vollzeit(-)
secretarial [,sekrə'teəriəl] Sekretariats-
business studies ['bɪznəs stʌdiz] Betriebswirtschaftslehre
diploma [dɪ'pləʊmə] Abschluss, Diplom
thanks to ['θæŋks tə] dank
to send out [,send 'aʊt] verschicken, versenden
CV (curriculum vitae) [,si: 'vi: kə,rɪkjələm 'vi:taɪ] Lebenslauf
letter of application [,letər əv æplɪ'keɪʃn] Bewerbungsschreiben
form [fɔ:m] Formular
manufacturer [,mænju'fæktʃərə] Hersteller/in, Produzent/in
employer [ɪm'plɔɪə] Arbeitgeber/in, Unternehmer/in
export sales [,ekspɔ:t 'seɪlz] Exportverkäufe

32	**background briefing** [ˌbækgraʊnd ˈbriːfɪŋ]	Hintergrundinformationen
	medium-sized [ˈmiːdiəmsaɪzd]	mittelgroß
	vocational [vəʊˈkeɪʃənl]	beruflich, Berufs-
	resumé [ˈrezjuːmeɪ]	Lebenslauf (AE)
	to state [steɪt]	feststellen, angeben, (im Text) vorkommen
	to manage [ˈmænɪdʒ]	(es) schaffen
	step [step]	Schritt, Stufe
	network [ˈnetwɜːk]	Netzwerk
	employment [ɪmˈplɔɪmənt]	Beschäftigung, Anstellung
	condition [kənˈdɪʃn]	Bedingung, Zustand
	wage [weɪdʒ]	Lohn, Gehalt
33	**round-the-world holiday** [raʊnd ðə wɜːld ˈhɒlədeɪ]	Weltreise
	travel industry [ˈtrævl ɪndəstri]	Tourismusbranche
	to last [lɑːst]	(an)dauern
	loads of [ˈləʊdz əv]	jede Menge (an)
	travel agency [ˈtrævl eɪdʒənsi]	Reisebüro
	culture [ˈkʌltʃə]	Kultur
	to suggest [səˈdʒest]	vorschlagen, andeuten, nahelegen
	Congratulations! [kənˌgrætʃʊˈleɪʃnz]	Herzlichen Glückwunsch! Ich gratuliere!
	informal [ɪnˈfɔːml]	ungezwungen, informell
	formal [ˈfɔːml]	formell, förmlich
	staff [stɑːf]	Angestellte, Personal
	junior [ˈdʒuːniə]	untergeordnet, rangniedriger
	senior [ˈsiːniə]	vorgesetzt, leitend
	closeness [ˈkləʊsnəs]	Nähe
	style [staɪl]	Stil
34	**including** [ɪnˈkluːdɪŋ]	einschließlich, darunter
	structure [ˈstrʌktʃə]	Struktur, Aufbau
	to show sb round [ˌʃəʊ ˈraʊnd]	jdn herumführen
	You're welcome. [jɔː ˈwelkəm]	Bitte (schön).
	department [dɪˈpɑːtmənt]	Abteilung
	reception [rɪˈsepʃn]	Empfang, Rezeption
	receptionist [rɪˈsepʃənɪst]	Empfangsdame, -chef
	meeting room [ˈmiːtɪŋ ruːm]	Besprechungsraum
	personnel [ˌpɜːsəˈnel]	Personal, Mitarbeiter
	staff development [ˈstɑːf dɪveləpmənt]	Personalentwicklung
	staff development officer [ˌstɑːf dɪˈveləpmənt ɒfɪsə]	Personalentwickler
	finance [ˈfaɪnæns]	Buchhaltung
	accountant [əˈkaʊntənt]	(Bilanz-)Buchhalter/in
	canteen [kænˈtiːn]	Kantine
	Research and Development [rɪˌsɜːtʃ ən dɪˈveləpmənt]	Forschung und Entwicklung
	for short [fə ˈʃɔːt]	abgekürzt
	product [ˈprɒdʌkt]	Produkt, Erzeugnis
	designer [dɪˈzaɪnə]	Konstrukteur/in, Designer/in
	to design [dɪˈzaɪn]	konstruieren, entwerfen, entwickeln, gestalten
	manufacturing [ˌmænjuˈfæktʃərɪŋ]	Herstellung, Produktion, Fertigung
	by far [baɪ ˈfɑː]	bei weitem
	quality controller [ˈkwɒləti kəntrəʊlə]	Qualitätskontrolleur
	conference [ˈkɒnfərəns]	Konferenz, Besprechung
	sales conference [ˌseɪlz ˈkɒnfərəns]	Vertriebsbesprechung
	entrance [ˈentrəns]	Eingang, Einfahrt
	distribution [ˌdɪstrɪˈbjuːʃn]	Vertrieb, Auslieferung
	finished goods [ˌfɪnɪʃt ˈgʊdz]	Fertigwaren
	sales [seɪlz]	Verkauf, Vertrieb
	survey [ˈsɜːveɪ]	Umfrage, Untersuchung, Erhebung
	questionnaire [ˌkwestʃəˈneə]	Fragebogen
	advertising [ˈædvətaɪzɪŋ]	Werbung, Reklame
	to come under [ˌkʌm ˈʌndə]	*hier:* unterstehen
	publicity [pʌbˈlɪsəti]	Publicity, Werbung
	head [hed]	Chef, Leiter
	to fit together [fɪt təˈgeðə]	zusammen passen
	to rush [rʌʃ]	eilen, sich beeilen
	to control [kənˈtrəʊl]	kontrollieren, (über-)prüfen
	to develop [dɪˈveləp]	(sich) entwickeln
	to label [ˈleɪbl]	benennen, etikettieren
	to swop [swɒp]	(aus-, ver-)tauschen
35	**society** [səˈsaɪəti]	Gesellschaft
	member [ˈmembə]	Mitglied
	state [steɪt]	(Bundes-)Staat
	unemployment [ˌʌnɪmˈplɔɪmənt]	Arbeitslosigkeit
	to be on the move [bi ɒn ðə ˈmuːv]	unterwegs, in Bewegung sein
	departure [dɪˈpɑːtʃə]	Abreise
	buyer [ˈbaɪə]	Einkäufer/in
	tough [tʌf]	hart
	retail [ˈriːteɪl]	Einzelhandel
	chain [tʃeɪn]	(Handels-)Kette
	branch [brɑːntʃ]	Niederlassung, Filiale
	citizen [ˈsɪtɪzn]	Bürger/in
	economic [ˌiːkəˈnɒmɪk]	wirtschaftlich, Wirtschafts-
	skills [skɪlz]	Fertigkeiten
	ambition [æmˈbɪʃn]	Ehrgeiz
	previous [ˈpriːviəs]	vorherig
	technical support [ˌteknɪkl səˈpɔːt]	technische Unterstützung
	economy [ɪˈkɒnəmi]	Wirtschaft, Konjunktur
	steady [ˈstedi]	stetig, gleichmäßig
	vacancy [ˈveɪkənsi]	freie Stelle
	skilled worker [ˌskɪld ˈwɜːkə]	Facharbeiter/in, gelernte/r Arbeiter/in
	to attract [əˈtrækt]	anziehen, -locken
	growth [grəʊθ]	Wachstum, Zunahme
	to remain [rɪˈmeɪn]	bleiben, verbleiben
	to behave [bɪˈheɪv]	sich verhalten, sich benehmen
	free-market economy [friː ˌmɑːkɪt ɪˈkɒnəmi]	freie Marktwirtschaft

	tax [tæks]	Steuer
	job protection [dʒɒb prəˈtekʃn]	Arbeitsschutz
	social security [ˌsəʊʃl sɪˈkjʊərəti]	soziale Absicherung, Sozialversicherung
	to fire [ˈfaɪə]	feuern, entlassen
	to hire [ˈhaɪə]	ein-, anstellen
	to take a risk [ˌteɪk ə ˈrɪsk]	ein Risiko eingehen
	to suit [suːt]	passen, recht sein
	to aim [eɪm]	zielen; beabsichtigen, bezwecken
36	**total** [ˈtəʊtl]	(ins)gesamt, Gesamtsumme
	workforce [ˈwɜːkfɔːs]	arbeitende Bevölkerung, Berufstätige
	politician [ˌpɒləˈtɪʃn]	Politiker/in
	unemployed [ˌʌnɪmˈplɔɪd]	arbeitslos, ohne Beschäftigung
	mother-in-law [ˈmʌðər ɪn lɔː]	Schwiegermutter
	to do well [ˌduː ˈwel]	gut sein, gut abschneiden
	technical knowledge [ˌteknɪkl ˈnɒlɪdʒ]	Fachwissen
	the big picture [ðə ˌbɪg ˈpɪktʃə]	das große Ganze
	re-united [ˌriːjuːˈnaɪtɪd]	wiedervereinigt
	sub-title [ˈsʌbtaɪtl]	Untertitel
	graph [grɑːf]	Grafik, Diagramm
	highly skilled [ˌhaɪli ˈskɪld]	gut ausgebildet, hoch qualifiziert
	to rise [raɪz]	(an)steigen, anwachsen
37	**to interpret** [ɪnˈtɜːprɪt]	interpretieren, deuten
	chart [tʃɑːt]	Diagramm, Tabelle
	slightly [ˈslaɪtli]	leicht, geringfügig
	steadily [ˈstedɪli]	stetig, gleichmäßig
	unchanged [ʌnˈtʃeɪndʒd]	unverändert
	to decrease [dɪˈkriːs]	sinken, fallen, abnehmen
	to shrink [ʃrɪŋk]	zurückgehen, schrumpfen
	average [ˈævərɪdʒ]	Durchschnitt
	expansion [ɪkˈspænʃn]	Erweiterung, Ausdehnung
	to employ [ɪmˈplɔɪ]	ein-, anstellen, beschäftigen
	to economize [ɪˈkɒnəmaɪz]	haushalten, (sparsam) wirtschaften
	survival [səˈvaɪvl]	Überleben
	to succeed [səkˈsiːd]	Erfolg haben, gelingen
	to direct [dəˈrekt]	leiten
	advert [ˈædvɜːt]	Anzeige, Werbespot
	operation [ˌɒpəˈreɪʃn]	Betrieb, Einsatz
	fastest-growing [ˌfɑːstɪstˈgrəʊɪŋ]	wachstumsintensivste/r/s
	to experience [ɪkˈspɪəriəns]	erfahren, erleben
	experienced [ɪkˈspɪəriənst]	erfahren
	approximately [əˈprɒksɪmətli]	ungefähr, etwa, zirka
	ability [əˈbɪləti]	Fähigkeit, Können
	strength [streŋθ]	Stärke, Kraft
	weakness [ˈwiːknəs]	Schwäche
38	**volunteer** [ˌvɒlənˈtɪə]	Freiwillige/r, Helfer/in
	to run [rʌn]	führen, betreiben, leiten
	to care for [ˈkeə fə]	sich kümmern um, pflegen
	elderly [ˈeldəli]	ältere Menschen, Senioren
	experimental [ɪkˌsperɪˈmentl]	Versuchs-, experimentell
	charity [ˈtʃærəti]	Wohltätigkeit, Wohltätigkeitsorganisation
	to volunteer [ˌvɒlənˈtɪə]	freiwillig arbeiten
	organic [ɔːˈgænɪk]	organisch; Bio-
	to analyze [ˈænəlaɪz]	analysieren
	to repaint [ˌriːˈpeɪnt]	neu anstreichen
	DIY (do-it-yourself) [ˌdiː aɪ ˈwaɪ]	Heimwerken, Do it yourself
	to take part in [teɪk ˈpɑːt ɪn]	teilnehmen an, mitmachen bei
	archaeological [ˌɑːkiəˈlɒdʒɪkl]	archäologisch
	dig [dɪg]	Ausgrabung
	injured [ˈɪndʒəd]	verletzt
	booklet [ˈbʊklət]	Broschüre
	to mind [maɪnd]	etw dagegen haben; aufpassen, beachten
	I'd rather … [aɪd ˈrɑːðə]	Ich möchte lieber …
39	**instructions** [ɪnˈstrʌkʃnz]	Bedienungsanleitung
	even though [ˈiːvn ðəʊ]	obwohl, doch
	sales [seɪlz]	Verkaufszahlen, Absatz
	slight [slaɪt]	gering, leicht
	unpleasant [ʌnˈpleznt]	unangenehm, unfreundlich
	used to [ˈjuːs tə]	früher …
	fortunately [ˈfɔːtʃənətli]	glücklicherweise
	to enclose [ɪnˈkləʊz]	beilegen, beifügen
	site map [ˈsaɪt mæp]	Lageplan
	ID (identification) [ˌaɪ ˈdiː]	Ausweis(dokument)
	label [ˈleɪbl]	Etikett, Marke
	to produce [prəˈdjuːs]	herstellen, produzieren
	ladder [ˈlædə]	Leiter
	overalls [ˈəʊvərɔːlz]	Overall, Arbeitsanzug
	to gasp [gɑːsp]	nach Luft ringen, japsen
	to stare [steə]	starren, anstarren

Unit 2 Reaching the market

40	**advertisement** [ədˈvɜːtɪsmənt]	Reklame, Werbung, Anzeige
	pop-up [ˈpɒpʌp]	Aufklapp-
	ad [æd]	*Kurzform von* advert
	neon sign [ˌniːɒn ˈsaɪn]	Neonreklame
	brochure [ˈbrəʊʃə]	Broschüre, Prospekt
	leaflet [ˈliːflət]	Broschüre, Prospekt
	commercial [kəˈmɜːʃl]	*hier:* Werbespot, Werbung
	full-(page) [ˌfʊlˈpeɪdʒ]	ganzseitig
	classified ad [ˌklæsɪfaɪd ˈæd]	Kleinanzeige
	sponsorship [ˈspɒnsəʃɪp]	Sponsoring
	glamorous [ˈglæmərəs]	glanzvoll, glamourös
	shocking [ˈʃɒkɪŋ]	schrecklich, schockierend
	disgusting [dɪsˈgʌstɪŋ]	ekelhaft, unerhört
	aim [eɪm]	Ziel, Absicht

	to vary ['veəri]	unterschiedlich sein, variieren
	to promote [prə'məʊt]	bewerben, unterstützen
	brand [brænd]	Marke
	image ['ɪmɪdʒ]	Image, Bild
	play on words [pleɪ ɒn 'wɜ:dz]	Wortspiel
41	**fashion** ['fæʃn]	Mode
	mover ['mu:və]	*etwa:* treibende Kraft
	whatever [wɒt'evə]	was auch immer
	odd [ɒd]	ungewöhnlich; sonderbar
	creation [kri'eɪʃn]	Kreation, Erfindung
	taste [teɪst]	Geschmack
	kind of ['kaɪnd əv]	irgendwie, ein bisschen
	to turn to ['tɜ:n tə]	sich wenden an, zuwenden
	inventive [ɪn'ventɪv]	erfinderisch
	cutting-edge [ˌkʌtɪŋ 'edʒ]	topaktuell, innovativ
	billion ['bɪliən]	Milliarde
	to ship [ʃɪp]	versenden
	researcher [rɪ'sɜ:tʃə]	Forscher
	influencer ['ɪnfluənsə]	jd mit Einfluss
	to invent [ɪn'vent]	erfinden
	to adopt [ə'dɒpt]	annehmen, übernehmen
	status ['steɪtəs]	Status, Ansehen
	equally ['i:kwəli]	gleichermaßen
	mainstream ['meɪnstri:m]	massentauglich
	gothic look [ˌgɒθɪk 'lʊk]	*Moderichtung*
	constantly ['kɒnstəntli]	ständig
	outfit ['aʊtfɪt]	Kleidung, Aufzug
	to move on [ˌmu:v 'ɒn]	weiter sein
	sense [sens]	Sinn
	to make up [ˌmeɪk 'ʌp]	ausmachen, bilden
	importance [ɪm'pɔ:tns]	Bedeutung
	largely ['lɑ:dʒli]	weitgehend, zum größten Teil
42	**trade** [treɪd]	Handel
	textile ['tekstaɪl]	Textilie, Textil-
	source [sɔ:s]	Quelle
	quota ['kwəʊtə]	Quote, Mengenbegrenzung
	dramatically [drə'mætɪkli]	dramatisch
	to flood [flʌd]	überfluten
	to set up [ˌset 'ʌp]	einrichten, gründen
	longer-term [ˌlɒŋgə 'tɜ:m]	längerfristig
	share [ʃeə]	Anteil
	to estimate ['estɪmeɪt]	schätzen
	pressure ['preʃə]	Druck
	similarity [ˌsɪmə'lærəti]	Ähnlichkeit
	to create [kri'eɪt]	(er)schaffen, machen
	liking ['laɪkɪŋ]	Geschmack
43	**invention** [ɪn'venʃn]	Erfindung
	productive [prə'dʌktɪv]	produktiv
	to go for sth ['gəʊ fə]	etw nehmen, gut finden
	man-made ['mænmeɪd]	künstlich, Kunst-
	cloth [klɒθ]	Stoff
	to express [ɪk'spres]	ausdrücken
	proportion [prə'pɔ:ʃn]	Verhältnis
	to manufacture [ˌmænju'fæktʃə]	herstellen, produzieren
	shopping mall ['ʃɒpɪŋ mɔ:l]	Einkaufspassage
	mainly ['meɪnli]	hauptsächlich, vor allem
	summary ['sʌməri]	Zusammenfassung
	in addition [ɪn ə'dɪʃn]	darüber hinaus
44	**first of all** [fɜ:st əv 'ɔ:l]	zu(aller)erst, zunächst
	to recognize ['rekəgnaɪz]	erkennen, wieder erkennen
	mind [maɪnd]	Bewusstsein, Gedächtnis
	partly ['pɑ:tli]	teilweise, zum Teil
	frequent ['fri:kwənt]	häufig, oft
	feeling ['fi:lɪŋ]	Gefühl
	to trust [trʌst]	vertrauen
	reliable [rɪ'laɪəbl]	zuverlässig
	reasonable ['ri:znəbl]	vernünftig, angemessen
	emotional [ɪ'məʊʃənl]	gefühlsmäßig, -betont
	feminine ['femənɪn]	feminin, weiblich
	competitor [kəm'petɪtə]	Konkurrent/in, Wettbewerber/in
	to keep a promise [ˌki:p ə 'prɒmɪs]	ein Versprechen halten
	to deliver [dɪ'lɪvə]	*hier:* halten, was es verspricht
	brand loyalty [brænd 'lɔɪəlti]	Markentreue
	to advertise ['ædvətaɪz]	werben (für), Werbung machen für
	precious metal ˌpreʃəs 'metl]	Edelmetall
	stainless steel [ˌsteɪnləs 'sti:l]	rostfreier Stahl
	craftsmanship ['krɑ:ftsmənʃɪp]	Handwerkskunst
	scratch-resistant ['skrætʃ rɪzɪstənt]	kratzfest
	akin to [ə'kɪn tə]	(einer Sache) ähnlich
	jewellery ['dʒu:əlri]	Schmuck
	watchmaking ['wɒtʃmeɪkɪŋ]	Uhrmacherei
	suited to ['su:tɪd tə]	geeignet für
	high-performance [ˌhaɪ pə'fɔ:məns]	Hochleistungs-
	feature ['fi:tʃə]	Merkmal, besondere Eigenschaft
	reinforced glass screen [ˌri:ɪnfɔ:st 'glɑ:s skri:n]	verstärkter Glasbildschirm
	advanced [əd'vɑ:nst]	fortschrittlich
	handset ['hændset]	Handapparat
	work of art [ˌwɜ:k əv 'ɑ:t]	Kunstwerk
	iconic [aɪ'kɒnɪk]	mit Kultsymbolcharakter
	above all [əˌbʌv 'ɔ:l]	vor allem
	high-quality [ˌhaɪ 'kwɒləti]	hochwertig
	desire [dɪ'zaɪə]	Verlangen, Wunsch
	elegantly ['elɪgəntli]	elegant
	owner ['əʊnə]	Besitzer/in, Eigentümer/in
	at the edge of technology [ət ði ˌedʒ əv tek'nɒlədʒi]	mit Spitzentechnik
	plastic ['plæstɪk]	Plastik, Kunststoff
	traditional [trə'dɪʃənl]	traditionell
	to provide [prə'vaɪd]	(an)bieten, zur Verfügung stellen
	after all [ˌɑ:ftər 'ɔ:l]	schließlich (doch)
45	**expenditure** [ɪk'spendɪtʃə]	Ausgabe(n), Kosten
	spending ['spendɪŋ]	Ausgaben

	account for [ə'kaʊnt fə]	ausmachen, betragen
	services ['sɜːvɪsɪz]	Dienstleistungen
	to define [dɪ'faɪn]	definieren
	comparison [kəm'pærɪsn]	Vergleich
	analysis [ə'næləsɪs]	Analyse
	well-known [ˌwel'nəʊn]	sehr bekannt, berühmt
	mark [mɑːk]	Marke; Markierung
	tool [tuːl]	Werkzeug, Instrument
	humour ['hjuːmə]	Humor
	basically ['beɪsɪkli]	grundsätzlich, eigentlich
	trainers ['treɪnəz]	Turn-, Tennisschuhe
	to be serious [bi 'sɪəriəs]	etw ernst meinen
46	**opposite** ['ɒpəzɪt]	Gegenteil, Gegensatz
	masculine ['mæskjəlɪn]	maskulin, männlich
	co-director [ˌkəʊdə'rektə]	*etwa:* Mitgeschäftsführer
	generally speaking ['dʒenrəli spiːkɪŋ]	im Allgemeinen
	excitement [ɪk'saɪtmənt]	Aufregung
	gold medal [ˌgəʊld 'medl]	Goldmedaille
	media council ['miːdiə kaʊnsl]	Medienrat
	ups and downs [ˌʌps ən 'daʊnz]	Auf und Ab, Höhen und Tiefen
	valuable ['væljuəbl]	wertvoll
	account [ə'kaʊnt]	Konto, Kunde
	event [ɪ'vent]	Ereignis, Veranstaltung
	relationship [rɪ'leɪʃnʃɪp]	Beziehung, Verhältnis
	tobacco [tə'bækəʊ]	Tabak
	to suffer ['sʌfə]	leiden, erleiden
	to present [prɪ'zent]	vorstellen, präsentieren
	to rewrite [ˌriː'raɪt]	umschreiben
	concept ['kɒnsept]	Konzept, Idee
	competition [ˌkɒmpə'tɪʃn]	Konkurrenz, Wettbewerb
	development [dɪ'veləpmənt]	Entwicklung
	stage [steɪdʒ]	Abschnitt, Stufe, Phase
	detailed ['diːteɪld]	ausführlich, genau
	completion [kəm'pliːʃn]	Abschluss, Erledigung
	account executive [əˌkaʊnt ɪg'zekjətɪv]	Kundenbetreuer
	responsible [rɪ'spɒnsəbl]	verantwortlich
	commercial matters [kəˌmɜːʃl 'mætəz]	kaufmännische Angelegenheiten
	business manager ['bɪznəs mænɪdʒə]	kaufmännischer Leiter
47	**job description** [dʒɒb dɪ'skrɪpʃn]	Stellenbeschreibung
	copywriter ['kɒpiraɪtə]	(Werbe-)Texter/in
	media planner [ˌmiːdiə 'plænə]	Medienplaner
	print media ['prɪnt miːdiə]	Printmedien
	to link [lɪŋk]	verbinden
	closely ['kləʊsli]	eng
	to sort out [ˌsɔːt 'aʊt]	in Ordnung bringen, klären
	payment ['peɪmənt]	Zahlung, Bezahlung
	at last [ət 'lɑːst]	endlich, schließlich
	to pitch for ['pɪtʃ fə]	ein Angebot für etw abgeben
	campaign [kæm'peɪn]	Kampagne, Aktion
	to take over [ˌteɪk 'əʊvə]	übernehmen
	rough [rʌf]	Rohentwurf
	creative team [kriˌeɪtɪv 'tiːm]	*etwa:* kreative Mannschaft
	Not too bad. [nɒt ˌtuː 'bæd]	Es geht so. Ganz gut.
	screen [skriːn]	Bildschirm
	launch [lɔːntʃ]	Start (einer Kampagne)
	Ltd = Limited ['lɪmɪtɪd]	GmbH
	to shadow ['ʃædəʊ]	begleiten
	addressee [ˌædre'siː]	Empfänger/in, Adressat/in
	appropriately [ə'prəʊpriətli]	geeignet, angemessen
	to refer [rɪ'fɜː]	verweisen (auf), sich beziehen (auf)
	to look forward to [ˌlʊk 'fɔːwəd tə]	sich freuen auf
	appropriate [ə'prəʊpriət]	geeignet, angemessen
	greeting ['griːtɪŋ]	Begrüßung, Gruß(formel)
	section head ['sekʃn hed]	Abteilungsleiter/in
	employee [ɪm'plɔɪiː]	Angestellte/r, Arbeitnehmer/in
48	**formula** ['fɔːmjələ]	Formel
	to attract attention [əˌtrækt ə'tenʃn]	Aufmerksamkeit erregen
	to raise [reɪz]	erhöhen
	to encourage [ɪn'kʌrɪdʒ]	ermuntern, fördern
	action ['ækʃn]	Handlung, Aktion
	real-life [ˌrɪəl 'laɪf]	wie im wirklichen Leben
	small print [ˌsmɔːl 'prɪnt]	das Kleingedruckte
	series ['sɪəriːz]	Reihe
	sub-heading ['sʌbhedɪŋ]	Untertitel
	ringtone ['rɪŋtəʊn]	Klingelton
	to depend on [dɪ'pend ɒn]	abhängen von, abhängig sein von
	musical ['mjuːzɪkl]	musikalisch, Musik-
	lovable ['lʌvəbl]	liebenswert
	heading ['hedɪŋ]	Überschrift
	order line ['ɔːdə laɪn]	Bestellhotline
	digit code ['dɪdʒɪt kəʊd]	Zahlencode
	tourist sight ['tʊərɪst saɪt]	Touristenattraktion
	back-up ['bækʌp]	Unterstützungs-, Reserve-
	vote [vəʊt]	Abstimmung
49	**presentation** [ˌprezn'teɪʃn]	Vorführung, Präsentation
	to manage ['mænɪdʒ]	verwalten, führen
	progress ['prəʊgres]	Verlauf, Fortschritt
	to finalize ['faɪnəlaɪz]	endgültig festlegen
	slot [slɒt]	Sendeplatz
	final ['faɪnl]	endgültig, letzte/r/s
	script [skrɪpt]	Drehbuch, Skript
	artwork ['ɑːtwɜːk]	Illustrationen, Bildmaterial
	space [speɪs]	Raum, Platz
	instruction [ɪn'strʌkʃn]	Anweisung, Aufforderung
	on board [ɒn 'bɔːd]	an Bord
	hand luggage ['hænd lʌgɪdʒ]	Handgepäck
	name tag ['neɪm tæg]	Namensschild
	at all times [ət ɔːl 'taɪmz]	jederzeit
	oil/water level ['ɔɪl, 'wɔːtə levl]	Öl-/Wasserstand
	tyre pressure ['taɪə preʃə]	Reifendruck
	to leave out [ˌliːv 'aʊt]	weg-, auslassen
	agent ['eɪdʒənt]	Handelnde/r

	to print [prɪnt]	drucken
	to invest [ɪn'vest]	investieren, anlegen
	greatly ['greɪtli]	in hohem Maße

Unit 3 The road to the future

50	**tailback** ['teɪlbæk]	Autoschlange
	commuter [kə'mju:tə]	Pendler/in
	misery ['mɪzəri]	Elend
	to worsen ['wɜ:sn]	sich verschlechtern
	headline ['hedlaɪn]	Schlagzeile, Überschrift
	scene [si:n]	Szene, Szenerie
	to imagine [ɪ'mædʒɪn]	sich vorstellen, sich einbilden
	calm [kɑ:m]	ruhig, gelassen
	relaxed [rɪ'lækst]	entspannt, locker
	anxious ['æŋkʃəs]	ängstlich, besorgt
	worried ['wʌrid]	besorgt, beunruhigt
	frustrated [frʌ'streɪtɪd]	frustriert
	present ['preznt]	gegenwärtig, aktuell
	distance to go [ˌdɪstəns tə 'gəʊ]	zurückzulegende Entfernung
	cause [kɔ:z]	Ursache, Grund, Anlass
	to commute [kə'mju:t]	pendeln, zum Arbeitsplatz fahren
	office manager [ˌɒfɪs 'mænɪdʒə]	Büroleiter/in
	cellphone ['selfəʊn]	Handy, Mobiltelefon
	technician [tek'nɪʃn]	Techniker/in
	dry cleaning [ˌdraɪ 'kli:nɪŋ]	chemische Reinigung
51	**overcrowding** [ˌəʊvə'kraʊdɪŋ]	Überfüllung
	traffic congestion ['træfɪk kəndʒestʃən]	Verkehrsstauung
	delivery [dɪ'lɪvəri]	Zustellung, (Aus-)Lieferung
	fuel ['fju:əl]	Kraftstoff, Treibstoff
	people carrier ['pi:pl kæriə]	Kleinbus
	awful ['ɔ:fl]	furchtbar, schrecklich
	exhaust emission [ɪg'zɔ:st ɪˌmɪʃn]	Abgasemission
	car sharing ['kɑ: ʃeərɪŋ]	Carsharing
	to share ['ʃeə]	sich etw teilen
	vehicle ['vi:əkl]	Fahrzeug, Verkehrsmittel
	pollution [pə'lu:ʃn]	(Umwelt-, Luft-)-Verschmutzung
	Secretary of State for Transport [sekrətri əv ˌsteɪt fə 'trænspɔ:t]	Verkehrsminister/in
	to keep up [ˌki:p 'ʌp]	Schritt halten, mithalten
	amount [ə'maʊnt]	Menge, Ausmaß
	various ['veəriəs]	verschiedene(r)
	permit ['pɜ:mɪt]	Erlaubnis, Genehmigung
	motorway ['məʊtəweɪ]	Autobahn
	to get one's money's worth [ˌget wʌnz mʌniz 'wɜ:θ]	auf seine Kosten kommen
	toll [təʊl]	Maut(gebühr)
	to cross [krɒs]	überqueren, *hier:* hinüberfahren
	to avoid [ə'vɔɪd]	(ver)meiden, aus dem Weg gehen
	charges ['tʃɑ:dʒɪz]	Gebühren, Kosten
	congestion charge [kən'dʒestʃən tʃɑ:dʒ]	Staugebühr
	efficiently [ɪ'fɪʃntli]	effizient, erfolgreich, tüchtig, wirksam
	to cut [kʌt]	reduzieren, senken
	damage ['dæmɪdʒ]	Schaden, Schäden
52	**congestion charging** [kən'dʒestʃən tʃɑ:dʒɪŋ]	Erhebung von Staugebühren
	globally ['gləʊbəli]	global
	passenger ['pæsɪndʒə]	Passagier/in, Mitifahrer/in
	scheme [ski:m]	Plan, Programm
	to be charged [bi 'tʃɑ:dʒd]	(eine Gebühr) zahlen müssen
	to enter ['entə]	hereinkommen, -fahren; eintreten (in)
	reduction [rɪ'dʌkʃn]	Verringerung, Senkung
	to push [pʊʃ]	drängen
	close to ['kləʊs tə]	nahe (bei)
	to consider [kən'sɪdə]	in Erwägung ziehen, nachdenken über
	increase ['ɪŋkri:s]	Zunahme, Wachstum
	benefit ['benɪfɪt]	Vorteil, Nutzen
53	**load** [ləʊd]	Ladung, Fracht
	drop [drɒp]	*hier:* Lieferung
	tunnel ['tʌnl]	Tunnel
	border ['bɔ:də]	Grenze
	via ['vaɪə]	über
	to deliver [dɪ'lɪvə]	liefern, zustellen
	area ['eəriə]	Gebiet, Bereich
54	**to work** [wɜ:k]	funktionieren
	impossible [ɪm'pɒsəbl]	unmöglich, undenkbar
	to construct [kən'strʌkt]	bauen
	to reduce [rɪ'dju:s]	verringern, senken
	to damage ['dæmɪdʒ]	beschädigen, schaden
	to refuse [rɪ'fju:z]	sich weigern
	in particular [ɪn pə'tɪkjələ]	insbesondere
	soft [sɒft]	mild
	intonation [ˌɪntə'neɪʃn]	Tonfall
	polite [pə'laɪt]	höflich
	definite ['defɪnət]	bestimmt, fest, definitiv
	school run ['sku:l rʌn]	Fahrt zur Schule
	to be frightened of [bi 'fraɪtnd əv]	Angst haben vor
	rush hour ['rʌʃ aʊə]	Hauptverkehrszeit, Stoßzeit
	a tiny little bit [ə ˌtaɪni lɪtl 'bɪt]	ein klitzekleines Bisschen
55	**to face** [feɪs]	sich gegenübersehen, rechnen müssen mit
	pricing ['praɪsɪŋ]	Preisfestsetzung, -gestaltung
	be based on [bi 'beɪst ɒn]	beruhen auf, basieren auf
	location [ləʊ'keɪʃn]	Standort, Position
	to track [træk]	verfolgen, aufspüren
	to record [rɪ'kɔ:d]	aufzeichnen
	distance travelled ['dɪstəns trævld]	zurückgelegte Entfernung
	to criticize ['krɪtɪsaɪz]	kritisieren
	to hide [haɪd]	(sich) verstecken, (sich) verbergen

	to fear [fɪə]	(be-)fürchten, Angst haben
	to destroy [dɪ'strɔɪ]	zerstören, vernichten
	haulier ['hɔ:liə]	Spediteur, Transportunternehmer
	to balance ['bæləns]	(sich) ausgleichen, im Gleichgewicht halten
	provided that [prə'vaɪdɪd ðət]	vorausgesetzt, dass
	urban ['ɜ:bən]	städtisch, Stadt-
	to gain [geɪn]	gewinnen
	environmentalist [ɪnˌvaɪrən'mentəlɪst]	Umweltschützer/in
	earth [ɜ:θ]	Erde
	electric [ɪ'lektrɪk]	elektrisch
	performance [pə'fɔ:məns]	Leistung
	limited ['lɪmɪtɪd]	beschränkt, begrenzt
	range [reɪndʒ]	Auswahl, Bandbreite
	to plug in [ˌplʌg 'ɪn]	anschließen, einstecken
	to recharge [ˌri:'tʃɑ:dʒ]	aufladen
	power station ['paʊə steɪʃn]	Kraftwerk
	to supply [sə'plaɪ]	liefern, versorgen
	electricity [ɪˌlek'trɪsəti]	Elektrizität, Strom
	hybrid vehicle [ˌhaɪbrɪd 'vi:əkl]	Hybridauto
	movement ['mu:vmənt]	Bewegung
	to support [sə'pɔ:t]	unterstützen, stützen
	for instance [fə'rɪnstəns]	zum Beispiel
	to perform [pə'fɔ:m]	Leistung bringen
	to power ['paʊə]	antreiben
	fuel cell ['fju:əl sel]	Brennstoffzelle
	hydrogen ['haɪdrədʒən]	Wasserstoff
	oxygen ['ɒksɪdʒən]	Sauerstoff
	waste product [weɪst 'prɒdʌkt]	Abfallprodukt
	except for [ɪk'sept fə]	außer, abgesehen von
	renewable [rɪ'nju:əbl]	erneuerbar
	environmentally friendly [ɪnˌvaɪrənˌmentəli 'frendli]	umweltfreundlich
	running costs [ˌrʌnɪŋ 'kɒsts]	Unterhaltskosten, Betriebskosten
56	**supplies** [sə'plaɪz]	Vorräte
	coal [kəʊl]	Kohle
	nuclear energy [ˌnju:kliə 'enədʒi]	Kernenergie
	hydro energy [ˌhaɪdrəʊ 'enədʒi]	Wasserkraft
	solar energy [ˌsəʊlə 'enədʒi]	Sonnenenergie
	biomass energy [ˌbaɪəʊmæs 'enədʒi]	Bioenergie
	to predict [prɪ'dɪkt]	vorhersagen
	to double ['dʌbl]	(sich) verdoppeln
	previously ['pri:viəsli]	vorher
	to reject [rɪ'dʒekt]	ablehnen, zurückweisen
	rural ['rʊərəl]	ländlich
	to solve [sɒlv]	lösen
	cute [kju:t]	niedlich, knuffig
	No way. [ˌnəʊ 'weɪ]	Auf gar keinen Fall.
57	**greenhouse** ['gri:nhaʊs]	Treibhaus
	income ['ɪnkʌm]	Einkommen
	solution [sə'lu:ʃn]	Lösung
	to represent [ˌreprɪ'zent]	vertreten, repräsentieren
	to disagree [ˌdɪsə'gri:]	anderer Meinung sein
	campaign group [kæm'peɪn gru:p]	Aktionsgruppe
	to quote [kwəʊt]	zitieren
	to get into a mess [ˌget ɪntə ə 'mes]	in einen Schlamassel geraten
	proposal [prə'pəʊzl]	Vorschlag
	to put forward [ˌpʊt 'fɔ:wəd]	vorbringen, aufstellen
	nightmare ['naɪtmeə]	Alptraum
	novel ['nɒvl]	Roman
	essential [ɪ'senʃl]	wesentlich, unbedingt notwendig
	enormous [ɪ'nɔ:məs]	enorm, gewaltig
	saving ['seɪvɪŋ]	Ersparnis, Einsparung
	to save [seɪv]	(Geld) sparen, einsparen
	certain ['sɜ:tn]	bestimmt
	to summarize ['sʌməraɪz]	zusammenfassen
	(point of) view [ˌpɔɪnt əv 'vju:]	Standpunkt, Ansicht
	to cope [kəʊp]	(damit) zurechtkommen
	to afford [ə'fɔ:d]	(es) sich leisten (können)
58	**factsheet** ['fæktʃi:t]	Informationsblatt
	population [ˌpɒpju'leɪʃn]	Bevölkerung, Einwohner(zahl)
	industrial [ɪn'dʌstriəl]	Industrie-, industriell
	conurbation [ˌkɒnɜ:'beɪʃn]	Ballungsgebiet, -raum
	to contain [kən'teɪn]	enthalten
	bus service ['bʌs sɜ:vɪs]	Busverbindung
	fare [feə]	Fahrpreis
	unreliable [ˌʌnrɪ'laɪəbl]	unzuverlässig
	tram [træm]	Straßenbahn
	extension [ɪk'stenʃn]	Ausdehnung, Erweiterung
	ministry ['mɪnɪstri]	Ministerium
	official [ə'fɪʃl]	offiziell, amtlich
	councillor ['kaʊnsələ]	Ratsmitglied
	to compare [kəm'peə]	vergleichen, sich vergleichen lassen
	Dear sir or madam, [ˌdɪə sɜ: ɔ: 'mædəm]	Sehr geehrte Damen und Herren,
	to state [steɪt]	vortragen
	position [pə'zɪʃn]	Position, Standpunkt
	opponent [ə'pəʊnənt]	Gegner/in, Gegenüber
59	**return** [rɪ'tɜ:n]	Rückfahrkarte
	ferry ['feri]	Fähre
	enjoyable [ɪn'dʒɔɪəbl]	angenehm
	urgently ['ɜ:dʒəntli]	dringend
	long-distance [ˌlɒŋ'dɪstəns]	Fern-, Langstrecken-
	comparison [kəm'pærɪsn]	Steigerung

Unit 4 Have to have!

60	**retail outlet** ['ri:teɪl aʊtlet]	Einzelhandelsgeschäft
	delicatessen [ˌdelɪkə'tesn]	Feinkost(laden)
	department store [dɪ'pɑ:tmənt stɔ:]	Kauf-, Warenhaus
	electrical goods [ɪˌlektrɪkl 'gʊdz]	Elektrowaren

	fast-food takeaway [,fɑːst fuːd 'teɪkəweɪ]	Imbiss
	jeweller's ['dʒuːələz]	Juwelier(geschäft)
	to go mad [gəʊ 'mæd]	durchdrehen
	display [dɪ'spleɪ]	Auslage, Dekoration
	canned [kænd]	in der Dose
	bottled ['bɒtld]	aus der Flasche
	frozen ['frəʊzn]	tiefgefroren
	special offer [,speʃl 'ɒfə]	Sonderangebot
	purchase ['pɜːtʃəs]	(Ein-)Kauf
	debit card ['debɪt kɑːd]	Bankkarte
	loyalty card ['lɔɪəlti kɑːd]	Kundenkarte
	checkout ['tʃekaʊt]	Kasse
	impulse ['ɪmpʌls]	Impuls
61	**brand name** ['brænd neɪm]	Markenzeichen, -name
	value-added ['væljuː 'ædɪd]	Mehrwert-
	pre-cooked [,priː'kʊkt]	vorgekocht
	profitable ['prɒfɪtəbl]	gewinnbringend, rentabel
	to display [dɪ'spleɪ]	aus-, aufstellen
	at eye level [æt 'aɪ levl]	auf Augenhöhe
	to watch out [,wɒtʃ 'aʊt]	aufpassen
	basics ['beɪsɪks]	Grundnahrungsmittel
	to grab [græb]	greifen, packen
	trolley ['trɒli]	Einkaufswagen
	basket ['bɑːskɪt]	Korb
	to slow down [,sləʊ 'daʊn]	(sich) verlangsamen
	natural ['nætʃrəl]	natürlich, echt
	rainbow ['reɪnbəʊ]	Regenbogen
	packet ['pækɪt]	Packung, Schachtel
	peppers ['pepəz]	Paprika(schoten)
	delicious [dɪ'lɪʃəs]	köstlich, lecker
	to resist [rɪ'zɪst]	widerstehen
	decor ['deɪkɔː]	Ausstattung, Dekor
	bakery ['beɪkəri]	Bäckerei
	counter ['kaʊntə]	Theke, Schalter
	freshness ['freʃnəs]	Frische
	memory ['meməri]	Erinnerung
	hypermarket ['haɪpəmɑːkɪt]	großer Einkaufsmarkt
	captive ['kæptɪv]	gefangen, Gefangene/r
	essentials [ɪ'senʃlz]	(absolut) notwendige Dinge
	demand [dɪ'mɑːnd]	Bedarf, Nachfrage
	item ['aɪtəm]	Artikel, Stück
	far apart [,fɑːr ə'pɑːt]	weit auseinander
	semi- ['semi]	halb-
62	**percentage** [pə'sentɪdʒ]	Prozentsatz
	consumer [kən'sjuːmə]	Verbraucher/in, Konsument/in
	out-of-town [,aʊt əv 'taʊn]	außerstädtisch
	competitive [kəm'petətɪv]	konkurrenzfähig
	high street ['haɪ striːt]	Hauptgeschäftsstraße
	survivor [sə'vaɪvə]	Überlebende/r
	to include [ɪn'kluːd]	enthalten, einbeziehen, umfassen
	up-market [,ʌp'mɑːkɪt]	im oberen Marktsegment
	to gather ['gæðə]	sich versammeln
	wholesale distributor [,həʊlseɪl dɪ'strɪbjətə]	Großhändler
	to handle ['hændl]	umschlagen, abwickeln
	quantity ['kwɒntəti]	Menge
	in bulk [ɪn 'bʌlk]	en gros
	producer [prə'djuːsə]	Erzeuger, Hersteller/in
	mail order [,meɪl 'ɔːdə]	Versandhandel
	individual [,ɪndɪ'vɪdʒuəl]	Einzel-
	efficiency [ɪ'fɪʃnsi]	Effizienz
63	**carton** ['kɑːtn]	Packung, Paket, Karton
	jar [dʒɑː]	(Marmeladen-)Glas
	loaf [ləʊf]	Laib
	slice [slaɪs]	Scheibe
	to pack [pæk]	(ein-, ver-)packen
	dozen ['dʌzn]	Dutzend
	produce ['prɒdjuːs]	*hier:* landwirtschaftliche(s) Erzeugnis(se)
	medium-size(d) ['miːdiəmsaɪzd]	mittelgroß
	small change [,smɔːl 'tʃeɪndʒ]	Wechsel-, Kleingeld
	note [nəʊt]	Geldschein, Banknote
	rubbish ['rʌbɪʃ]	Müll
	scales [skeɪlz]	Waage
	rate [reɪt]	Tarif
	size [saɪz]	Größe
	changing room ['tʃeɪndʒɪŋ ruːm]	Umkleideraum, -kabine
	loose [luːs]	weit (geschnitten), lose, locker
	waist [weɪst]	Taille
	sleeve [sliːv]	Ärmel
	pure [pjʊə]	rein, echt
	cotton ['kɒtn]	Baumwolle
	synthetic [sɪn'θetɪk]	synthetisch
64	**politeness** [pə'laɪtnəs]	Höflichkeit
	indirectness [,ɪndə'rektnəs]	Indirektheit
	to request [rɪ'kwest]	bitten um
	parcel ['pɑːsl]	Paket, Päckchen
	colleague ['kɒliːg]	Kollege/Kollegin
	to adapt [ə'dæpt]	anpassen, adaptieren
	to act out [,ækt 'aʊt]	vorspielen, aufführen
65	**everyday life** [,evrideɪ 'laɪf]	Alltag
	worth [wɜːθ]	wert, im Wert von
	specialty shop ['speʃəlti ʃɒp]	Fachgeschäft
	gift [gɪft]	Geschenk
	advantage [əd'vɑːntɪdʒ]	Vorteil, Vorzug
	convenient [kən'viːniənt]	günstig, angenehm
	rapidly ['ræpɪdli]	schnell, rasch
	crowded ['kraʊdɪd]	überfüllt, voll
	at one's expense [ət wʌnz ɪk'spens]	auf jds Kosten
	e-tail ['iː teɪl]	Einzelhandel im Internet
	level ['levl]	Niveau
	dot com [dɒt'kɒm]	Internetfirma
	to fail [feɪl]	scheitern
	to go bankrupt [gəʊ 'bæŋkrʌpt]	Pleite gehen
	channel ['tʃænl]	Kanal, (Vertriebs-)Weg
	warehouse ['weəhaʊs]	Lager
	to mix [mɪks]	mischen

	dealer ['di:lə]	Händler/in
	imaginative [ɪ'mædʒɪnətɪv]	phantasievoll, einfallsreich
	efficient [ɪ'fɪʃnt]	effizient, (leistungs)fähig
66	**to charge** [tʃɑ:dʒ]	in Rechnung stellen, berechnen
	warmth [wɔ:mθ]	Wärme
	insurance [ɪn'ʃʊərəns]	Versicherung
	to comment ['kɒment]	kommentieren, bemerken
67	**hardly** ['hɑ:dli]	(wohl) kaum
	to purchase ['pɜ:tʃəs]	(ein)kaufen
	auction ['ɔ:kʃn]	Versteigerung, Auktion
	to compete [kəm'pi:t]	konkurrieren, im Wettbewerb stehen
	ever since [,evə 'sɪns]	seitdem
	founder ['faʊndə]	Gründer/in
	treasure ['treʒə]	Schatz
	convenience [kən'vi:niəns]	Komfort, Annehmlichkeit
	method ['meθəd]	Art, Verfahren
	postage ['pəʊstɪdʒ]	Porto
	pre-addressed [pri: ə'drest]	adressiert
	postage-paid ['pəʊstɪdʒ peɪd]	freigemacht
	cheque [tʃek]	Scheck
68	**roughly** ['rʌfli]	ungefähr, etwa
	allowance [ə'laʊəns]	Taschengeld
	earnings ['ɜ:nɪŋz]	Verdienst, Einkünfte
	pie chart ['paɪ tʃɑ:t]	Tortendiagramm
	necessity [nə'sesəti]	Notwendigkeit, Bedürfnis
	requirement [rɪ'kwaɪəmənt]	Bedingung, Voraussetzung
	savings ['seɪvɪŋz]	Ersparnisse
	bar chart ['bɑ: tʃɑ:t]	Balkendiagramm
	brief [bri:f]	kurz
	to read out [,ri:d 'aʊt]	vorlesen
69	**checkout assistant** [,tʃekaʊt ə'sɪstənt]	Kassierer/in
	to press [pres]	drücken
	button ['bʌtn]	Taste, Knopf
	permission [pə'mɪʃn]	Erlaubnis, Genehmigung
	to ring [rɪŋ]	läuten, klingeln
	to consist [kən'sɪst]	bestehen
	indeed [ɪn'di:d]	in der Tat, allerdings
	treat [tri:t]	besondere Freude
	teabag ['ti:bæg]	Teebeutel
	stuff [stʌf]	Zeug
	addict ['ædɪkt]	Süchtige/r, Abhängige/r
	case [keɪs]	Fall

Unit 5 Our global market

70	**to communicate** [kə'mju:nɪkeɪt]	sich verständigen, kommunizieren
	engineer [,endʒɪ'nɪə]	Ingenieur/in, Techniker/in
	underground ['ʌndəgraʊnd]	Untergrund, unterirdisch
	health-conscious ['helθkɒnʃəs]	gesundheitsbewusst
	scientist ['saɪəntɪst]	(Natur-)Wissenschaftler/in
	tropical ['trɒpɪkl]	tropisch, Tropen-
	jungle ['dʒʌŋgl]	Dschungel, Urwald
71	**foreign** ['fɒrən]	ausländisch
	make [meɪk]	Marke, Fabrikat
	channel ['tʃænl]	Kanal, Sender
	steel worker ['sti:l wɜ:kə]	Stahlarbeiter/in
	steel mill ['sti:l mɪl]	Stahlwerk, Walzwerk
	import duties ['ɪmpɔ:t dju:ti:z]	Einfuhrzölle
	security guard [sɪ'kjʊərəti gɑ:d]	Sicherheitsbeamte/r
	programmer ['prəʊgræmə]	Programmierer/in
	to graduate ['grædʒueɪt]	einen Abschluss machen
	despite [dɪ'spaɪt]	trotz
	data transmission [,deɪtə træns'mɪʃn]	Daten(fern)übertragung
	well off [,wel 'ɒf]	gut dran, wohlhabend
	standard ['stændəd]	Maßstab, Norm
	clerical worker [,klerɪkl 'wɜ:kə]	Schreibkraft, Bürokraft
	quotation [kwəʊ'teɪʃn]	(Preis-)Angebot
	to beat [bi:t]	schlagen, übertreffen
	production schedule [prə'dʌkʃn ʃedju:l]	Produktionsplan, Fertigungsplan
	to go on strike [,gəʊ ɒn 'straɪk]	in Streik treten
	to feed [fi:d]	füttern, ernähren
	brand-new [,brænd'nju:]	nagelneu
	maintenance ['meɪntənəns]	Wartung
	fantastically [fæn'tæstɪkli]	fantastisch
	annual ['ænjuəl]	jährlich
72	**reason** ['ri:zn]	Grund, Begründung
	data processing [,deɪtə 'prəʊsesɪŋ]	Datenverarbeitung
	telecommunications [,telikə,mju:nɪ'keɪʃnz]	Fernmeldewesen
	rapid ['ræpɪd]	schnell, rasch
	target ['tɑ:gɪt]	Ziel
	low-cost [,ləʊ'kɒst]	billig, Billig-
	high-value [haɪ 'vælju:]	hochwertig, hochpreisig
	transfer ['trænsfɜ:]	Transfer, Verlagerung
	high-cost [,haɪ'kɒst]	hochwertig, kapitalintensiv
	high-level [,haɪ'levl]	auf hohem Niveau, anspruchsvoll
	locally ['ləʊkəli]	vor Ort
	wide [waɪd]	breit, weit
	to globalize ['gləʊblaɪz]	globalisieren
	to save sb from sth ['seɪv frəm]	jdn vor etw bewahren
	to emphasize ['emfəsaɪz]	betonen, hervorheben
	bright future [braɪt 'fju:tʃə]	glänzende Zukunft
73	**dictionary entry** ['dɪkʃənri entri]	Stichwort im Wörterbuch
	to look up [,lʊk 'ʌp]	nachschlagen
	flour ['flaʊə]	Mehl
	powder ['paʊdə]	Pulver
	pepper ['pepə]	Pfeffer
	technologically [,teknə'lɒdʒɪkli]	technologisch
	to repeat [rɪ'pi:t]	wiederholen
	literature ['lɪtrətʃə]	Literatur
	to treat [tri:t]	behandeln
	moral ['mɒrəl]	moralisch

	to obey [ə'beɪ]	befolgen, gehorchen
	economist [ɪ'kɒnəmɪst]	Wirtschaftswissenschaftler/in
	loss [lɒs]	Schaden, Verlust
	graduation [ˌgrædʒu'eɪʃn]	Erlangung eines akademischen Grades
	hopeful ['həʊpfl]	hoffnungsvoll
	ethnic group ['eθnɪk gru:p]	Volksgruppe
74	**poverty** ['pɒvəti]	Armut
	supplier [sə'plaɪə]	Anbieter/in, Lieferant/in
	to force [fɔ:s]	zwingen
	depressing [dɪ'presɪŋ]	bedrückend, deprimierend
	casual worker [ˌkæʒuəl 'wɜ:kə]	Gelegenheitsarbeiter
	bonus ['bəʊnəs]	Zulage, Prämie
	to pick [pɪk]	pflücken
	overtime ['əʊvətaɪm]	Überstunden
	to sew [səʊ]	nähen
	underwear ['ʌndəweə]	Unterwäsche
	crop [krɒp]	Ernte, Anbaupflanzen
	value ['vælju:]	Wert
	to collapse [kə'læps]	einbrechen, abstürzen
	existing [ɪg'zɪstɪŋ]	bestehend, vorhanden
	to form [fɔ:m]	bilden
	to examine [ɪg'zæmɪn]	untersuchen, prüfen
	to guarantee [ˌgærən'ti:]	garantieren
	gradually ['grædʒuəli]	allmählich, schrittweise
	meanwhile ['mi:nwaɪl]	inzwischen, zwischenzeitlich
	craft [krɑ:ft]	Handwerk
	middleman ['mɪdlmən]	Zwischenhändler
	breakdown ['breɪkdaʊn]	Aufteilung, -schlüsselung
	commission [kə'mɪʃn]	Provision, Gebühr
	labour ['leɪbə]	Arbeit, Arbeitskraft
	packaging ['pækɪdʒɪŋ]	Verpackung
	customs ['kʌstəmz]	Zoll
	shipping ['ʃɪpɪŋ]	Versand
	handling ['hændlɪŋ]	Abwicklung
75	**foundation** [faʊn'deɪʃn]	Stiftung
	turnover ['tɜ:nəʊvə]	Umsatz
	consumption [kən'sʌmpʃn]	Konsum, Verbrauch
	own-brand [ˌəʊn 'brænd]	Eigenmarke, Hausmarke
	council services ['kaʊnsl sɜ:vɪsɪz]	*etwa:* öffentliche Einrichtungen
	key [ki:]	Schlüssel
	involved in [ɪn'vɒlvd ɪn]	beteiligt an
	extra ['ekstrə]	zusätzlich
	foreigner ['fɒrənə]	Ausländer/in
76	**failure** ['feɪljə]	Pleite
	dependent [dɪ'pendənt]	abhängig
	to exclude [ɪk'sklu:d]	ausschließen
	aid [eɪd]	Hilfe
	raw material [ˌrɔ: mə'tɪəriəl]	Rohstoff(e)
	ground [graʊnd]	(Erd-)Boden
	investment [ɪn'vestmənt]	Investition, Anlage
	old-fashioned [ˌəʊld'fæʃənd]	altmodisch, veraltet
	due to ['dju: tə]	wegen, aufgrund von, dank
	explanation [ˌeksplə'neɪʃn]	Erklärung
	workshop ['wɜ:kʃɒp]	Werkstatt
	pan [pæn]	Pfanne
	to force down [ˌfɔ:s 'daʊn]	niederdrücken
	grateful ['greɪtfl]	dankbar
77	**body language** ['bɒdi læŋgwɪdʒ]	Körpersprache
	face-to-face [ˌfeɪs tə 'feɪs]	direkt (gegenüber), persönlich
	to interact [ˌɪntər'ækt]	interagieren, miteinander umgehen
	acceptable [ək'septəbl]	annehmbar, akzeptabel
	firm [fɜ:m]	fest
	handshake ['hændʃeɪk]	Händedruck
	to touch [tʌtʃ]	anfassen, berühren
	eye contact ['aɪ kɒntækt]	Blickkontakt
	uncomfortable [ʌn'kʌmftəbl]	unwohl, unangenehm
	rarely ['reəli]	selten
	confidence ['kɒnfɪdəns]	(Selbst-)Vertrauen, Selbstsicherheit
	pushy ['pʊʃi]	aufdringlich, penetrant
78	**to explore** [ɪk'splɔ:]	erforschen, erkunden
	association [əˌsəʊsi'eɪʃn]	Verband
	topic ['tɒpɪk]	Thema
	scale [skeɪl]	Skala
	spread [spred]	Verbreitung, Verteilung
	base [beɪs]	Basis
	concerning [kən'sɜ:nɪŋ]	bezüglich, hinsichtlich
	to spread [spred]	verbreiten, verteilen
	widely ['waɪdli]	weit (verbreitet)
	public relations [ˌpʌblɪk rɪ'leɪʃnz]	Öffentlichkeitsarbeit
79	**so as to** ['səʊ əz tə]	so dass, um … zu
	travel agent ['trævl eɪdʒənt]	Reisebüro(angestellte/r)
	to borrow ['bɒrəʊ]	(sich etw) borgen, (sich) (aus)leihen
	guidebook ['gaɪdbʊk]	Reiseführer
	library ['laɪbrəri]	Bibliothek
	to hire ['haɪə]	leihen, mieten
	to need sth badly [ˌni:d 'bædli]	etw dringend benötigen

Unit 6 The serious business of holidays

80	**adventure holiday** [ədˌventʃə 'hɒlədeɪ]	Abenteuerurlaub
	final exam [ˌfaɪnl ɪg'zæm]	Abschlussprüfung
81	**encounter** [ɪn'kaʊntə]	Begegnung
	harbour ['hɑ:bə]	Hafen
	preparation [ˌprepə'reɪʃn]	Vorbereitung
	to turn out [ˌtɜ:n 'aʊt]	sich herausstellen
	chef [ʃef]	Koch/Köchin
	resort [rɪ'zɔ:t]	Urlaubsort, Hotelanlage
	to tour [tʊə]	bereisen, eine Rundreise machen
	conversion [kən'vɜ:ʃn]	Umbau
	quote [kwəʊt]	Angebot, Preis
	to discover [dɪ'skʌvə]	entdecken
	deposit [dɪ'pɒzɪt]	Kaution, Anzahlung
	savings account ['seɪvɪŋz əkaʊnt]	Sparkonto

	loan [ləʊn]	Kredit, Darlehen
	to turn down [ˌtɜːn ˈdaʊn]	ablehnen
	to operate [ˈɒpəreɪt]	laufen, arbeiten
	cash flow [ˈkæʃ fləʊ]	Liquidität, Bargeldfluss
	paperwork [ˈpeɪpəwɜːk]	Formalitäten, Papierkram
	licence [ˈlaɪsns]	Genehmigung, Lizenz
	to convert [kənˈvɜːt]	umbauen
	in time [ɪn ˈtaɪm]	rechtzeitig
	to approve [əˈpruːv]	genehmigen
	to shake [ʃeɪk]	schütteln
	to hurry away [ˌhʌri ˈəweɪ]	davoneilen
	to greet [griːt]	(be)grüßen
	to appear [əˈpɪə]	erscheinen, auftauchen
82	**transition** [trænˈzɪʃn]	Übergang
	Eastern bloc [ˌiːstən ˈblɒk]	Ostblock
83	**to jump in** [ˌdʒʌmp ˈɪn]	auf etw anspringen, loslegen
	regular [ˈregjələ]	regelmäßig, regulär
	to hate [heɪt]	hassen, überhaupt nicht mögen
	insecurity [ˌɪnsɪˈkjʊərəti]	Unsicherheit
	translation [trænsˈleɪʃn]	Übersetzung
	risky [ˈrɪski]	riskant
84	**to be in credit** [ˌbi ɪn ˈkredɪt]	ein Guthaben haben
	overdrawn [ˌəʊvəˈdrɔːn]	überzogen
	to deposit [dɪˈpɒzɪt]	einzahlen
	to withdraw [wɪðˈdrɔː]	abheben
	in the black [ɪn ðə ˈblæk]	in den schwarzen Zahlen
	in the red [ɪn ðə ˈred]	in den roten Zahlen
	term [tɜːm]	Semester, Trimester
	overdraft facility [ˌəʊvədrɑːft fəˈsɪləti]	Überziehungskredit
	to overdraw [ˌəʊvəˈdrɔː]	überziehen
	separately [ˈseprətli]	getrennt
	secret [ˈsiːkrɪt]	geheim
	automated teller machine [ˌɔːtəmeɪtɪd ˈtelə məʃiːn]	Geldautomat
	cashpoint [ˈkæʃpɔɪnt]	Geldautomat
	to key in [ˌkiː ˈɪn]	eingeben
	to debit [ˈdebɪt]	belasten
	cheque book [ˈtʃek bʊk]	Scheckbuch, -heft
	register [ˈredʒɪstə]	Register, charakteristische Redeweise
	exchange [ɪksˈtʃeɪndʒ]	Austausch
	to take turns [teɪk ˈtɜːnz]	(sich) abwechseln
85	**debate** [dɪˈbeɪt]	Debatte
	instructor [ɪnˈstrʌktə]	Lehrer/in, Ausbilder/in
	trail [treɪl]	Spur
	surely [ˈʃʊəli]	sicherlich
	beauty [ˈbjuːti]	Schönheit
	footprint [ˈfʊtprɪnt]	Fußabdruck
	unknown [ˌʌnˈnəʊn]	unbekannt
	rainforest [ˈreɪnfɒrɪst]	Regenwald
	to disappear [ˌdɪsəˈpɪə]	verschwinden
	destruction [dɪˈstrʌkʃn]	Zerstörung, Vernichtung
	harm [hɑːm]	Schaden
	long-haul flight [ˌlɒŋ hɔːl ˈflaɪt]	Langstreckenflug
	required by [rɪˈkwaɪəd baɪ]	erforderlich für
	fully [ˈfʊli]	völlig, vollständig
	tourist spot [ˈtʊərɪst spɒt]	Urlaubsort
86	**decline** [dɪˈklaɪn]	Rückgang
	to decline [dɪˈklaɪn]	zurückgehen, sinken
	recovery [rɪˈkʌvəri]	Erholung, Aufschwung
	budget airline [ˌbʌdʒɪt ˈeəlaɪn]	Billigflieger
	to carry [ˈkæri]	befördern
	carrier [ˈkæriə]	Fluggesellschaft
	to overtake [ˌəʊvəˈteɪk]	überholen
	drunk [drʌŋk]	betrunken
	stereotype [ˈsteriətaɪp]	Stereotyp
	truth [truːθ]	Wahrheit
	nationality [ˌnæʃəˈnæləti]	Staatsangehörigkeit
	to associate [əˈsəʊʃieɪt]	in Verbindung bringen, assoziieren
	ambitious [æmˈbɪʃəs]	ehrgeizig
	determined [dɪˈtɜːmɪnd]	(fest) entschlossen, bestimmt
	dynamic [daɪˈnæmɪk]	dynamisch
	good-humoured [gʊd ˈhjuːməd]	gut gelaunt
	hardworking [ˌhɑːdˈwɜːkɪŋ]	fleißig
	loyal [ˈlɔɪəl]	treu, loyal
	practical [ˈpræktɪkl]	praktisch (veranlagt), realistisch
	sociable [ˈsəʊʃəbl]	gesellig
87	**exhausted** [ɪgˈzɔːstɪd]	erschöpft
	exhausting [ɪgˈzɔːstɪŋ]	anstrengend
	ski run [ˈskiː rʌn]	Skipiste
	landing [ˈlændɪŋ]	Landung
	terrified [ˈterɪfaɪd]	erschrocken, ängstlich
	terrifying [ˈterɪfaɪɪŋ]	erschreckend
	worrying [ˈwʌriɪŋ]	beunruhigend
	embarrassed [ɪmˈbærəst]	verlegen, bestürzt
	embarrassing [ɪmˈbærəsɪŋ]	peinlich
	death [deθ]	Tod
	to shorten [ˈʃɔːtn]	(ver-)kürzen
	to underline [ˌʌndəˈlaɪn]	unterstreichen
	to conclude [kənˈkluːd]	(ab)schließen, folgern
	to recommend [ˌrekəˈmend]	empfehlen
	to respond [rɪˈspɒnd]	reagieren (auf), antworten
	moreover [mɔːrˈəʊvə]	außerdem
	by contrast [baɪ ˈkɒntrɑːst]	im Gegensatz
88	**outward** [ˈaʊtwəd]	hier: Hinflug
	lively [ˈlaɪvli]	lebendig, rege, lebhaft
	single room [ˌsɪŋgl ˈruːm]	Einzelzimmer
	twin room [ˌtwɪn ˈruːm]	Zweibettzimmer
	half board [ˌhɑːfˈbɔːd]	Halbpension
	pppw = per person, per week	
	family-run [ˈfæməli rʌn]	in Familienhand
	bed and breakfast [ˌbed ən ˈbrekfəst]	Frühstückspension, Zimmer mit Frühstück
	downtown [ˈdaʊntaʊn]	(im/ins) Stadtzentrum
	pppn = per person, per night	
	equipped [ɪˈkwɪpt]	ausgerüstet, ausgestattet
	air conditioning (AC) [ˈeə kəndɪʃnɪŋ]	Klimaanlage
	budget [ˈbʌdʒɪt]	Budget, Etat

	pros and cons [ˌprəʊz ənd ˈkɒnz]	Für und Wider
	to add up [ˌæd ˈʌp]	zusammenzählen, -rechnen
	self-catering [ˌselfˈkeɪtərɪŋ]	mit Selbstversorgung
	facilities [fəˈsɪlətiz]	Einrichtungen, Möglichkeiten
89	**error** [ˈerə]	Fehler, Irrtum
	mixture [ˈmɪkstʃə]	Mischung
	sun tan [ˈsʌn tæn]	Sonnenbräune
	champion [ˈtʃæmpiən]	Meister/in, Champion

Unit 7 Eco-choices

90	**eco-** [ˈiːkəʊ]	Öko-
	eco-friendly [ˈiːkə frendli]	umweltfreundlich
	environment [ɪnˈvaɪrənmənt]	Umwelt
	saloon car [səˈluːn kɑː]	Limousine
	fuel economy [ˈfjuːəl ɪkɒnəmi]	geringer Kraftstoffverbrauch
	catalytic converter [ˌkætəˌlɪtɪk kənˈvɜːtə]	Katalysator
	smoothly [ˈsmuːðli]	ruhig, glatt
	sharp [ʃɑːp]	scharf
	acceleration [əkˌseləˈreɪʃn]	Beschleunigung
	braking [ˈbreɪkɪŋ]	Bremsen
	well-established [ˌwel ɪˈstæblɪʃt]	etabliert
91	**conventional** [kənˈvenʃənl]	herkömmlich, konventionell
	polluting [pəˈluːtɪŋ]	umweltschädlich
	resources [rɪˈsɔːsɪz]	Mittel, Ressourcen
	to consume [kənˈsjuːm]	verbrauchen, konsumieren
	to accelerate [əkˈseləreɪt]	beschleunigen
	brake [breɪk]	Bremse
	to waste [weɪst]	vergeuden, verschwenden
	heat [hiːt]	Hitze
	to extend [ɪkˈstend]	erweitern, ausbauen
	recycling [ˌriːˈsaɪklɪŋ]	Recycling, Wiederverwertung
	to re-use [ˌriː ˈjuːz]	wiederverwenden
	to throw away [ˌθrəʊ əˈweɪ]	wegwerfen
	bargain [ˈbɑːgɪn]	Angebot, Schnäppchen
	atmosphere [ˈætməsfɪə]	Atmosphäre
	community [kəˈmjuːnəti]	Allgemeinheit, Gemeinschaft
	heating [ˈhiːtɪŋ]	Heizung
	fossil fuel [ˈfɒsl fjuːəl]	fossiler Brennstoff
	powerful [ˈpaʊəfl]	leistungsstark
	artificial [ˌɑːtɪˈfɪʃl]	künstlich, Kunst-
	score [skɔː]	Ergebnis, Punktestand
92	**automatic** [ˌɔːtəˈmætɪk]	automatisch
	carbon [ˈkɑːbən]	Kohlenstoff
	impact [ˈɪmpækt]	(Aus-)Wirkung, Effekt
	activity kit [ækˈtɪvəti kɪt]	*etwa:* Bausatz
	to rate [reɪt]	bewerten, einstufen, (ein)schätzen
	response [rɪˈspɒns]	Antwort, Rückmeldung
	approximate [əˈprɒksɪmət]	ungefähr
	to score [skɔː]	Punkte erzielen
93	**pump** [pʌmp]	Pumpe
	rail [reɪl]	Schiene, Gleis
	seaside [ˈsiːsaɪd]	Küste, Strand
	stewardess [ˌstjuːəˈdes]	Stewardess
	hostess [ˈhəʊstəs]	Gastgeberin
	wood [wʊd]	Holz
	pharmaceuticals salesman [ˌfɑːməˈsuːtɪklz seɪlzmən]	Arzneimittelvertreter
	playhouse [ˈpleɪhaʊs]	Theater
	wooden crate [ˌwʊdn ˈkreɪt]	Holzkiste
	pile [paɪl]	Haufen, Stapel
	to landfill [ˈlændfɪl]	(Müll) deponieren
	recycler [ˌriːˈsaɪklə]	Wiederverwerter
	to guess [ges]	raten, vermuten
	to recycle [ˌriːˈsaɪkl]	recyceln, wieder verwerten
	nationally [ˈnæʃnəli]	landesweit
	builder [ˈbɪldə]	Bauunternehmer/in
	to turn over [ˌtɜːn ˈəʊvə]	umsetzen
	to reckon [ˈrekən]	glauben, schätzen
	long-term [ˌlɒŋˈtɜːm]	langfristig, Langzeit-
	chemicals [ˈkemɪklz]	Chemikalien
	to throw out [ˌθrəʊ ˈaʊt]	aussondern, wegwerfen
	grade [greɪd]	(Güte-)Klasse
	resaleable [riːˈseɪləbl]	wiederverkäuflich
	compost bin [ˈkɒmpɒst bɪn]	Komposttonne
	reusable [ˌriːˈjuːzəbl]	erneut verwendbar
	broken [ˈbrəʊkən]	kaputt, zerbrochen
	bits and pieces [ˌbɪts ənd ˈpiːsɪz]	kleine Stücke
	chipboard [ˈtʃɪpbɔːd]	Spanplatte
94	**green** [griːn]	umweltfreundlich
	utility [juːˈtɪləti]	Versorgungsbetrieb
	to announce [əˈnaʊns]	bekannt geben, ankündigen
	ridge [rɪdʒ]	Bergkamm, Grat
	phase [feɪz]	Phase, Abschnitt
	city council [ˈsɪti kaʊnsl]	Stadtrat, Gemeinderat
	to call [kɔːl]	einberufen
	memorial hall [məˌmɔːriəl ˈhɔːl]	Gedenkhalle
	mayor [meə]	Bürgermeister/in
	to sum up [ˌsʌm ˈʌp]	zusammenfassen
	to risk [rɪsk]	riskieren
	polluted [pəˈluːtɪd]	verschmutzt
	disastrous [dɪˈzɑːstrəs]	unglücklich, katastrophal
95	**at times** [ət ˈtaɪmz]	manchmal
	easily [ˈiːzəli]	zweifellos, bestimmt
	site [saɪt]	Stelle, Standort
	generator [ˈdʒenəreɪtə]	Generator
	to pump [pʌmp]	pumpen
	tower [ˈtaʊə]	Turm
	rotor [ˈrəʊtə]	Rotor
	to reach up [ˌriːtʃ ˈʌp]	emporragen
	peace [piːs]	Frieden, Ruhe
	non-stop [ˌnɒnˈstɒp]	ununterbrochen
	global warming [ˌgləʊbl ˈwɔːmɪŋ]	Erderwärmung
	carbon dioxide [ˌkɑːbən daɪˈɒksaɪd]	Kohlendioxid

temperature ['temprətʃə] Temperatur
human ['hju:mən] menschlich, Menschen-
violent ['vaɪələnt] heftig
sea level ['si: levl] Meeresspiegel
agreement [ə'gri:mənt] Vereinbarung, Abkommen
industrialized nations [ɪn,dʌstriəlaɪzd 'neɪʃnz] Industrienationen
to achieve [ə'tʃi:v] erreichen, erlangen
energy-efficient [,enədʒi ɪ'fɪʃnt] energiesparend
96 **hemisphere** ['hemɪsfɪə] Halbkugel
surface ['sɜ:fɪs] Oberfläche
ice core ['aɪs kɔ:] Eis-Bohrkern
sample ['sɑ:mpl] Probe
domestic [də'mestɪk] Inland(s)-, inländisch
scenario [sə'nɑ:riəʊ] Szenario
to displace [dɪs'pleɪs] verdrängen, vertreiben
coastal ['kəʊstl] Küsten-
wetland ['wetlənd] Feuchtgebiet, Sumpfgebiet
at risk [ət 'rɪsk] gefährdet
flooding ['flʌdɪŋ] Überschwemmung
inch [ɪntʃ] Inch, Zoll
97 **available** [ə'veɪləbl] erhältlich, verfügbar
on time [ɒn 'taɪm] pünktlich
to run out of time [,rʌn aʊt əf 'taɪm] die Zeit wird knapp
postman ['pəʊstmən] Briefträger
wedding ['wedɪŋ] Hochzeit, Trauung
purpose ['pɜ:pəs] Zweck, Absicht
briefly ['bri:fli] kurz
98 **tired** ['taɪəd] müde
ready-prepared [,redi prɪ'peəd] Fertig-
meal [mi:l] Essen, Mahlzeit
normally ['nɔ:məli] normalerweise
disadvantage [,dɪsəd'vɑ:ntɪdʒ] Nachteil, Schaden
developer [dɪ'veləpə] Bauunternehmer
99 **to mention** ['menʃn] erwähnen, nennen
female ['fi:meɪl] weiblich, Frauen-
stupidly ['stju:pɪdli] dummerweise
to fail [feɪl] versäumen
to put off [,pʊt 'ɒf] verschieben
to pass on [,pɑ:s 'ɒn] weiterleiten
guy [gaɪ] Typ, Junge

Unit 8 Your world of work

100 **to dislike** [dɪs'laɪk] nicht mögen
estate agent [ɪ'steɪt eɪdʒənt] Immobilienmakler/in
salesperson ['seɪlzpɜ:sn] Verkäufer/in
low-skilled ['ləʊ skɪld] angelernt
low-paid [,ləʊ'peɪd] niedrig bezahlt
shift [ʃɪft] Schicht
work placement ['wɜ:k pleɪsmənt] Praktikum
101 **hard-working** [,hɑ:d 'wɜ:kɪŋ] fleißig
to input ['ɪnpʊt] eingeben
to process ['prəʊses] verarbeiten, bearbeiten
accurately ['ækjərətli] genau
vital ['vaɪtl] unerlässlich, unbedingt notwendig
numeracy ['nju:mərəsi] rechnerische Fähigkeiten
code [kəʊd] (Bestell-)Nummer
mental ['mentl] geistig
stamina ['stæmɪnə] Ausdauer
to meet a deadline [mi:t ə 'dedlaɪn] einen Termin einhalten
promotional event [prə'məʊʃənl ɪ'vent] Werbeveranstaltung
trade show ['treɪd ʃəʊ] Fachmesse
team player ['ti:m pleɪə] *etwa:* jd mit gutem Gruppenverhalten
problem solver ['prɒbləm sɒlvə] Problemlöser
to multi-track ['mʌlti træk] mehrgleisig arbeiten
demanding [dɪ'mɑ:ndɪŋ] anstrengend, anspruchsvoll
careers officer [kə'rɪəz ɒfɪsə] Berufsberater/in
to require [rɪ'kwaɪə] erfordern, verlangen
enthusiastic [ɪn,θju:zi'æstɪk] begeisterungsfähig, begeistert
commitment [kə'mɪtmənt] Engagement, Einsatz
goal [gəʊl] Ziel
to take responsibility [teɪk rɪ,spɒnsə'bɪləti] Verantwortung übernehmen
punctuality [,pʌŋktʃu'æləti] Pünktlichkeit
accuracy ['ækjərəsi] Genauigkeit
attention to detail [ə,tenʃn tə 'di:teɪl] Detailgenauigkeit
interpersonal [,ɪntə'pɜ:sənl] zwischenmenschlich
102 **punctual** ['pʌŋktʃuəl] pünktlich
accurate ['ækjərət] genau, akkurat
key [ki:] Schlüssel-, Haupt-
103 **flexibility** [,fleksə'bɪləti] Flexibilität
creativity [,kri:eɪ'tɪvəti] Kreativität
determination [dɪ,tɜ:mɪ'neɪʃn] Entschlossenheit
enthusiasm [ɪn'θju:ziæzəm] Begeisterung(sfähigkeit)
committed [kə'mɪtɪd] engagiert
realism ['ri:əlɪzəm] Realismus
production process [prə,dʌkʃn 'prəʊses] Produktionsprozess
degree [dɪ'gri:] (akademischer) Abschluss
sales representative ['seɪlz reprɪzentətɪv] (Handels-)Vertreter/in
fiancé [fi'ɒnseɪ] Verlobter
to be committed to [bi kə'mɪtɪd tə] sich engagieren für
to specialize in ['speʃəlaɪz ɪn] sich spezialisieren auf
sales lead ['seɪlz li:d] Verkaufsvorsprung
firm [fɜ:m] fest, beständig
challenge ['tʃælɪndʒ] Herausforderung, Aufgabe
104 **neatly** ['ni:tli] ordentlich, sauber
tidily ['taɪdi] aufgeräumt, ordentlich
achievement [ə'tʃi:vmənt] Leistung, Errungenschaft

	in-job training [ˌin dʒɒb 'treɪnɪŋ]	firmeninterne Ausbildung
105	**great-grandparents** [ˌgreɪt 'grænpeərənts]	Urgroßeltern
	workplace ['wɜ:kpleɪs]	Arbeitsplatz
	farming ['fɑ:mɪŋ]	Landwirtschaft
	computing [kəm'pju:tɪŋ]	Computerwesen
	to re-invent [ˌri:ɪn'vent]	sich ein neues Image geben, sich neu definieren
	strategy ['strætədʒi]	Strategie, Taktik
	downsizing ['daʊnsaɪzɪŋ]	Personal-, Stellenabbau
	to exist [ɪg'zɪst]	existieren
	qualified ['kwɒlɪfaɪd]	ausgebildet, geeignet
	to perform [pə'fɔ:m]	(Tätigkeit) ausüben
	case study ['keɪs stʌdi]	Fallstudie
	grammar school ['græmə sku:l]	Gymnasium
	pointless ['pɔɪntləs]	sinnlos
	demotivated [ˌdi:'məʊtɪveɪtɪd]	demotiviert
	to serve [sɜ:v]	servieren
	apprenticeship [ə'prentɪʃɪp]	Lehre, Ausbildung
106	**to de-layer** [di:'leɪə]	Hierarchien abbauen
	to get rid of [get 'rɪd əv]	beseitigen, abschaffen
	layer ['leɪə]	Ebene, Schicht
	pyramid ['pɪrəmɪd]	Pyramide
	shape [ʃeɪp]	Form
	flat [flæt]	flach
	to downsize ['daʊnsaɪz]	Stellen abbauen
	to merge [mɜ:dʒ]	fusionieren
	to outsource ['aʊtsɔ:s]	(Arbeitsprozesse) auslagern
	individual [ˌɪndɪ'vɪdʒuəl]	Einzelperson
	to restructure [ˌri:'strʌktʃə]	umstrukturieren
	flexitime ['fleksitaɪm]	Gleitzeit
	responsibilities [rɪˌspɒnsə'bɪlətiz]	Tätigkeiten, Aufgaben
	author ['ɔ:θə]	Autor/in
	disappointed [ˌdɪsə'pɔɪntɪd]	enttäuscht
107	**useless** ['ju:sləs]	nutzlos, sinnlos
	caffeinated ['kæfɪneɪtɪd]	mit Koffein
	legible ['ledʒəbl]	lesbar
	logical ['lɒdʒɪkl]	logisch
	patient ['peɪʃnt]	geduldig
	relevant ['reləvənt]	relevant
	illegible [ɪ'ledʒəbl]	unleserlich
	illogical [ɪ'lɒdʒɪkl]	unlogisch
	imbalance [ɪm'bæləns]	Unausgeglichenheit
	immoral [ɪ'mɒrəl]	unmoralisch
	impersonal [ɪm'pɜ:sənl]	unpersönlich
	irrational [ɪ'ræʃnəl]	irrational, unvernünftig
	to panic ['pænɪk]	in Panik geraten
	essay ['eseɪ]	Aufsatz, Essay
	to make sense [meɪk 'sens]	sinnvoll sein, Sinn haben
108	**telephone directory** ['telɪfəʊn dərektəri]	Telefonbuch
	picker ['pɪkə]	Pflücker/in
	depending on [dɪ'pendɪŋ ɒn]	je nach, abhängig von
	relief [rɪ'li:f]	Erleichterung
	relief worker [rɪ'li:f wɜ:kə]	Aushilfe
	dispatch [dɪ'spætʃ]	Versand
	minibus ['mɪnɪbʌs]	Kleinbus
	FAO = for the attention of [fə ði ə'tenʃn əv]	z. Hdn. = zu Händen von
	temp [temp]	Zeitarbeiter/in
	holiday cover ['hɒlɪdeɪ kʌvə]	Urlaubsvertretung
	duty ['dju:ti]	Aufgabe
	to restock [ˌri:'stɒk]	wieder auffüllen
	GCSE [ˌdʒi: si: es 'i:]	mittlere Reife
	quoting ['kwəʊtɪŋ]	unter Angabe von
	ref = reference number [ref]	(Akten-)Zeichen
	preferable ['prefərəbl]	erwünscht
	discount ['dɪskaʊnt]	Rabatt, Nachlass
	manpower ['mænpaʊə]	Arbeitskräfte, Personal
109	**embassy** ['embəsi]	Botschaft
	to congratulate [kən'grætʃuleɪt]	gratulieren, beglückwünschen
	amazed [ə'meɪzd]	erstaunt
	to shout at sb ['ʃaʊt ət]	jdn anschreien
	to store [stɔ:]	lagern, aufheben
	copier ['kɒpiə]	Kopierer
	on purpose [ɒn 'pɜ:pəs]	absichtlich
	by mistake [baɪ mɪ'steɪk]	aus Versehen, irrtümlich
	as a matter of fact [əz ə ˌmætər əv 'fækt]	eigentlich, sogar, tatsächlich

File 1 The form and layout of business letters

110	**ref = reference number** [ref]	(Akten-)Zeichen
	full stop [ˌfʊl 'stɒp]	Punkt
	Attn = attention [ə'tenʃn]	z. Hdn. = zu Händen von)
	wholesale catalogue [ˌhəʊlseɪl 'kætəlɒg]	Großhandelskatalog
	subject line ['sʌbdʒɪkt laɪn]	Bezugszeile, Betreffzeile
	to enclose [ɪn'kləʊz]	beilegen, beifügen
	current ['kʌrənt]	aktuell, gegenwärtig (gültig)
	haircare product [ˌheəkeə 'prɒdʌkt]	Haarpflegeprodukt
	to be well received [bi ˌwel rɪ'si:vd]	gut aufgenommen werden
	retail trade [ˌri:teɪl 'treɪd]	Einzelhandel
	fashion press ['fæʃn pres]	Modepresse
	delighted [dɪ'laɪtɪd]	(sehr) erfreut
	to supply [sə'plaɪ]	(be)liefern, versorgen
	sample ['sɑ:mpl]	Muster, Probe(exemplar)
	firm offer [ˌfɜ:m 'ɒfə]	Festangebot, festes Angebot
	to look forward to [ˌlʊk 'fɔ:wəd tə]	sich freuen auf
	Yours sincerely [jɔ:z sɪn'sɪəli]	Mit freundlichen Grüßen
	firm [fɜ:m]	Firma
	to sign off [ˌsaɪn 'ɒf]	(einen Brief) schließen
	Yours faithfully [jɔ:z 'feɪθfəli]	Mit freundlichen Grüßen, Hochachtungsvoll
	position [pə'zɪʃn]	Stellung
	Limited (Ltd) ['lɪmɪtɪd]	GmbH
	sales [seɪlz]	Vertrieb, Verkauf
	enc = enclosure [ɪŋk ɪn'kləʊʒə]	Anlage

111 **individual** [ˌɪndɪ'vɪdʒuəl] Einzelperson, Einzelne/r
matter ['mætə] Angelegenheit, Sache, Ding
receiver [rɪ'si:və] Empfänger
addressee [ˌædre'si:] Empfänger/in, Adressat/in
to apply [ə'plaɪ] gelten, zur Anwendung kommen
casual ['kæʒuəl] salopp, lässig
familiar [fə'mɪliə] vertraulich, vertraut
senior ['si:niə] vorgesetzt
to lay out [ˌleɪ 'aʊt] gestalten, layouten
globalization [ˌgləʊbəlaɪ'zeɪʃn] Globalisierung
increasingly [ɪn'kri:sɪŋli] zunehmend
advantage [əd'vɑ:ntɪdʒ] Vorteil, Vorzug
letterhead ['letəhed] Briefkopf
logical ['lɒdʒɪkl] logisch
complimentary close [ˌkɒmplɪˌmentri 'kləʊz] Schlussformel
body text ['bɒdi tekst] Haupttext
reference ['refərəns] Zeichen, Bezug
salutation [ˌsælju'teɪʃn] Anrede
signature block ['sɪgnətʃə blɒk] Unterschriftsabschnitt, Unterschriften
to obey [ə'beɪ] befolgen, gehorchen
accurate ['ækjərət] genau, akkurat
to make sure [ˌmeɪk 'ʃʊə] sicherstellen, sich vergewissern
e.g. [ˌi: 'dʒi:] z.B.
brief [bri:f] kurz
plain [pleɪn] schnörkellos, schlicht
natural ['nætʃrəl] natürlich, echt
style [staɪl] Stil
formal ['fɔ:ml] formell, förmlich
112 **delivery** [dɪ'lɪvəri] Lieferung
supplier [sə'plaɪə] Anbieter/in, Lieferant/in
in modern practice [ɪn ˌmɒdn 'præktɪs] nach moderner Geschäftspraxis
space [speɪs] Leerstelle
enquiry [ɪn'kwaɪəri] Anfrage
textiles ['tekstaɪlz] Textilien
denim ['denɪm] Denim (Jeansstoff)
purchasing assistant ['pɜ:tʃəsɪŋ əsɪstənt] Einkäufer/in, Assistent im Einkauf
cloth [klɒθ] Stoff, Tuch
intended for [ɪn'tendɪd fə] gedacht für, dazu dienend
range [reɪndʒ] Sortiment, Auswahl
further to ['fɜ:ðə tʊ] in Bezug auf, im Anschluss an
grateful ['greɪtfl] dankbar
to evaluate [ɪ'væljueɪt] bewerten, auswerten
to get in touch [get ɪn 'tʌtʃ] (sich) in Verbindung setzen
discount ['dɪskaʊnt] Rabatt, Nachlass
volume order ['vɒlju:m ɔ:də] Großauftrag, Mengenbestellung
113 **to turn into** ['tɜ:n ɪntə] umarbeiten zu/in
to underline [ˌʌndə'laɪn] unterstreichen
advertisement [əd'vɜ:tɪsmənt] Werbung
enclosed [ɪn'kləʊzd] (einem Brief) beigelegt, beigefügt
image ['ɪmɪdʒ] Image, Bild
brochure ['brəʊʃə] Broschüre, Prospekt
incidentally [ˌɪnsɪ'dentli] übrigens, nebenbei
manufacturer [ˌmænju'fæktʃərə] Hersteller/in, Produzent/in
related [rɪ'leɪtɪd] verwandt
attached [ə'tætʃt] beigefügt
leading ['li:dɪŋ] führend
maker ['meɪkə] Hersteller/in, Produzent/in
stuff [stʌf] Zeug
advert ['ædvɜ:t] Anzeige
glad [glæd] froh
by the way [baɪ ðə 'weɪ] übrigens, nebenbei
keen on ['ki:n ɒn] (sehr) interessiert an

File 2 Enquiries

114 **opening** ['əʊpnɪŋ] Briefanfang
to obtain [əb'teɪn] erhalten, besorgen, sich verschaffen
reason ['ri:zn] Grund
request [rɪ'kwest] Anfrage
close [kləʊs] (Brief-)Schluss
closing ['kləʊzɪŋ] abschließend
comment ['kɒment] Bemerkung
to act [ækt] handeln, reagieren
promptly ['prɒmptli] unverzüglich, prompt
cosmetics [kɒz'metɪks] Kosmetik(a)
wholesaler ['həʊlseɪlə] Großhändler/in
drugstore ['drʌgstɔ:] Drogerie
perfumery [pɜ:'fju:məri] Parfümerie
throughout [θru:'aʊt] überall (in), in ganz
beauty products [ˌbju:ti 'prɒdʌkts] Kosmetikartikel
to expand [ɪk'spænd] erweitern, vergrößern
purchasing manager ['pɜ:tʃəsɪŋ mænɪdʒə] Einkaufsleiter/in, Chefeinkäufer/in
producer [prə'dju:sə] Produzent/in, Hersteller/in
high-quality [ˌhaɪ 'kwɒləti] hochwertig
stand [stænd] (Messe-)Stand
possibility [ˌpɒsə'bɪləti] Möglichkeit
115 **speaking** ['spi:kɪŋ] am Apparat
display material [dɪ'spleɪ mətɪəriəl] Dekorationsmaterial
extra ['ekstrə] zusätzlich, extra, Extra-
seasonal ['si:zənl] Saison-
campaign [kæm'peɪn] Kampagne, Werbeaktion
sunscreen ['sʌnskri:n] Sonnencreme
to come up [ˌkʌm 'ʌp] zur Sprache kommen
monthly ['mʌnθli] monatlich
at present [ət 'preznt] momentan, derzeit
to damage ['dæmɪdʒ] beschädigen
surface ['sɜ:fɪs] Oberfläche
to drop [drɒp] fallen lassen, hinfallen
shower ['ʃaʊə] Dusche
say [seɪ] beispielsweise

	to harm [hɑ:m]	schaden
	sales [seɪlz]	Verkäufe, Verkaufszahlen
	available [ə'veɪləbl]	erhältlich, verfügbar, lieferbar
	unbreakable [ʌn'breɪkəbl]	unzerbrechlich
	disadvantage [ˌdɪsəd'vɑ:ntɪdʒ]	Nachteil
	to pack [pæk]	packen, verpacken
	packaging ['pækɪdʒɪŋ]	Verpackung(smaterial)
116	**trial** ['traɪəl]	Probe-
	consignment [kən'saɪnmənt]	Lieferung, (Waren-)Sendung
	case [keɪs]	Karton, Kiste
	boxed [bɒkst]	in Schachtel(n)
	tube [tju:b]	Tube
	to fix up [ˌfɪks 'ʌp]	arrangieren, herrichten
	agreed [ə'gri:d]	vereinbart
	to quote [kwəʊt]	ein Angebot abgeben
	DDP = delivered duty paid [dɪˌlɪvəd ˌdju:ti 'peɪd]	geliefert verzollt
	store [stɔ:]	Laden, Geschäft, Lager
	trade terms ['treɪd tɜ:mz]	Handelsbedingungen
	statement ['steɪtmənt]	Aussage
	brand name ['brænd neɪm]	Markenzeichen, -name
	to deliver [dɪ'lɪvə]	liefern
117	**freight** [freɪt]	Fracht
	logistics department [ləˌdʒɪstɪks 'dɪpɑ:tmənt]	Logistik, Auslieferung, Spedition
	quotation [kwəʊ'teɪʃn]	Angebot
	to ship [ʃɪp]	(ver)senden
	repeat order [rɪ'pi:t ɔ:də]	Folgeauftrag
	ready-packed ['redi pækt]	fertig verpackt
	europallet ['jʊərəʊpælət]	Euro-Palette
	goods [gʊdz]	Ware(n), Güter
	protected [prə'tektɪd]	geschützt
	impact ['ɪmpækt]	Stoß
	expanded polystyrene [ɪkˌspændɪd pɒli'staɪri:n]	Polystyrol
	corner-piece ['kɔ:nə pi:s]	Eckstück
	damp [dæmp]	Feuchtigkeit
	layer ['leɪə]	Schicht, Lage
	heavy-duty polythene sheeting [heviˌdju:ti 'pɒliθi:n ʃi:tɪŋ]	schwere Polyäthylenfolie
	invoiced value [ˌɪnvɔɪst 'vælju:]	Rechnungswert
	prompt [prɒmpt]	unverzüglich, prompt
	at the latest [ət ðə 'leɪtɪst]	spätestens
	With best regards [wɪð ˌbest rɪ'gɑ:dz]	Viele Grüße
118	**toolbox** ['tu:lbɒks]	Werkzeugkasten
	availability [əˌveɪlə'bɪləti]	Verfügbarkeit
119	**with reference to** [wɪð 'refrəns tə]	mit Bezug auf
	protective clothing [prəˌtektɪv 'kləʊðɪŋ]	Schutzkleidung
	leather ['leðə]	Leder
	knee pad ['ni: pæd]	Knieschützer
	belt [belt]	Gürtel, Gurt
	to imagine [ɪ'mædʒɪn]	sich vorstellen
120	**to take notes** [ˌteɪk 'nəʊts]	sich Notizen machen
	based on ['beɪst ɒn]	auf der Grundlage von

File 3 Offers and quotations

121	**on what terms** [ɒn ˌwɒt 'tɜ:mz]	zu welchen Konditionen
	to be willing [bi 'wɪlɪŋ]	bereit/gewillt sein
	services ['sɜ:vɪsɪz]	Dienstleistungen
	special terms [ˌspeʃl 'tɜ:mz]	Sonderkonditionen
	terms and conditions [ˌtɜ:mz ənd kən'dɪʃnz]	allgemeine Geschäftsbedingungen
	to print [prɪnt]	drucken, abdrucken
	payment ['peɪmənt]	Zahlung, Bezahlung
	to refer to [rɪ'fɜ: tə]	sich beziehen auf, verweisen auf
	to quote [kwəʊt]	angeben, zitieren
	quantity ['kwɒntəti]	Menge
	tabular form [ˌtæbjələ 'fɔ:m]	Tabellenform
	to point out [ˌpɔɪnt 'aʊt]	hinweisen auf, aufmerksam machen auf
	to avoid [ə'vɔɪd]	vermeiden
	to appreciate [ə'pri:ʃieɪt]	zu schätzen wissen
	to overdo [ˌəʊvə'du:]	übertreiben
	introductory offer [ˌɪntrə'dʌktəri ɒfə]	Einführungsangebot
	additional [ə'dɪʃənl]	zusätzlich
	introductory discount [ɪntrəˌdʌktəri 'dɪskaʊnt]	Einführungsrabatt
	trade price ['treɪd praɪs]	Großhandelspreis
	on a positive note [ɒn ə 'pɒzətɪv nəʊt]	*etwa:* freundlich
	query ['kwɪəri]	Frage, Rückfrage, Anfrage
122	**as requested** [əz rɪ'kwestɪd]	wie erwünscht, wunschgemäß
	premises ['premɪsɪz]	(Betriebs-)Gelände
	first order [fɜ:st 'ɔ:də]	Erstbestellung
	immediate [ɪ'mi:diət]	sofort, umgehend
	to allow [ə'laʊ]	gestatten, gewähren
	cash discount ['kæʃ dɪskaʊnt]	Barzahlungsrabatt
123	**consignee** [ˌkɒnsaɪ'ni:]	(Waren-)Empfänger, Adressat
	to include [ɪn'klu:d]	enthalten, umfassen
	loading ['ləʊdɪŋ]	Ver-, Beladung
	unloading [ˌʌn'ləʊdɪŋ]	Entladung, Löschung
	insurance [ɪn'ʃʊərəns]	Versicherung
	pallet ['pælət]	Palette
	satisfactory [ˌsætɪs'fæktəri]	zufriedenstellend
	to return [rɪ'tɜ:n]	zurückschicken, -senden
	confirmation of acceptance [kɒnfəˌmeɪʃn əv ək'septəns]	Auftragsbestätigung
	ending ['endɪŋ]	Schluss, Ende
	midday [ˌmɪd'deɪ]	Mittag, mittags
124	**extract** ['ekstrækt]	Auszug
	depending on [dɪ'pendɪŋ ɒn]	je nach, abhängig von
	in addition to [ɪn ə'dɪʃn tə]	zusätzlich (zu)
	to negotiate [nɪ'gəʊʃieɪt]	aushandeln, verhandeln

	prospect ['prɒspekt]	Aussicht, Chance
	to circulate ['sɜ:kjəleɪt]	(an alle) verschicken
	to submit [səb'mɪt]	unterbreiten, einreichen
	estimate ['estɪmət]	(Kosten-)Voranschlag, Schätzung
	distribution [ˌdɪstrɪ'bju:ʃn]	Lieferung, Vertrieb
	location [ləʊ'keɪʃn]	(Stand-)Ort, Firmensitz
	to confirm [kən'fɜ:m]	bestätigen
	to ensure [ɪn'ʃʊə]	sicherstellen, gewährleisten
	favour ['feɪvə]	Gefallen
	rebate ['ri:beɪt]	Rabatt, Nachlass
	duplicate ['dju:plɪkət]	doppelt, zweifach
	worth [wɜ:θ]	Wert
	value ['vælju:]	Wert
	amount [ə'maʊnt]	Summe, Betrag
	extent [ɪk'stent]	Ausmaß, Umfang
	to dispatch [dɪ'spætʃ]	ausliefern, versenden
	receipt [rɪ'si:t]	Empfang
	transmission [træns'mɪʃn]	Sendung, Übertragung
125	**to depend on** [dɪ'pend ɒn]	abhängen von, darauf ankommen
	satisfied ['sætɪsfaɪd]	zufrieden
	valid ['vælɪd]	gültig
	key [ki:]	Schlüssel-, Haupt-
	to take a call [ˌteɪk ə 'kɔ:l]	einen Anruf entgegennehmen
	initials [ɪ'nɪʃlz]	Initialen
127	**plant** [plɑ:nt]	Werk, Betrieb(sanlage)

File 4 Orders, acknowledgements and reminders

129	**acknowledgement** [ək'nɒlɪdʒmənt]	Bestätigung
	reminder [rɪ'maɪndə]	Mahnung, Mahnschreiben
	to place an order [ˌpleɪs ən 'ɔ:də]	einen Auftrag erteilen
	item ['aɪtəm]	Artikel, Posten
	to note [nəʊt]	feststellen, zur Kenntnis nehmen
	to deal with ['di:l wɪð]	bearbeiten, sich befassen mit
130	**to acknowledge** [ək'nɒlɪdʒ]	bestätigen
	article ['ɑ:tɪkl]	Artikel
	to handle ['hændl]	erledigen
131	**with regard to** [wɪð rɪ'gɑ:d tə]	in Bezug auf
	purchase ['pɜ:tʃəs]	Kauf, Einkauf
	candle ['kændl]	Kerze
	equivalent [ɪ'kwɪvələnt]	Entsprechung, Übersetzung
	advice of dispatch [ədˌvaɪs əv dɪ'spætʃ]	Versandanzeige
	relationship [rɪ'leɪʃnʃɪp]	Beziehung, Verhältnis
	as stated [əz 'steɪtɪd]	wie dargelegt
	profitable ['prɒfɪtəbl]	gewinnbringend, erfolgreich
133	**prompt** [prɒmpt]	Stichwort, Vorgabe
135	**overdue** [ˌəʊvə'dju:]	überfällig
	to abolish [ə'bɒlɪʃ]	abschaffen, streichen
	three-stage ['θri: steɪdʒ]	dreistufig
	legal proceedings [ˌli:gl prə'si:dɪŋz]	rechtliche Schritte, Gerichtsverfahren
	Customer Accounts ['kʌstəmə əkaʊnts]	*(Abteilung)* Kundenkonten
	to remind [rɪ'maɪnd]	(jdn an etw) erinnern
	to overlook [ˌəʊvə'lʊk]	übersehen
	to misdirect [ˌmɪsdə'rekt]	fehlleiten
	to extend [ɪk'stend]	verlängern
	generous ['dʒenərəs]	großzügig
	margin ['mɑ:dʒɪn]	(Zeit-)Spanne
	to arrange for [ə'reɪndʒ fə]	einrichten, organisieren
	to settle ['setl]	bezahlen, begleichen
	in the meantime [ɪn ðə 'mi:ntaɪm]	in der Zwischenzeit
136	**skin cream** ['skɪn kri:m]	Hautcreme
	to assume [ə'sju:m]	annehmen, davon ausgehen
	chemists ['kemɪsts]	Apotheke
	threat [θret]	Drohung
	to react [ri'ækt]	reagieren
	personally ['pɜ:sənəli]	persönlich
	to retire [rɪ'taɪə]	in den Ruhestand gehen
	outstanding [aʊt'stændɪŋ]	ausstehend
137	**dissatisfied** [dɪs'sætɪsfaɪd]	unzufrieden
	disturbed [dɪ'stɜ:bd]	beunruhigt, gestört
	legitimate cause [lɪˌdʒɪtɪmət 'kɔ:z]	triftiger Grund
	to look into sth ['lʊk ɪntə]	etw untersuchen, prüfen
	meet obligations [mi:t ˌɒblɪ'geɪʃnz]	Verbindlichkeiten regeln erfüllen
	to insist [ɪn'sɪst]	(darauf) bestehen
	delay [dɪ'leɪ]	Verzögerung
	to trouble ['trʌbl]	belästigen, Umstände bereiten
	unpaid [ˌʌn'peɪd]	unbezahlt
	bill [bɪl]	Rechnung
	unhappy [ʌn'hæpi]	unglücklich
	swimwear ['swɪmweə]	Badebekleidung
138	**polite** [pə'laɪt]	höflich
	commercial [kə'mɜ:ʃl]	gewerblich
	dishwasher ['dɪʃwɒʃə]	Geschirrspüler
	mixer ['mɪksə]	Mixer

File 5 Dealing with complaints

139	**defective** [dɪ'fektɪv]	fehlerhaft
	faulty ['fɔ:lti]	fehlerhaft, defekt
	aim [eɪm]	Ziel, Absicht
	to hand out blame [hænd ˌaʊt 'bleɪm]	Schuldzuweisungen machen
	solution [sə'lu:ʃn]	Lösung
	to complain [kəm'pleɪn]	sich beschweren, reklamieren
	to suggest [sə'dʒest]	vorschlagen
	replacement [rɪ'pleɪsmənt]	Ersatz, Austausch
	at sb's expense [ət ɪk'spens]	auf jds Kosten
	to apologize [ə'pɒlədʒaɪz]	sich entschuldigen
	investigation [ɪnˌvestɪ'geɪʃn]	Nachforschung, Untersuchung
	reduction [rɪ'dʌkʃn]	Preisnachlass, Ermäßigung
	to reject [rɪ'dʒekt]	ablehnen, zurückweisen

	pressure ['preʃə]	Druck
	stocks [stɒks]	Lagerbestand, Warenbestand
	urgent ['ɜ:dʒənt]	dringend, eilig
	to treat [tri:t]	behandeln
	awful ['ɔ:fl]	furchtbar, schrecklich
140	**damaged** ['dæmɪdʒd]	beschädigt
	as scheduled [əz 'ʃedju:ld]	wie vorgesehen, wie geplant
	presumably [prɪ'zju:məbli]	vermutlich
	insurance claim [ɪn'ʃʊərəns kleɪm]	Versicherungsanspruch
	forwarding agent ['fɔ:wədɪŋ eɪdʒənt]	Spediteur
	to dispose of [dɪ'spəʊz əv]	entsorgen, beseitigen
	at your end [ət 'jɔ:r end]	bei Ihnen/Dir
	in fact [ɪn 'fækt]	tatsächlich, eigentlich
141	**staff** [stɑ:f]	Mitarbeiter, Angestellte
	snap-on cap ['snæp ɒn kæp]	Schnappverschluss(kappe)
	screw-on cap ['skru: ɒn kæp]	Schraubverschluss(kappe)
	assorted [ə'sɔ:tɪd]	gemischt
	confusion [kən'fju:ʒn]	Verwirrung
	mix-up ['mɪks ʌp]	Missverständnis, Verwechslung
	identical [aɪ'dentɪkl]	identisch
	package ['pækɪdʒ]	Paket
	packing ['pækɪŋ]	Verpackung
	to instruct [ɪn'strʌkt]	anweisen
	shipment ['ʃɪpmənt]	Sendung
	inconvenience [ˌɪnkən'vi:niəns]	Unannehmlichkeit
	inexperienced [ˌɪnɪk'spɪəriənst]	unerfahren
	temporary worker ['temprəri wɜ:kə]	Zeitarbeiter/in
	to mix up [ˌmɪks 'ʌp]	verwechseln, durcheinander bringen
142	**can** [kæn]	Dose
	styling mousse ['staɪlɪŋ mu:s]	Frisierschaum
	print [prɪnt]	Druck, Druckschrift
	version ['vɜ:ʃn]	Version, Fassung
	impossible [ɪm'pɒsəbl]	unmöglich
	magnifying glass ['mægnɪfaɪɪŋ glɑ:s]	Lupe
	instructions [ɪn'strʌkʃnz]	Bedienungsanleitung, Anweisungen
	essential [ɪ'senʃl]	unbedingt erforderlich, wichtig
	worried ['wʌrid]	beunruhigt, besorgt
	to care for ['keə fə]	sich kümmern um
	appearance [ə'pɪərəns]	Äußeres, (äußere) Erscheinung
	to provide [prə'vaɪd]	zur Verfügung stellen, sorgen für, liefern
143	**relatively** ['relətɪvli]	relativ, verhältnismäßig
	at management level [ət 'mænɪdʒmənt 'levl]	auf Managementebene
	illegible [ɪ'ledʒəbl]	unleserlich
	to sympathize with ['sɪmpəθaɪz wɪð]	Verständnis haben für
	internal [ɪn'tɜ:nl]	intern
	memo ['meməʊ]	Notiz, Kurzmitteilung
	product development [ˌprɒdʌkt dɪ'veləpmənt]	Produktentwicklung
	to operate ['ɒpəreɪt]	bedienen, anwenden
	designer [dɪ'zaɪnə]	Designer/in, Konstrukteur/in
	competitive market [kəmˌpetətɪv 'mɑ:kɪt]	hart umkämpfter Markt
	competition [ˌkɒmpə'tɪʃn]	Konkurrenz
	legal requirement [li:gl rɪ'kwaɪəmənt]	gesetzliche Vorschrift
	warning ['wɔ:nɪŋ]	Warnung
	direct [də'rekt]	direkt, unmittelbar
	to require [rɪ'kwaɪə]	verlangen, benötigen
144	**to produce** [prə'dju:s]	produzieren, herstellen
	unacceptable [ˌʌnək'septəbl]	unannehmbar, inakzeptabel
	highly ['haɪli]	äußerst
	legislation [ˌledʒɪs'leɪʃn]	Gesetzgebung, gesetzliche Regelung(en)
	container [kən'teɪnə]	Behälter, Gefäß
	to reduce [rɪ'dju:s]	reduzieren, verkleinern
	indeed [ɪn'di:d]	wirklich, in der Tat
	competitor [kəm'petɪtə]	Konkurrent/in, Wett-, Mitbewerber/in
	to suggest [sə'dʒest]	hindeuten auf
145	**incomplete** [ˌɪnkəm'pli:t]	unvollständig
	computer failure [kəm'pju:tə feɪljə]	Computer-, Systemabsturz
	rough handling [rʌf 'hændlɪŋ]	grobe Behandlung
	teddy bear ['tedibeə]	Teddybär
	considerable [kən'sɪdərəbl]	beträchtlich, beachtlich
	loss [lɒs]	Schaden, Verlust
	insurer [ɪn'ʃʊərə]	Versicherungsgeber, Versicherer
	due to ['dju: tə]	wegen, aufgrund von
	apology [ə'pɒlədʒi]	Entschuldigung
	responsibility [rɪˌspɒnsə'bɪləti]	Verantwortung
	compensation [ˌkɒmpən'seɪʃn]	Schaden(s)ersatz, Kompensation
	sufficient [sə'fɪʃnt]	ausreichend, genug
	to cover ['kʌvə]	abdecken
	with respect [wɪð rɪ'spekt]	bei allem Respekt
	to take up [ˌteɪk 'ʌp]	aufgreifen, sich einer Sache annehmen
	voice mail ['vɔɪs meɪl]	Sprachmitteilung
	valve [vælv]	Ventil
	inspector [ɪn'spektə]	Kontrolleur/in
	just in case [dʒʌst ɪn 'keɪs]	nur für den Fall
148	**to unpack** [ˌʌn'pæk]	auspacken
	discrepancy [dɪs'krepənsi]	Diskrepanz, Unstimmigkeit
	design [dɪ'zaɪn]	*hier:* Muster

	anxious ['æŋkʃəs]	bemüht
149	**technical** ['teknɪkl]	technisch, fachbezogen
	background ['bækgraʊnd]	Hintergrund
	to role-play ['rəʊl pleɪ]	als Rollenspiel durchführen

File 6 Applying for a job

150	**application** [ˌæplɪ'keɪʃn]	Bewerbung
	to consist [kən'sɪst]	bestehen
	stage [steɪdʒ]	Stufe, Phase, Abschnitt
	letter of application [ˌletər əv æplɪ'keɪʃn]	Bewerbungsschreiben
	CV = curriculum vitae [ˌsiː 'viː kəˌrɪkjələm 'viːtaɪ]	Lebenslauf
	invitation [ˌɪnvɪ'teɪʃn]	Einladung
	notification [ˌnəʊtɪfɪ'keɪʃn]	Benachrichtigung
	rejection [rɪ'dʒekʃn]	Ablehnung
	unsolicited [ˌʌnsə'lɪsɪtɪd]	unaufgefordert, unverlangt
	vacancy ['veɪkənsi]	offene Stelle
	as follows [əz 'fɒləʊz]	wie folgt
	suitability [ˌsuːtə'bɪləti]	Eignung
	briefly ['briːfli]	kurz
	qualifications [ˌkwɒlɪfɪ'keɪʃnz]	Ausbildung, Qualifikation
	skills [skɪlz]	Fertigkeiten
	to achieve [ə'tʃiːv]	erreichen
	post [pəʊst]	Posten
151	**internship** ['ɪntɜːnʃɪp]	Praktikum, Volontariat
	business studies ['bɪznəs stʌdiz]	Betriebswirtschaftslehre (BWL)
	to be required to [bi rɪ'kwaɪəd tə]	verpflichtet sein, etw zu tun
	foreign ['fɒrən]	Auslands-, ausländisch
	intern ['ɪntɜːn]	Praktikant/in, Volontär/in
	to consider [kən'sɪdə]	in Erwägung ziehen
	distributor [dɪ'strɪbjətə]	Vertragshändler
	fashion industry ['fæʃn 'ɪndəstri]	Modebranche
	to qualify ['kwɒlɪfaɪ]	Abschluss(prüfung) machen
	ideal [aɪ'diːəl]	ideal
	school-leaving certificate [ˌskuːl liːvɪŋ sə'tɪfɪkət]	(Schul-)Abgangszeugnis
	reasonably ['riːznəbli]	einigermaßen
	fluent ['fluːənt]	fließend
	academic year [ækəˌdemɪk 'jɪə]	akademisches Jahr
	vacation [və'keɪʃn]	Urlaub, Ferien
	period ['pɪəriəd]	Zeitraum
	to hesitate ['hezɪteɪt]	zögern
152	**nationality** [ˌnæʃə'næləti]	Staatsangehörigkeit
	education [ˌedʒu'keɪʃn]	(Schul-)Bildung, Ausbildung
	A-levels ['eɪ levlz]	(*entspricht*) Abitur
	grade [greɪd]	Note
	scale [skeɪl]	Skala
	unsatisfactory [ˌʌnˌsætɪs'fæktəri]	ungenügend
	office duties [ˌɒfɪs 'djuːtiz]	Bürodienst, Bürotätigkeit
	employment [ɪm'plɔɪmənt]	Arbeit, Beschäftigung
	administrative [əd'mɪnɪstrətɪv]	administrativ, Verwaltungs-
	community service [kə'mjuːnəti sɜːvɪs]	gemeinnützige Tätigkeit
	volunteer [ˌvɒlən'tɪə]	Freiwillige/r, freiwillig
	carer ['keərə]	Pfleger/in
	the elderly [ði 'eldəli]	ältere Menschen
	advanced [əd'vɑːnst]	fortgeschritten
	intermediate [ˌɪntə'miːdiət]	fortgeschrittene/r Anfänger/in
	references ['refərənsɪs]	Empfehlungsschreiben
	reverse chronological order [rɪˌvɜːs krɒnəlɒdʒɪkl 'ɔːdə]	umgekehrte zeitliche Reihenfolge
153	**career** [kə'rɪə]	(beruflicher) Werdegang, Karriere
	challenging ['tʃælɪndʒɪŋ]	herausfordernd, anstrengend
	to gain [geɪn]	gewinnen, erlangen
	well-qualified [wel'kwɒlɪfaɪd]	gut/hoch qualifiziert
	college of further education [ˌkɒlɪdʒ əv ˌfɜːðər ˌedʒu'keɪʃn]	berufsbildende Schule
	engineering [ˌendʒɪ'nɪərɪŋ]	Ingenieurwesen, Maschinenbau
	convenient [kən'viːniənt]	passend, günstig
	to catch sb's attention [kætʃ ə'tenʃn]	jds Aufmerksamkeit erregen
	to advertise ['ædvətaɪz]	annoncieren, ausschreiben
	bilingual secretary [baɪˌlɪŋgwəl 'sekrətri]	Fremdsprachensekretärin
	requirement [rɪ'kwaɪəmənt]	Anforderung, Voraussetzung
	drive [draɪv]	Schwung, Drive
	team spirit [ˌtiːm 'spɪrɪt]	Teamgeist
	to contribute [kən'trɪbjuːt]	beitragen, beisteuern
	to involve [ɪn'vɒlv]	mit sich bringen, beinhalten
	challenge ['tʃælɪndʒ]	Herausforderung, Aufgabe
	at your convenience [ət ˌsʌmbədis kən'viːniəns]	wenn es Ihnen passt
154	**specific** [spə'sɪfɪk]	speziell
	specialization [ˌspeʃəlaɪ'zeɪʃn]	Spezialisierung
	job training ['dʒɒb treɪnɪŋ]	berufliche Ausbildung
155	**office assistant** [ˌɒfɪs ə'sɪstənt]	Büroangestellte/r
	opening ['əʊpnɪŋ]	(freie) Stelle
	secretarial duties [sekrəˌteəriəl 'djuːtiz]	Sekretariatsaufgaben
	papermaking ['peɪpəmeɪkɪŋ]	Papierherstellung
	confident ['kɒnfɪdənt]	zuversichtlich
	to acquire [ə'kwaɪə]	erwerben
	to qualify ['kwɒlɪfaɪ]	qualifizieren
	favourable response [ˌfeɪvərəbl rɪ'spɒns]	positive Reaktion
	in due course [ɪn ˌdjuː 'kɔːs]	zu gegebener Zeit

	contribution [ˌkɒntrɪˈbjuːʃn]	Beitrag
	temping agency [ˈtempɪŋ eɪdʒənsi]	Zeitarbeitsfirma
	receptionist [rɪˈsepʃənɪst]	Empfangsdame, -chef
	work placement [ˈwɜːk pleɪsmənt]	Praktikum

File 7 Telephoning: making contacts and arranging appointments

156	**means of communication** [ˌmiːnz əv kəmjuːnɪˈkeɪʃn]	Kommunikationsmittel
	economy [ɪˈkɒnəmi]	Wirtschaft
	parcel [ˈpɑːsl]	Paket, Päckchen
	word spider [ˈwɜːd spaɪdə]	Wortnetz
	answerphone [ˈɑːnsəfəʊn]	Anrufbeantworter
	landline [ˈlændlaɪn]	Festnetz(leitung)
	multimedia [ˌmʌltiˈmiːdiə]	Multimedia(-)
	messaging [ˈmesɪdʒɪŋ]	Nachrichtenübermittlung
	text messaging [tekst ˈmesɪdʒɪŋ]	SMS
	to compare [kəmˈpeə]	vergleichen
157	**outdoor** [ˈaʊtdɔː]	im Freien, Outdoor
	to market [ˈmɑːkɪt]	vermarkten
	consultancy [kənˈsʌltənsi]	Beratungsfirma
	to enter a market [ˌentər ə ˈmɑːkɪt]	in einen neuen Markt eindringen
	to run [rʌn]	führen, betreiben
	to take a message [ˌteɪk ə ˈmesɪdʒ]	etw ausrichten
158	**to mind** [maɪnd]	etw dagegen haben
	to spell [spel]	buchstabieren
	to pronounce [prəˈnaʊns]	aussprechen
	to ring [rɪŋ]	anrufen
	united [juˈnaɪtɪd]	vereint, vereinigt
	digital [ˈdɪdʒɪtl]	digital
	to put through [ˌpʊt ˈθruː]	durchstellen, verbinden
	to hold the line [həʊld ðə ˈlaɪn]	am Apparat/dran bleiben
	to be available [bi əˈveɪləbl]	zu sprechen sein
159	**surname** [ˈsɜːneɪm]	Nach-, Familienname
	dot [dɒt]	Punkt
	to dictate [dɪkˈteɪt]	diktieren
	to swap [swɒp]	vertauschen
	underscore [ˌʌndəˈskɔː]	Unterstrich
	hyphen [ˈhaɪfn]	Bindestrich, Trennstrich
	slash [slæʃ]	Schrägstrich
	backslash [ˈbækslæʃ]	Backslash
	colon [ˈkəʊlən]	Doppelpunkt
160	**lobby** [ˈlɒbi]	Foyer, Eingangshalle
161	**entrance** [ˈentrəns]	Eingang, Einfahrt
	signposted [ˈsaɪnpəʊstɪd]	ausgeschildert
162	**heading** [ˈhedɪŋ]	Überschrift
	to have in mind [həv ɪn ˈmaɪnd]	denken an
	to suit (fine) [ˌsuːt ˈfaɪn]	(gut) passen, recht sein
	misunderstanding [ˌmɪsʌndəˈstændɪŋ]	Missverständnis

File 8 Emailing: making appointments, travel arrangements

164	**travel arrangements** [ˈtrævl əreɪndʒmənts]	Reisepläne
	informal [ɪnˈfɔːml]	ungezwungen, nicht förmlich, informell
	precise [prɪˈsaɪs]	genau, präzise
	topic [ˈtɒpɪk]	Thema
	shortened [ˈʃɔːtnd]	verkürzt, abgekürzt
	casing [ˈkeɪsɪŋ]	Gehäuse, Hülle
	the Channel Tunnel [ˈtʃænl tʌnl]	der Kanaltunnel
165	**at the beginning** [ət ðə bɪˈgɪnɪŋ]	am Anfang, anfangs
	mill [mɪl]	Mühle
	agenda [əˈdʒendə]	Tagesordnung
	scratch-resistant [ˈskrætʃ rɪzɪstənt]	kratzfest
	impact-resistant [ˈɪmpækt rɪzɪstənt]	stoßfest
	That's about it. [ˌðæts əbaʊt ˈɪt]	Das wär's erst einmal.
166	**apart from** [əˈpɑːt frəm]	außer, abgesehen von
167	**reservation** [ˌrezəˈveɪʃn]	Reservierung, Buchung
	en suite [ɒn ˈswiːt]	mit Bad
	assistance [əˈsɪstəns]	Hilfe, Unterstützung
	purpose [ˈpɜːpəs]	Zweck, Sinn
168	**pleasantly situated** [ˌplezntli ˈsɪtʃueɪtɪd]	reizvoll gelegen
	accountant [əˈkaʊntənt]	Buchhalter/in
	to manage [ˈmænɪdʒ]	(es/etw) schaffen
169	**travel agent** [ˈtrævl eɪdʒənt]	Reisebüro(angestellte/r)
	itinerary [aɪˈtɪnərəri]	Reiseroute, Reiseplan
	to hire [ˈhaɪə]	mieten, leihen
	to mention [ˈmenʃn]	erwähnen, nennen
	means of transport [miːnz əf ˈtrænspɔːt]	Beförderungsmittel, Verkehrsmittel
171	**to depart** [dɪˈpɑːt]	abreisen, abfahren, abfliegen
	arrival [əˈraɪvl]	Ankunft
	mixed up [ˌmɪkst ˈʌp]	durcheinander
	registration number [ˌredʒɪˈstreɪʃn nʌmbə]	Autokennzeichen
172	**car hire** [ˈkɑː haɪə]	Autovermietung
	deal [diːl]	(günstiges) Angebot
	to drop off [ˌdrɒp ˈɒf]	zurückgeben
	unlimited mileage [ʌnˌlɪmɪtɪd ˈmaɪlɪdʒ]	unbegrenzte Meilen
	surcharge [ˈsɜːtʃɑːdʒ]	Aufschlag
	on top of [ɒn ˈtɒp əv]	auf

File 9 Toolbox for business communication

174	**on top of** [ɒn ˈtɒp əv]	auf

Alphabetisches Wörterverzeichnis

Diese Liste enthält alle Wörter des chronologischen Wörterverzeichnisses in alphabetischer Reihenfolge. Die Zahl nach dem Stichwort bezieht sich auf die Seite, auf der das Wort zum ersten Mal erscheint. Sind mehrere Seitenzahlen aufgeführt, beziehen sich diese auf unterschiedliche Bedeutungen des Wortes und/oder auf ein Vorkommen sowohl im *Main Course* als auch im *Business Communication Course*. Der Buchstabe *T* nach einer Seitenzahl bedeutet, dass das Wort im Hörverständnistext erscheint.

A

A-levels *152* (*entspricht*) Abitur
abbreviation *181* Abkürzung
ability *37* Fähigkeit, Können
to abolish *135* abschaffen, streichen
about: That's ~ it. *165* Das wär's erst einmal.
above all *44* vor allem
academic year *151* akademisches Jahr
to accelerate *91* beschleunigen
acceleration *90* Beschleunigung
acceptable *77* annehmbar, akzeptabel
access *31* Zugang, Zugriff
to accompany *179* begleiten
accordance: in ~with *132* gemäß, in Übereinstimmung mit
according to *22* zufolge, nach, gemäß
account *46* Konto, Kunde
account executive *46* Kundenbetreuer
to account for *45* ausmachen, betragen
accountant *34 T, 168* (Bilanz-)Buchhalter/in
accuracy *101* Genauigkeit
accurate(ly) *101, 111* genau, akkurat
to achieve *95, 150* erreichen, erlangen
achievement *104* Leistung, Errungenschaft
to acknowledge *130* bestätigen
acknowledgement *129* Bestätigung
to acquire *155* erwerben
to act *114* handeln, reagieren
to act out *64* vorspielen, aufführen
action *48 T* Handlung, Aktion
activity kit *92* etwa: Bausatz
ad *40* *Kurzform von* advert
to adapt *64* anpassen, adaptieren
to add up *88* zusammenzählen, -rechnen
addict *69* Süchtige/r, Abhängige/r
addition: in ~ *43* darüber hinaus
addition: in ~ to *124* zusätzlich (zu)
additional *121* zusätzlich
addressee *47, 111* Empfänger/in, Adressat/in
to adjust *25* anpassen, einstellen
administrative *152* administrativ, Verwaltungs-
to adopt *41* annehmen, übernehmen
advance *180* Fortschritt
advance: in ~ *126* im Voraus
advanced *44, 152* fortschrittlich
advantage *65, 111* Vorteil, Vorzug
adventure holiday *80* Abenteuerurlaub
advert *37, 113* Anzeige, Werbespot
to advertise *44, 119, 153* werben (für), Werbung machen für, ausschreiben
advertisement *40, 113* Reklame, Werbung, Anzeige
advertising *34 T* Werbung, Reklame
advice of dispatch *131* Versandanzeige
to advise *23* (be-)raten, empfehlen
to afford *57* (es) sich leisten (können)
after all *44* schließlich (doch)
age: for ~s *12* eine Ewigkeit
agenda *165* Tagesordnung
agent *49* Handelnde/r
agony *7* Qual
agreed *116* vereinbart
agreement *95* Vereinbarung, Abkommen
ahead of *26* vor
aid *76* Hilfe
aim *40, 139* Ziel, Absicht
to aim *35* zielen; beabsichtigen, bezwecken
air conditioning (AC) *88* Klimaanlage
air waybill *179* Luftfrachtbrief,
airfreight *126* Luftfracht
aisle seat *170* Gangplatz
akin to *44* (einer Sache) ähnlich
alcohol *10* Alkohol
to allow *15, 122* erlauben, gestatten
allowance *68* Taschengeld
amazed *109* erstaunt
ambition *35* Ehrgeiz
ambitious *86* ehrgeizig
amount *51, 124* Menge, Ausmaß, Summe, Betrag
analysis *45* Analyse
to analyze *38* analysieren
to announce *94* bekannt geben, ankündigen
to annoy *22* ärgern
annual *71* jährlich
answerphone *156* Anrufbeantworter
anxious *50* ängstlich, besorgt
anxious *148* bemüht
anyhow *8* jedenfalls, sowieso
apart from *166* außer, abgesehen von
to apologize *139* sich entschuldigen
apology *145* Entschuldigung
to appear *81* erscheinen, auftauchen
appearance *142* Äußeres, (äußere) Erscheinung
application *150* Bewerbung
to apply *22, 111* gelten, zutreffen, zur Anwendung kommen
to apply for *31* sich bewerben um
appointment *13* Termin, Verabredung
to appreciate *121* zu schätzen wissen
apprentice *14* Auszubildende/r
apprenticeship *105* Lehre, Ausbildung
appropriate(ly) *47* geeignet, angemessen
approval: on ~ *180* zur Ansicht
to approve *81* genehmigen
approximate(ly) *37, 92* ungefähr, etwa, zirka
archaeological *38* archäologisch
area *53* Gebiet, Bereich
to arrange *14* arrangieren, vereinbaren
to arrange for *135* einrichten, organisieren
arrangements *25* Vorbereitungen, Pläne, Abmachungen
arrival *171* Ankunft
article *130* Artikel
artificial *91* künstlich, Kunst-
artwork *49* Illustrationen, Bildmaterial
as a matter of fact *109* eigentlich, sogar, tatsächlich
as follows *133* wie folgt
as requested *122* wie erwünscht, wunschgemäß
as scheduled *140* wie vorgesehen, wie geplant
as stated *131* wie dargelegt
aspect *27* Aspekt, Seite
assistance *167* Hilfe, Unterstützung
to associate *86* in Verbindung bringen, assoziieren
association *78* Verband
assorted *141* gemischt
to assume *136* annehmen, davon ausgehen
athletics *22* Leichtathletik
atmosphere *91* Atmosphäre
attached *113* beigefügt
attention: ~ to detail *101* Detailgenauigkeit
attention: to attract ~ *48 T* Aufmerksamkeit erregen
attitude *15* Einstellung, Haltung
Attn = attention *110* z.Hd. = zu Händen von
to attract *35* anziehen, -locken
attractive *177* attraktiv
auction *67* Versteigerung, Auktion
authentic *174* echt, authentisch
author *106* Autor/in
automated teller machine (ATM) *84 T* Geldautomat
automatic *92* automatisch
automatic transmission *170* Automatik(getriebe)
automatically *26* automatisch
availability *118* Verfügbarkeit
available *97, 115* erhältlich, verfügbar, lieferbar
available: to be ~ *158* zu sprechen sein
average *37* Durchschnitt
to avoid *51, 121* (ver)meiden, aus dem Weg gehen
avoidable *26* vermeidbar
awful *51, 139* furchtbar, schrecklich

B

back-up *48* Unterstützungs-, Reserve-
background *149* Hintergrund
backslash *159* Backslash
badly-paid *30* schlecht bezahlt
bakery *61* Bäckerei
to balance *55* (sich) ausgleichen, im Gleichgewicht halten
balanced *22* ausgeglichen, ausgewogen
ban *25* Verbot
bar chart *68* Balkendiagramm
bargain *91* Angebot, Schnäppchen
base *78* Basis
based: ~ on *120* auf der Grundlage von
based: to be ~ on *55* beruhen auf, basieren auf
basically *45* grundsätzlich, eigentlich
basics *61* Grundnahrungsmittel
basket *61* Korb
to beat *71* schlagen, übertreffen

beauty *85* Schönheit
beauty products *114* Kosmetikartikel
bed and breakfast *88* Frühstückspension, Zimmer mit Frühstück
beginning: at the ~ *165* am Anfang, anfangs
to behave *35* sich verhalten, sich benehmen
belt *119* Gürtel, Gurt
benefit *52* Vorteil, Nutzen
benefits *30* Vergünstigungen
bilingual secretary *153* Fremdsprachensekretärin
bill *137* Rechnung
bill of exchange *180* Wechsel
bill of lading *179* Seefrachtbrief, Konnossement
billion *41* Milliarde
binding *119* verbindlich, bindend
biomass energy *56* Bioenergie
bits and pieces *93 T* kleine Stücke
black: in the ~ *84* in den schwarzen Zahlen
board: on ~ *49, 180* an Bord
body language *77* Körpersprache
body mass index (BMI) *22* Körpermassenzahl
body text *111* Haupttext
bonus *74* Zulage, Prämie
booking *30* Buchung, Reservierung
booklet *38* Broschüre
border *53, 178* Grenze
to borrow *79* (sich etw) borgen, (sich) (aus)leihen
bottled *60* aus der Flasche
boxed *116* in Schachtel(n)
brackets: in ~ *25* in Klammern
brake *91* Bremse
braking *90* Bremsen
branch *35* Niederlassung,Filiale
brand *40* Marke
brand loyalty *44* Markentreue
brand name *61* Markenzeichen, -name
brand name *116* Markenzeichen, -name
brand-new *71* nagelneu
breakdown *74* Aufteilung, -schlüsselung
brief(ly) *68, 111* kurz
bright future *72* glänzende Zukunft
brochure *40, 113* Broschüre, Prospekt
broken *93 T, 146* kaputt, zerbrochen
budget *88* Budget, Etat
budget airline *86* Billigflieger
builder *93 T* Bauunternehmer/in
bulk: in ~ *62* en gros
burger *22* Hamburger
bus service *58* Busverbindung
business manager *46* kaufmännischer Leiter
business studies *31, 151* Betriebswirtschaftslehre (BWL)
button *69* Taste, Knopf
buyer *35* Einkäufer/in

C

caffeinated *107* mit Koffein
to call *94* einberufen
calm *50* ruhig, gelassen
campaign *47 T, 115* Kampagne, Werbeaktion
campaign group *57 T* Aktionsgruppe
campsite *25* Campingplatz
can *142* Dose
to cancel *12* stornieren, absagen
candle *131* Kerze
canned *60* in der Dose
canteen *34 T* Kantine
capitalization *177* Kapitalstruktur, Kapitalisierung
caption *27* Bildunterschrift
captive *61* gefangen, Gefangene/r
car hire *172* Autovermietung
car sharing *51* Carsharing
carbon *92* Kohlenstoff
carbon dioxide *95* Kohlendioxid
to care for *38, 142* sich kümmern um, pflegen
career *30, 153* Karriere, (beruflicher) Werdegang
careers officer *101* Berufsberater/in
careless *23* leichtsinnig, unvorsichtig
carer *152* Pfleger/in
cargo *179* Fracht, Ladung
cargo officer *180* Frachtoffizier
carrier *86, 178* Fluggesellschaft, Transportunternehmen, Frachtführer
to carry *86* befördern
to carry on *15* weitermachen, fortfahren
carton *63* Packung, Paket, Karton
cartoon *27* Karikatur
case *15, 69* Karton, Kiste; Fall
case: just in ~ *145* nur für den Fall
case study *105* Fallstudie
cash discount *122* Barzahlungsrabatt
cash flow *81* Liquidität, Bargeldfluss
cashpoint *84 T* Geldautomat
casing *164* Gehäuse, Hülle
casual *111* salopp, lässig
casual worker *74* Gelegenheitsarbeiter
catalytic converter *90* Katalysator
to catch sb's attention *153* jds Aufmerksamkeit erregen
cause *50* Ursache, Grund, Anlass
to cause *23* verursachen, verschulden
cellphone *50* Handy, Mobiltelefon
certain *57 T* bestimmt
certificate of origin *179* Ursprungszeugnis
chain *35* (Handels-)Kette
challenge *103 T, 153* Herausforderung, Aufgabe
challenging *30, 153* herausfordernd, anstrengend
champion *89* Meister/in, Champion
changing room *63 T* Umkleideraum, -kabine
channel *65, 71* Kanal, (Vertriebs-)Weg, Sender
the Channel Tunnel *164* der Kanaltunnel
charge: in ~ of *7* verantwortlich für
to charge *66* in Rechnung stellen, berechnen
to charge: to be ~d *52* (eine Gebühr) zahlen müssen
charges *51* Gebühren, Kosten
charity *38* Wohltätigkeit, Wohltätigkeitsorganisation
chart *37* Diagramm, Tabelle
check-in *30* Abfertigung, Check-In
to check in *170* einchecken
checkout *60* Kasse
checkout assistant *69* Kassierer/in
chef *81* Koch/Köchin
chemicals *93 T* Chemikalien
chemist's *136* Drogerie, Apotheke
cheque *67, 180* Scheck
cheque book *84 T* Scheckbuch, -heft
chess *9* Schach
chipboard *93 T* Spanplatte
to circulate *124* (an alle) verschicken
circumstance *16* Umstand, Bedingung
citizen *35* Bürger/in
city council *94* Stadtrat, Gemeinderat
classification *22* Klassifizierung, Einstufung
classified ad *40* Kleinanzeige
clerical worker *71* Schreibkraft, Bürokraft
clerk *30* Angestellte/r
client *10* Kunde, Kundin
climate *26* Klima
climate change *26* Klimawandel
close *114* (Brief-)Schluss
close corporation *177* GmbH
close to *52* nahe (bei)
closely *47* eng
closeness *33* Nähe
closing *114* abschließend
closing time *17* Geschäftsschluss, Ladenschlusszeit
cloth *43, 112* Stoff, Tuch
clothing *26* Kleidung, Kleider
co-director *46* etwa: Mitgeschäftsführer
coal *56* Kohle
coastal *96* Küsten-
code *101* (Bestell-)Nummer
to collapse *74* einbrechen, abstürzen
colleague *64* Kollege/Kollegin
college of further education (CFE) *31, 153* berufsbildende Schule,
colon *159* Doppelpunkt
to combine *18* verbinden, kombinieren
combined transport waybill *179* kombinierter Warenbegleitschein
to come under *34 T* hier: unterstehen
to come up *115* zur Sprache kommen
comment *114* Bemerkung
to comment *66* kommentieren, bemerken
commercial *40* Werbespot, Werbung
commercial *138* gewerblich
commercial matters *46* kaufmännische Angelegenheiten
commission *74* Provision, Gebühr
commitment *101* Engagement, Einsatz
committed *103* engagiert
committed: to be ~ to *103 T* sich engagieren für
to communicate *70* sich verständigen, kommunizieren
community *91* Allgemeinheit, Gemeinschaft
community service *152* gemeinnützige Tätigkeit
to commute *50* pendeln, zum Arbeitsplatz fahren
commuter *50* Pendler/in
company *10* Unternehmen, Firma, Gesellschaft
to compare *58, 156* vergleichen, sich vergleichen lassen
comparison *45, 59* Vergleich; Steigerung
compensation *145* Schaden(s)ersatz, Kompensation
to compete *67* konkurrieren, im Wettbewerb stehen
competition *46, 143* Konkurrenz, Wettbewerb
competitive *62* konkurrenzfähig
competitive market *143* hart umkämpfter Markt
competitor *44, 144* Konkurrent/in, Wett-, Mitbewerber/in
to complain *139* sich beschweren, reklamieren
complaint *137* Beschwerde, Reklamation, Mängelrüge
completion *46* Abschluss, Erledigung

complimentary close *111* Schlussformel
compost bin *93 T* Komposttonne
computer failure *145* Computer-, Systemabsturz
computing *105* Computerwesen
concept *46* Konzept, Idee
concerning *78* bezüglich, hinsichtlich
to conclude *87* (ab)schließen, folgern
condition *32, 179* Bedingung, Zustand
conference *34 T* Konferenz, Besprechung
conference facilities *168* Einrichtungen für Konferenzen
confidence *77, 133* (Selbst-)Vertrauen, Selbstsicherheit
confident *155* zuversichtlich
to confirm *124* bestätigen
confirmation of acceptance *123* Auftragsbestätigung
confusion *141* Verwirrung
congestion charge *51* Staugebühr
congestion charging *52* Erhebung von Staugebühren
to congratulate *109* gratulieren, beglückwünschen
Congratulations! *33* Herzlichen Glückwunsch! Ich gratuliere!
connected *12* angeschlossen, verbunden
to consider *52, 151* in Erwägung ziehen, nachdenken über
considerable *145* beträchtlich, beachtlich
consignee *123* (Waren-)Empfänger, Adressat
consignment *116* Lieferung, (Waren-)Sendung
consignor *179* Versender, (Waren-)Absender
to consist *69, 150* bestehen
constantly *41* ständig
to construct *54* bauen
consultancy *157* Beratungsfirma
to consume *91* verbrauchen, konsumieren
consumer *62* Verbraucher/in, Konsument/in
consumption *75* Konsum, Verbrauch
contact page *7* etwa: Kontaktvermittlungs-Seite
to contain *58* enthalten
container *144* Behälter, Gefäß
contents *146* Inhalt
continental breakfast *168* kleines Frühstück
contract of carriage *179* Beförderungsvertrag
contrast: by ~ *87* im Gegensatz
to contribute *153* beitragen, beisteuern
contribution *155* Beitrag
to control kontrollieren, (über-)prüfen
conurbation *58* Ballungsgebiet, -raum
convenience *67* Komfort, Annehmlichkeit
convenience: at your ~ *153* wenn es Ihnen passt
convenient *65, 153* günstig, angenehm, passend
conventional *91* herkömmlich, konventionell
conversion *81* Umbau
to convert *81* umbauen
to cope *57* (damit) zurechtkommen
copier *109* Kopierer
copywriter *47* (Werbe-)Texter/in
corner-piece *117* Eckstück
to correspond to *146* entsprechen
cosmetics *114* Kosmetik(a)
cotton *63 T* Baumwolle
council services *75* etwa: öffentliche Einrichtungen
councillor *58* Ratsmitglied
counter *61* Theke, Schalter
course: in due ~ *155* zu gegebener Zeit
court *16* Gericht(shof)
to cover *31, 145* (be-, zu-, ab)decken
craft *74* Handwerk
craftsmanship *44* Handwerkskunst
crate *146* (Holz-)Kiste
to create *42, 180* (er)schaffen, machen
creation *41* Kreation, Erfindung
creative team *47 T* etwa: kreative Mannschaft
creativity *103* Kreativität
credit: to be in ~ *84* ein Guthaben haben
to credit *146* gutschreiben
credit transfer *180* (Bank-)Überweisung
to criticize *55* kritisieren
crop *74* Ernte, Anbaupflanzen
to cross *51* überqueren, hier: hinüberfahren
cross-country skiing *9* Skilanglauf
crowded *65* überfüllt, voll
culture *33* Kultur
current *110* aktuell, gegenwärtig (gültig)
currently *10* momentan, zurzeit
Customer Accounts *135* (Abteilung) Kundenkonten
customs *74, 179* Zoll, Zollbehörde
customs duties *177* Zollabgaben
to cut *51* reduzieren, senken
cute *56* niedlich, knuffig
cutting-edge *41* topaktuell, innovativ
CV = curriculum vitae *31, 150* Lebenslauf

D

damage *51* Schaden, Schäden
to damage *54, 115* beschädigen, schaden
damaged *140* beschädigt
damp *117* Feuchtigkeit
data processing *72* Datenverarbeitung
data projector *168* Beamer
data transmission *71* Daten(fern)übertragung
to de-layer *106* Hierarchien abbauen
dead-end job *31* Stelle ohne Aufstiegschancen
deal *172* (günstiges) Angebot
to deal with *30, 129* umgehen mit, sich befassen mit, bearbeiten, erledigen
dealer *65, 119* Händler/in
Dear sir or madam, *58* Sehr geehrte Damen und Herren,
death *87* Tod
debate *85* Debatte
to debit *84 T* belasten
debit card *60* Bankkarte
decline *86* Rückgang
to decline *86* zurückgehen, sinken
decor *61* Ausstattung, Dekor
to decrease *37* sinken, fallen, abnehmen
defective *139* fehlerhaft
to define *45* definieren
definite *54* bestimmt, fest, definitiv
definitely *22* bestimmt, sicher,, auf jeden Fall
degree *103 T* (akademischer) Abschluss
delay *137* Verzögerung
delicatessen *60* Feinkost(laden)
delicious *61* köstlich, lecker
delighted *110* (sehr) erfreut
to deliver *44, 53, 116* liefern, zustellen; halten, was es verspricht
delivery *51, 112* Zustellung, (Aus-)Lieferung
demand *61* Bedarf, Nachfrage
demanding *101* anstrengend, anspruchsvoll
to demonstrate *17* demonstrieren
demotivated *105* demotiviert
denim *112* Denim (Jeansstoff)
to depart *170* abreisen, abfahren, abfliegen
department *34 T* Abteilung
department store *60* Kauf-, Warenhaus
departure *35, 170* Abfahrt, Abreise, Abflug
to depend on *48 T, 125* abhängen von, abhängig sein von, darauf ankommen
dependent *76* abhängig
depending on *108, 124* je nach, abhängig von
deposit *81* Kaution, Anzahlung
to deposit *84* einzahlen
depressing *74* bedrückend, deprimierend
design *148* hier: Muster
to design *34 T* konstruieren, entwerfen, entwickeln, gestalten
designer *34 T, 143* Konstrukteur/in, Designer/in
desire *44* Verlangen, Wunsch
desk *170* Schalter
despite *71* trotz
destination *18* (Reise-)Ziel
to destroy *55* zerstören, vernichten
destruction *85* Zerstörung, Vernichtung
detailed *46, 119* ausführlich, genau
determination *103* Entschlossenheit
determined *86* (fest) entschlossen, bestimmt
to develop *34* (sich) entwickeln
developer *98* Bauunternehmer
development *46* Entwicklung
to dictate *159* diktieren
dictionary entry *73* Stichwort im Wörterbuch
diet *22* Diät, Ernährung
dig *38* Ausgrabung
digit code *48* Zahlencode
digital *158* digital
diploma *31* Abschluss, Diplom
to direct *37* leiten
direct *143* direkt, unmittelbar
direct service *170* Direktverbindung
disadvantage *98, 115* Nachteil, Schaden
to disagree *57* anderer Meinung sein
disagreement *177* Meinungsverschiedenheit
to disappear *85* verschwinden
disappointed *106* enttäuscht
disaster *177* Katastrophe, Unglück
disastrous *94* unglücklich, katastrophal
discount *108, 112* Rabatt, Nachlass
to discover *81* entdecken
discrepancy *148* Diskrepanz, Unstimmigkeit
disgusting *40* ekelhaft, unerhört
dishwasher *138* Geschirrspüler
to dislike *100* nicht mögen
dispatch *108* Versand
to dispatch *124* ausliefern, versenden
to displace *96* verdrängen, vertreiben
display *60* Auslage, Dekoration
to display *61* aus-, aufstellen
display material *115* Dekorationsmaterial
to dispose of *140* entsorgen, beseitigen
dissatisfied *137* unzufrieden
distance: ~ to go *50* zurückzulegende Entfernung
distance: ~ travelled *55* zurückgelegte Entfernung
distribution *34 T, 124* Vertrieb, Auslieferung, Lieferung

ferry *59* Fähre
fiancé *103 T* Verlobter
to file *11* ablegen, zu den Akten legen
filing *13* Ablage
final *49* endgültig, letzte/r/s
final exam *80* Abschlussprüfung
to finalize *49* endgültig festlegen
finance *34 T* Buchhaltung
financial(ly) *18* finanziell
fingernail *11* Fingernagel
finished goods *34 T* Fertigwaren, -güter
to fire *35* feuern, entlassen
firm *110* Firma
firm *77* fest, beständig
firm offer *110* Festangebot, festes Angebot
first aid kit *25* Verbandskasten
first of all *44* zu(aller)erst, zunächst
first order *122* Erstbestellung
to fit together *34 T* zusammen passen
to fix *25* festsetzen, ausmachen
to fix up *116* arrangieren, herrichten
flat *106* flach
flexibility *103* Flexibilität
flexitime *106* Gleitzeit
flight *12* Flug
flight attendant *30* Flugbegleiter/in
to flood *42* überfluten
flooding *96* Überschwemmung
florist *30* Blumenhändler/in
flour *73* Mehl
fluent *151* fließend
footprint *85* Fußabdruck
to force *74* zwingen
to force down *76 T* niederdrücken
foreign *71* ausländisch
foreign *151* Auslands-, ausländisch
foreign: ~ trade *180* Außenhandel
foreigner *75* Ausländer/in
form *10, 31* Form; Formular
to form *74* bilden
formal *33, 111* formell, förmlich
formality *178* Formalität
formula *48 T* Formel
fortunately *39* glücklicherweise
forwarding agent *140* Spediteur
fossil fuel *91* fossiler Brennstoff
foundation *75* Stiftung
founder *67* Gründer/in
free-market economy *35* freie Marktwirtschaft
freight *117* Fracht, Frachtkosten
frequent *44* häufig, oft
freshness *61* Frische
fries *22* Pommes frites
frightened: to be ~ of *54* Angst haben vor
frozen *60* tiefgefroren
frustrated *50* frustriert
fuel *51* Kraftstoff, Treibstoff
fuel cell *55* Brennstoffzelle
fuel economy *90* geringer Kraftstoffverbrauch
full-page *40* ganzseitig
full stop *110* Punkt
full-time *31* ganztags, Vollzeit(-)
fully *85* völlig, vollständig
further education *31* etwa: höhere Schulbildung
further to *112* in Bezug auf, im Anschluss an

G

gadget *26* Gerät
to gain *55, 153* gewinnen, erlangen
gap *27* Lücke
to gasp *39* nach Luft ringen, japsen
to gather *62* sich versammeln
GCSE *108* mittlere Reife
generally speaking *46* im Allgemeinen
generator *95* Generator
generous *135* großzügig
to get about *26* herumkommen, sich fortbewegen
to get bored *13* sich langweilen
to get hurt *17* (sich) verletzen, (sich) wehtun
to get in touch *18, 112* (sich) in Verbindung setzen
to get into a mess *57 T* in einen Schlamassel geraten
to get one's money's worth *51* auf seine Kosten kommen
to get real *18* etw endlich begreifen
to get rid of *106* beseitigen, abschaffen
gift *65* Geschenk
glad *113* froh
glamorous *40* glanzvoll, glamourös
global warming *95* Erderwärmung
globalization *111* Globalisierung
to globalize *72* globalisieren
globally *52* global
glossary *177* Glossar
to go bankrupt *65* Pleite gehen
to go clubbing in die Disko gehen
to go for sth *43* etw nehmen, gut finden
to go mad *60* durchdrehen
to go on strike *71* in Streik treten
goal *101* Ziel
gold medal *46* Goldmedaille
good-humoured *86* gut gelaunt
goods *117* Ware(n), Güter
gothic look *41* *Moderichtung*
government *26* Regierung
to grab *61* greifen, packen
grade *93 T, 152* (Güte-)Klasse; Note
gradually *74* allmählich, schrittweise
to graduate *71* einen Abschluss machen
graduation *73* Erlangung eines akademischen Grades
grammar school *105* Gymnasium
to grant *132* gewähren, bewilligen
graph *36* Grafik, Diagramm
grateful *76 T, 112* dankbar
great-grandparents *105* Urgroßeltern
greatly *49* in hohem Maße
green *94* umweltfreundlich
greenhouse *57* Treibhaus
to greet *81* (be)grüßen
greeting *47* Begrüßung, Gruß(formel)
gridlock *26* Verkehrsinfarkt
ground *76* (Erd-)Boden
growing *119* wachsend
growth *35* Wachstum, Zunahme
growth *177* Wachstum, Zunahme
to guarantee *74* garantieren
guarantee *147* Garantie
to guarantee *181* garantieren
to guess *93 T* raten, vermuten
guide *22* Richtlinie
guidebook *79* Reiseführer
guy *99* Typ, Junge
gym *22* Fitnessstudio

H

haircare product *110* Haarpflegeprodukt
half board *88* Halbpension
hand luggage *49* Handgepäck
to hand out blame *139* Schuldzuweisungen machen
to hand over *178* aushändigen, übergeben
to handle *62, 130* umschlagen, abwickeln, erledigen
handling *74* Abwicklung
handset *44* Handapparat
handshake *77* Händedruck
harbour *81* Hafen
hard-working *101* fleißig
hardly *67* (wohl) kaum
hardworking *86* fleißig
harm *85* Schaden
to harm *115* schaden
to hate *83* hassen, überhaupt nicht mögen
haulier *55* Spediteur, Transportunternehmer
to have in mind *162* denken an
head *34 T* Chef, Leiter
heading *48 T, 162* Überschrift
headline *50* Schlagzeile, Überschrift
health-conscious *70* gesundheitsbewusst
heat *91* Hitze
heating *91* Heizung
heavy-duty polythene sheeting *117* schwere Polyäthylenfolie
height *22* Höhe, Größe
hemisphere *96* Halbkugel
to hesitate *151* zögern
to hide *55* (sich) verstecken, (sich) verbergen
high street *62* Hauptgeschäftsstraße
high-cost *72* hochwertig, kapitalintensiv
high-level *72* auf hohem Niveau, anspruchsvoll
high-performance *44* Hochleistungs-
high-quality *44, 114* hochwertig
high-value *72* hochwertig, hochpreisig
highly *144* äußerst
highly skilled *36* gut ausgebildet, hoch qualifiziert
highway patrol *26* Verkehrspolizei
to hire *35, 79, 169* ein-, anstellen, leihen, mieten
to hold the line *158* am Apparat/dran bleiben
holiday cover *108* Urlaubsvertretung
honest *22* ehrlich, anständig
to honour *180* (Wechsel) akzeptieren, einlösen
hopeful *73* hoffnungsvoll
hostess *93 T* Gastgeberin
household *26* Haushalt
huge *31* riesig
human *95* menschlich, Menschen-
humour *45* Humor
to hurry away *81* davoneilen
hybrid vehicle *55* Hybridauto
hydro energy *56* Wasserkraft
hydrogen *55* Wasserstoff
hypermarket *61* großer Einkaufsmarkt
hyphen *159* Bindestrich, Trennstrich

I

i.e. *181* d.h.
ice core *96* Eis-Bohrkern
iconic *44* mit Kultsymbolcharakter
ICT *31* Informations- und Kommunikationstechnologie
ID (identification) *39* Ausweis(dokument)
ideal *151* ideal
identical *141* identisch
ignorance *177* Unwissenheit, Unkenntnis
illegible *107, 143* unleserlich
illogical *107* unlogisch
to illustrate *27* illustrieren, veranschaulichen

image *40, 113* Image, Bild
imaginative *65* phantasievoll, einfallsreich
to imagine *50, 119* sich vorstellen, sich einbilden
imbalance *107* Unausgeglichenheit
immediate *122* sofort, umgehend
immoral *107* unmoralisch
impact *92, 117* (Aus-)Wirkung, Effekt; Stoß
impact-resistant *165* stoßfest
impersonal *107* unpersönlich
import duties *71* Einfuhrzölle
importance *41* Bedeutung
importer *178* Importeur/in
impossible *54, 142* unmöglich, undenkbar
impulse *60* Impuls
in-job training *104* firmeninterne Ausbildung
inadequate *146* unzulänglich
inch *96* Inch, Zoll
incidentally *113* übrigens, nebenbei
to include *62, 123* enthalten, einbeziehen, umfassen
including *34 T* einschließlich, darunter
income *57* Einkommen
incomplete *145* unvollständig
inconvenience *141* Unannehmlichkeit
inconvenient *167* ungünstig
incorporated company (Inc.) *177* (als Kapitalgesellschaft) eingetragen
incoterm *119* Incoterm
to increase *29* zunehmen, steigen, erhöhen
increase *52* Zunahme, Wachstum
increasingly *111* zunehmend
indeed *69, 144* in der Tat, allerdings, wirklich
independent *30* unabhängig
indirectness *64* Indirektheit
individual *62, 106, 111* Einzelperson, Einzelne/r; Einzel-,
industrial *58* Industrie-, industriell
industrialized nations *95* Industrienationen
inexperienced *141* unerfahren
influencer *41* jd mit Einfluss
informal *33, 164* ungezwungen, informell
information technology *31* Informationstechnologie
initials *125* Initialen
to injure *23* verletzen
injured *38* verletzt
injury *26* Verletzung
innovative *119* innovativ
to input *101* eingeben
insecurity *83* Unsicherheit
to insist *137* (darauf) bestehen
inspector *145* Kontrolleur/in
instance: for ~ *55* zum Beispiel
instead *8* stattdessen, anstatt
to instruct *141* anweisen
instruction *49* Anweisung, Aufforderung
instructions *39* Bedienungsanleitung
instructions *142* Bedienungsanleitung, Anweisungen
instructor *85* Lehrer/in, Ausbilder/in
insurance *66, 123* Versicherung
insurance certificate *179* Versicherungszertifikat
insurance claim *140* Versicherungsanspruch
to insure *179* versichern
insurer *145* Versicherungsgeber, Versicherer
to integrate *19* integrieren, einbauen
intended for *112* gedacht für, dazu dienend
to interact *77* interagieren, miteinander umgehen
intermediate *152* fortgeschrittene/r Anfänger/in
intern *151* Praktikant/in, Volontär/in
internal *143* intern
International Chamber of Commerce *177* Internationale Handelskammer
internship *151* Praktikum, Volontariat
interpersonal *101* zwischenmenschlich
to interpret *37* interpretieren, deuten
intonation *54* Tonfall
introductory discount *121* Einführungsrabatt
introductory offer *121* Einführungsangebot
to invent *41* erfinden
invention *43* Erfindung
inventive *41* erfinderisch
to invest *49* investieren, anlegen
investigation *139* Nachforschung, Untersuchung
investment *76* Investition, Anlage
invitation *150* Einladung
invoice *10* Rechnung
invoiced value *117* Rechnungswert
to involve *153* mit sich bringen, beinhalten
involved in *75* beteiligt an
irrational *107* irrational, unvernünftig
irregular *30* unregelmäßig
irresponsible *23* unverantwortlich
irrevocable *126* unwiderruflich
issue *23* Frage, Angelegenheit, Thema, Problem
to issue *179* ausstellen
It's a pity. *25* Schade.
italics *14* Kursivschrift
item *61, 129* Artikel, Stück, Posten
itinerary *169* Reiseroute, Reiseplan

J

jar *63* (Marmeladen-)Glas
jeweller's *60* Juwelier(geschäft)
jewellery *44* Schmuck
job applicant *10* Stellenbewerber/in
job description *47* Stellenbeschreibung
job protection *35* Arbeitsschutz
job training *154* berufliche Ausbildung
to jump in *83* auf etw anspringen, loslegen
jungle *70* Dschungel, Urwald
junior *33* untergeordnet, rangniedriger

K

keen on *113* (sehr) interessiert an
to keep a promise *44* ein Versprechen halten
to keep up *51* Schritt halten, mithalten
key *75, 102, 125* Schlüssel; Schlüssel-, Haupt
to key in *84 T* eingeben
to kid oneself *22* sich etwas vormachen
kind of *41* irgendwie, ein bisschen
kite-surfing *8* Kitesurfen
knee pad *119* Knieschützer

L

to label *34* benennen, etikettieren
label *39* Etikett, Marke
labour *74* Arbeit, Arbeitskraft
ladder *39* Leiter
to landfill *93 T* (Müll) deponieren
landing *87* Landung
landline *156* Festnetz(leitung)
largely *41* weitgehend, zum größten Teil
to last *33* (an)dauern
last: at ~ *47 T* endlich, schließlich
last name *174* Nach-, Familienname
late: at the ~st *117* spätestens
late: the ~st *26* das Allerneueste
launch *47 T* Start (einer Kampagne)
law *26* Gesetz
law firm *13* Anwaltskanzlei
lawyer *13* (Rechts-)Anwalt/Anwältin
to lay out *111* gestalten, layouten
layer *106, 117* Ebene, Schicht, Lage
leading *113* führend
leaflet *40* Broschüre, Prospekt
leather *119* Leder
to leave out *49* weg-, auslassen
legal proceedings *135* rechtliche Schritte, Gerichtsverfahren
legal requirement *143* gesetzliche Vorschrift
legible *107* lesbar
legislation *144* Gesetzgebung, gesetzliche Regelung(en)
legitimate cause *137* triftiger Grund
leisure *8* Freizeit, Freizeit-
letter of application *31, 150* Bewerbungsschreiben
letterhead *111* Briefkopf
level *65* Niveau
liability *177* Haftung
liar *15* Lügner/in
library *79* Bibliothek
licence *26, 81* Führerschein, Genehmigung, Lizenz
lifestyle *7* Lebensstil, Lifestyle
likely *29* wahrscheinlich
liking *42* Geschmack
limit *26* Beschränkung, Begrenzung
to limit *26* beschränken, begrenzen
limited *55* beschränkt, begrenzt
Limited (Ltd) *110* GmbH
link *9* verbinden
to link *47* verbinden
literature *73* Literatur
lively *88* lebendig, rege, lebhaft
living expenses *31* Lebenshaltungskosten
load *53* Ladung, Fracht
to load *178* verladen
loading *123* Ver-, Beladung
loads of *33* jede Menge (an)
loaf *63* Laib
loan *81* Kredit, Darlehen
lobby *160* Foyer, Eingangshalle
local *27* örtlich, einheimisch
locally *72* vor Ort
location *55, 124* Standort, Position, Firmensitz
logical *107, 111* logisch
logistics department *117* Logistik, Auslieferung, Spedition
long-distance *59* Fern-, Langstrecken-
long-haul flight *85* Langstreckenflug
long-term *93 T* langfristig, Langzeit-
longer-term *42* längerfristig
to look after *7* sich kümmern um, betreuen
to look forward to *47, 110* sich freuen auf
to look up *73* nachschlagen
loose *63 T* weit (geschnitten), lose, locker
to lose weight *24* abnehmen
loss *73, 145* Schaden, Verlust
lovable *48 T* liebenswert
low-cost *72* billig, Billig-
low-paid *100* niedrig bezahlt
low-skilled *100* angelernt
loyal *86* treu, loyal
loyalty card *60* Kundenkarte
Ltd = Limited *47* GmbH

M

N

O

P

perfumery *114* Parfümerie
period *151* Zeitraum
permission *69* Erlaubnis, Genehmigung
permit *51* Erlaubnis, Genehmigung
personal *27* persönlich, privat
personality *26* Persönlichkeit
personally *136* persönlich
personnel *34 T* Personal, Mitarbeiter
petrol *26* Benzin
pharmaceuticals salesman *93 T* Arzneimittelvertreter
phase *94* Phase, Abschnitt
physical *22* körperlich
to pick *74* pflücken
picker *108* Pflücker/in
picture: the big ~ *36* das große Ganze
pie chart *68* Tortendiagramm
pile *93 T* Haufen, Stapel
piracy *177* Piraterie
to pitch for *47 T* ein Angebot für etw abgeben
to place an order *129* einen Auftrag erteilen
plain *111* schnörkellos, schlicht
plant *127* Werk, Betrieb(sanlage)
plastic *44* Plastik, Kunststoff
play on words *40* Wortspiel
playhouse *93 T* Theater
pleasantly situated *168* reizvoll gelegen
to plug in *55* anschließen, einstecken
(point of) view *57* Standpunkt, Ansicht
to point out *121* hinweisen auf, aufmerksam machen auf
pointless *105* sinnlos
polite *54, 138* höflich
politeness *64* Höflichkeit
politician *36* Politiker/in
polluted *94* verschmutzt
polluting *91* umweltschädlich
pollution *51* (Umwelt-, Luft-)Verschmutzung
pop-up *40* Aufklapp-
population *58* Bevölkerung, Einwohner(zahl)
port *178* Hafen, Hafenstadt
position *58, 110* Position, Standpunkt, Stellung
positive: on a ~ note *121* etwa: freundlich
possibility *114* Möglichkeit
post *150* Posten
postage *67* Porto
postage-paid *67* freigemacht
postman *97* Briefträger
to postpone *167* verschieben
poverty *74* Armut
powder *73* Pulver
to power *55* antreiben
power station *55* Kraftwerk
powerful *91* leistungsstark
practical *86* praktisch (veranlagt), realistisch
practice : in ~ *180* in der Praxis
practice : in modern ~ *112* nach moderner Geschäftspraxis
pre-addressed *67* adressiert
pre-cooked *61* vorgekocht
precious metal *44* Edelmetall
precise *164* genau, präzise
to predict *56* vorhersagen
preferable *108* erwünscht
premises *122* (Betriebs-)Gelände
preparation *81* Vorbereitung
prepared *126* bereit
present *50* gegenwärtig, aktuell
present: at ~ *115* momentan, derzeit
to present *46* vorstellen, präsentieren
presentation *49* Vorführung, Präsentation
to press *69* drücken
pressure *42, 139* Druck
presumably *140* vermutlich
previous *35* vorherig
previously *56* vorher
pricing *55* Preisfestsetzung, -gestaltung
print *142* Druck, Druckschrift
to print *49, 121* (ab)drucken
print media *47* Printmedien
pro-forma invoice *179* Proforma-Rechnung
probationary period *26* Probezeit
problem solver *101* Problemlöser
to process *101* verarbeiten, bearbeiten
produce *63 T* hier: landwirtschaftliche(s) Erzeugnis(se)
to produce *39, 144* herstellen, produzieren
producer *62, 114* Erzeuger, Hersteller/in, Produzent/in
product *34 T* Produkt, Erzeugnis
product development *143* Produktentwicklung
production *31* Produktion, Herstellung, Fertigung
production process *103* Produktionsprozess
production schedule *71* Produktionsplan, Fertigungsplan
productive *43* produktiv
profitable *61, 131* gewinnbringend, rentabel, erfolgreich
programmer *71* Programmierer/in
progress *49* Verlauf, Fortschritt
to promote *40* bewerben, unterstützen
promotional event *101* Werbeveranstaltung
prompt *133* Stichwort, Vorgabe
prompt(ly) *114* unverzüglich, prompt
to pronounce *158* aussprechen
propaganda *22* Propaganda
proportion *43* Verhältnis
proposal *57 T, 167* Vorschlag
proprietary company (Pty) *177* GmbH
pros and cons *88* Für und Wider
prospect *124* Aussicht, Chance
protected *117* geschützt
protective clothing *119* Schutzkleidung
to provide *44, 142* (an)bieten, zur Verfügung stellen, sorgen für, liefern
provided that *55* vorausgesetzt, dass
provisional *180* provisorisch, vorläufig
psychologist *26* Psychologe/in
public *23* öffentlich
public limited company (PLC) *177* AG, Aktiengesellschaft
public relations *78* Öffentlichkeitsarbeit
publicity *34 T* Publicity, Werbung
pump *93* Pumpe
to pump *95* pumpen
punctual *102* pünktlich
punctuality *101* Pünktlichkeit
purchase *60, 131* Kauf, Einkauf
to purchase *67* (ein)kaufen
purchasing assistant *112* Einkäufer/in, Assistent im Einkauf
purchasing manager *114* Einkaufsleiter/in, Chefeinkäufer/in
pure *63 T* rein, echt
purpose *97, 167* Zweck, Absicht, Sinn
purpose: on ~ *109* absichtlich
push *31* Stoß, Anstoß
to push *52* drängen
pushy *77* aufdringlich, penetrant
to put forward *57 T* vorbringen, aufstellen
to put off *99* verschieben
to put through *158* durchstellen, verbinden
pyramid *106* Pyramide

Q

qualifications *150* Ausbildung, Qualifikation
qualified *105* ausgebildet, geeignet
to qualify *151, 155* qualifizieren, Abschluss(prüfung) machen
quality controller *34 T* Qualitätskontrolleur
quantity *62, 121* Menge
query *121* Frage, Rückfrage, Anfrage
questionnaire *34 T* Fragebogen
quota *42* Quote, Mengenbegrenzung
quotation *71, 117* (Preis-)Angebot
to quote *57 T* zitieren
quote *81* Angebot, Preis
to quote *116, 121* ein Angebot abgeben; angeben, zitieren
quoting *108* unter Angabe von

R

rail *93, 126* (Eisen-)Bahn, Schiene, Gleis
rail consignment note *180* Bahnfrachtbrief
rainbow *61* Regenbogen
rainforest *85* Regenwald
to raise *48 T* erhöhen
range *55, 112* Auswahl, Bandbreite, Sortiment
rapid(ly) *65* schnell, rasch
rarely *77* selten
rate *63 T* Tarif
to rate *92* bewerten, einstufen, (ein)schätzen
rather: I'd ~ ... *38* Ich möchte lieber ...
raw material *76* Rohstoff(e)
to re-invent *105* sich ein neues Image geben, sich neu definieren
re-united *36* wiedervereinigt
to re-use *91* wiederverwenden
to reach up *95* emporragen
to react *136* reagieren
to read out *68* vorlesen
ready-packed *117* fertig verpackt
ready-prepared *98* Fertig-
real-life *48 T* wie im wirklichen Leben
realism *103* Realismus
to realize *22* sich klar werden, (be)merken
reason *72, 114* Grund, Begründung
reasonable *44* vernünftig, angemessen
reasonably *151* einigermaßen
rebate *124* Rabatt, Nachlass
receipt *124, 179* Empfang; Beleg, Quittung
to receive: to be well ~d *110* gut aufgenommen werden
receiver *111* Empfänger
reception *34 T* Empfang, Rezeption
receptionist *34 T, 155* Empfangsdame, -chef
to recharge *55* aufladen
to reckon *93 T* glauben, schätzen
to recognize *44* erkennen, wieder erkennen
to recommend *87* empfehlen
to record *55, 179* aufzeichnen, verzeichnen, festhalten
recovery *86* Erholung, Aufschwung
to recycle *93 T* recyceln, wieder verwerten
recycler *93 T* Wiederverwerter
recycling *91* Recycling, Wiederverwertung
red: in the ~ *84* in den roten Zahlen
to reduce *54, 144* verringern, senken, reduzieren, verkleinern

reduction *52, 139* Verringerung, Senkung, Preisnachlass, Ermäßigung
redundancy pay *31* Arbeitslosengeld, Abfindung
redundant *31* überflüssig, arbeitslos
ref = reference number *108, 110* (Akten-) Zeichen
to refer *47* verweisen (auf), sich beziehen (auf)
to refer to *121* sich beziehen auf, verweisen auf
reference *111* Zeichen, Bezug
references *152* Empfehlungsschreiben
to refuse *54, 180* sich weigern
regard: With best ~s *117* Viele Grüße
register *84* Register, charakteristische Redeweise
registered *177* registriert, eingetragen
registration number *171* Autokennzeichen
to regret *147* bedauern, bereuen
regular *83* regelmäßig, regulär
regulated *180* reguliert
reinforced glass screen *44* verstärkter Glasbildschirm
to reject *56, 139* ablehnen, zurückweisen
rejection *150* Ablehnung
related *113* verwandt
relationship *46, 131* Beziehung, Verhältnis
relatively *143* relativ, verhältnismäßig
relaxed *50* entspannt, locker
relevant *107* relevant
reliable *44* zuverlässig
relief *108* Erleichterung
relief worker *108* Aushilfe
to remain *35* bleiben, verbleiben
to remind *135* (jdn an etw) erinnern
reminder *129* Mahnung, Mahnschreiben
renewable *55* erneuerbar
to repack *179* neu verpacken, umpacken
to repaint *38* neu anstreichen
to repair *29* reparieren
to repeat *73* wiederholen
repeat order *117* Folgeauftrag
repetitive *30* (sich dauernd) wiederholend, monoton
to replace *14* ersetzen, austauschen
replacement *139* Ersatz, Austausch
to represent *57* vertreten, repräsentieren
representative *119* Vertreter/in, Repräsentant/in
request *9, 114* Bitte, Anfrage
to request *64* bitten um
to require *101, 126* erfordern, verlangen, benötigen
to require: to be ~d to *151* verpflichtet sein, etw zu tun
required by *85* erforderlich für
requirement *68, 153* Bedingung, Voraussetzung, Anforderung
resaleable *93 T* wiederverkäuflich
Research and Development *34 T* Forschung und Entwicklung
researcher *41* Forscher
reservation *167* Reservierung, Buchung
resident *26* Einwohner, Bewohner
to resist *61* widerstehen
resort *81* Urlaubsort, Hotelanlage
resources *91* Mittel, Ressourcen
to respond *87* reagieren (auf), antworten
response *92* Antwort, Rückmeldung
responsibilities *106* Tätigkeiten, Aufgaben
responsibility *145* Verantwortung
responsible *46* verantwortlich
to restock *108* wieder auffüllen
to restructure *106* umstrukturieren
resumé *32* Lebenslauf (AE)
retail *35* Einzelhandel
retail outlet *60* Einzelhandelsgeschäft
retail trade *110* Einzelhandel
retailer *13* (Einzel-)Händler
to retain *146* behalten, übernehmen
to retake (a test) *26* (eine Prüfung) nochmals machen
to retire *136* in den Ruhestand gehen
return *59* Rückfahrkarte
return: by ~ *132* postwendend
to return *123* zurückschicken, -senden
return flight *170* (Hin- und) Rückflug
reusable *93 T* erneut verwendbar
reverse chronological order *152* umgekehrte zeitliche Reihenfolge
to rewrite *46* umschreiben
ridge *94* Bergkamm, Grat
to ring *69, 158* läuten, klingeln; anrufen
ringtone *48 T* Klingelton
to rise *36* (an)steigen, anwachsen
risk: at ~ *96* gefährdet
to risk *94* riskieren
risky *83, 177* riskant
to role-play *149* als Rollenspiel durchführen
rotor *95* Rotor
rough *47 T* Rohentwurf
rough handling *145* grobe Behandlung
roughly *68* ungefähr, etwa
round-the-world holiday *33* Weltreise
rubber plant *11* Gummibaum
rubbish *63 T* Müll
rude *15* unhöflich, ungezogen, rücksichtslos
to run *38, 157* führen, betreiben, leiten
to run out of time *97* die Zeit wird knapp
running costs *55* Unterhaltskosten, Betriebskosten
rural *56* ländlich
to rush *34 T* eilen, sich beeilen
rush hour *54* Hauptverkehrszeit, Stoßzeit

S

safely *178* sicher, heil, wohlbehalten
salary *30* Gehalt, Lohn
sales *34 T, 39, 110* Verkauf, Vertrieb; Verkaufszahlen, Absatz
sales assistant *30* Verkäufer/in
sales conference *34 T* Vertriebsbesprechung
sales lead *103 T* Verkaufsvorsprung
sales representative *103 T* (Handels-)Vertreter/in
salesperson *100* Verkäufer/in
saloon car *90* Limousine
salutation *111* Anrede
sample *96, 110* Probe(exemplar), Muster
satisfactory *123* zufriedenstellend
satisfied *125* zufrieden
to save *57 T* (Geld) sparen, einsparen
to save sb from sth *72* jdn vor etw bewahren
saving *57 T* Ersparnis, Einsparung
savings *68* Ersparnisse
savings account *81* Sparkonto
say *115* beispielsweise
scale *78, 152* Skala
scales *63 T* Waage
to scare *29* Angst machen
scenario *96* Szenario
scene *50* Szene, Szenerie
schedule *16* Terminplan, Fahrplan
scheme *52* Plan, Programm
school run *54* Fahrt zur Schule
school-leaver *19* Schulabgänger/in
school-leaving certificate *151* (Schul-) Abgangszeugnis
scientist *70* (Natur-)Wissenschaftler/in
scooter *26* Motorroller
score *91* Ergebnis, Punktestand
to score *92* Punkte erzielen
scratch-resistant *44, 165* kratzfest
scratched *146* zerkratzt
screen *47 T* Bildschirm
screw-on cap *141* Schraubverschluss(kappe)
script *49* Drehbuch, Skript
sea level *95* Meeresspiegel
seafreight *126* Seefracht
to search *18* suchen
sea: at ~ *177* auf See
seaside *93* Küste, Strand
seasonal *115* Saison-
secret *84 T* geheim
secretarial *31* Sekretariats-
secretarial duties *155* Sekretariatsaufgaben
Secretary of State for Transport *51* Verkehrsminister/in
section head *47* Abteilungsleiter/in
secure *30* sicher
security guard *71* Sicherheitsbeamte/r
seldom *9* selten
selection *174* Auswahl
self-catering *88* mit Selbstversorgung
semi- *61* halb-
to send out *31* verschicken, versenden
senior *33, 111* vorgesetzt, leitend
sense *41* Sinn
separately *84 T* getrennt
series *48 T* Reihe
serious: to be ~ *45* etw ernst meinen
to serve *105* servieren
services *45, 121* Dienstleistungen
set *27* Satz
to set up *42* einrichten, gründen
to settle *135* bezahlen, begleichen
settlement *126* Zahlung
to sew *74* nähen
to shadow *47* begleiten
to shake *81* schütteln
shape *106* Form
share *42, 177* Anteil, Aktie
to share *51* sich etw teilen
shareholder *177* Gesellschafter, Teilhaber/in, Aktionär/in
sharp *90* scharf
shelf-filling *13* Regalbestückung, -auffüllung
shift *100* Schicht
to ship *41, 117* (ver)senden
shipment *141* Sendung
shipping *74* Versand
shipping documents *179* Versandpapiere
shipping line *179* Schifffahrtslinie, Reederei
shipping note *180* Schiffszettel, Warenbegleitschein
shocking *40* schrecklich, schockierend
shopping mall *43* Einkaufspassage
short: for ~ *34 T* abgekürzt
to shorten *87* (ver-)kürzen
shortened *164* verkürzt, abgekürzt
shortly *132* in Kürze, kurz
to shout at sb *109* jdn anschreien
to show sb round *34 T* jdn herumführen
shower *115* Dusche

to shrink *37* zurückgehen, schrumpfen
to sign off *110* (einen Brief) schließen
signature block *111* Unterschriftsabschnitt, Unterschriften
signposted *161* ausgeschildert
similar *14* ähnlich
similarity *42* Ähnlichkeit
sincere *147* aufrichtig, ehrlich
single administrative document *180* Einheitspapier
single household *27* Einpersonenhaushalt
single market *180* Binnenmarkt
single room *88* Einzelzimmer
site *95* Stelle, Standort
site map *39* Lageplan
size *63 T* Größe
ski run *87* Skipiste
skilled worker *35* Facharbeiter/in, gelernte/r Arbeiter/in
skills *35, 150* Fertigkeiten
skin cream *136* Hautcreme
slash *159* Schrägstrich
sleeve *63 T* Ärmel
slice *63* Scheibe
slight(ly) *37, 146* gering, leicht, geringfügig
slot *49* Sendeplatz
to slow down *61* (sich) verlangsamen
small change *63 T* Wechsel-, Kleingeld
small print *48 T* das Kleingedruckte
smoothly *90* ruhig, glatt
snap-on cap *141* Schnappverschluss(kappe)
so as to *79* so dass, um ... zu
sociable *86* gesellig
social security *35* soziale Absicherung, Sozialversicherung
society *35* Gesellschaft
soft *54* mild
solar energy *56* Sonnenenergie
solution *57, 139* Lösung
to solve *56, 174* lösen
to sort out *47 T* in Ordnung bringen, klären
source *42* Quelle
space *49, 112* Raum, Platz, Leerstelle
speaking *115* am Apparat
special offer *60* Sonderangebot
special terms *121* Sonderkonditionen
specialization *154* Spezialisierung
to specialize in *103 T* sich spezialisieren auf
specialty shop *65* Fachgeschäft
specific *154* speziell
to specify *174* angeben
speed *29* Geschwindigkeit
speed camera *29* Radargerät, Blitzer
speed limit *29* Geschwindigkeitsbegrenzung
to spell *158* buchstabieren
spending *45* Ausgaben
sponsorship *40* Sponsoring
spread *78, 180* Verbreitung, Verteilung
to spread *78* verbreiten, verteilen
square *22* Quadrat
staff *33, 141* Angestellte, Personal, Mitarbeiter
staff development *34 T* Personalentwicklung
staff development officer *34 T* Personalentwickler
stage *46, 150* Abschnitt, Stufe, Phase
stainless steel *44* rostfreier Stahl
stamina *101* Ausdauer
stand *114* (Messe-)Stand
standard *71* Maßstab, Norm
to stare *39* starren, anstarren
state *35* (Bundes-)Staat
to state *32* feststellen, angeben, (im Text) vorkommen, vortragen
statement *14, 116* Aussage, Behauptung
stationery *17* Briefpapier, Büromaterial
status *41, 180* Status, Ansehen
stead(il)y *35* stetig, gleichmäßig
steel mill *71* Stahlwerk, Walzwerk
steel worker *71* Stahlarbeiter/in
step *32* Schritt, Stufe
stereotype *86* Stereotyp
stewardess *93* Stewardess
stock control *31* Lagerhaltung, Inventur
stock market *177* Börse
stocks *139* Lagerbestand, Warenbestand
store *13, 116* Laden, Geschäft, Lager
to store *109* lagern, aufheben
strategy *105* Strategie, Taktik
strength *37* Stärke, Kraft
stressful *30* sehr anstrengend, stressig
structure *34 T* Struktur, Aufbau
stuff *69, 113* Zeug
stupidly *99* dummerweise
style *33, 111* Stil
styling mousse *142* Frisierschaum
sub-heading *48 T* Untertitel
sub-title *36* Untertitel
subject line *110* Bezugszeile, Betreffzeile
to submit *124* unterbreiten, einreichen
to succeed *37* Erfolg haben, gelingen
to suffer *46* leiden, erleiden
sufficient *145* ausreichend, genug
to suggest *33, 139, 144* vorschlagen, andeuten, nahelegen, hindeuten auf
suggestion *25* Vorschlag
to suit (fine) *35, 162* (gut) passen, recht sein
suitability *150* Eignung
suitable *18* geeignet, angemessen
suited to *44* geeignet für
to sum up *94* zusammenfassen
to summarize *57* zusammenfassen
summary *43* Zusammenfassung
summer camp *21* Sommer(ferien)lager
sun tan *89* Sonnenbräune
sunscreen *115* Sonnencreme
supplier *74, 112* Anbieter/in, Lieferant/in
supplies *56* Vorräte
to supply *55, 110* (be)liefern, versorgen
to support *55* unterstützen, stützen
surcharge *172* Aufschlag
surely *85* sicherlich
surface *96, 115* Oberfläche
surname *159* Nach-, Familienname
survey *34 T* Umfrage, Untersuchung, Erhebung
survival *37* Überleben
to survive *18* überleben
survivor *62* Überlebende/r
to swap *159* vertauschen
swimwear *137* Badebekleidung
to switch off *8* ausschalten
to swop *34* (aus-, ver-)tauschen
to sympathize with *143* Verständnis haben für
synthetic *63 T* synthetisch

T

tabular form *121* Tabellenform
tailback *50* Autoschlange
to take a call *125* einen Anruf entgegennehmen
to take a message *157* etw ausrichten
to take a risk *35* ein Risiko eingehen
to take advantage of *126* Gebrauch machen von
to take dictations *13* Diktate aufnehmen
to take notes *120* sich Notizen machen
to take over *47 T* übernehmen
to take over *177* übernehmen
to take part in *38* teilnehmen an, mitmachen bei
to take place *180* stattfinden
to take possession of *179* in Besitz nehmen
to take responsibility *101* Verantwortung übernehmen
to take time out *18* Pause machen, Auszeit nehmen
to take turns *84* (sich) abwechseln
to take up *24, 145* anfangen, etw zu tun; aufgreifen, sich einer Sache annehmen
target *72* Ziel
taste *41* Geschmack
tax *35* Steuer
taxes *178* Steuern
teabag *69* Teebeutel
team player *101* etwa: jd mit gutem Gruppenverhalten
team spirit *153* Teamgeist
technical *149* technisch, fachbezogen
technical knowledge *36* Fachwissen
technical support *35* technische Unterstützung
technician *50* Techniker/in
technologically *73* technologisch
teddy bear *145* Teddybär
telecommunications *72* Fernmeldewesen
telephone directory *108* Telefonbuch
temp *108* Zeitarbeiter/in
temperature *95* Temperatur
temping agency *155* Zeitarbeitsfirma
temporary job *18* Aushilfstätigkeit
temporary worker *141* Zeitarbeiter/in
term *84 T, 177* Semester, Trimester; Begriff, Fachwort
term: on what ~s *121* zu welchen Konditionen
terms and conditions *121* allgemeine Geschäftsbedingungen
terms of delivery *177* Lieferbedingungen
terms of payment *180* Zahlungsbedingungen
terrified *87* erschrocken, ängstlich
terrifying *87* erschreckend
text messaging *156* SMS
textile *42* Textilie, Textil-
textiles *112* Textilien
thanks to *31* dank
threat *136* Drohung
three-stage *135* dreistufig
throughout *114* überall (in), in ganz
to throw away *91* wegwerfen
to throw out *93 T* aussondern, wegwerfen
tidily *104* aufgeräumt, ordentlich
tight *17* fest; knapp
till *17* (Laden-)Kasse
time: at ~s *95* manchmal
time: at all ~s *49* jederzeit
time: in ~ *81* rechtzeitig
time: on ~ *97* pünktlich
tiny: a ~ little bit *54* ein klitzekleines Bisschen
tired *98* müde
tobacco *46* Tabak
toll *51* Maut(gebühr)

tool *45* Werkzeug, Instrument
toolbox *118* Werkzeugkasten
top: on ~ of *172* auf
topic *78, 164* Thema
total *36* (ins)gesamt, Gesamtsumme
to touch *77* anfassen, berühren
tough *35* hart
to tour *81* bereisen, eine Rundreise machen
touring holiday *19* Rundreise
tourist sight *48* Touristenattraktion
tourist spot *85* Urlaubsort
tower *95* Turm
to track *55* verfolgen, aufspüren
trade *42* Handel
trade price *121* Großhandelspreis
trade show *101* Fachmesse
trade terms *116* Handelsbedingungen
traditional *44* traditionell
traffic congestion *51* Verkehrsstauung
traffic lights *29* (Verkehrs-)Ampel
trail *85* Spur
trainers *45* Turn-, Tennisschuhe
tram *58* Straßenbahn
transaction *181* Geschäftsabschluss
transfer *72* Transfer, Verlagerung
transition *82* Übergang
translation *83* Übersetzung
transmission *124* Sendung, Übertragung
travel agency *33* Reisebüro
travel agent *79, 169* Reisebüro(angestellte/r)
travel arrangements *164* Reisepläne
travel industry *33* Tourismusbranche
treasure *67* Schatz
treat *69* besondere Freude
to treat *73, 139* behandeln
trial *116* Probe-
trolley *61* Einkaufswagen
tropical *70* tropisch, Tropen-
to trouble *137* belästigen, Umstände bereiten
to trust *44, 126* (darauf) vertrauen
truth *86* Wahrheit
tube *116* Tube
tunnel *53* Tunnel
to turn down *81* ablehnen
to turn into *113* umarbeiten zu/in
to turn out *81* sich herausstellen
to turn over *93 T* umsetzen
to turn to *41* sich wenden an, zuwenden
turnover *75* Umsatz
twin room *88* Zweibettzimmer
tyre pressure *49* Reifendruck

U

unacceptable *144* unannehmbar, inakzeptabel
unbreakable *115* unzerbrechlich
unchanged *37* unverändert
uncomfortable *77* unwohl, unangenehm
undamaged *179* unbeschädigt
underground *70* Untergrund, unterirdisch
to underline *87, 113* unterstreichen
underscore *159* Unterstrich
underwear *74* Unterwäsche
underweight *22* untergewichtig
unemployed *36* arbeitslos, ohne Beschäftigung
unemployment *35* Arbeitslosigkeit
unhappy *137* unglücklich
unified *180* einheitlich
united *158* vereint, vereinigt
United Nations *174* Vereinte Nationen
unknown *85* unbekannt
unlike *179* anders als, im Gegensatz zu
unlimited mileage *172* unbegrenzte Meilen
unloading *123* Entladung, Löschung
to unpack *148* auspacken
unpaid *137* unbezahlt
unpleasant *39* unangenehm, unfreundlich
unreliable *58* unzuverlässig
unsatisfactory *152* ungenügend
unsolicited *150* unaufgefordert, unverlangt
up-market *62* im oberen Marktsegment
up-to-date *180* aktuell
ups and downs *46* Auf und Ab, Höhen und Tiefen
urban *55* städtisch, Stadt-
urgent(ly) *59, 139* dringend, eilig
used to *39* früher ...
useless *107* nutzlos, sinnlos
utility *94* Versorgungsbetrieb

V

vacancy *35, 150* offene Stelle
vacation *151* Urlaub, Ferien
valid *125* gültig
validity *126* Gültigkeit
valuable *46* wertvoll
value *74, 124* Wert
value-added *61* Mehrwert-
valve *145* Ventil
varied *30* vielfältig, abwechslungsreich
various *51* verschiedene(r)
to vary *40* unterschiedlich sein, variieren
vehicle *51* Fahrzeug, Verkehrsmittel
version *142* Version, Fassung
via *53* über
view *13* Ansicht
violent *95* heftig
virtually *15* praktisch, nahezu
vital *101* unerlässlich, unbedingt notwendig
vocational *32* beruflich, Berufs-
vocational training *154* Berufsausbildung
voice mail *145* Sprachmitteilung
volume order *112* Großauftrag, Mengenbestellung
volunteer *38, 152* Freiwillige/r, Helfer/in; freiwillig
to volunteer *38* freiwillig arbeiten
vote *48* Abstimmung

W

wage *32* Lohn, Gehalt
waist *63 T* Taille
war *177* Krieg
warehouse *65, 133* Lager
warmth *66* Wärme
warning *143* Warnung
warranty *147* Gewährleistung, Garantie
to waste *91* vergeuden, verschwenden
waste product *55* Abfallprodukt
to watch out *61* aufpassen
watchmaking *44* Uhrmacherei
to water plants *11* Blumen gießen
way: by the ~ *113* übrigens, nebenbei
weakness *37* Schwäche
weather forecast *21* Wettervorhersage
wedding *97* Hochzeit, Trauung
to weigh *22* wiegen
well off *71* gut dran, wohlhabend
well-established *90* etabliert
well-known *45* sehr bekannt, berühmt
well-paid *30* gut bezahlt
well-qualified *153* gut/hoch qualifiziert
wetland *96* Feuchtgebiet, Sumpfgebiet
whatever *41* was auch immer
wheel *27* Rad
wholesale catalogue *110* Großhandelskatalog
wholesale distributor *62* Großhändler
wholesaler *114* Großhändler/in
wide *72* breit, weit
widely *78* weit (verbreitet)
widely used *174* weit verbreitet
willing: to be ~ *121* bereit/gewillt sein
window seat *170* Fensterplatz
with reference to *119* mit Bezug auf
with regard to *131* in Bezug auf
with respect *145* bei allem Respekt
to withdraw *84* abheben
wood *93 T* Holz
wooden crate *93 T* Holzkiste
word spider *156* Wortnetz
to work *54* funktionieren
work experience *13* Berufs-, Arbeitserfahrung
to work ... hours *30* ... Arbeitszeiten haben
work of art *44* Kunstwerk
to work out well *31* gut klappen, gut funktionieren
work placement *100, 155* Praktikum
workforce *36* arbeitende Bevölkerung, Berufstätige
workplace *105* Arbeitsplatz
workshop *76 T* Werkstatt
worried *50* besorgt, beunruhigt
worried *142* beunruhigt, besorgt
worrying *87* beunruhigend
to worsen *50* sich verschlechtern
worth *65, 124* wert, im Wert von

Y

You're welcome. *34 T* Bitte (schön).
Yours faithfully *110* Mit freundlichen Grüßen, Hochachtungsvoll
Yours sincerely *210* Mit freundlichen Grüßen
youth *24* Jugend

Unregelmäßige Verben

arise, arose, arisen	entstehen
be, was/were, been	sein
beat, beat, beaten	schlagen
become, became, become	werden
begin, began, begun	starten, anfangen
bind, bound, bound	fesseln, binden
break, broke, broken	brechen, kaputtmachen
bring, brought, brought	bringen
broadcast, broadcast, broadcast	senden, ausstrahlen
build, built, built	bauen
burn, burnt (burned), burnt (burned)	brennen
buy, bought, bought	kaufen
catch, caught, caught	fangen
choose, chose, chosen	wählen
come, came, come	kommen
cost, cost, cost	kosten
cut, cut, cut	schneiden
deal, dealt, dealt	handeln, sich beschäftigen mit
dig, dug, dug	graben, bohren
do, did, done	tun, machen
draw, drew, drawn	zeichnen
dream, dreamt (dreamed), dreamt (dreamed)	träumen
drink, drank, drunk	trinken
drive, drove, driven	fahren
eat, ate, eaten	essen
fall, fell, fallen	fallen
feel, felt, felt	fühlen
fight, fought, fought	(be)kämpfen
find, found, found	finden
fly, flew, flown	fliegen
forget, forgot, forgotten	vergessen
freeze, froze, frozen	frieren
get, got, got	bekommen
give, gave, given	geben
go, went, gone	gehen
grow, grew, grown	wachsen
have, had, had	haben
hear, heard, heard	hören
hide, hid, hidden	(sich) verstecken
hit, hit, hit	schlagen
hold, held, held	halten
hurt, hurt, hurt	weh tun
input, input (inputted), input (inputted)	eingeben
keep, kept, kept	behalten
know, knew, known	wissen, kennen
lay, laid, laid	legen
lead, led, led	führen
learn, learnt, learnt (learned)	lernen
leave, left, left	(weg)gehen, (ver)lassen
let, let, let	lassen, erlauben
light, lit (lighted), lit (lighted)	erleuchten, entzünden
lose, lost, lost	verlieren
make, made, made	machen, tun
mean, meant, meant	bedeuten
meet, met, met	treffen
pay, paid, paid	bezahlen
put, put, put	legen, stellen
read, read, read	lesen
ride, rode, ridden	fahren, reiten
rise, rose, risen	steigen, sich erheben
ring, rang, rung	klingeln
run, ran, run	laufen, verwalten
say, said, said	sagen
see, saw, seen	sehen
seek, sought, sought	suchen
sell, sold, sold	verkaufen
send, sent, sent	senden
set, set, set	setzen, stellen, legen
shake, shook, shaken	schütteln
show, showed, shown (showed)	zeigen
shut, shut, shut	schließen
sing, sang, sung	singen
sink, sank, sunk	(ver)senken
sit, sat, sat	sitzen
sleep, slept, slept	schlafen
smell, smelt (smelled), smelt (smelled)	riechen
speak, spoke, spoken	sprechen
speed, sped, sped (speeded)	rasen
spell, spelt (spelled), spelt (spelled)	buchstabieren
spend, spent, spent	ausgeben
stand, stood, stood	stehen
steal, stole, stolen	stehlen
swim, swam, swum	schwimmen
take, took, taken	nehmen
teach, taught, taught	unterrichten
tear, tore, torn	zerreißen
tell, told, told	erzählen
think, thought, thought	denken
throw, threw, thrown	werfen
understand, understood, understood	verstehen
wake, woke, woken	wecken
wear, wore, worn	tragen
win, won, won	gewinnen
write, wrote, written	schreiben

Quellenverzeichnis

Grafiken/Cartoons: Oxford Designers & Illustrators; Landkarten: Carlos Borrell, Berlin

Titelfoto: Gettyimages/W. Krecichwost

The Advertising Archives: S. 40; Alamy: S.26/4/G.Crabbe; S.26/6/RF; P.Austin: S.63/1; C.Buckstegen: S.6(4)RF; C.Caridia: S.88/1; Corel: S.63/3; S.70/1; S.70/3; S.71/2/4; S.80/1/3/4/6; S.85/1/2/3/4; S.88/2/3; S.102; Corbis: S.6 /T.Bozi; S.7/RF; S.8/2/3/RF; S.18/1/RF; S.18/2/K.Kulish; S.18/3/R.Gehman; S.23/1/E.Robert; S.23/2/M.Prince; S.23/4/M.Prince; S.23/5/RF/WV; S.26/2/RF; S.30/1/RF; S.30/2/RF; S.30/3/RF; S.30/5/T.Stewart; S.30/6/RF; S.36/2/RF/WV; S.50/J.Sohm; S.51/1/E.Robert; S.68/RF; S.71/1/RF; S.72/1/Reuters; S.76/M.Freeman; S.80/2/J.McDonald; S.84/W.Whitehurst; S.86/RF; S.95/RF; S.100/1/H.King; S.100/2/RF; S.105/RF; S.108/1/2/RF; S.114/1/C.Carroll; S.114/4/Left Lane Productions; S.156/1/G.Steiner; S.156/2/S.Chenn; S.156/3/H.Winkler; S.156/5/M.Moellenberg; Comstock: S.114/3/5RF; Fotofinder: S.8/5/J.Lantelme; S.13/2/N.Michalke; S.13/3/Blickwinkel/M.Baumann; S.18/4/P.Eckenroth/Joker; S.26/3/Schapowalow/Brand X; S.30/4/Bildagentur-online/Kroener; S.35/mediacolors; S.36/1/vario-images; S.65,S.90/F1-online; S.101/1/Photothek; S.101/2/Stock4B; S.114/2/a-location; Gettyimages: S.7/1/2/3/4 RF; S.8/1RF; S.8/4/RF; S.13/1/RF; S.22/1/RF; S.22/2/RF S.23/3/RF; S.23/3/RF/WV; S.23/6/RF; S.26/1/RF; S.41/T.Howell; S.51/2/RF; S.51/3/M.Barraud; S.53/D. de Lossy; S.67/A.Harper ; S.70/5/RF/WV; S.71/3/R.Mackechnie; S.156/4/RF; D.Graham: S.26/5; S.31/1/2; S.33/1/2; S.38; S.63/4; S.70/6/7/8; S.83; S.84; S.93; S.94/2; S.96; S.97; H.Holtkamp: S.81 ; V.Maly: S.70/2WV; Picture Alliance: S.63/2/KPA-Hackenberg;S.72/2; S.80/5/J.Büttner; S.94/1/P.Pleul; Mit freundlicher Unterstützung folgender Unternehmen: S.44/Nokia; S.55/REVA Electric Car Company; S.70/BMW; Textrechte: S.58/http://www.worldenergy.org/wec-geis/wec_info/about_wec/tandc.asp.

Nicht alle Copyright-Inhaber konnten ermittelt werden; deren Urheberrechte werden hiermit vorsorglich und ausdrücklich anerkannt.